KT-481-189

Scotland's referendum on 18 September 2014 is a choice between two futures.

If we vote Yes, we take the next step on Scotland's journey. We will move forward with confidence, ready to make the most of the many opportunities that lie ahead. The most important decisions about our economy and society will be taken by the people who care most about Scotland, that is by the people of Scotland. The door will open to a new era for our nation.

Scotland's future will be in Scotland's hands.

If we vote No, Scotland stands still. A once in a generation opportunity to follow a different path, and choose a new and better direction for our nation, is lost. Decisions about Scotland would remain in the hands of others.

We, the people who live here, have the greatest stake in making Scotland a success. With independence we can make Scotland the fairer and more successful country we all know it should be. We can make Scotland's vast wealth and resources work much better for everyone in our country, creating a society that reflects our hopes and ambition. Being independent means we will have a government that we choose – a government that always puts the people of Scotland first.

This is what being independent can deliver for Scotland and it is why the Scottish Government believes the people of Scotland, individually and collectively, will be better off with independence.

CONTENTS

PART 3

3 CHAPTER

FINANCE AND THE ECONOMY

4 CHAPTER

HEALTH, WELLBEING AND SOCIAL PROTECTION

 **CHAPTER 5**
EDUCATION,
SKILLS AND
EMPLOYMENT

CHAPTER 6
INTERNATIONAL
RELATIONS AND
DEFENCE

CHAPTER 7 — JUSTICE, SECURITY AND HOME AFFAIRS

CHAPTER 8 — ENVIRONMENT, RURAL SCOTLAND, ENERGY AND RESOURCES

PART 5

Q&A

QUESTIONS AND ANSWERS

ANNEXES

ENDNOTES

The Rt Hon Alex Salmond MSP
First Minister

Scotland is an ancient nation, renowned for the ingenuity and creativity of our people, the breathtaking beauty of our land and the brilliance of our scholars. Our national story has been shaped down the generations by values of compassion, equality, an unrivalled commitment to the empowerment of education, and a passion and curiosity for invention that has helped to shape the world around us. Scots have been at the forefront of the great moral, political and economic debates of our times as humanity has searched for progress in the modern age.

It is in that spirit of progress that you will be asked on 18 September 2014,

'Should Scotland be an independent country?'

The answer we give to that question will determine how we can shape our nation for the future. The year ahead should be a national celebration of who we are and what we could be.

The debate we are engaged in as a nation is about the future of all of us lucky enough to live in this diverse and vibrant country. It is a rare and precious moment in the history of Scotland – a once in a generation opportunity to chart a better way.

At its heart independence is not about this Government or any political party. It is about a fundamental democratic choice for the people of Scotland. It is about the power to choose who we should be governed by and the power to build a country that reflects our priorities as a society and our values as a people.

I believe in independence because I believe it will be better for all of us if decisions about Scotland are taken by the people who care most about Scotland – the people who live and work here. It is my absolute conviction that Scotland's future should be in Scotland's hands.

I also believe that the bonds of family, friendship, history and culture between Scotland and the other parts of the British Isles are precious. England, Wales and Northern Ireland will always be our family, friends and closest neighbours. But with Scotland as an independent country, our relationship will be one of equals. I have no doubt that it will flourish.

I want to be clear about what independence means and why the Scottish Government is asking you to vote Yes.

The vote in September 2014 is about becoming independent from the parliamentary union of 1707 and passing to the Scottish Parliament the powers Westminster has over matters such as taxation, welfare and the economy, and securing for Scotland our own place in the world as an independent country.

Last year, in the Edinburgh Agreement, the Scottish and Westminster Governments agreed to continue to work together constructively in the light of the outcome of the referendum, whatever it may be, in the best interests of the people of Scotland and of the rest of the United Kingdom. That is an important commitment from both Governments. It will help to ensure a smooth transition of powers from Westminster to Scotland.

That constructive working together will continue after independence.

We will work in partnership with the rest of the UK to share the pound for our mutual benefit, but we will pursue a Scottish tax and economic policy to boost jobs, growth and social justice.

Westminster governments, rejected at the ballot box in Scotland, will no longer be able to inflict the poll tax or the bedroom tax on the most vulnerable people in our society.

We will continue to work in partnership with the rest of the UK in defence alliances to promote peace and security, but we will be able to remove Trident from Scotland's soil and stop paying towards the £100 billion lifetime cost of a new generation of nuclear weapons.

We will work in partnership with the rest of the UK inside the European Union. But we will be able to represent Scotland at the top tables of Europe as a constructive member state and stand up for vital Scottish interests.

Scotland will remain within the Union of the Crowns with Her Majesty The Queen as our head of state, but we will have a modern, written constitution.

And the social ties between Scotland and the rest of the UK will continue and thrive.

That is the independent Scotland we will negotiate following a Yes vote. We will do so in time for Scotland to become independent on 24 March 2016 and be ready for the first elections to an independent Scottish Parliament in the spring of that year.

Of course some would prefer Scotland to become a republic, to leave the EU or NATO, or to have our own currency. After Scotland becomes independent, any political party seeking to make these kinds of changes would first have to win support to do so in an election.

That is the real democratic value of independence – the people of Scotland are in charge. It will no longer be possible for governments to be elected and pursue policies against the wishes of the Scottish people. So other choices can be made, different from those we propose in this guide – but these will be the choices of the Scottish people.

Independence will put the people of Scotland in charge of our own destiny.

No-one is suggesting an independent Scotland would not face challenges. We would be unique if that was not the case.

But we are rich in human talent and natural resources. We are one of the wealthiest nations in the world. With independence, we can build the kind of country we want to be.

People down the decades have wondered if a country blessed with such wealth, talent and resources could and should have done more to realise the potential we know exists for everyone. Those generations could only imagine a better Scotland.

Our generation has the opportunity to stop imagining and wondering and start building the better Scotland we all know is possible.

This is our country. This is Scotland's future. It is time to seize that future with both hands.

Alex Salmond

Gains from independence – whichever party is elected

- Decisions about Scotland will be taken by the people who care most about Scotland – those who live and work here

- An independent Parliament elected entirely by people in Scotland will replace the current Westminster system. Under that system, elected representatives from Scotland make up just 9 per cent of the 650 members of the House of Commons; the House of Lords is wholly unelected

- Governments will always be formed by parties that win elections in Scotland. It will no longer be possible for key decisions to be made by governments that do not command the support of the Scottish electorate

- A guarantee that tax and social security rates will be set in line with the wishes of the people of Scotland. That will mean an end to the imposition on Scotland of policies like the "bedroom tax"

- Public services can be kept in public hands. The Scottish Parliament has the power to keep the NHS in public hands but it could not stop other services such as the Royal Mail being privatised by Westminster

- An economic policy aimed at economic stability and job security in Scotland will replace an economic policy which disproportionately benefits London and the South East of England

- Access to our own resources – for every one of the last 32 years estimates show Scotland has generated more tax per head than the UK as a whole. With independence, decisions about the level and allocation of public spending will be taken here in Scotland

- An economic policy that can be tailored to take advantage of Scotland's world-class universities and key growth industries like food and drink, life sciences, and tourism

- An independent Scotland can invest our oil wealth for future generations. By value there is estimated to be as much North Sea oil still to come as has already been extracted. Norway has a savings fund worth more than £470 billion

- Our taxes will not be used to pay for nuclear weapons and we can remove Trident from Scotland for good

Gains from independence – if we are the first government of an independent Scotland

- A transformational extension of childcare, giving our children the best start in life, making it easier for parents – especially mothers – to return to work and delivering new job opportunities

- Abolition of the "bedroom tax" which will save 82,500 households in Scotland – including 63,500 households with a disabled adult and 15,500 households with children – an average of £50 per month

- A halt to the rollout of Universal Credit and Personal Independence Payments in Scotland allowing future Scottish governments to develop reforms to our welfare system that meet our needs

- The first steps towards a fairer tax system by ensuring that basic rate tax allowances and tax credits rise at least in line with inflation, and ending of the married couples tax allowance and abolishing the Shares for Rights scheme

- Pensioners' incomes protected with the triple lock so that pensions increase by either inflation, earnings, or 2.5 per cent, whichever is highest

- Simplification of the tax system to reduce compliance costs, streamline reliefs and help to reduce tax avoidance, with a target revenue gain of £250 million a year by the end of the first term

- Return of the Royal Mail to public ownership in Scotland, guaranteeing the quality of service that all parts of our country currently enjoy

- A Fair Work Commission and a guarantee that the minimum wage will rise at least in line with inflation. Over the last five years, this would have improved the earnings of the lowest paid Scots by the equivalent of £675. Continued support for the living wage for central government staff and promotion of it for other sectors of the Scottish economy

- A timetable for reducing the rate of corporation tax by up to three percentage points to counter the gravitational business pull of London

- Examination of further help for small businesses, for example with national insurance costs to encourage them to create more jobs

- Reduction in Air Passenger Duty by 50 per cent, with a view to abolishing it when public finances allow

- Support for energy efficiency and the roll out of green technology from central government budgets to reduce energy bills by around 5 per cent

What you can expect from this guide to an independent Scotland

The Scottish Government supports independence for Scotland.

On 18 September 2014 you will be asked to vote in a referendum on the question:

> **'Should Scotland be an independent country?'**

The Scottish Government believes you should vote Yes.

This guide sets out the gains of independence for Scotland – whichever party is in government – and this Government's vision and priorities for action if we are the first government of an independent Scotland. It also explains the process by which Scotland will become independent following a Yes vote and how our newly independent Scotland will work.

Scotland has many natural advantages. The foundations of our economy are strong. We have abundant natural resources. We have a talented population with many world-class businesses and institutions. We have a proud history, progressive traditions, fine intellectual and artistic accomplishments, a strong identity and many friends across the world.

Through devolution, the people of Scotland have experienced some of the benefits of independence. The advantages of taking decisions for ourselves have been clear. Crime is lower. Health outcomes have improved. In many ways – like our unemployment rate – our economy is stronger than the UK as a whole. The Scottish Parliament has protected the NHS from privatisation and restored our tradition of free education.

This guide lays out how we can complete Scotland's journey to home rule and become a fully independent country.

If Scotland votes Yes in the referendum the Scottish Government will negotiate so that Scotland becomes independent on 24 March 2016.

In detail, this guide sets out:

The case for independence. Decisions about Scotland – decisions that affect us, our families, our communities and the future of our country – should be taken in Scotland to reflect the views and concerns of the Scottish people, rather than by governments at Westminster with different priorities, often rejected by voters in Scotland.

The strong foundations already in place for the economy and public finances of an independent Scotland. Scotland can afford to be independent. We can pay for, and protect, our public services. Even those who currently argue against independence accept that Scotland can be a successful independent country. Independence will give us the powers we need to build an even stronger economy. It will equip us to compete effectively in the global economy, rather than remain under Westminster which has created an unequal society and an unbalanced economy.

How Scotland will become independent. Following a vote for independence on 18 September 2014, Scotland will prepare to become an independent country. There will be negotiations with the rest of the UK, the EU and other international partners. Planning for independence in March 2016 allows a realistic time to reach agreement in those discussions and to complete the legal processes to transfer power to the Scottish Parliament.

The first parliamentary election in an independent Scotland will take place on 5 May 2016.

What an independent Scotland will look like. The shape of Scotland in the future will be determined by how the people of Scotland vote in elections in 2016 and thereafter. The current Scottish Government will lead Scotland from a Yes vote in September 2014 to independence in March 2016. This guide sets out what Scotland will look like at the point of independence – on issues such as the currency, the monarchy and membership of the EU.

The gains of independence for you, your family and community. Independence will give the Scottish Parliament new powers in areas like the economy, taxation, welfare, energy and defence, and control over key national assets like the postal system. In this guide we set out the many opportunities these powers will give Scotland, and some of the current Scottish Government's priorities for action if we are elected to be the government of an independent Scotland in May 2016.

Answers to your questions. In this guide we answer detailed questions we have been asked about independence.

Structure of this guide

Part one of the guide sets out an overview of the case for independence:

■ why Scotland needs independence

■ what Scotland will look like on independence

■ what will happen between a Yes vote and Scotland becoming independent

■ our financial and economic strengths

■ the benefits of independence and the priorities for action of the current Government if it is the first government of an independent Scotland

■ the consequences of Scotland voting No to independence

Part two describes the strengths of Scotland's national finances over recent decades compared to the UK as a whole. It also estimates Scotland's opening financial position at the point of independence – 2016/17 – and sets out this Government's priorities for the first term of a Scottish Parliament.

Part three provides detailed analysis of the changes needed across Scotland, the opportunities that independence provides for any future Scottish government to make those changes, and the particular priorities for action identified by this Government. These chapters cover:

- Finance and the Economy, including measures to boost the economy, create jobs and ensure we have a skilled, motivated and fairly-rewarded workforce, and proposals on our currency, the tax system, and financial regulation

- Transport, including proposals to strengthen connections within and to Scotland, support decarbonisation and reduce Air Passenger Duty

- Health, Wellbeing and Social Protection, including proposals to improve pensions, build a fairer welfare system in an independent Scotland, and continue to protect our NHS

- Education, Skills and Employment, including the opportunities for our schools, universities and colleges to flourish with independence, our transformational childcare proposals, and the need to address inequalities in educational attainment in our schools, protect free university education and strengthen Scotland's academic research base

- International Relations and Defence, including Scotland's transition to independent membership of the EU, and our proposals for Scotland's armed forces and international representation

- Justice, Security and Home Affairs, including the opportunities to make our communities safe, protect ourselves against terrorism and other security threats, and establish a system of immigration and citizenship that meets Scotland's needs

- Environment, Rural Scotland and Energy & Resources, including the opportunities for our food and drink, agriculture and fishing industries, and our rural and island communities, and proposals to support our energy industries – oil and gas and renewables – and manage our energy wealth for the future with the creation of a Scottish Energy Fund

- Culture and Communications, including the future of broadcasting and the Royal Mail in Scotland

Part four sets out the timescale and process for Scotland to become an independent country following a Yes vote in the referendum. It describes the transition that will take place and the negotiations that will be required on assets and liabilities, and to ensure continued delivery of public services. It also sets out the opportunities for a modern democracy with our own written constitution and describes how equality and human rights will be protected and promoted on independence.

Finally, in **Part five** we answer detailed questions we have been asked about independence.

SUMMARY

SCOTLAND IN NUMBERS

5.3 MILLION PEOPLE*

16% OF THE POPULATION AGED UNDER **15** (850,000*)

*SOURCE: 2011 CENSUS
**SOURCE: TIMES HIGHER EDUCATION UNIVERSITY RANKINGS

83%* OF THE SCOTTISH POPULATION FEEL THEY HAVE A **SCOTTISH** NATIONAL IDENTITY

20%* OF THE POPULATION **SHARE THEIR SCOTTISH CONNECTION WITH** ANOTHER IDENTITY

SCOTLAND HAS **FIVE UNIVERSITIES** IN THE WORLD'S TOP 200,*

INCLUDING ST ANDREWS **THE THIRD** OLDEST UNIVERSITY IN THE ENGLISH-SPEAKING **WORLD** IF SCOTLAND BECAME INDEPENDENT NOW

54TH MEMBER OF THE COMMONWEALTH

194TH INDEPENDENT COUNTRY TO JOIN THE UN

29TH MEMBER OF **THE EU**

Part One – The case for independence

Independence means that Scotland's future will be in our own hands. Decisions currently taken for Scotland at Westminster will instead be taken by the people of Scotland.

A vote for independence will be the clearest possible declaration of confidence in ourselves and our nation. Independence will release a period of energy, effort and ambition which has the power to realise our hopes and expectations and transform our country.

Independence is not an end in itself. The Scottish Government wants us to have the powers of independence so that people who live here can build a different and better Scotland, where the many benefits of our rich and vibrant society are cherished and shared and where we work together to advance our nation as a whole.

At the heart of the case for independence are the principles of democracy, prosperity and fairness:

- the people of Scotland will always get governments we vote for

- we will control our own resources and make our own decisions about our economy

- we can decide how we use our wealth to benefit all the people in our society

If we vote for independence, the eyes of the world will be on Scotland as our ancient nation emerges – again – as an independent country. Scotland will become the 29th member of the European Union and the 194th member of the United Nations.

We can already all be proud of the democratic and peaceful process we are engaged in through the referendum. It shows the world that Scotland is ready to be a nation and will be a good and active global citizen.

At the first independent election on 5 May 2016, voters will have the chance to choose a government and policies for Scotland's future. Independence will give that government the powers it needs to build a more prosperous country and a fairer society.

Part Two – Scotland's national finances

Scotland is a wealthy country and can more than afford to be independent. Our public finances have consistently been healthier than those elsewhere in the UK, giving us a strong platform upon which to build economic success and maintain strong services.

Over each of the last 32 years, estimates show Scotland has contributed more tax per head of population than the the UK as whole. Total Scottish tax receipts in 2011/12 (the latest year for which figures are available) were equivalent to £10,700 per head. This compares to a figure of £9,000 per head in the UK as a whole.

Taking tax and spending together, over the last five years Scotland's public finances have been stronger than the UK as a whole by a total of £12.6 billion – almost £2,400 per head. Over the period from 2007/08 to 2011/12 the ratio of public spending to GDP was estimated to be lower for Scotland than in the UK as a whole.

On independence in 2016, Scotland's estimated financial position will continue to be healthier than the UK as a whole. We will set out on a firm financial footing. The Government has identified measures to raise revenue and reduce spending that will provide scope for our immediate priorities for action: transformation of our childcare system, ending the "bedroom tax", and competitive business taxation.

Part Three – The opportunities of independence

Economy

Even without North Sea oil and gas, GDP (national economic output) per head in Scotland is virtually identical to that of the UK as a whole. With oil it is almost one-fifth bigger.

The Scottish economy has key strengths in growth industries such as food and drink, energy, creative industries, tourism and life sciences. Per head of population we have more top universities than any other country in the world. We perform strongly as a location for inward investment and we have a strong financial services industry.

The economic choice in the independence referendum is therefore how to build on this sound economic base to create sustainable jobs, ensure that more people share in Scotland's wealth and build long-term resilience and security in our economy.

Under the Westminster system Scotland is treated as a regional economy within the UK. Our ability to meet future challenges and seize opportunities is constrained and many major decisions are taken by Westminster. Currently, the Scottish Parliament is responsible for just 7 per cent of taxes raised in Scotland; new tax powers will only increase this to around 15 per cent. With independence Scotland will control 100 per cent of our resources.

Under the Westminster system, Scotland is also locked in to one of the most unequal economic models in the developed world: since 1975 income inequality among working-age people has increased faster in the UK than in any other country in the OECD. The increasing geographical imbalance concentrates jobs, population growth and investment in London and the South East of England, but no action has been taken to address this by successive Westminster governments.

The UK economic model is also vulnerable to instability. The UK recession and recovery has been more prolonged and damaging than first thought and debt levels remain amongst the highest in the developed world.

The gap between rich and poor, the increasing concentration of economic activity in one part of the UK and the imbalances in the structure and composition of the UK economic model all suggest that continuing as a regional economy will hamper job creation in Scotland and reduce economic resilience and security in the long-term.

The Scottish Government believes that Scotland needs to become independent to address these issues. Only independence provides the opportunity to build an economy to take advantage of our unique strengths and size, and to deliver a more prosperous, resilient and fairer Scotland, fully engaged in Europe and the wider world.

The Scottish Government plans to use the powers of independence to achieve higher levels of growth and job opportunities through:

- a strong external focus on competing in the global economy
- promoting areas of comparative advantage to develop a distinctive economy
- emphasising innovation, technology and manufacturing
- fostering high levels of trust and reducing income inequality, encouraging a stronger and shared sense of national purpose
- improving workforce skills and opportunities, particularly for women and young people

Our priorities would include:

- increasing female and parental participation in the workforce through a transformational expansion in childcare provision
- giving Scottish businesses a competitive edge by providing a clear timetable for reducing corporation tax by up to three percentage points; and improving international connectivity by cutting Air Passenger Duty by 50 per cent
- introducing a package of employment measures designed to improve company performance and develop a greater sense of cohesion and opportunity in the workplace, including employee representation and greater female participation on company boards

- examining how to help small businesses, for example with their national insurance contributions

We plan to establish a Fair Work Commission which will guarantee that the minimum wage will rise at the very least in line with inflation and provide advice on fairness at work and business competitiveness. The Commission will work with a Convention on Employment and Labour Relations to transform the relationship between government, employers and employees.

Currency

The pound is Scotland's currency just as much as it is the rest of the UK's.

The expert Fiscal Commission Working Group concluded that retaining Sterling as part of a formal Sterling Area with the UK would be the best option for an independent Scotland and the rest of the UK.

The Scottish Government agrees with that view. Using Sterling will provide continuity and certainty for business and individuals, and an independent Scotland will make a substantial contribution to a Sterling Area. We will therefore retain the pound in an independent Scotland.

Taxation

With independence the Scottish Parliament will make decisions about all aspects of taxation. Independence will provide an opportunity to design a Scottish tax system based on specific Scottish circumstances, preferences and principles.

Tax rates and allowances will be set by future governments in an independent Scotland. As Scotland's public finances are healthier than those of the UK as a whole, there will no requirement for an independent Scotland to raise the general rate of taxation to fund existing levels of spending.

As well as the changes to business taxation outlined above, the current Scottish Government would make the following changes to personal taxation during the first term of an independent Scottish Parliament:

- we will ensure that the personal tax allowance and tax credits increase in line with inflation
- we will end the proposed tax allowance for some married couples which does not help all families and parents
- we will abolish the Shares for Rights scheme which offers tax incentives to those giving up employment rights, creating tax avoidance opportunities and risks to employees
- we will simplify the tax system to reduce compliance costs, streamline reliefs and help to reduce tax avoidance, with a target revenue gain of £250 million a year by the end of the first term

Transport

Scotland's geographical position makes strong international and cross-border transport links vital for our economic success and our social wellbeing. Within the UK, Westminster focuses on the transport needs of London and the South East, as the plans for high-speed rail demonstrate. Independence will provide us with more choices for our transport system, and we will be able to decide our forward investment based on our own finances rather than within boundaries set by Westminster. We will be able to consider options such as different ownership models for the rail network, and address Scotland's international connections to the global marketplace, developing our air and sea access to the most important markets. We will also be able to consider tax measures to help transport in Scotland, like reducing Air Passenger Duty and examining the benefits of a Fuel Duty Regulator mechanism to stabilise prices for business and consumers.

Early years

Parents in the UK face some of the highest childcare costs in Europe. Parents in Scotland spend around 27 per cent of household income on childcare, compared to the OECD average of 12 per cent.

Independence will give us the opportunity to make a transformational change to the way that Scotland provides childcare services, which will allow parents, in particular women, to choose to work without worrying about the cost of looking after their children. With independence the benefits of their work – in economic growth and tax revenues – will stay in Scotland, contributing over time to the costs of this provision.

This Government plans a universal system of high quality early learning and childcare for children from the age of one to when they enter school. By the end of the first independent Scottish Parliament, every three and four year old and vulnerable two year old will be entitled to 1,140 hours of child care a year. This is the same amount of time as children spend in primary school in a year (the equivalent of 30 hours per week over 38 weeks).

This extension in the provision of early learning and childcare will be achieved in a way that is affordable and sustainable. It will include investment in training and require a substantial increase in the workforce. We estimate that it will create around 35,000 new jobs. The additional investment will also cover regulation, inspection and quality through Education Scotland, the Care Inspectorate and the Scottish Social Services Council.

Schools and universities

In Scotland's secondary schools, attainment levels have increased year-on-year. Substantial programmes of investment in new schools and teacher numbers have also been put in place. Scotland's schools are now implementing the Curriculum for Excellence to equip young people with the skills they need for the 21st century.

However, Scotland still has a long-standing problem with equality of attainment in our schools. Pupils from the most deprived 20 per cent of areas leave school with significantly lower qualifications than those in the least deprived 20 per cent. That gap is greater than most of the developed nations against which we measure ourselves. Independence gives us the opportunity to address this gap and the wider issues of deprivation and poverty which lie behind it.

Independence will also allow Scotland to protect the principle of free education, and the current Scottish Government guarantees that, on independence, Scottish students will continue to have free access to higher education.

We plan to continue to participate in the current common research area ensuring that Scotland's research continues to be available across the UK to benefit both Scotland and the rest of the UK. Scotland will pay our way within the common research area, and contribute to arrangements for research funding through the existing Research Councils.

State Pensions

The proportion of tax revenues taken up by social protection (including state pensions) is lower in Scotland than the UK, so these benefits are currently more affordable here.

We will ensure that current pensioners will receive their pensions as now, on time and in full. All accrued rights will be honoured and protected, and planned reforms will be rolled out, including the single-tier pension.

While we accept that the State Pension Age should rise to 66 according to the existing timetable, the Westminster Government's plan for a rapid move to 67 is a concern. The timetable is significantly faster than that announced by the previous Westminster Government and it fails to take account of the fact that, due to lower life expectancy, Scots currently enjoy fewer years, on average, in receipt of state pensions than pensioners elsewhere in the UK.

This Scottish Government plans to:

- set up an Independent Commission on the State Pension Age to consider the appropriate State Pension Age for Scotland over the long term

- uprate the State Pension by the triple-lock from 2016. This means that pensions increase by average earnings, CPI inflation, or 2.5 per cent – whichever of these is highest – and provides protection for the value of pensions over time

- ensure that from 6 April 2016, new pensioners will receive a Scottish single-tier pension, set at the rate of £160 per week – £1.10 a week higher than the rate currently expected for the UK

- retain the Savings Credit (the full Savings Credit payment is currently £18 per week for a single person) benefiting around 9,000 low income pensioners

Private and public service pensions

This Scottish Government supports the continued roll-out of automatic enrolment, introduced last year, to help address the historic decline in private pension saving. With independence, we would establish a Scottish Employment Savings Trust to provide a workplace pension scheme focused on people with low to moderate earnings, which will accept any employer wishing to use it.

In an independent Scotland, all public service pension rights and entitlements will be fully protected and accessible.

The organisation and infrastructure needed to pay state and public sector pensions is already in place in Scotland, through the pensions centres in Motherwell and Dundee, the Scottish Public Pensions Agency and the local authority teams that manage public sector pensions.

Social protection

In an independent Scotland we envisage a welfare system based on clear principles and values: support for people who work; a safety net for people who cannot work; and a climate of social solidarity.

The current Westminster Government's approach to welfare has consistently been rejected by a majority of Scottish MPs and MSPs. If we leave welfare in Westminster's hands, our welfare state is likely to be changed beyond recognition. Universal Credit and Personal Independence Payments have suffered from controversy and delay, and have created significant anxiety amongst some of our most vulnerable people. The unfairness of the "bedroom tax" is well known.

We believe it is possible to design an efficient and fair welfare system that meets the needs of those who depend on it, and treats them with dignity and respect while supporting those who can to find work.

Following independence, the immediate priorities will be to reverse the most damaging and counterproductive of the UK welfare changes. On independence the current Government will:

■ abolish the "bedroom tax" within the first year of the first year of the independent Scottish Parliament

■ halt the further roll out of Universal Credit and Personal Independence Payments in Scotland

■ ensure that benefits and tax credits increase at least in line with inflation to avoid the poorest families falling further into poverty

If there is a vote for independence in the referendum, the Scottish Government will ask the Westminster Government to stop the roll-out in Scotland of Universal Credit and Personal Independence Payments immediately. This will give the Scottish Government elected in 2016 maximum flexibility to reform the welfare system in line with Scotland's priorities.

Health

In an independent Scotland, we will continue to provide high quality, world-leading health and social care in a way that reflects the founding principles of the NHS and our social care services.

Scotland faces long-standing challenges in health outcomes which are strongly associated with economic and social disadvantage. With independence, Scotland can work towards a fairer society that will address these health inequalities.

Independence will not affect the day-to-day management of the NHS in Scotland, nor how people access NHS services. Similarly, it will not mean ending current cross-border arrangements with health services in the rest of the UK, which have continued even though the NHS in Scotland already operates independently.

International relations

An independent Scotland will have a firm commitment to international partnership and co-operation, not only in these Isles, but also in the EU and other international organisations, to secure shared interests and protect Scotland's people and resources.

Scotland and the rest of the UK will have a close and constructive relationship both at home and on many foreign policy issues. The current Scottish Government would intend to support the rest of the UK in maintaining its seat on the UN Security Council.

We plan to establish a network of overseas embassies and consulates to represent Scotland's interests internationally.

We estimate that the running costs of our initial proposed network of 70 to 90 overseas missions will be £90-120 million. This is expected to be below Scotland's population share of the UK's total expenditure on overseas representation in 2016/17, giving opportunities for savings. Scotland would also be entitled to a fair share of the UK's assets.

European Union

The Scottish Government, supported by the overwhelming majority of Members of the Scottish Parliament, believes that membership of the EU is in the best interests of Scotland. It is our policy, therefore, that an independent Scotland will continue as a member of the EU.

Following a vote for independence, the Scottish Government will immediately seek discussions with the Westminster Government and with the member states and institutions of the EU to agree the process whereby a smooth transition to full EU membership can take place on the day Scotland becomes an independent country.

We will approach EU membership negotiations on the basis of the principle of *continuity of effect*. That means that Scotland's transition to independent membership will be based on the EU Treaty obligations and provisions that currently apply to Scotland under our present status as part of the UK. It will avoid disruption to Scotland's current fully integrated standing within the legal, economic, institutional, political and social framework of the EU.

While the Scottish Government recognises the political and economic objectives of the Eurozone, an independent Scotland will not seek membership. Scotland's participation in the Sterling Area will not conflict with wider obligations under the EU Treaties.

Nor will we seek membership of the Schengen area. Instead, an independent Scotland will remain part of the Common Travel Area (CTA) with the rest of the UK, Ireland, the Isle of Man and the Channel Islands. The CTA, which dates back to the early 1920s, is part of the broader "social union" that is the expression of the close economic, social and cultural ties across the nations of these islands.

International development
Part of being a good global citizen is a commitment to international development. In line with the target recognised by the United Nations as long ago as 1970, we plan to spend 0.7 per cent of Gross National Income on Official Development Assistance, and to enshrine it as a binding, statutory commitment.

Defence
By removing nuclear weapons and maintaining defence forces appropriate to our circumstances, we can save a substantial proportion of Scotland's current defence contribution to the UK, while still having levels of defence spending that allow us to deliver the capabilities we need and make a significant investment in procurement, supporting key Scottish industries including the shipbuilding industry.

Following a vote for independence, we would make early agreement on the speediest safe removal of nuclear weapons a priority. This would be with a view to the removal of Trident within the first term of the Scottish Parliament following independence.

Following a vote for independence in 2014, the Scottish Government will notify NATO of our intention to join the alliance and will negotiate our transition from being a NATO member as part of the UK to becoming an independent member of the alliance. Scotland would take our place as one of the many non-nuclear members of NATO.

The current Scottish Government has identified five defence priorities for an independent Scotland:

■ maintaining the commitment to a budget for defence and security in an independent Scotland of £2.5 billion

- securing the speediest safe withdrawal of nuclear weapons from Scotland

- building a focus on maritime capabilities, such as air and sea-based patrol, and specialist forces able to operate around our coasts, protecting Scotland's maritime assets and contributing to collective security in the North Atlantic

- progressively building to a total of 15,000 regular and 5,000 reserve personnel following independence

- reconfiguring the defence estate inherited at the point of independence to meet Scotland's needs, including the transition of Faslane to a conventional naval base and joint headquarters of Scottish defence forces

We are prepared to negotiate arrangements for the continued use of defence infrastructure in Scotland by UK forces and vice versa, at least for a transitional period. Such arrangements could be carried forward into the longer term, where both the countries consider them the most effective means of delivering defence capabilities.

Justice

It is our more deprived communities that suffer most from the impact of crime and are most vulnerable to the influence of organised crime. An independent Scotland will have control over policy on welfare, employment and public expenditure. As a result, rather than just dealing with the consequences of crime and disadvantage through the criminal justice system, an independent Scotland will be able to use the full range of powers available to government to make our communities safer, stronger and more secure.

There are some specific issues that would become the responsibility of the Scottish Parliament on independence, such as firearms, drugs – including the proceeds of drug trafficking – and gambling. Responsibility for these will allow Scotland to take an integrated approach to issues that affect our communities.

Security

An independent Scotland will have national security arrangements that reflect Scotland's needs, values and the risks and threats we face, based on a full review of security requirements and a regular cycle of threat assessments.

A new security and intelligence agency will have a range of responsibilities focused on intelligence-gathering, analysis and reporting, assessment of risk and threat, cyber security and protection of critical infrastructure. Although independent, it would work closely with Police Scotland.

Given the interest of both Scotland and the rest of the UK in our mutual security, the Scottish Government will work closely with the current UK security and intelligence agencies both to ensure that there is a seamless, secure transition and for the continuing security of both countries.

Immigration

Scotland's differing demographic and migration needs mean that the current UK immigration system has not served our interests.

This Government plans, following independence, a points-based immigration system, targeted at particular Scottish needs. The system will enable us to meet the needs of Scottish society with greater flexibility. For example, it could provide incentives to migrants who move to live and work in remoter geographical areas – assisting with community sustainability, or adding new categories of skills.

We will also reintroduce student visas removed by Westminster to encourage more talented people from around the world to further their education in Scotland, providing income for Scotland's education institutions and contributing to diversity.

Citizenship and passports

In taking forward the result of a vote for independence, we will ensure that British citizens "habitually resident" in Scotland on independence will automatically be considered Scottish citizens. This will include British citizens who hold dual citizenship with another country. Scottish-born British citizens currently living outside of Scotland will also automatically be considered

Scottish citizens. Other people will be able to register or apply for Scottish citizenship on independence based on clear criteria.

All Scottish citizens will have the right to acquire a Scottish passport, although there will be no requirement to hold one. We plan that citizens will be able to apply for Scottish passports from the date of independence.

Rural Scotland

Scottish farmers, crofters and rural and remote communities should be able to compete on a level playing field with their counterparts across Europe.

The interests of rural Scotland have been repeatedly traded off against other UK priorities in EU negotiations where Scotland has no direct voice.

Successive Westminster governments have argued for a significant reduction in agricultural support payments despite Scotland's already low share of funding and the need for support given our geographical and climatic challenges. These payments are vital to ensure our farmers and crofters continue to produce food, deliver environment benefits and sustain our rural communities.

An independent Scotland will engage with the EU as an independent member state to secure a fairer return, boosting support to Scotland's farmers, increasing business start-up assistance for young farmers, supporting more infrastructure investments in broadband and renewables, and providing greater investment in rural tourism.

As an independent member state, Scotland will be negotiating as one of the foremost and most respected fishing nations in Europe. This status will give Scotland the opportunity to take a leadership role in reforming the Common Fisheries Policy to deliver fisheries management at regional and Member State level and to keep Scottish quota in Scotland.

Food and drink

Scotland's Food and Drink sector contributes 18 per cent of our overseas exports, but less than 1.5 per cent of overseas exports for the UK as a whole. Scotland's food and drink industry does an excellent job promoting the Scottish brand, but Scotland is constrained by the current constitutional settlement from directly engaging on a level footing with other countries. Independence will boost Scotland's international profile, delivering new opportunities for food and drink exports, as well as attracting new visitors to our country to enjoy our produce.

Energy

Scotland is an energy-rich nation. We have the largest oil reserves in the EU as well as huge renewable energy potential. But under successive Westminster governments our energy wealth has not been invested, instead it has gone straight to the UK Treasury.

Independence gives Scotland the opportunity to harness this energy wealth for the people of Scotland. With independence we can ensure that taxation revenues from oil and gas support Scottish public services, and that Scotland sets up an Energy Fund to ensure that future generations also benefit from our oil and gas reserves. The principles of stability and certainty that will guide this Government's approach will guarantee new investment in energy: we have no plans to increase the overall tax burden on the oil industry and no changes will be made to the fiscal regime without consultation.

A well-functioning energy market, delivering the best outcome for consumers, is a prerequisite for a flourishing economy and society. With our plans for independence, Scotland's substantial energy resources and balanced generation mix will provide enhanced security of supply, greater long-term stability in energy prices, decarbonisation of electricity generation, the protection and creation of jobs and further community empowerment. We propose that a single GB-wide market for electricity and gas will continue, helping the rest of the UK secure its supply and meet its renewables obligations, provided that the system also meets Scottish requirements for security of supply.

The government of an independent Scotland will be able to use all the powers available to us to help people with their energy bills. The current Scottish Government intends to meet the costs of programmes like the Energy Company Obligation and Warm Homes Discount from central resources. This will allow energy companies to reduce bills to consumers by around five per cent.

Culture

In an independent Scotland we will build on our cultural ambitions for Scotland. Our approach has been, and will continue to be, distinct from that of Westminster in that we recognise the intrinsic value of culture and heritage, and do not just value them for their economic benefit, substantial though that is. We view culture and heritage as fundamental to our wellbeing and quality of life. Our ambition is to build an independent nation where our cultural and historic life can continue to flourish. With independence we will have new powers over the economy to encourage our culture and creative sectors. And the process of becoming independent will, itself, stimulate new creativity and energy in Scotland.

An independent Scotland will enjoy increased opportunities to build our international reputation for culture, heritage and creativity. The development of a Scottish overseas diplomatic and trade network will provide Scotland with the opportunity to promote and share our culture and traditions with nations across the world.

Broadcasting

Independence will create new opportunities in broadcasting and production in Scotland. A new publicly funded, public service broadcaster should help strengthen our democracy, encourage production and participation. It should be a trusted, reliable, impartial source of information and reflect the diversity of the nation and our world to the people of Scotland, and it should seek opportunities to collaborate beyond our borders to pioneer innovation in entertainment, education and journalism.

Following independence the Scottish Government plans to honour all existing TV and radio broadcasting licences to their expiry, maintaining access to all the existing programming and content that people currently enjoy.

Alongside the commercial channels serving Scotland, we plan to create a new public service broadcaster, the Scottish Broadcasting Service (SBS), which will initially be based on the staff and assets of BBC Scotland. Over time the SBS would develop services to reflect the broad interests and outlook of the people of Scotland. Broadcasting on TV, radio and online, the SBS will be funded by licence fee, which on independence will be the same as the UK licence fee. All current licence fee payment exemptions and concessions will be retained. We propose that the SBS enters into a new formal relationship with the BBC as a joint venture, where the SBS would continue to supply the BBC network with the same level of programming, in return for continuing access to BBC services in Scotland. This will ensure that the people of Scotland will still have access to all current programming, including *EastEnders, Dr Who,* and *Strictly Come Dancing* and to channels like CBeebies.

Part Four – Transition

Between the referendum in 2014 and independence in 2016
The period between the referendum and independence will see negotiations with the rest of the UK, represented by the Westminster Government, and with the EU and other international partners and organisations. **Following these preparations and negotiations, Scotland will assume our status as an independent country on 24 March 2016.**

Following a vote for independence in 2014, agreements will be made between the Scottish and Westminster Governments, in the spirit of the Edinburgh Agreement, setting the parameters for Scotland's transition to independence. These will:

- set out the precise timetable towards independence day in 2016

- determine the principles, process and timetable for the negotiation and conclusion of the agreements which will form the final independence settlement

- provide the Scottish Government and Scottish Parliament with the legal powers they need to prepare for independence

Soon after a vote for independence, we will seek a transfer of the necessary powers to the Scottish Parliament so that it can establish the constitutional platform for an independent Scotland – the laws and administrative arrangements to establish Scotland as an independent state.

In addition to discussions with the UK, negotiations will be held with the EU in advance of independence to settle the terms of an independent Scotland's continuing membership.

The final agreement with the rest of the UK will cover a range of matters, including the approach to assets and liabilities and the delivery of services. The over-riding priority will be the seamless delivery of public services to citizens of both countries.

The apportionment of the UK national debt will be negotiated and agreed. The national debt could be apportioned by reference to the historic contribution made to the UK's public finances by Scotland, or on the basis of our population share. We may choose to offset Scotland's share of the value of UK assets against our inherited debt. On any realistic calculation Scotland's inherited debt is projected to be a lower proportion of GDP than is the case for the UK as a whole.

Government and Civil Service

Independence will see the Scottish Government develop new functions as it takes on the responsibilities of serving an independent country. Scotland already has a civil service that is politically impartial, appointed on merit and supports the elected government of the day. If the present Scottish Government is re-elected we plan to spread government jobs and decision-making, delivering the direct economic benefits of independent government to more parts of Scotland.

The Westminster Government employs nearly 30,000 civil servants in Scotland at present. On independence many will transfer to the employment of the Scottish Government and its agencies. We will work with the Westminster Government to preserve continuity of employment for all staff, either by transfer to the Scottish Government or through continued employment by the Westminster Government where it still requires their skills.

A modern constitution

Independence provides an opportunity to modernise Scottish democracy on the basis of a written constitution setting out the way the country is governed and the rights of its citizens.

The Scottish Government believes a constitutional convention will ensure a participative and inclusive process by which the people of Scotland, as well as politicians, civic society organisations, business interests, trade unions, local authorities and others, can have a direct role in shaping the constitution.

The Scottish Government will be just one of many voices contributing to the debate and helping to shape Scotland's written constitution. However, there are certain provisions that the Government believes should be considered by the constitutional convention, such as equality of opportunity and the right to live free of discrimination and prejudice, a constitutional ban on nuclear weapons being based in Scotland, and certain social and economic rights, such as the right to education, the right to healthcare and protections for children.

The Monarchy and the Crown

On independence Scotland will be a constitutional monarchy, continuing the Union of the Crowns that dates back to 1603, pre-dating the Union of the Parliaments by over one hundred years. On independence in 2016, Her Majesty The Queen will be head of state.

Earlier in 2013, the rules on succession to the Crown (as they affect Scotland and elsewhere) were amended to remove outdated gender discrimination. This Government intends to support, and promote amongst the other Commonwealth States with the Queen as head of state, a similar measure to remove religious discrimination from the succession rules.

Top questions and answers

We know that you want to know as much as possible about an independent Scotland and what it will mean for you, your family and Scotland as whole. You can find answers to some of the most common questions here, with cross-references to the relevant sections of the guide. In Part 5 we answer 650 detailed questions we have been asked about independence.

Why should Scotland be independent?

Independence means Scotland's future will be in Scotland's hands. It means we can make more of Scotland's wealth, talent and resources for the benefit of the people who live in Scotland through a stronger economy, more jobs and people getting a fairer return for their hard work and efforts.

It will allow Scottish governments to do specific things like improve childcare, make the tax system fairer, cut energy bills and scrap the "bedroom tax".

Independence is about improving the quality of life for all people across Scotland. We will be able to take decisions on our economy designed for Scotland's particular needs and based on our own priorities.

Similar countries to Scotland have seen higher levels of economic growth over the past generation. That is because they have the bonus of being independent and are able to make the right choices for their nation and economy. If Scotland had matched the levels of growth of these other independent nations between 1977 and 2007, GDP per head in Scotland would now be 3.8 per cent higher, equivalent to an additional £900 per head.

Can Scotland afford to be independent?

Yes. Scotland is one of the wealthiest nations in the world. In terms of our total economic output per head we ranked eighth out of the 34 developed countries in the OECD in 2011. We raise more tax and our public finances have been stronger than those of the UK as a whole over the past 32 years.

Despite all these strengths, many families in Scotland are struggling to make ends meet. We are a wealthy country and yet the full benefit of our vast wealth is not felt by the people who live and work here. With independence, we can make sure Scotland's wealth and resources work better for the people of Scotland.

To find out more about Scotland's public finances go to Chapter 2.

What will happen to my pension?

Under our plans your state pension and any personal or occupational pensions will be paid in the same way as they are today. The rights you have accrued will be protected. Scotland is better able to afford pension and welfare payments than the rest of the UK. Social protection (which includes pensions and benefits) takes up a smaller share of our national output and our tax revenues than it does in the UK as a whole.

Under the Scottish Government's proposals you will, as a minimum, receive the same state pension payments on independence as in the rest of the UK. The current Scottish Government also proposes some added protections.

Given that life expectancy for both men and women in Scotland has consistently remained below the UK level, the present Scottish Government is committed to reviewing the Westminster Government's plan to speed up the timetable for increasing the State Pension Age to 67 between 2026 and 2028.

You can find out more about the state pension in Chapter 4.

Will independence change the tax I pay?

The process of independence itself will not change the tax rates we pay. As Scotland's public finances are healthier than those of the UK as a whole, there will no requirement to raise the general rate of taxation to fund existing levels of spending after independence.

However, being able to make changes to the tax system is one of the advantages of independence. If the present Scottish Government is elected in 2016 as the first government of an independent Scotland, our first budget would:

- increase tax allowances and tax credits in line with inflation

- simplify the tax system to reduce compliance costs, streamline reliefs and help to reduce tax avoidance, with a target revenue gain of £250 million per year by the end of the first term

- end the proposed tax allowance for some married couples, which does not benefit all parents or families

- abolish the UK's Shares for Rights scheme which encourages tax avoidance

You can find out more about tax in an independent Scotland in Chapters 2 and 3.

Who will form the government of an independent Scotland?

The first government of an independent Scotland will be elected at the next Scottish election in May 2016.

The 2016 elections will happen in the same way as previous elections, with both constituency and regional MSPs elected. The votes cast in 2016 will determine which party or parties form the government. That could be SNP, Scottish Labour, or any other party – or coalition of parties – that secures the support of the electorate. It will be for the people of Scotland to decide.

To find out more about an independent government and parliament go to Chapter 10.

Will Scotland be a member of the EU?

Yes. It is the current Scottish Government's policy that Scotland remains part of the European Union. Between a Yes vote in 2014 and independence day, Scotland will agree the terms of our continuing membership of the EU. This will happen while we are still part of the UK and part of the EU, ensuring a smooth transition to independent membership.

You can find out more about Scotland in the EU in Chapter 6.

How can you guarantee our future security?
Scotland will have our own defence forces to protect Scotland and its seas. The present Scottish Government is committed to NATO membership.

The current Scottish Government will ensure a strong conventional military presence on Scottish soil and in Scottish waters, but we will ensure that nuclear weapons on the Clyde are removed. To find out more about defence go to Chapter 6.

Scotland will also be more financially secure. The lessons from the financial crisis are being learned and across the world new rules are being put in place to reduce and where possible remove the risks that led to the crisis of 2008. There are more details in Chapter 3.

An independent Scotland will also have one of the best safety nets for the future with our offshore energy reserves providing a guarantee that we can protect ourselves in hard times.

We will establish an Energy Fund, which will save a proportion of our current oil wealth for future generations. You can find out more about Scotland's Energy Fund in Chapter 8.

Will we be able to keep the pound or will we be forced to join the euro?
Scotland will continue to use the pound, just as we do today. The Scottish Government's expert advisers, the Fiscal Commission, have set out a clear framework for this. It will be in the interests of the rest of the UK as well as Scotland. You can find out more about the currency in Chapter 3.

EU law sets down a series of conditions a country must meet before it can join the euro. This includes entering the Exchange Rate Mechanism (ERM) II. Joining ERM II is voluntary and that means Scotland cannot be forced to join the euro. To find out more about Scotland in the EU go to Chapter 6.

How can Scotland be independent if we keep the pound?
Independent countries around the world share currencies.
Countries like France, Germany, and the Netherlands do not
have their own currency but are clearly independent, and
control their own resources. This approach makes sense for
Scotland and the rest of the UK, because it will make it easier
for us to trade with each other and will also mean that our
mortgages and pensions continue to be in pounds and pence,
just as they are today.

To find out more about keeping the pound, go to Chapter 3.

Will it cost too much to become independent?
No. Scotland already pays our share of the cost of UK-wide
services, like the benefits system and the tax system. We pay
our share of the UK's armed forces and overseas embassies.
After independence we will no longer be paying for these UK
services and bodies, but will use the money to pay for our own
Scottish equivalent. We propose to save money on some things
like defence as we will not be paying towards the UK's nuclear
weapons. So money that we currently send to Westminster to
be spent in other parts of the UK – or on things we in Scotland
do not want – will stay in Scotland to invest in a modern and
efficient system of government for our newly independent
country, and to pay for things that we do want. We might decide
to continue to share some services with the UK, at least for a
transitional period.

You can find out more about the transition to independence in
Chapter 10.

What makes you think an independent Scotland will be a fairer
country?
The sort of country we become will be up to the people of
Scotland. Scotland has all the wealth it needs to be a fairer
country. We are one of the richest nations on the planet
and could choose to use that wealth in a different way from
Westminster. For example, we can choose to invest in childcare
instead of spending money on nuclear weapons. We can
choose not to impose the "bedroom tax" and to have a more

efficient tax system that ensures everyone pays their fair share. With independence we can make different choices in line with our values and the views of the people of Scotland.

To find out more about the democratic opportunities of independence, go to Chapter 1.

You can find out more about social justice in an independent Scotland at Chapter 4.

What will independence deliver for me?

With independence the Scottish Parliament will have all the powers we need in Scotland to make life better for the people who live here. The present Scottish Government's policies for an independent Scotland include:

- delivering a transformational change in childcare so that over time, every child from age one to starting school is guaranteed 30 hours of provision for 38 weeks of the year. This will reduce costs for families and improve support for people with children to return to work (see Chapter 5)

- reducing your energy bills by around five per cent by moving the costs of some environmental schemes from your energy bill and funding them from central government resources (see Chapter 8)

- protecting your state pension, with stronger guarantees that the real value of your pension will not fall (see Chapter 4)

- ensuring that the minimum wage rises in line with inflation (see Chapter 3)

- protecting the value of benefits, tax allowances and tax credits by uprating these in line with inflation (see Chapter 3)

- building a fairer Scotland by stopping the roll out of Universal Credit, scrapping the "bedroom tax" and halting some of the most damaging welfare changes being introduced by the Westminster Government (see Chapter 4)

What will happen to our relationships with the other parts of the UK?

Scotland will continue to have a close and special relationship with the other nations of these isles. This will be a new, updated partnership of equals between the people of Scotland and the rest of the UK.

Under our proposals, we will keep our close links of family and friendship through a continuing social union and will continue to share the Queen as head of state (as 16 Commonwealth countries currently do) and share the pound as our currency. We'll be equal partners within the EU and as part of a common defence partnership in NATO.

But independence will end the parliamentary union and that means we will no longer send MPs to Westminster. Decisions about Scotland's future and about our economy and society will be taken here. The people of Scotland will be in charge.

To find out more about our continuing special relationship with England, Wales and Northern Ireland, go to Chapter 6.

What about a Scottish passport?

Our proposals for independence mean that, as a Scottish citizen you will be entitled to a Scottish passport. A Scottish passport will cost the same as a UK passport and you will be able to continue using your existing UK passport until it is the normal time for you to change it. To find out more about passports and citizenship, go to Chapter 7.

Scotland is already part of a Common Travel Area (CTA) with the rest of the UK, Ireland, the Channel Islands and the Isle of Man, which dates back to the 1920s. We plan to remain part of the CTA which means that there will be no border controls, and you will not need a passport to travel to other parts of the UK, Ireland, the Channel Islands and the Isle of Man (although of course some airlines require proof of identity for domestic flights). You can read more in Chapter 6.

How will we become independent?

Scotland will become independent if the people of Scotland vote Yes in the referendum on 18 September 2014. After a vote for independence, the Scottish Government will reach agreement with the Westminster Government and the EU on arrangements for the transition to independence, based on our proposed date of **24 March 2016**. You can find out more about the transition to independence in Chapter 10.

Will we keep The Queen?

Yes. The Queen will remain head of state in Scotland. An independent Scotland will have a written constitution which sets out how we are to be governed. There are more details about government and parliament in an independent Scotland in Chapter 10.

What about our share of the national debt?

Scotland and the rest of the UK will agree a share of the national debt. This could be by reference to the historical contribution made to the UK's public finances by Scotland. An alternative approach would be to use our population share. Either way, our share of the UK's debt is projected to be smaller as a proportion of our economic output than for the UK as a whole, which means Scotland is better placed for the future.

However, we will also be entitled to a fair share of the UK's assets, which are estimated to be worth £1,267 billion. We may choose to offset part of our share of UK assets against the debt we agree to take on from the UK.

To find out more about our share of the UK debt and how we will manage it, go to Chapter 10.

What will happen to the benefits and tax credits I receive?

On independence you will continue to receive benefit payments and tax credits in the same way as you do now. Becoming independent will not, in itself, change your entitlement. However, future Scottish governments can choose to do things differently from the UK. For example, this Government will stop the damaging changes to our welfare system being introduced by Westminster. We will scrap the "bedroom tax" and stop the roll out of Universal Credit and Personal Independence Payments. You can see more of our proposals for a fairer welfare system in Chapter 4.

Will civil servants working in UK departments still have jobs?
Independence will mean the civil service in Scotland will cover a range of services currently provided by Westminster. Responsibility for services such as benefits will transfer to the Scottish Government. New jobs will be created for services currently delivered from other parts of the UK. We will work with the Westminster Government to preserve continuity of employment for all staff, either by transfer to the Scottish Government or through continued employment by the Westminster Government where it continues to require their skills. The pension entitlements and other terms and conditions of employment of civil servants transferring from the Westminster Government will be fully honoured. Staff who transfer will join a skilled and diverse workforce in the civil service in Scotland, which is based on the principles of honesty, integrity, objectivity and impartiality, committed to good employment practice and with a continued commitment to no compulsory redundancies.

You can find out more about our plans for the public sector in Scotland in Chapter 10.

Is it Scotland's oil and gas?
The vast bulk of oil and gas in the UK comes from the Scottish part of the UK Continental Shelf and will be in Scotland after independence. Analysis tells us that in excess of 90 per cent of the oil and gas revenues are from fields in Scottish waters (based on well-established principles of international law). To find out more, go to Chapter 8.

Do we depend on oil and gas to become independent?
No. Scotland's economic output per head, even without oil and gas, is virtually the same as the UK as a whole. So oil and gas is a bonus. When we include the output of the North Sea, Scotland produces almost a fifth more per head that the UK average.

Oil and gas revenues make up 15 per cent of Scotland's overall public sector receipts, compared to 30 per cent for Norway and yet Norway has prospered and has a oil fund worth £470 billion.

To find out more about our oil and gas wealth, go to Chapter 8.

PART 1

CHAPTER 1 | THE CASE FOR INDEPENDENCE

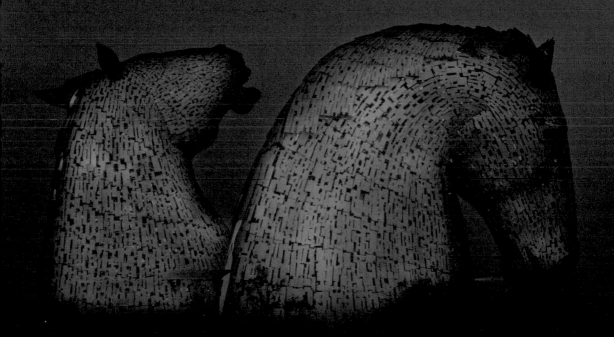

GAINS OF INDEPENDENCE

ECONOMIC POLICY AIMED AT **ECONOMIC** STABILITY AND JOB SECURITY IN **SCOTLAND**

ABILITY TO USE OUR OIL WEALTH FOR FUTURE GENERATIONS **BY VALUE** THERE IS ESTIMATED TO BE AS MUCH **NORTH SEA OIL** STILL TO COME AS HAS ALREADY BEEN EXTRACTED

AN INDEPENDENT **PARLIAMENT ELECTED** ENTIRELY BY **PEOPLE IN SCOTLAND**

ECONOMIC POLICY CAN BE TAILORED TO TAKE ADVANTAGE OF SCOTLAND'S **WORLD-CLASS UNIVERSITIES** AND KEY GROWTH INDUSTRIES LIKE **FOOD & DRINK LIFE SCIENCES AND TOURISM**

SCOTTISH PARLIAMENT HAS POWER TO **STOP** SERVICES BEING PRIVATISED

DECISIONS ABOUT SCOTLAND WILL BE TAKEN BY THE PEOPLE **WHO CARE** MOST ABOUT **SCOTLAND** THOSE WHO **WORK &** LIVE HERE

TAXES FROM PEOPLE IN **SCOTLAND** NO LONGER USED TO PAY FOR NUCLEAR **WEAPONS**

A GUARANTEE **THAT TAX** AND SOCIAL **SECURITY** RATES WILL BE SET IN LINE WITH THE WISHES OF THE PEOPLE OF **SCOTLAND**

ACCESS TO OUR OWN RESOURCES **DECISIONS ABOUT LEVEL** AND ALLOCATION OF PUBLIC SPENDING WILL BE TAKEN HERE IN SCOTLAND

Since the Scottish Parliament was re-established in 1999, responsibility for governing Scotland has been split.

The Scottish Parliament and Scottish Government in Edinburgh are responsible for a range of "devolved" matters, including the National Health Service, education, justice, social services, housing, the environment, farming, fisheries and aspects of transport.

The Westminster Government – currently a coalition of the Conservative and Liberal Democrat parties – and the Westminster Parliament have "reserved" responsibilities including defence, foreign affairs, macroeconomic policy, the welfare system, financial and business regulation and most aspects of taxation (see Annex B).

Taxes raised in Scotland pay for both governments, but our taxes generally go directly to Westminster[1]. Devolved services are largely funded by a "block grant" determined by Westminster[2].

Under independence, the Scottish Parliament and Scottish Government would take over all Westminster's remaining powers and responsibilities for Scotland. Decisions on economic policy, international relations, defence spending and priorities, social security benefits, taxation and other public spending would be made in Scotland by governments accountable to the Scottish people and not by Westminster governments we often do not support.

This chapter gives an overview of:

- why Scotland needs independence
- what Scotland will look like on independence
- what will happen between a Yes vote and Scotland becoming independent
- our financial and economic strengths
- the benefits of independence and the priorities for action of the current Scottish Government if it becomes the first government of an independent Scotland
- the consequences of Scotland voting No to independence

HOW SCOTLAND IS GOVERNED NOW

Constitution based on sovereignty of the Crown in Parliament
Her Majesty The Queen As Head of State

DEALING DIRECTLY WITH
OTHER GOVERNMENTS

NEGOTIATING TREATIES
ON SCOTLAND'S BEHALF

REPRESENTING SCOTLAND
INTERNATIONALLY

UK GOVERNMENT, INCLUDING
PRIME MINISTER AND SECRETARY
OF STATE FOR SCOTLAND FORMED BY
PARTY OF PARTIES WINNING MOST
SEATS IN HOUSE OF COMMONS
(SCOTLAND HAS 59 OUT OF 650 SEATS)

HOUSES OF PARLIAMENT

UPHOLDING
THE LAW OF

SUPREME COURT OF
THE UNITED KINGDOM

MAKES
DECISIONS

MAKES
LAWS

HOUSES OF COMMONS
(WITH 59 SCOTTISH
MPs OUT OF 650)

HOUSE OF LORDS,
MEMBERS APPOINTED
NOT ELECTED

HEARING APPEALS
ON CIVIL MATTERS
AND HUMAN RIGHTS
FROM

RESPONSIBLE FOR RESERVED ISSUES
LIKE TAX, WELFARE, FOREIGN AFFAIRS
AND DEFENCE

DEVOLVED POWERS
GIVEN IN 1998 & 2012

POWERS CAN BE ADDED
OR TAKEN AWAY

SCOTTISH COURTS:
COURT OF SESSION, HIGH COURT
OF JUSTICIARY AND OTHER
SCOTTISH COURTS

SCOTTISH GOVERNMENT
INCLUDING
FIRST MINISTER

RESPONSIBLE
TO

SCOTTISH PARLIAMENT,
ELECTED SOLELY BY
PROPORTIONAL
REPRESENTATION
("HOLYROOD")

MAKES
DECISIONS

MAKES
LAWS

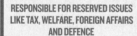

RESPONSIBLE FOR DEVOLVED ISSUES LIKE HEALTH,
EDUCATION, LOCAL GOVERNMENT, JUSTICE,
THE ENVIRONMENT, HOUSING, SOCIAL WORK

DEALING DIRECTLY WITH
OTHER GOVERNMENTS

HOW SCOTLAND WILL BE
GOVERNED ON INDEPENDENCE

Constitution based on sovereignty of the people of Scotland
Her Majesty The Queen As Head of State

NEGOTIATING TREATIES
ON SCOTLAND'S BEHALF

REPRESENTING SCOTLAND
INTERNATIONALLY

SCOTTISH GOVERNMENT
INCLUDING
FIRST MINISTER

RESPONSIBLE
TO

SCOTTISH PARLIAMENT,
ELECTED SOLELY BY PROPORTIONAL
REPRESENTATION
("HOLYROOD")

UPHOLDING
THE LAW OF

COURT OF SESSION AND
HIGH COURT OF JUSTICIARY
ACTING AS THE SUPREME COURT
OF SCOTLAND

MAKES
DECISIONS

MAKES
LAWS

HEARING APPEALS
FROM

RESPONSIBLE FOR ALL ISSUES, INCLUDING HEALTH, EDUCATION,
LOCAL GOVERNMENT, JUSTICE, THE ENVIRONMENT, HOUSING,
SOCIAL WORK, TAX, WELFARE, FOREIGN AFFAIRS AND DEFENCE

OTHER SCOTTISH COURTS

Later chapters of this guide look at these issues in greater detail.

Why Scotland needs independence

The central purpose of independence is to make life better for people living in Scotland. Only a Scottish Parliament and Government will always be able to put the interests of the people of Scotland first. We only have to look at the track record of devolution since 1999 to know this is the case; these powers have been good for Scotland, but in those areas still controlled by Westminster there have been many costs for families and communities in Scotland.

Democracy, prosperity and fairness are the principles at the heart of the case for independence. Independence means that the people of Scotland will take responsibility for our future into our own hands. It will also give us the economic and social powers that any country needs to build a more prosperous and fairer society. As this guide will demonstrate, Scotland can afford to be independent.

Crucially, these principles work in harmony. If we transfer decision-making powers from Westminster to Scotland we are more likely to see policies that are in tune with the values of the people of Scotland, that close the gap between rich and poor, and provide greater opportunities for everyone in Scotland regardless of their background. We can build a fairer society. And in doing so we can create a more prosperous country because we know that successful countries are more equal and cohesive. They make full use of everyone's talents and have a sense of shared national purpose.

There are three over-riding reasons for Scotland to become an independent country. These are:

1. To create a more democratic Scotland
   The Scottish Government believes that the people of Scotland are the ones who will do the best job of running our country. We will not get every decision right, but more often than not the choices we make for our economy and our society will be better for Scotland than those made at Westminster.

A Scottish Parliament with limited devolved powers has already shown what is possible. The Scottish Parliament has delivered free personal care for the elderly, kept our NHS in the public sector and restored free education for our students. With powers over our tax system, social security, immigration and defence, the Scottish Parliament will also be able to make better choices for Scotland on these issues.

With independence, Scotland will always get the governments we vote for. For 34 of the 68 years since 1945, Scotland has been ruled by Westminster governments with no majority in Scotland. Policies are imposed on Scotland even when they have been opposed by our elected Westminster MPs. Under the current Westminster Government this democratic deficit has resulted in:

- the privatisation of the Royal Mail
- unfair welfare changes such as the "bedroom tax"
- cuts in capital spending, harming economic recovery
- a commitment to spend as much as £100 billion on the lifetime costs of a replacement nuclear weapon system

Being able to decide our own government really matters. The costs of decisions being made at Westminster are being paid by families and communities across Scotland. Many of the consequences will be long-lasting: as a direct result of the Westminster Government's welfare changes, the child poverty rate in Scotland is predicted to rise to 22.7 per cent, equivalent to an additional 50,000 children by 2020[3]. None of this needs to happen. These consequences are a direct result of Scotland getting governments we did not vote for.

With independence, Scotland will have the tools we need to turn our rich country into a rich society. This will require hard work and effort, but the prize is worth it: we can create a more prosperous, sustainable and successful future for our families, our nation and for ourselves.

2. To build a more prosperous country
   Both before and after devolution, the key economic
   powers necessary to deliver growth and prosperity
   remained with Westminster. Control of taxation, public
   spending limits, regulation of business and industry,
   and competition policy all rest in London. Successive
   devolved Scottish governments have had considerable
   success in reducing unemployment, increasing
   employment and promoting inward investment. But the
   fundamental economic decisions that affect Scotland are
   taken in Westminster, often by governments that have
   no popular mandate in Scotland, and in the interests
   of an economy and society with different priorities from
   Scotland.

   Scotland is blessed with a range of economic strengths
   and advantages: substantial natural resources, a
   strong international brand, world-class universities
   and research, and a range of world-leading industries
   including food and drink, life sciences, the creative
   industries, energy, tourism, insurance, wealth
   management and engineering.

   Because of those strengths and advantages, our national
   output per head of population puts us near the top of the
   OECD[4] – the association of the wealthiest countries in
   the world[5].

   Even without North Sea oil, Scotland's economy
   produces almost exactly the same amount of output per
   head as the rest of the UK. With oil and gas, we produce
   nearly a fifth more.

   However, despite all of Scotland's strengths, over the
   past 30 years our economic growth rate has been lower
   than the UK average and lower than that of comparable
   nations across Europe (see Chapter 3). That reflects a
   number of factors, including lower population growth.

   Our economic output is the product of our collective hard
   work and ingenuity as a nation, and reflects the many
   advantages we enjoy. Yet life expectancy is lower in

Scotland than in similar countries[6], and poverty levels are too high[7].

Nations that are similar to Scotland – such as Norway, Finland, Denmark and Sweden – sit at the top of world wealth and well-being league tables[8]. Unlike Scotland, they are independent and are able to take decisions in the best interests of their own economies. They do not leave the important decisions about their economy to parliaments whose interests necessarily lie elsewhere. That is their independence advantage and they have used it to build societies that deliver a higher quality of life for their citizens.

If Scotland moved from the rates of growth it has experienced in the past to instead match the levels of growth of other small European countries, the benefits for people in Scotland in terms of prosperity and employment would be significant. As an illustration, had Scotland's growth matched these other independent nations between 1977 and 2007, GDP per head would now be 3.8 per cent higher, equivalent to an additional £900 per head (see Chapter 3). We would also enjoy the higher revenues that accompany greater prosperity.

Independence would make the Scottish Parliament and Government responsible for the full range of economic powers. Decisions on taxation and other economic levers, as well as employment law and all aspects of economic regulation, would be taken in Scotland and tailored to Scotland's needs. In some cases – such as our proposal to continue to share the pound as our currency – the choices would involve partnership and co-operation with other countries. However, the decisions on when to co-operate would be entirely ours to make.

The ability to make our own decisions is the point of independence. It will provide the best conditions for sustainable economic growth, and enable us to protect living standards, reduce poverty and inequality, and build a better society.

3. To become a fairer society

   Within the UK, Scotland is part of an increasingly unequal society. The UK ranks 28th out of 34 nations in the OECD on a measure of overall inequality[9]. OECD analysis shows that since 1975, income inequality among working-age people has increased faster in the UK than in any other country in the organisation[10]. This is not the result of the policies of one government, but of almost 40 years of decisions at Westminster.

   Seeking to become a more equal society is not just the right thing to do. It also makes sense for the economy.

   We know that the most equal societies also have the highest levels of well-being and are most prosperous. They are also, more often than not, nations like Scotland; the fairest and most successful countries in the world are independent European nations of similar size[11].

   We want the powers of independence so that we can build a different and better Scotland, where the many benefits of a rich and active society are cherished and where we work together to advance our nation as a whole. Progress under devolution has shown us what is possible, but it is not enough.

For these important reasons of democracy, prosperity and fairness, it is time for the people of Scotland to take responsibility for our own future as we look towards the third decade of this 21st century. Rather than remaining a peripheral concern for Westminster governments that we did not elect and do not necessarily support, we can forge our own path. With independence we can create a social nation: a country that acts and feels like a community, a vibrant society where we know the benefits of looking out for each other. Independence is about empowering the people and communities of Scotland as much as it is about empowering our Parliament and government. It will give us the ability, collectively, to choose the path ahead that is right for us and for those we work with and live beside.

Driving our ambition is the firm knowledge that Scotland, and all of the people who live here, should be enjoying the benefits of higher levels of sustainable economic growth. There is so much more we can achieve with all the advantages that we enjoy.

What a newly independent Scotland will look like

Immediately following a vote for independence next year, Scotland will look familiar, but will already have changed, and for the better. The Yes vote will be a resounding statement of national self-confidence.

There will be a transition period between a Yes vote in September 2014 and Scotland becoming independent. Negotiations will take place in this period with the Westminster Government and international partners, particularly the European Union (EU). Setting a date of March 2016 for those to be completed will allow a realistic time period for all of the preparations needed for the Scottish Parliament to take on the necessary powers of independence (see Chapter 10).

On independence, Her Majesty The Queen will remain our head of state, just as she is for 16 Commonwealth countries. Scotland will be a constitutional monarchy for as long as the people of Scotland wish us to be so. Scotland will take our place amongst the member states of the EU and the United Nations.

Scotland's existing institutions and structures of government will continue, but independence will extend their powers and responsibilities. The Scottish Parliament will become the Parliament of an independent Scotland. It will continue to have 129 members, representing constituencies and regions across Scotland, and will be located in the existing Parliament building at Holyrood. The Scottish Parliament will take over responsibilities currently exercised at Westminster.

We will replace a costly, remote and unrepresentative Westminster system with a Parliament elected entirely by the people of Scotland, saving the Scottish taxpayers around £50 million a year in their contributions to the costs of the House of Commons and the House of Lords.

However, the biggest difference will come from the opportunity to take action to meet Scotland's needs, across all areas of the nation's life, to make the most of Scotland's strengths and build on key principles supported by the people of Scotland.

The first election to the new independent Scottish Parliament will take place on 5 May 2016. People will vote in the usual way using the existing proportional system. The newly elected independent Parliament will have responsibility for establishing a constitutional convention which will take forward the drafting of a written constitution for Scotland, based on extensive engagement with the people of Scotland, as well as civic groups and organisations.

Independence will see the Scottish Government develop new functions as it takes on the responsibilities of serving an independent country. If the present Scottish Government is re-elected, we will spread government jobs and decision-making across the country, delivering the direct economic benefits of independent government to more parts of Scotland.

During the transition period, many more countries will set up embassies and consulates in Scotland. We can expect an increase in transport connections to and from Scotland, and the new independent Scottish Government will start to be created – bringing jobs which are currently based in London to Scotland.

For public services that are currently reserved, there will be arrangements for the continued delivery of services to the public across the UK where this is in the interests of service users and the two governments. In most cases, this will be for a transitional period, but in some it may be for the longer term. The underlying principle in all cases will be the seamless delivery of services to people in Scotland (and the rest of the UK), with decisions for Scotland being made in Scotland by the Scottish Government and Scottish Parliament.

Scotland already has an independent legal system. The Inner House of the Court of Session and the High Court of Justiciary sitting as the Court of Criminal Appeal will collectively be Scotland's Supreme Court.

References on points of EU law will continue to be made to the European Court of Justice in Luxembourg, and applications on human rights issues to the European Court of Human Rights in Strasbourg will continue. The structure of Sheriff Courts and other courts will remain the same. The Crown Office will continue to be the sole independent public prosecuting authority and will continue to investigate all suspicious and unexplained deaths. The structure of police and other emergency services will be also be unaffected by the move to independence.

On independence, the structure of local government in Scotland will remain the same, with local councils continuing to deliver the full range of services they do today. This will include schools, leisure and social services. The next election to Scotland's local authorities will take place as planned in 2017. Independence will give us the power to embed the role of local authorities in a written constitution and consider the most appropriate responsibilities for local government and communities. The NHS, which is already the responsibility of the Scottish Parliament, will operate on exactly the same basis the day after independence as it does the day before.

The most important point, however, in considering what an independent Scotland will look like is this: it will look like the kind of Scotland we as a people choose to build. We will take the decisions. What happens to our country will be our responsibility.

The Government of an independent Scotland

The structure and location of government in an independent Scotland will be for the elected government of the day to decide. This box sets out the approach proposed by the current Government, which is to structure the Scottish Government into nine portfolios, each of which will comprise at least one Cabinet Secretary and supporting Ministers. This structure is designed to continue the current Scottish Government's approach of more flexible and more efficient government, allowing us to take full advantage of some of the key benefits of independence: agility, accessibility and short lines of decision-making. The nine portfolios we are planning are:

■ Office of the First Minister

■ Finance and Economy

■ Health, Wellbeing and Social Protection

■ Education, Skills and Employment

■ International Relations and Defence

■ Justice, Security and Home Affairs

■ Environment, Rural Scotland, Energy and Resources

■ Culture, Communications and Digital

■ Law Officers

Office of the First Minister
The First Minister will have overall responsibility for the Scottish Government, transition agreements and the constitution, and will be supported by a Minister for Parliamentary Business who will attend Cabinet.

Finance and Economy
The Cabinet Secretary for Finance will have responsibility for Scotland's budget and public service reform, and will be supported by a Minister for Communities and Public Services who will have responsibilities including local government,

equalities and community empowerment. A Cabinet Secretary for Trade and Economic Development will have responsibility for competitiveness, business and tourism, and will be supported by a Minister for Transport. Revenue Scotland will have major operational centres based in East Kilbride and offices around Scotland.

Health, Wellbeing and Social Protection
The Cabinet Secretary for Health will have responsibility for the NHS and will be supported by a Minister for Public Health and Sport and a Minister for Children and Families. There will be a Cabinet Secretary for Social Protection who will be supported by a Minister for Pensions and Older People. NHS services will be based in existing facilities. A Working Age and Disability Benefits HQ will be based in Glasgow. There will be national pensions centres at existing sites in Dundee and Motherwell and a national child maintenance centre in Falkirk, plus a network of centres around the country.

Education, Skills and Employment
The Cabinet Secretary for Education will have responsibility for primary, secondary, further and higher education, as well as Gaelic and Scots, and will be supported by a Minister for Schools and a Minister for Youth Employment.

International Relations and Defence
The Cabinet Secretary for International Relations will have responsibility for relations with the rest of the UK and Ireland, the EU, and the wider international community, and will be supported by a Minister for International Development. The Cabinet Secretary for Defence will have responsibility for defence policy and will be supported by a Minister for the Armed Forces and Veterans. Scotland's Military HQ will be at Faslane and there will be delivery functions in East Kilbride, at Kentigern House in Glasgow, and in international embassies and missions.

Justice, Security and Home Affairs

The Cabinet Secretary for Justice will have responsibility for police, security and intelligence, and the justice system, and will be supported by a Minister for Home Affairs with responsibilities including immigration and borders.

Environment, Rural Scotland, Energy and Resources

The Cabinet Secretary for Natural Resources will have responsibility for energy, sustainability and the environment. The Cabinet Secretary for Food and Rural Affairs will have responsibility for food and drink, agriculture, fishing and rural communities.

Culture, Communications and Digital

The Cabinet Secretary for Culture will be responsible for culture, broadcasting, postal services and digital delivery, and will be supported by a Minister for Communications.

Law Officers

The Lord Advocate and Solicitor General will continue as head of the systems of criminal prosecution and investigation of deaths in Scotland and will provide legal advisory functions across the whole range of government activity, including currently reserved functions.

In addition to these government departments, significant functions currently delivered for Scotland from elsewhere in the UK will be transferred to Scotland. This means that jobs which Scottish taxpayers currently fund in London and elsewhere will instead come to Scotland, providing a boost for our economy, and creating new jobs and career opportunities. This Government proposes to locate these functions around Scotland.

In an independent Scotland, we will establish a new security and intelligence body, a Scottish Border and Migration Service and a Scottish Motor Services Agency. At present spending on these functions in other parts of the UK is funded, in part, by taxes and fees collected from people and businesses in Scotland. With independence these taxes and fees would be spent in Scotland.

SEPTEMBER 2014	BY MARCH 2016	MAY 2016
The Referendum decides whether Scotland should be an independent country.	Negotiations settle the terms and transition arrangements, for approval by both Parliaments.	Elections determine who will form the first government of an independent Scotland.

Becoming independent - the transition

Timetable for negotiations

Following a vote for independence in the referendum on 18 September 2014, there will be a period of preparation for Scotland to become an independent country. Setting a realistic independence date of **24 March 2016** will allow time for the preparations necessary for the Scottish Parliament to take on the new powers of independence to be completed.

This period between the referendum and independence will see negotiations with the rest of the UK, represented by the Westminster Government, and with the EU and other international partners and organisations. Following these preparations and negotiations, Scotland will assume our status as an independent country before the Scottish parliamentary elections in May 2016.

In the Edinburgh Agreement signed by the First Minister and the Prime Minister on 15 October 2012, the Scottish and Westminster Governments committed to work together constructively in light of the outcome of the referendum in the best interests of the people of Scotland and the rest of the UK[12]. Following a vote for independence in 2014, agreements will be needed between the Scottish and Westminster Governments, in the spirit of the Edinburgh Agreement, setting the parameters for Scotland's transition to independence. These will set out:

- the precise timetable towards independence day in 2016

- the constitutional platform for an independent Scotland – the laws and administrative arrangements to establish Scotland as an independent state

- the process and timetable for the negotiations, and conclusion of the agreements which will form the final independence settlement

It will be in the interests of both countries for the governments to make rapid and constructive progress on these negotiations, in line with the commitments made in the Edinburgh Agreement. It would assist in preparing for the negotiations if discussions between the governments were to take place prior to the referendum, and the Scottish Government will continue to press for such engagement.

A Yes vote will require work to be undertaken within the Scottish Government, drawing on external advice and expertise from within civic society and our academic and business communities.

The negotiating team will be led by the First Minister, and the process will include figures from across Scottish public life and Scotland's other political parties. During the transition period the Government will seek the agreement of the Scottish Parliament to extend its sitting days to ensure full democratic scrutiny of the process and to provide adequate time for the necessary legislation to be passed.

Constitutional platform for independence

Scotland's current governmental arrangements are based on the Scotland Act 1998, which is an Act of the Westminster Parliament. With independence, Scotland's government will not be based on the authority of Westminster but on the sovereignty of the people of Scotland.

To prepare for this new status a number of steps will need to be taken to provide a constitutional platform for Scotland to make a seamless transition to independence and to provide a secure underpinning to the legal and governmental system.

Soon after a Yes vote in the referendum, the Westminster and Scottish Parliaments will need to pass legislation to give the Scottish Parliament powers to: declare independent statehood for Scotland in the name of the sovereign people of Scotland; amend the Scotland Act 1998; and extend the powers of the Scottish Parliament and Scottish Government into all policy areas currently reserved to Westminster, in order to make preparations for independence.

With the transfer of the appropriate legislative competences, the Scottish Parliament will be in a position to make the necessary preparations for Scotland to become independent.

Agreement with the rest of the UK

The independence agreement with the rest of the UK will cover a range of matters, mainly the approach to the assets and liabilities of the UK, the delivery of services and the position of individuals working within public services. There will also need to be agreements on cross-border operational matters, as is the case now, and on transitional arrangements for those areas where a period of adjustment will be the most sensible approach.

The over-riding priority will be the seamless delivery of public services on independence to citizens of both countries. This applies both to those services currently delivered to Scotland from locations elsewhere in the UK, and to those services currently delivered from Scotland to citizens elsewhere in the UK.

Agreement with international organisations and partners

In addition to discussions with the Westminster Government, negotiations will be held in advance of independence with the EU to agree the terms of an independent Scotland's continuing membership. Scotland will continue to be part of the UK – and, therefore, an integral part of the EU – during these negotiations. The UK and Scottish Governments, along with the EU institutions and member states, will have a shared interest in working together to conclude these negotiations to transfer Scotland's EU membership from membership as part of the UK to membership as an independent member state.

Discussions and negotiations will also be required about the terms of Scotland's (and indeed the rest of the UK's) membership of other international bodies to which Scotland currently belongs as a component nation of the UK. Such negotiations will necessarily involve both the Scottish and Westminster Governments, together with our international partners (see Chapter 6). Such arrangements will cover Scotland's membership of international organisations such as the UN and NATO. On independence, Scotland will also become a Non-Nuclear Weapons State party to the Nuclear Non-Proliferation Treaty and a party to other major international treaties.

Scotland will succeed to international treaties by sending notifications of succession to the depositaries of multilateral treaties (for example, the Secretary-General of the UN is the depositary for the 500 UN Treaties), and by writing to the other states in relation to each of the UK's existing bilateral treaties to which Scotland would wish to succeed. This is in line with normal international practice.

Strong foundations - Scotland's financial and economic strengths

There are now few people who still argue that Scotland does not have the strength or capacity to be independent. The UK Prime Minister, David Cameron, has recognised that this is the case[13].

Most countries in the world generate less wealth per head than Scotland – including the UK as a whole. If Scotland cannot afford to be independent, neither can the UK.

We pay our own way
Over each of the last 32 years, estimates show that Scotland has contributed more tax per head of population than the rest of the UK. In 2011/12 we generated £10,700 of tax revenues per head, compared to £9,000 for the UK[14].

We spend a lower proportion of both our national output and our tax revenues on social protection – things like pensions and welfare – than the UK, which means that Scotland is wealthy enough to look after our most vulnerable people.

Taken as a whole, Scotland's national accounts are healthier than the UK's. Over the last five years they have been stronger to the tune of £12.6 billion – almost £2,400 for every person living in Scotland. That is money that could have been used to deliver more for public services such as our schools and hospitals, to reduce taxes or to cut the amount we need to borrow. More importantly, it shows that Scotland has firm financial foundations. We have the economic and financial strength we need to choose independence.

By independence in 2016/17, Scotland's fiscal deficit is forecast to have fallen to between 2.5 per cent and 3.2 per cent of GDP, assuming that we take on a population share of UK public sector debt; with a historic share of UK debt, our deficit is forecast to be lower still, at between 1.6 per cent and 2.4 per cent of GDP. By contrast, the UK is forecast to run a deficit of 3.4 per cent of GDP in the same year[15]. The International Monetary Fund estimates that the average deficit across the G7 economies will be 3.2 per cent in 2016[16].

On independence, Scotland will accept a fair share of the existing UK debt. The amount of the debt that we accept will be subject to negotiations. We will also be entitled to a fair share of UK assets (assets that our taxes have helped to pay for). The debt could be apportioned by reference to the historic contribution made to the UK's public finances by Scotland. An alternative approach would be to use a population share. In either case, Scotland's debt is projected to be lower as a proportion of GDP than that of the UK as a whole.

The question, therefore, is not "Can we afford to be independent?" Instead, given all these strengths, we should be asking "How do we make people in Scotland better off?" With independence, we will be better able to get our resources working for all the people of Scotland.

We will only be able to do that if we make the most of the talents and potential of everyone in the country. That means creating a fairer society so that everyone has the opportunity to get on in life, both for themselves and for the contribution they can make to their communities and to Scotland.

Greater security through independence
Some who support the current Westminster system argue that Scotland benefits from a pooling and sharing of resources across the UK. However, this is far from the reality. Our resources may be pooled, but they are not fairly shared.

The Westminster system has created a country with some of the biggest regional differences in GDP per head of any EU nation. Growth has been concentrated in London and the South East.

Within the UK, half of the population owns just 9.9 per cent of the wealth, while the very richest 10 per cent own 43.8 per cent[17]. Income inequality is amongst the highest in the developed world[18].

This situation has been getting progressively worse. Even though Scotland is economically strong, it will become harder to cope with an economic policy which funnels so much activity into one corner of the UK and to one section of society.

In addition, Westminster is making welfare changes that threaten the security of all of us, especially the most vulnerable.

This is in contrast to the Scottish Parliament's protection of the universal principle, which recognises that people pay into the system and should get some reward or help in time of need.

The idea of pooling and sharing wealth is the mark of a fair society. The evidence shows that it is small independent European nations that have the best record of generating more wealth for all and of sharing it more fairly across society[19].

The evidence is clear that Scotland is ideally placed to deliver the economic and social gains that are normal in similar nations. The strength of our economy, our natural resources, and the degree of political consensus we enjoy gives us confidence that choices will be made to use the wealth of our nation to transform our economically productive country into a rich and fair society. But only independence can deliver this outcome and secure a Scottish Parliament with the necessary responsibilities, political balance and political will to achieve genuine social advances.

Across the world, nations face a range of challenges, from climate change and energy and water security to demographic changes that will alter the composition of society. With independence, we will have the powers to respond to these challenges and their impact in Scotland ourselves, rather than relying on the decisions of others. Independence will also give us the opportunity to play an active part in shaping global and European solutions to these problems. With independence, we will be better placed to meet the challenges of the future.

Over time, we will also have the opportunity to save a proportion of the revenues that flow from our offshore energy wealth for the benefit of future generations (see Chapter 8).

Energy and resources

Scotland has energy security. We produce six times our current demand for oil and three times our demand for gas. We have extraordinary potential in renewable energy, including a quarter of Europe's offshore wind and tidal potential.

Investment in the oil and gas sector is at the record level of £13.5 billion this year, and planned future investment is estimated at £100 billion. Industry projections also point to an increase in output in the first years of independence. Production is expected to extend beyond the middle of the century, with the industry estimating remaining reserves of up to 24 billion barrels of oil and gas that can still be recovered. In terms of wholesale value, North Sea reserves could be worth £1.5 trillion – a greater value than the amount extracted to date. As the vast bulk of the reserves are beneath Scottish waters, that gives us one of the best financial safety nets of any country in the world[20].

While projections of the price for oil and gas vary, everyone now acknowledges that Scotland's oil and gas wealth is an extremely valuable resource and will last for a long time to come. Scotland can also look forward to a further energy bonus from our green energy resources, with expected sales of £14 billion by 2050 from offshore tidal and wind energy[21].

Given the breadth and depth of our economic strengths, Scotland is better placed than most to ensure a secure future for the people who live here. By making the most of our strengths, we can provide the strongest guarantees in the years to come. In this way, we can prepare for future economic and financial pressures, enabling us to respond in a more effective way to economic downturns or unexpected challenges.

Population

Developed countries across the world face pressures on public services, as there are fewer people of working age and a larger proportion of children and people in retirement in the population. For at least the next 15 years, Scotland will be in a more advantageous position than the rest of the UK, and with independence[22] we will be able to take the most important steps to address this challenge for the longer term. With the economic powers of independence, we can do more to generate higher levels of economic growth, which will in turn boost revenue levels. We will be able to create more opportunities for young people, allowing us to retain more of our working age population, and to attract back people who have chosen to work elsewhere. We will also be able to encourage suitably qualified new talent to settle and work in Scotland, and retain more of the students who come to study at our world-class universities. Right now, detrimental policies from Westminster are a major factor in preventing many Scottish-educated graduates from choosing to live and work in Scotland.

Scotland has the talent, resources, wealth and ingenuity to meet the challenges of the future. Greater certainty in the future comes not from leaving decisions to others, but from taking responsibility ourselves. Scotland has greater security when we have greater control over the direction we take as a nation. We can respond with action based on Scotland's particular circumstances, and take decisions that put us in a stronger position to meet the longer-term challenges that we can see emerging in the years ahead.

Government policies and public services with independence

On day one of independence, public services will continue to be delivered in a way that will be seamless for those who rely on them. Policy changes will be decided not in the 2014 referendum, but at future elections, both national and local. The benefit of independence is that all the important decisions affecting the quality of public services in Scotland will be taken in Scotland and not at Westminster. Westminster will no longer be able to reduce the funding available to the Scottish Parliament. Instead our Parliament will decide the right level of public spending for Scotland.

The success of those public services already under the control of the Scottish Parliament – free personal care for the elderly and world-leading improvements in hospital safety, to take just two examples – demonstrates the gains that come when decisions are made in Scotland.

As with devolution, the full gains from independence will come over time. The aim of the Scottish Government, through the process of becoming independent, is to protect the things we know are important to people living in Scotland, while also providing some immediate advantages from the move to independence and building for the long term.

With independence, decisions on the taxes we pay, the state pension, the delivery of all public services, and policies that affect our economy and society will be taken in Scotland based on the needs and interests of the people who live here.

Looking at neighbouring independent nations, such as Norway and Denmark, it is clear that they enjoy an independence bonus that allows them to deliver fairer societies. They are able to provide more targeted support for families with children and better levels of care for older citizens, and deliver measures to boost their economies, support higher standards of living and create more jobs.

These independence gains did not come overnight. They required effort and a focus on what was best for their societies, but they are a signal of what can be achieved when Scotland too becomes an independent nation.

Independence will give us the opportunity to better provide the public services we all value and rely on. It will put decisions on the level and allocation of Scotland's budget into the hands of the Scottish Government and Parliament, rather than leaving these decisions to Westminster. That means we can choose to guarantee free personal care and decent pensions for our older people and free tuition fees for students, instead of replacing Trident. Indeed, making different choices from Westminster on nuclear weapons and defence will allow this Scottish Government to save £500 million – money that can deliver direct benefits for people in Scotland.

The policies that will be pursued in an independent Scotland will be down to the government elected by the people of Scotland, starting with the first election following independence in May 2016.

This may be the SNP, Labour or any other party – or coalition of parties – that wins enough support.

The consequences of Scotland voting No in the referendum

The referendum is a choice between two futures: taking control in Scotland of our own affairs, or remaining under the control of Westminster. It is a choice about who can be trusted to make the best decisions for Scotland – our own Parliament elected in Scotland, or Westminster.

If the result of the referendum is No, decisions on welfare, defence and foreign policy will continue to be taken by Westminster for Scotland, whatever the views of the Scottish electorate. For example, with a No vote we will see a new generation of nuclear weapons on the Clyde. There is no assurance that decisions on the key issues that affect Scotland's prosperity, security and future will be made in line with the interests and values of the people who live here. Decisions with damaging effects on Scottish society – such as the "bedroom tax" which was introduced despite the opposition of 90 per cent of Scottish MPs – will continue to be made in Westminster.

The overall level of public spending in Scotland will continue to be driven by decisions on priorities for England through the Barnett formula – which determines Scotland's block grant by reference to spending by Westminster – rather than by Scottish priorities. There is the prospect that the funding system for devolved government in Scotland will be scrapped, with the risk of further significant cuts to the Scottish Parliament's budget and serious consequences for Scottish public services. Westminster politicians from all parties have indicated that reviewing the basis of Scotland's spending is a real possibility.

If we remain in the UK, the Conservative Party's promise of an in/out referendum on EU membership raises the serious possibility that Scotland will be forced to leave the EU against the wishes of the people of Scotland.

Despite much talk of further devolution and more powers for Scotland, with a No vote there is no assurance that there will be any new powers for the Scottish Parliament within the UK. Neither the Westminster Government nor the campaign opposing independence has made concrete proposals for further devolution to the Scottish Parliament following a No vote in the referendum. A vote against independence would not in itself lead to an extension of the powers of the Scottish Parliament; any proposals to strengthen the Scottish Parliament would require the agreement of Westminster through legislation, and there is no guarantee that any of the UK parties will propose – or follow through on – any such legislation.

Following the referendum in 1979, we saw that, despite the promises made during that campaign and the clear public support for devolution, it took a further 20 years for a democratic Scottish Parliament to be established. The only way to secure and guarantee greater powers for the Scottish Parliament is to vote Yes in the referendum.

PART 2

CHAPTER **2** | SCOTLAND'S FINANCES

■ Scotland is a wealthy country and can afford to be independent

■ Our public finances are healthier than those of the UK as a whole

■ Tax receipts per head in Scotland are estimated to have been higher than in the UK as a whole in each and every year since 1980/81

■ In 2011/12, Scottish tax receipts were equivalent to £10,700 per head – £1,700 higher than the equivalent UK figure

■ Over the last five years, Scotland's public finances have been stronger than the UK as a whole by a total of £12.6 billion – almost £2,400 per head

■ Projections set out here demonstrate that Scotland's public finances are expected to strengthen over the next few years

■ Independence will provide us with the opportunity to manage our public finances more securely and to create a more vibrant and resilient economy

Why we need a new approach

The strength of a country's public finances depends on the balance between public spending, revenues and the stock of government debt.

These in turn depend upon the health of the economy and choices around the level and composition of taxes and provision of public services.

This chapter sets out Scotland's public finances and demonstrates that Scotland has the financial foundations to be a successful independent country.

It also provides an overview of the financial position that the Scottish Government expects an independent Scotland to inherit and this Government's early priorities for public spending and revenue.

The starting point for this analysis is the National Statistics publication, Government Expenditure and Revenue Scotland (GERS). GERS is the authoritative publication on Scotland's public finances.

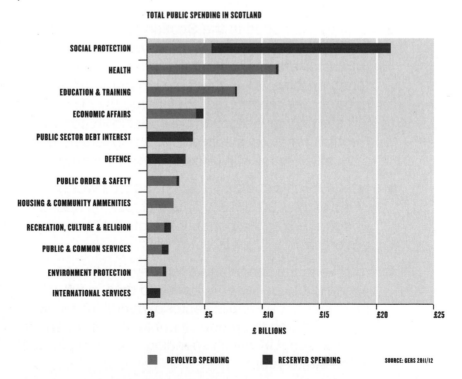

TOTAL PUBLIC SPENDING IN SCOTLAND

£ BILLIONS

■ DEVOLVED SPENDING   ■ RESERVED SPENDING   SOURCE: GERS 2011/12

GERS provides estimates of the tax revenue generated in Scotland and the public spending undertaken for Scotland within the current constitutional framework[23].

The facts are as follows:

- even when oil and gas revenues are excluded, estimated tax receipts per head in Scotland are broadly equivalent to the UK figure[24]. When Scotland's oil and gas receipts are added, tax revenue per head in Scotland is nearly 20 per cent higher than the UK average

- in 2011/12, the most recent year for which information is available, Scotland generated £10,700 of tax revenues per head compared to £9,000 per head for the UK as a whole[25, 26]

- indeed, in every year from 1980/81 to 2011/12, Scottish tax receipts per head are estimated to have been higher than in the UK as a whole

- some decisions on taxes are already devolved to Scotland, notably on council tax and local business rates. However, together these taxes account for just 7 per cent of total Scottish tax receipts[27]

- changes included in the Scotland Act 2012, due to come into effect over the next one to two years, will give the Scottish Parliament control over two additional taxes which together raise about £400 million per year, and some limited control over a proportion of income tax. These changes will still only give Scotland responsibility for 15 per cent of Scottish receipts. Decisions on the overwhelming majority of Scottish taxes will remain at Westminster[28]

- total public spending for Scotland was worth an estimated £64 billion in 2011/12[29]. This includes all spending undertaken for the benefit of Scotland by every tier of government in the UK

- relative to the size of the economy, public spending is estimated to be lower in Scotland than in the UK as a whole. In 2011/12, total public sector expenditure for Scotland was estimated to be equivalent to 42.7 per cent of GDP. In comparison, UK public spending was 45.5 per cent of GDP in the same year[30]

- as a share of GDP, public spending in Scotland is also lower than in the majority of EU-15 countries[31]

The overall level of public spending for Scotland is primarily decided by the Westminster Government.

In terms of reserved programmes affecting Scotland, the Westminster Government sets levels of spending on matters such as welfare payments and defence. This covers around 40 per cent of all spending for Scotland.

For devolved programmes such as health, education and transport, the total budget is set by the Westminster Government using the Barnett Formula. The Barnett Formula uses the size of Scotland's population relative to other parts of the UK to calculate changes in the budget available for devolved services, depending on decisions taken about funding levels for Whitehall departments.

Public spending in Scotland is therefore set without reference to the needs or preferences of Scottish households or businesses. Nor does it directly reflect the substantial contribution that Scotland makes to UK tax receipts.

Taking revenues and expenditures together provides a picture of the overall health of the public finances.

The facts show that, over the last five years, Scotland's public finances, despite being in deficit, are estimated to have been relatively stronger than the UK as a whole by a total of £12.6 billion – almost £2,400 per head[32].

This relatively stronger fiscal position is consistent with a longer-term trend.

The Fiscal Commission Working Group ("the Fiscal Commission")[33] has estimated, that since 1980/81, Scotland has run an average annual net fiscal surplus of 0.2 per cent of GDP, compared to an average annual deficit for the UK of around 3 per cent of GDP.

The Fiscal Commission has also illustrated that, had Scotland had control of our own resources, and assuming no change in tax revenues or spending priorities, our relatively stronger fiscal position from 1980/81 would have allowed us to not only eliminate a per head share of UK net debt, but actually accumulate assets worth between £82 billion and £116 billion by 2011/12[34].

This would have equated to an asset of between £15,500 and £22,000 per head. In contrast, by the end of 2011/12, the UK had accumulated net debt of over £1.1 trillion, equivalent to a liability of £17,500 per head.

The opportunities available to Scotland
Despite these underlying strengths, Scotland is disadvantaged by not being independent.

Scotland does not have full control of our economy or public finances.

The Scottish Parliament is unable to determine the level and composition of taxation or the overall value of public spending.

It is not possible to realise the financial benefits of successful economic policies – such as increased revenues or reduced welfare payments. Under current arrangements, these benefits are passed straight to the Westminster Government. For example, because Scotland has proportionately more social housing, spending on housing benefit is lower, but the benefit of this goes to the Westminster Government not the Scottish Government.

Without independence, Scotland is also exposed to the approach that successive Westminster governments have taken to managing the public finances.

Between 2001/02 and 2007/08, the then Labour Westminster Government increased debt year on year, despite strong economic growth[35]. As a result, just as the recession hit, the UK had the third highest structural deficit in the OECD[36].

In surveying the UK's public finances, the Fiscal Commission concluded that:

> the decision not to manage government borrowing more prudently during the years prior to the financial crisis weakened the resilience of the public finances and meant that they were not well placed to respond to the sharp drop in tax revenues, and increase in government spending, which occurred with the onset of the recession in 2008[37].

This position has since been compounded by the current Westminster Government's decision to cut public expenditure too quickly – especially public sector capital investment – and before the recovery had gained momentum. This damaged economic growth, depressed tax revenues and resulted in borrowing exceeding forecasts.

In contrast, the Scottish Government has developed a reputation for sound financial management. In the areas that we control, we have taken tough decisions, delivered significant efficiencies and prioritised spend to the areas which have the most significant economic impact and offer the greatest protection for those who rely on public services.

Independence will provide the opportunity to safeguard Scotland's financial sustainability more effectively and ensure that our public finances are managed to reflect the needs of Scotland's economy.

Scotland's public finances on independence

It is clear that Scotland currently pays our way within the UK.

As we move to independence, our strong public finances will provide the foundations for policy decisions on taxation, growth and welfare.

As with most developed countries – including the UK – Scotland is currently running an estimated fiscal deficit, which means that the revenues from taxation fall short of public spending[38]. Of the 31 members of the OECD for which data are available, 27 are estimated to have been in deficit during 2012[39].

As a result of the recession, Scotland will inherit challenging fiscal position that will require careful stewardship in the years immediately following independence. The first Government of an independent Scotland will need to make decisions based on the prevailing conditions.

To enable an informed assessment of the financial position of an independent Scotland, the Scottish Government has prepared projections of Scotland's public finances under the current constitutional framework to 2016/17, the year when Scotland will become independent[40]. Such projections reflect the decisions and priorities of the Westminster Government. In contrast, the strength of Scotland's public finances in the years after 2016/17 will depend on the economic and fiscal decisions of future Scottish governments and our ability to grow the economy.

Scotland's public finances are forecast to improve as the economy continues to strengthen.

The financial position that Scotland will inherit on independence will also reflect, in part, negotiations between the Scottish and Westminster Governments following a Yes vote. For example, the proportion of UK public sector debt which an independent Scotland will assume responsibility for will have implications for our annual debt interest payments. Negotiations will enable phasing and the financial consequences of the transition to be agreed, planned and managed by all parties.

To reflect the range of possible outcomes, the analysis in this guide uses two scenarios for Scotland's share of UK public sector debt and annual interest payments:

- Scotland's share of UK public sector net debt could be apportioned by reference to the historical balance of public spending and taxation since 1980/81, the earliest year for which figures are available. This provides a measure of our contribution to the UK's finances over the years. As Scotland has been in a relatively stronger position than the UK over this period, a historical share of public sector debt would be lower than a population share[41]

- Alternatively, Scotland could take responsibility for a population share of UK public sector net debt

Under either outcome, Scotland's projected debt to GDP ratio would be smaller than the UK's. Negotiations will also take into account the degree to which Scotland's share of UK public sector debt, and in turn its annual debt interest payments, could be reduced in return for forgoing rights to certain UK assets (see Part 4).

Based on the Westminster Government's current spending plans, public spending excluding debt interest payments for Scotland is forecast to fall by 4 per cent in real terms between 2011/12 and 2016/17.

UK debt interest payments are projected to rise by over 20 per cent in real terms between 2011/12 and 2016/17, reflecting higher levels of UK borrowing in recent years[42]. Based on such figures, Scotland's historical share of UK debt interest is projected to be £3.9 billion in 2016/17 or £5.5 billion based on a per head share.

Assuming onshore tax revenues in Scotland follow the path forecast for the UK as a whole, they are projected to grow by approximately £5 billion (10 per cent) in real terms between 2011/12 and 2016/17[43].

Tax revenues from oil and gas production will depend on a range of different factors, including future production in the North Sea, wholesale oil and gas prices and profitability. The Fiscal Commission has set out proposals for how such revenues could be managed successfully in an independent Scotland.

The Scottish Government has published forecasts for North Sea tax receipts under a range of scenarios[44]. Two scenarios are used here.

In the first, production is assumed to remain unchanged at current levels, whilst oil prices are assumed to remain unchanged in cash terms at their average level over the two years to March 2013. Under such a scenario, Scottish oil and gas receipts are forecast to generate £6.8 billion in tax revenue in 2016/17.

In the second scenario, production is forecast to increase more in line with industry forecasts, although at a lower level of profitability. Under this scenario, oil and gas receipts could reach £7.9 billion in 2016/17.

The table below provides forecasts of key elements of public sector expenditure and revenue for Scotland in 2016/17 based on the above scenarios and projections.

TABLE – ESTIMATES OF SCOTLAND'S FINANCIAL POSITION (2016/17) £ BILLIONS – UNDER CURRENT CONSTITUTIONAL ARRANGEMENTS	
Total Expenditure (Non-Debt Interest)	**£63.7**
Currently Devolved	£37.3
Defence	£3.0
Reserved Social Protection	£18.8
Other Reserved Spending	£4.6
Public Sector Debt Interest[1]	£3.9 to £5.5
Total Public Sector Receipts	**£63.7 to £64.8**
Onshore Receipts	**£56.9**
Offshore Receipts	**£6.8-£7.9**
Net Fiscal Balance[2]	
Including historical share of debt interest payments	-£2.7 to -£4.0
As percentage of GDP	-1.6 per cent to -2.4 per cent
Including population share of debt interest payments	-£4.3 to -£5.5
As percentage of GDP	-2.5 per cent to -3.2 per cent
UK Public Sector Net Borrowing[3]	**-£61**
As percentage of GDP	-3.4 per cent

Figures are rounded to the nearest hundred million and therefore may not sum
[1] Range based upon historical or population share
[2] Scottish Government projections
[3] Office for Budget Responsibility – March 2013 Economic and Fiscal Outlook

Scotland's deficit is forecast to fall to between 1.6 per cent and 2.4 per cent of GDP in 2016/17 with a historical share of UK debt and to be between 2.5 per cent and 3.2 per cent of GDP if we take on a population share of UK public sector debt. The Office for Budget Responsibility forecasts that the UK will run a deficit of 3.4 per cent of GDP in the same year[45]. The IMF estimates that the average deficit across the G7 economies will be 3.2 per cent in 2016[46]. Based on this approach, the net fiscal balance for an independent Scotland in 2016/17 is therefore forecast to be better than for the UK as a whole.

When assessing a country's finances, an important figure to consider is the current budget balance. This measures the degree to which current taxpayers meet the cost of paying for the public services they consume today and includes a contribution to debt interest payments. If a country is running near to a current budget balance or surplus, it may still have to borrow to fund capital expenditure. However, such borrowing will be for long-term investment which can be expected to increase the economy's productive capacity in future years. Such borrowing can therefore be part of a sustainable approach to managing the public finances.

Assuming a share of debt interest payments based upon Scotland's historical contribution to the UK public finances, Scotland's current budget balance is estimated to be between 0.1 per cent (i.e. a surplus) and -0.7 per cent of GDP in 2016/17. Assuming a population share of debt interest payments, Scotland's current budget balance in 2016/17 is projected to be between -0.8 per cent and -1.5 per cent of GDP. This compares to a forecast for the UK as a whole of -1.9 per cent.

Given this expected starting point, the following section sets out the early tax and expenditure priorities that the current Scottish Government would take forward following independence.

We recognise that, as with any financial projection, revenues and expenditure may be higher or lower than projected at this stage. As a responsible government, we will make plans for transition and contingency.

Early priorities for action within sound public finances
Robust public finances are an important prerequisite for delivering sustainable economic growth. The sharp increase In Westminster borrowing, and resulting austerity, highlights the significant implications for household incomes and the economy of not managing the public finances responsibly.

This Government will ensure that Scotland has stable and sustainable public finances, underpinned by the discipline of a framework designed to ensure that Scotland's finances are appropriate for the country's economy, and able to withstand changes in economic circumstances.

To support this, this Government will put in place an effective fiscal framework, including: the creation of an independent Scottish Fiscal Commission; fiscal rules; and an Energy Fund to manage oil revenues[47]. This will provide future Scottish governments with a sound basis on which to make appropriate choices about tax rates, spending levels, debt and borrowing.

Sound public finances will be an important part of the agreements underpinning a Sterling Area arrangement with the rest of the UK and for demonstrating our credibility to financial markets[48]. The record of Scotland's public finances, and the projections provided here, give us confidence that Scotland will be able to meet these requirements.

In an independent Scotland, the elected government will have control over all tax revenues and expenditure in Scotland. This will provide an opportunity to redirect currently reserved expenditure to reflect Scottish priorities and also to use key tax and regulatory powers to improve the Scottish economy – for example, by better linking our welfare and tax system.

This Government intends to raise revenue and reduce spending by:

■ reducing defence and security spending to £2.5 billion per year (which is still more than Westminster spends on defence in Scotland)

■ ending the married couples tax allowance, planned for introduction in 2015

■ cancelling the Westminster Government's Shares for Rights scheme in Scotland

■ providing for a streamlined system of overseas representation focused on Scottish citizens and priority business sectors

There will also be savings from no longer having to fund the Westminster Parliament.

We expect these changes to deliver savings or increases in revenue totalling around £600 million in a full year.

This will provide scope to take action in the first budget of an independent Scotland to create a fairer and more successful country. The priorities of the current Scottish Government for that first budget will be to:

■ maintain a commitment to protecting free personal care, free prescriptions, free higher education tuition for Scottish students and free concessionary travel

■ abolish the "bedroom tax"

■ extend the period of the triple lock for uprating of state pensions

■ reduce energy bills by moving the cost of the Energy Company Obligation and Warm Home Discount Scheme to the Scottish Government

■ provide 600 hours of childcare to around half of two year olds, as part of a longer term plan to deliver a transformational expansion in childcare

- equalise the earnings disregard between first and second earners for those already in receipt of Universal Credit

- increase tax allowances, tax credits and benefits in line with inflation

- meet international commitments to spend 0.7 per cent of Gross National Income on international aid

We expect these commitments to cost around £500-600 million per year in total to deliver.

Over the course of the first term of an independent Scottish Parliament, the Scottish Government proposes to work with Scotland's tax authority, Revenue Scotland, to simplify the tax system to reduce compliance costs, streamline reliefs and help to reduce tax avoidance, with a target revenue gain of £250 million per year by the end of the first term.

Alongside simplification, this Government plans for Revenue Scotland to deploy modern digital collection technologies to help ensure that all taxpayers pay their fair share of taxes, bearing down on the amount of revenues which are lost to error, avoidance and evasion.

Within our framework for robust and sustainable public finances, we propose to deliver the following measures to boost Scotland's competitiveness within the first term of an independent Scottish Parliament:

- provide childcare for 30 hours per week for 38 weeks per year – equivalent to primary school hours – for every three and four year old and vulnerable two year old, as part of a longer-term commitment to provide this level of provision to all children from age one until they start school

- cut Air Passenger Duty by 50 per cent, with a view to eventually abolishing it

- provide a clear timetable for cutting corporation tax by up to three percentage points for businesses paying tax in Scotland

We will also examine an increase in the National Insurance
Employment Allowance to help small businesses, and will
commence negotiations to return Royal Mail in Scotland to
public ownership.

PART 3

CHAPTER

3

FINANCE
AND THE
ECONOMY

SCOTLAND
HAS GOT WHAT IT TAKES

£17 BILLION CONSTRUCTION INDUSTRY[1]

£9 BILLION TOURISM INDUSTRY[2]

10% OF EU'S WAVE ENERGY POTENTIAL[10]

GDP PER HEAD SCOTLAND RANKS **8**TH OUT OF 34 OECD MEMBER COUNTRIES[3]

SCOTLAND

98.8% OF PREDICTED UK OFFSHORE **OIL** PRODUCTION[4]

£2.8 BILLION CREATIVE INDUSTRY[11]

25% OF EUROPE'S POTENTIAL **WIND** AND **TIDAL ENERGY**[5]

£32 BILLION RURAL AND **ISLAND** ECONOMY[12]

£13 BILLION **FOOD & DRINK** INDUSTRY[6]

5.3 MILLION PEOPLE[7]

11.6% OF UK FARMING PRODUCTION[8]

£2.3 BILLION ECONOMIC IMPACT OF THE HISTORIC ENVIRONMENT[13]

£4.3 BILLION WHISKY EXPORT INDUSTRY[9]

1, 3, 6, 8, 10, 11, 12. SOURCE: SCOTTISH GOVERNMENT
2. SOURCE: VISIT SCOTLAND
4. SOURCE: PROFESSOR ALEX KEMP, ABERDEEN UNIVERSITY (IN THE 30 YEARS FROM 2011)
5. SOURCE: SCOTTISH GOVERNMENT ANALYSIS
7. SOURCE: 2011 CENSUS
9. SOURCE: HER MAJESTY'S REVENUE AND CUSTOMS
13. SOURCE: HISTORIC ADVISORY COUNCIL FOR SCOTLAND

- Independence will allow us to use our own resources and shape our own fiscal and economic policies for Scottish needs and circumstances. This will ensure greater economic security and opportunity in the future

- We plan to prioritise job creation through measures to encourage growth

- We will support manufacturing, innovation and the transition to a low carbon economy

- Scotland will continue to use the pound, providing continuity and certainty for individuals and businesses in Scotland and the rest of the UK

- We will support a labour market that helps people into work that is sustainable and fairly rewarded

- Our Fair Work Commission will guarantee that the minimum wage rises – at the very least – in line with inflation to ensure that work is a route out of poverty

- We will bring together employers and employees in a convention on employment and labour relations to build a collaborative approach to work and create a responsive labour market

- We have identified the following priorities to support the Scottish economy for the first session of an independent Scottish parliament
  - a commitment to increase the personal tax allowance, benefits and tax credits in line with inflation
  - a pre-announced reduction in corporation tax of up to three percentage points
  - a reduction of Air Passenger Duty by 50 per cent
  - the simplification of the tax system to reduce compliance costs, streamline reliefs and help to reduce tax avoidance, with a target revenue gain of £250 million a year by the end of the first term

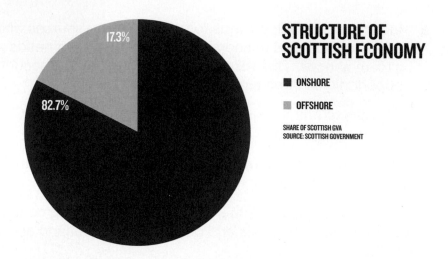

**STRUCTURE OF
SCOTTISH ECONOMY**

■ ONSHORE

■ OFFSHORE

SHARE OF SCOTTISH GVA
SOURCE: SCOTTISH GOVERNMENT

17.3%

82.7%

Why we need a new approach
Scotland has strong economic foundations.

We have substantial natural resources, a highly-skilled workforce, a long-standing reputation for innovation, and an internationally-recognised brand, with products and companies competing at the highest level in international markets.

The First Report of the Fiscal Commission provided an overview of Scotland's economy and assessed performance relative to both the UK and other comparable nations. The Group concluded that

> By international standards Scotland is a wealthy and productive country. There is no doubt that Scotland has the potential to be a successful independent nation[49].

Devolution has provided Scotland with some – albeit limited – ability to tailor policies to Scottish circumstances, and successive Scottish administrations have used these to help narrow a historic gap in economic performance with the UK.

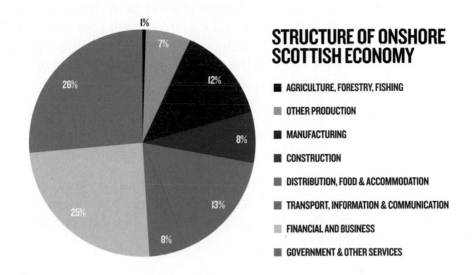

STRUCTURE OF ONSHORE SCOTTISH ECONOMY

- AGRICULTURE, FORESTRY, FISHING
- OTHER PRODUCTION
- MANUFACTURING
- CONSTRUCTION
- DISTRIBUTION, FOOD & ACCOMMODATION
- TRANSPORT, INFORMATION & COMMUNICATION
- FINANCIAL AND BUSINESS
- GOVERNMENT & OTHER SERVICES

Scotland's economic performance is now stronger than – or just as good as – the UK on key measures:

- even excluding the contribution of North Sea oil and gas, output per head in Scotland is 99 per cent of the UK average and the highest in the UK outside London and the South East[50]

- adding in a geographical share of North Sea output gives Scotland an output per head almost 20 per cent higher than the UK

- in 2010 Gross National Income per head in Scotland – including the North Sea – was approximately £26,000, which compares with around £24,000 for the UK as a whole, according to experimental estimates[51]

- productivity, measured as output per hour worked, is now identical in Scotland to that of the UK[52]

- amongst OECD economies, it is estimated Scotland would be ranked eighth in terms of output per head[53]

- in 2012, Scotland's share of all new UK Foreign Direct Investment projects was nearly 11 per cent[54] – well above a population share

- Scotland's relative labour market performance has also strengthened. Scotland's employment rate has been higher, and our unemployment rate lower than in the UK as a whole for most of the recent period. Our rates of economic participation have also been better

- Scotland's public finances are estimated to have been in a relatively stronger position over the last five years, than the UK as a whole – to the tune of £12.6 billion[55]

Scotland has a diverse economy with key strengths across a range of sectors such as food and drink, tourism, creative industries, life sciences, universities, financial services and manufacturing.

Scotland is rich in energy with around 25 per cent of Europe's offshore wind and tidal energy potential, and 10 per cent of Europe's wave potential[56]. It is estimated that there could be up to 24 billion barrels of recoverable oil and gas remaining in the North Sea with the potential for production to continue for decades to come[57].

As a regional economy within the UK, Scotland performs relatively well on aggregate measures of economic performance, but as an independent nation we could be doing significantly better. Many of our competitors are stronger, not just economically, but also in terms of equality and wellbeing[58].

For example, Scotland's economy has grown more slowly than other comparable independent European countries in recent decades. Over time, such differences can have substantial implications for economic prosperity.

If Scotland moved from the rates of growth it has experienced in the past to instead match the levels of growth of small European countries, the benefits for people in Scotland in terms of prosperity and employment would be significant. As an illustration, had growth in Scotland matched these other independent nations between 1977 and 2007, GDP per head would now be 3.8 per cent higher, equivalent to an additional £900 per head[59].

Growth and competitiveness are important, however there is a growing recognition that the characteristics of growth and the distribution of its benefits are just as important.

Under the Westminster system Scotland is locked in to one of the most unequal economic models in the OECD – with the UK ranked 28th out of 34 countries in terms of its Gini coefficient (a key measure of income inequality)[60]. Such inequalities have in fact widened rather than narrowed in recent decades[61]. Such patterns are not only damaging in their own right, but act to constrain growth over the long term[62].

There is also clear evidence of increasing geographical imbalances which have concentrated jobs, population growth and investment in London and the South-East of England[63]. At the same time, there has also been a gradual erosion of economic resilience with a declining manufacturing base, sustained current account deficits and higher levels of public and private sector debt.

The gap between rich and poor, the increasing concentration of economic activity in one small part of the UK, and growing imbalances in the structure of the UK economy all suggest that continuing as a regional economy will hamper job creation in Scotland and reduce economic security in the long term.

The economic choice in the independence referendum is about how we best equip ourselves to meet the challenges, seize the opportunities and secure the future for people living in Scotland now and in years to come.

The Scottish Government believes that the best option for Scotland is to become independent. It will create the opportunity to build an economy that takes advantage of Scotland's unique strengths and size, and which delivers a more outward focused, fairer and resilient economy.

The opportunities available to Scotland

Under the current constitutional arrangements, the Scottish Government has responsibility for devolved economic policy areas. However, responsibility for most important economic and social policies is reserved to Westminster. This includes welfare, employability, workplace relations, economic and financial regulation and consumer protection. The Scottish Parliament is responsible for just 7 per cent of taxes raised in Scotland. Even after the new tax powers of the Scotland Act 2012, this figure will only increase to around 15 per cent[64].

Remaining under the Westminster system restricts Scotland's ability to meet future challenges and opportunities.

We are clear about the longstanding issues to be tackled in order to drive growth and address inequality in the Scottish economy. We will need to:

- create more and better employment opportunities across all parts of the country and tackle long-standing social and economic inequalities that constrain our economic potential

- boost and diversify our businesses

- rebalance the economy and strengthen the role of manufacturing and innovation

- grow our export base and provide the framework to help support Scottish companies to compete in global markets

- encourage a longer-term focus on investment and economic sustainability

- support the transition to a low carbon economy

Since devolution our performance within the UK has strengthened[65]. This illustrates the advantages of Scotland making our own decisions to the benefit of our economy. But we can do much better.

Independence will provide the government of Scotland with access to economic and fiscal levers which the Westminster Government currently controls. Future Scottish governments will be able to set policy to Scotland's own circumstances, strengths and preferences.

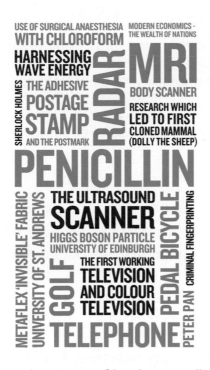

USE OF SURGICAL ANAESTHESIA WITH CHLOROFORM
HARNESSING WAVE ENERGY
SHERLOCK HOLMES
THE ADHESIVE POSTAGE STAMP AND THE POSTMARK
RADAR
MODERN ECONOMICS - THE WEALTH OF NATIONS
MRI BODY SCANNER
RESEARCH WHICH LED TO FIRST CLONED MAMMAL (DOLLY THE SHEEP)
PENICILLIN
METAFLEX 'INVISIBLE' FABRIC
UNIVERSITY OF ST. ANDREWS
THE ULTRASOUND SCANNER
HIGGS BOSON PARTICLE UNIVERSITY OF EDINBURGH
THE FIRST WORKING TELEVISION AND COLOUR TELEVISION
GOLF
PEDAL BICYCLE
PETER PAN
CRIMINAL FINGERPRINTING
TELEPHONE

Having responsibility for all economic levers in Scotland will allow us to transform our country. With independence we will be able to choose an economic approach that builds on our existing strengths and which helps deliver a more outward focused, dynamic and resilient economy. For example, independence will allow future Scottish governments to build on the progress already being made to tackle climate change and to capture Scotland's significant economic opportunities in the low carbon sector.

The performance of many small countries demonstrates the advantage of having a policy framework appropriate to local circumstances. Evidence shows that countries similar in size to Scotland have a strong track record[66]:

- currently nine of the top fifteen OECD economies measured by output per head are of similar size to Scotland[67]

- small countries make up a majority of the top 20 positions in the UN Human Development Index[68]

An independent Scotland will not replicate the economic structure of the UK; instead independence will bring opportunities to operate more effectively and efficiently.

This Government's aim is that, within a decade, Scotland will achieve and maintain a place in the top 10 nations in the UN Human Development Index[69]. Achieving this aim will show both an improved economic performance and that we have translated greater economic success into direct social and personal benefits for the people of Scotland.

The Scotland we can create

Since 2007, the Scottish Government has been pursuing an economic strategy with a clear purpose: increasing sustainable economic growth, with opportunities for all of Scotland to flourish.

Driving our ambition for a more successful economy are six key priorities:

■ creating a supportive business environment

■ delivering benefits from the transition to a low carbon economy

■ improving opportunities for learning, skills development and wellbeing

■ a focus on infrastructure

■ ensuring effective government

■ producing economic and social outcomes that are more equitable

These will remain at the centre of this government's approach in an independent Scotland.

An independent Scotland will be able to use our new powers to improve productivity, boost participation and build greater solidarity, cohesion and sustainability.

Productivity

More productive economies typically enjoy higher living standards. In 2011, Scotland's productivity was 100 per cent of the UK average measured by output per hour worked, and 99 per cent of the UK average in terms of output per filled job[70].

However, in comparison with our international competitors, Scotland's (and the UK's) performance is less favourable. Countries, such as Norway, Ireland, Denmark and Austria do better. For example, productivity in Denmark is around 12 per cent higher than in Scotland[71].

Independence will provide the opportunity to target policies to Scotland's unique circumstances and challenges, and to

boost productivity. Our plans for re-industrialisation, innovation, taxation, investment and internationalisation will help to achieve this by delivering the necessary changes to our economy.

Participation and population
An engaged and productive workforce is central to long-term economic success. Greater participation increases the economy's growth potential. It is also key to addressing important social objectives, such as tackling poverty. A labour market which is resilient, adaptable to changes in economic conditions, and able to respond quickly to new opportunities and challenges is a major competitive advantage.

In recent years, Scotland has had a stronger employment record than the UK. However, consistent with the trend at the UK level, the characteristics and composition of our labour market has changed, adversely affecting job security, the rewards of work and equality of opportunity.

Many other independent countries perform more strongly both in terms of participation and job outcomes[72]. Independence will give us control over labour market policies, including direct levers such as taxation, welfare and regulation, and indirect levers such as child care and employee and employer relations.

The most significant determinant of Scotland's long-term growth gap relative to the UK has been slower population growth. A country's population – in particular those of working age – is a key driver of long-term prosperity. Successive administrations have made boosting Scotland's population a top priority. The most recent Census showed that as at March 2011, Scotland's population stood at 5.295 million – the highest ever[73]. However, the recent growth has only served to reverse the impact of decades of emigration and the latest population projections suggest that Scotland's working age population will not grow as rapidly as the UK as a whole[74].

Independence will provide an opportunity to grow the economy more quickly, provide more opportunities for our young people to stay and build careers in Scotland and to attract skilled workers.

Solidarity, cohesion and sustainability
Scotland is currently a more equal country than the UK as a whole[75]. However, in 2010, Scotland would still have been ranked 17th in the OECD in terms of income inequality, so clearly we need to do better[76]. Too often the benefits of economic growth are not shared equally across the country. Independence will provide the levers to tackle inequalities in Scotland.

Aligning tax and welfare policies, helping people to move into sustained work and supporting people to develop the skills to progress will all help support better solidarity and cohesion in Scotland.

With independence, we will have the opportunity to:

■ set out a vision for the type of economy and society that captures Scotland's distinct values and build distinct economic, industrial and social policies which reflect these aims

■ use welfare and employment policies to tackle long-standing inequalities – both social and regional – that have persisted for decades

■ prioritise tax powers, regulation and Scotland's new global status to develop growth sectors and growth companies, widen the export base, attract investment, and support local firms to move into new and emerging markets

- develop an industrial strategy that promotes manufacturing and its links to the local supply chain

- use the full array of business policies – affecting small and large businesses – alongside the resources of the public sector and Scotland's universities and colleges to support innovation and expand the business base

- target policy to barriers that hold Scotland back – for example, by reducing Air Passenger Duty to boost international connectivity

- build a more stable macroeconomic framework

- design a more efficient tax system

- implement an improved and streamlined consumer protection and regulatory regime which cuts back on waste and duplication

- coordinate devolved powers with new tax and expenditure responsibilities – for example, in skills and employability, childcare, tax and welfare – to deliver more coherent policies

- use full responsibility for Scotland's natural resources, such as control of the sea bed and oil and gas reserves, to maximise the growth prospects for the future and to enable communities to benefit from our assets

- align education and skills policy with employment and industrial policies to facilitate more high value job opportunities and achieve the objective of full employment

- recognise that our island communities have challenges and opportunities that differ from those in other parts of the country in areas like transport and energy

This is not a prescriptive menu of policies, but illustrates what choices could be made with independence. It will enable future Scottish governments – whatever their political colour – to look at how we can best grow our economy and create jobs, with a broader range of options and opportunities to do things differently.

A supportive, competitive and dynamic business environment

The choices open to us

An independent Scotland will have the opportunity to pursue policies designed to grow the economy and create jobs. With responsibility for the full range of policy levers, the government of an independent Scotland will be able to create a more supportive, competitive and dynamic business environment.

Within the devolved powers currently available, the Scottish Government is pursuing a range of actions to support sustainable economic growth and higher quality jobs, including the Small Business Bonus Scheme, attracting international investment, the Scottish Investment Bank and investment in infrastructure.

With independence, future Scottish governments can build on these policies to enable Scotland's businesses to reach their full potential. Future Scottish governments will be able to make choices over tax, measures to boost innovation and exports, promote good industrial relations and support small and medium sized enterprises.

Our priorities for action
Each of Scotland's political parties will bring forward policy proposals at the future elections to an independent Scottish parliament. If elected in 2016, the current Scottish Government's priorities for action will be as follows.

A competitive and efficient tax environment
Being close to a global economic hub such as London can be an advantage for Scotland. However, London inevitably acts as an economic magnet, attracting jobs and investment (particularly headquarter operations) away from other parts of the UK. The ability to vary tax is essential to redress the unbalanced nature of the UK economy.

We plan to set out a timescale for reducing corporation tax by up to three percentage points below the prevailing UK rate. The intention of pre-announcing the cut is to stimulate economic activity in advance of it taking place and to retain and attract new investment. This will be one way to secure a competitive advantage and help to reverse the loss of corporate headquarters which has been a feature of the Scottish economy over the last 30 years.

Support for the reindustrialisation of Scotland
A key priority will be to re-balance and re-industrialise Scotland's economy, to secure a number of benefits including:

■ *boosting high-value jobs* – through increased manufacturing activity[77]

■ *promoting innovation* – although manufacturing firms account for only 12 per cent of Scottish (onshore) output[78], they account for 66 per cent of business R&D spending[79]

■ *addressing geographical disparities* – the decline in manufacturing has contributed to geographical imbalances across Scotland. Increasing manufacturing activity in a local area will help develop clusters of economic activity and support local supply chains[80]

■ *boosting exports* – around 62 per cent of Scottish international exports are manufactured and a greater focus on internationalisation across the economy will help boost competitiveness and support jobs[81]

One option for future governments to support manufacturing and boost innovation will be to use the tax system to improve incentives for investment, for example through more generous depreciation allowances for key growth sectors in Scotland.

The current Scottish Government will also develop a new industrial strategy for Scotland. Key elements of the industrial strategy will include:

■ support for investment, including research and development

■ support for indigenous companies and ownership by strengthening the role of the Scottish Investment Bank

■ expanding skills development by bringing together employment and skills policies and putting modern apprenticeships at the heart of our approach

■ expanding our manufacturing base, with a particular focus on maximising the manufacturing opportunities of our offshore energy potential

■ targeted use of loan guarantees

Boosting connectivity
In the modern global economy, air connections are vital to international connectivity. Benchmarking analysis, based on 2011 data, indicated that Scotland's short haul network had almost reached the level of connectivity that would be expected when compared to peer regional networks[82]. However, Scotland's long-haul network performance is not as strong and there are clear areas for improvement to destinations such as the Asia Pacific region and North America.

With independence, government policies – for example, careful design of Air Passenger Duty (APD) – can be used to encourage the types of flights that benefit Scotland. Analysis suggests that the current APD impacts negatively on the Scottish economy, with APD in the UK now the highest tax of its type anywhere in the world.

A recent study estimated that APD will cost Scotland more than £200 million a year in lost tourism spend alone by 2016[83]. We plan to reduce APD by 50 per cent in the first term of the independent parliament, with a view to abolishing it when public finances allow.

As an independent nation, Scotland will be better placed to work with airport, airline, tourism and other partners to sustain network development activity in long-haul markets, as part of a Team Scotland approach. The Irish Government has for example struck a deal with Customs Authorities in the US to allow passengers travelling through airports in Ireland to clear passport control before boarding the plane[84].

Maximising the opportunities of our overseas representation
At present Scottish Development International has offices across Asia, the Pacific, Europe, the Middle East and the Americas[85]. An independent Scotland will prioritise our effort and resources to strengthen our international presence in the nations and markets that are of greatest economic importance to us. It is worth noting that 91 per cent of total Scottish exports currently go to 21 countries[86].

A crucial part of the role of Scotland's proposed overseas representation (see Chapter 5) will be to identify opportunities to directly promote Scottish goods and services. The Team Scotland approach will be built on and with independence our government departments, the private sector and our diplomatic missions will work together to promote Scotland.

Other actions
In addition to the priorities outlined above – all of which are designed to improve productivity, participation and cohesion – we will also take the following actions:

Support small and medium-sized enterprises

This government will continue our commitment to the Small Business Bonus which has reduced, or eliminated entirely, business rates for tens of thousands of properties across Scotland and to maintaining Scottish business rates parity with the rest of the UK[87]. The tax system in Scotland will be designed to reduce compliance burdens facing small and medium-sized enterprises in particular.

The Government will also examine the case for an increase in the National Insurance employment allowance for small business.

Streamline competition and regulation policy

Competition is a key driver of productivity, exports and consumer value and choice. An independent Scotland, as part of the EU, will continue to meet the regulatory requirements associated with membership – many of which relate to the operation of the Single Market. We will also develop and deliver a streamlined and efficient regulatory model with a combined regulatory body with a single, strong voice, both in Scotland and internationally, on competition and consumer issues[88].

Strengthen consumer protection

Scottish consumers are an important part of the economy[89]. In order for economic activity to flourish it is important that consumers are able to trust businesses. We will establish a more integrated, simplified consumer landscape with a single consumer body to take into account Scottish specific issues, such as unfair parcel delivery charges in rural areas, building on the Scottish Government's proposal for a combined economic regulator.

Directly influence EU legislation

With independence Scotland's government will be able to represent Scotland's interests as a full and active participant in the EU.

Maximise investment

Investment in infrastructure will remain a central part of the Scottish Government's approach to supporting long-term sustainable economic growth. On independence the Scottish Government will make our own decisions about resources for capital investment. We will have full access to capital borrowing and will take forward infrastructure priorities as set out in our Infrastructure Investment Plan.

Increasing innovation throughout Scotland's economy
Innovation is a key driver of productivity and growth[90]. Firms innovate in order to stay ahead of their rivals, through the

production of new knowledge or the application of existing knowledge.

The top-performing small independent countries emphasise science and innovation in their economic strategies. Many small countries have been increasing their research and development (R&D) spending, as a percentage of GDP, more quickly than larger economies[91]. From 2001 to 2011 total R&D spend rose as a percentage of GDP in Finland, Denmark and Ireland. In contrast, R&D spend as a percentage of GDP in the UK and Scotland remained broadly unchanged over this period[92].

This investment in science and technology, and in education and training more generally, has allowed many of our competitors to strengthen their performance in export markets – in particular high technology export markets – and support economic growth.

The largest proportion of R&D spend comes from the private sector – on average around two thirds of total R&D expenditure across OECD countries[93]. However, in Scotland this proportion is considerably lower, with the largest contribution to total R&D spend coming from investment by the Higher Education sector[94].

Scotland's investment in Higher Education R&D is world class – the latest official statistics show that, in 2011, Scotland's Higher Education R&D expenditure as a percentage of GDP ranked top of the 12 countries/regions of the UK, and fourth highest among the OECD countries[95].

Key priorities for Scotland will be to find ways of boosting business spending on research and development, whilst enabling higher levels of commercialisation of the world-class research produced at Scottish universities.

With independence Scotland will further strengthen the relationships and linkages between key partners in innovation – including businesses, universities, funding providers, companies, and public sector agencies – in a coherent strategy with shared priorities.

Direct financing levers

With independence we will develop and expand direct financing instruments, including the provision of credit loans and guarantees and encouraging higher levels of equity financing and venture capital.

Indirect financing levers

Tax based incentives that are aimed at encouraging investment in innovation activities can be applied to either expenditure (related to R&D) or income that results from investment in R&D. Following independence this Government will examine how best to develop and target such tax relief to encourage Scotland's innovative industries.

Intellectual property

We will ensure continuity of the legal framework for protecting intellectual property rights. Independence will also allow Scotland to offer a simpler and cheaper, more business-friendly model than the current UK system, which is bureaucratic and expensive, especially for small firms. The UK is one of the few EU countries which does not offer a scheme which covers the basics of protection. Scotland could follow, for example, the German model which protects technical innovations.

Scotland also has a distinctive body of expertise in dispute resolution through the Scottish Arbitration Centre which could be developed as an international centre of excellence in arbitration.

We recognise that researchers are highly skilled, and globally mobile. Scottish universities recruit researchers from across the world, whilst many Scottish researchers work in institutions in other countries. With responsibility for immigration policy this Scottish Government will amend recent Westminster Government restrictions which impact in particular on the ability of our universities and colleges to attract international students. We will develop an approach to immigration to attract international talent at a level that would support high growth companies to develop and grow (see Chapter 7).

Innovation is not limited to high tech sectors. It can also drive growth across the economy by investing in new approaches to meeting customer needs and attracting attention to Scottish products. For example, VisitScotland developed a unique partnership with The Walt Disney Company to make the most of the opportunity of the animated feature *Brave* to boost tourism in Scotland. The Scottish Government and VisitScotland have continued to build on this innovative relationship with the world's largest entertainment organisation, showing Scottish food, drink and culture and promoting our assets as a tourism destination at the recent eighth Epcot International Food & Wine Festival at Walt Disney World in Orlando, Florida.

A valued and well-rewarded workforce

The choices open to us

A country's people are its greatest asset and it is vital that everyone in Scotland has the opportunity to fulfil their potential. Well rewarded and sustained employment is the best route out of poverty and the best way to tackle inequality.

All the actions described in this chapter are designed to improve job opportunities and long-term economic resilience. With independence, we will focus on creating better work opportunities, with the aim of creating maximum employment for the entire workforce and the long-term success of Scotland's economy.

Under devolution the Scottish Government has responsibilities for education and skills, but not for employment regulation, tax or welfare policies, all of which are crucial to support people entering and remaining in employment. The Scottish Government is responsible for training the present and future workforce, equipping them with the skills and knowledge they need, but has no say in how they are treated once they are in a job.

The Scottish Government has used our responsibilities to support employment, in particular to address the challenge of youth unemployment. The action we have taken includes a commitment to 25,000 new apprenticeship opportunities in each year of the current Parliament, the majority of which are targeted at young people; and Opportunities for All, which is a guaranteed place in education or training for all 16-19 year olds not already in learning, training or employment.

Independence will enable future Scottish governments to create a more coherent framework for employment and the labour market – one that links education, employability training, welfare, taxation and health with action aimed at creating a supportive business environment to foster job creation. It will also allow us to create joined up services which match job seekers and opportunities, within a supportive culture, offering help and assistance to those furthest from the labour market.

The success of Scotland in creating job opportunities and greater economic security than at present will also depend crucially on a sense of cohesion. There is good evidence that countries of Scotland's size that perform well have a sense of shared national purpose[96]. With independence steps can be taken to improve cohesion, and partnership within the economy.

Our priorities for action
The priorities for action for this Scottish Government in the first term of an independent Scottish parliament will be to:

- work directly with the trade unions, employer associations, employers and the voluntary sector to build a partnership approach to addressing labour market challenges

- create sustainable employment that pays fairly through changes to the minimum wage and a commitment to the living wage

- encourage people into work through a focus on early intervention and policies that support skills, training and opportunity

We will work with the STUC and the business community on mechanisms to formalise the relationship between government, employer associations and employee associations with a particular focus on encouraging wider trade union participation and in recognition of the positive role that can be played by collective bargaining in improving labour market conditions. For example, evidence from the OECD shows that stronger trade unions tend to reduce inequality in labour income and ensure a more equal distribution of earnings[97].

With independence powers over employment legislation will transfer from Westminster to Scotland. Employment law and regulations cover minimum terms and conditions, maternity and paternity rights, worker representation, the rules around unions and collective bargaining and the minimum wage.

The Scottish Government has adopted a strong social partnership approach, working with the voluntary sector, unions, employer associations and employers directly. With independence we will build on this approach.

We have proposed a Fair Work Commission which, as part of a remit, will deliver the mechanism for uprating the National Minimum Wage.

We will also establish a National Convention on Employment and Labour relations. Bringing together labour market regulation and other employment-related policies in a forum which encourages direct and constructive dialogue across all key stakeholders will be a major advantage. This could, in principle, range from a focus on high-level issues such as labour market reform, to sectoral issues such as addressing skills-shortages in key sectors and particular policy initiatives such as the Living Wage.

Employee representation
Analysis by the TUC shows that in 14 of the 28 EU member states workers have the right to be represented on company boards[98]. These countries have adopted different models in line with their own circumstances and cultures. There are differences for example in how worker representatives are nominated and elected and which companies are covered by the requirement.

Employee representation can help to bolster long-term decision-making and improve industrial relations. There are already examples of good practice here too – First Group has had an employee director since the company was created in 1989.

In an independent Scotland we will consult on the best form of employee representation on company boards.

We will also take steps to ensure that women have equal opportunities in terms of the quality as well as the number of jobs. Greater action needs to be taken to improve female representation and diversity on company boards.

Whilst the Westminster Government requires firms to report the number of men and women on their boards[99], and has a target to increase the number of women on FTSE 100 boards to 25 per cent by 2015[100], a number of European countries have adopted a more progressive attitude to gender balance on company boards. Belgium, Italy, France, Iceland and Norway have already introduced legislation requiring a gender quota on boards[101].

The Scottish Government will consult on a target for female representation on company – and public boards – and, if necessary, we will legislate as appropriate.

Independence will allow Scotland to bring together all of our resources and expertise, including academic and industry expertise, employee and employer organisations, in direct and constructive dialogue across Scotland's economic sectors – including new and emerging sectors, such as renewables – and on key issues, such as the Living Wage, zero-hours contracts and access to Employment Tribunals. An independent Scotland can examine innovative ways to support improvements in the productivity and well-being of the workforce.

Sustainable and fairly rewarded employment
The Scottish Government believes that it is absolutely vital for our economy and for our society that work pays, and that work pays fairly. The living wage and minimum wage will be central elements of our employment policy.

Living Wage

Achieving fair levels of pay is a fundamental aspect of building a more equal, socially just society. More of the people living in poverty today are in work than out of it and this trend has increased since the mid-1990s[102]. The Scottish Government fully supports the Living Wage campaign and its principle of encouraging employers to reward their staff fairly. We have led by example by ensuring all staff covered by the public sector pay policy are paid at least the Scottish Living Wage. This covers the 180,000 people in Scotland working for central government, our agencies and the NHS[103] benefiting directly up to 3,300 workers[104]. This is part of the Government's "social wage" – the contract between the people of Scotland and their government.

Our commitment to support the Scottish Living Wage for the duration of this Parliament is a commitment to those on the lowest incomes. However, over 400,000 people in Scotland are working for less than the living wage, which is nearly a fifth of the Scottish workforce and the majority of these low paid workers are women[105]. The Scottish Government is funding the Poverty Alliance to deliver a Living Wage Accreditation Scheme to promote the living wage and increase the number of private companies that pay it to make decent pay the norm in our country. We will continue to support and promote the living wage in an independent Scotland.

Minimum Wage

Around 70,000 people currently receive the minimum wage in Scotland[106]. In real terms the minimum wage has failed to increase in almost a decade and in every single year since the recession of 2008 it has failed to keep up with the cost of living – if the minimum wage had increased in line with the cost of living over the past five years some of the lowest paid Scots would now earn almost £675 a year more than they do today[107].

This Scottish Government is therefore giving a firm commitment that if we are the government in an independent Scotland, the minimum wage will in future rise at least in line with inflation.

This Scottish Government's Fair Work Commission, with members drawn from business, trade unions and wider society, will advise the government on the minimum wage. The Commission will also provide advice on other factors relating to individual and collective rights which contribute to fairness at work and business competitiveness, recognising that both are integral elements of sustainable economic growth in Scotland. The Commission will work with the larger Convention on Employment and Labour Relations. Together they will help the Scottish Government foster a constructive and collaborative approach to industrial relations policy and formalise the relationship between government, employers, trade unions and employee associations.

Other actions
Other specific policies that the current Scottish Government will pursue to improve the labour market will include:

A Youth Guarantee

The Youth Guarantee will establish the opportunity of education, training or employment as constitutional rights. In an independent Scotland this right could be extended to those aged up to 24 years old, building on the success of the current Opportunities for All guarantee of employment, apprenticeship or training for all young people age 16 to 19. This approach will put us in line with the rest of Europe where the EU Youth Guarantee aims to offer young people across Europe a job, apprenticeship, traineeship or education place within four months of becoming unemployed or leaving education. A new programme of EU funds will become available from 2014 to allow member states to make significant progress on this commitment.

A focus on early intervention

Employment services in an independent Scotland will be built on the principle of "early intervention", and seek to prevent individuals from becoming long-term unemployed with all of the associated problems for individuals and for society. An early assessment of needs can provide support when required rather than after nine or 12 months as happens under the current system.

Integration of skills and employability

Following independence, we will bring together job matching, employability training and career guidance, currently being delivered separately in Scotland by the Department for Work and Pensions and Skills Development Scotland. This will allow local service delivery to be customised more closely to the needs of individuals. We will also aim to provide more tailored and coherent provision and increase the involvement of the Third Sector.

Strengthening employment protection

While each element of employment regulation has individual impacts, taken together as a system, they need to balance the twin objectives of protecting the rights of employees and encouraging companies to grow and create good quality jobs. The current Scottish Government plans to reverse recent changes introduced at Westminster which reduce key aspects of workers' rights. For example on independence we will restore a 90 days consultation period for redundancies affecting 100 or more employees.

Abolish the Westminster Government's Shares for Rights scheme

This scheme encourages workers to give up employment rights in areas such as unfair dismissal and redundancy pay in return for tax incentives on shares in their employers. The TUC has criticised the scheme and notes that there was overwhelming opposition to the proposals during the consultation process[108]. The Institute for Fiscal Studies has described the policy as having all the hallmarks of another tax avoidance scheme[109].

An effective immigration policy

We plan to develop and operate a controlled, transparent and efficient immigration system that best meets Scotland's needs. This will include a points based approach targeted at particular Scottish circumstances. We will also reintroduce the post-study work visa, which was abolished by the Westminster Government in April 2012 (see Chapter 7). This visa will encourage more talented people from around the world to further their education in Scotland, providing income for Scotland's institutions and contributing to a growing economy.

Our currency, fiscal rules and financial regulation

The choices open to us

A robust macroeconomic framework is essential to deliver robust economic growth and to create jobs. The Fiscal Commission, comprising eminent economists including two Nobel laureates, has explored the full range of options available to Scotland.

Their first report analysed an independent Scotland's currency choices, and the inter-linkages between a framework for monetary policy, financial stability and fiscal sustainability[110]. Having considered in detail all the options, they put forward a robust framework – including retention of the pound – which will be workable from day one of independence.

Currency and monetary policy

An independent Scotland will be able to decide our currency and the arrangements for monetary policy.

Four currency options were examined by the Fiscal Commission – the continued use of Sterling (pegged and flexible), the creation of a Scottish currency and membership of the Euro.

They concluded that retaining Sterling as part of a formal monetary union with rest of the UK will be the best option. The Fiscal Commission proposed a practical and workable model, including governance and institutional arrangements that would create a successful and robust framework.

The Commission's analysis shows that it will not only be in Scotland's interests to retain Sterling but that – post independence – this will also benefit the rest of the UK.

Under such an arrangement, monetary policy will be set according to economic conditions across the Sterling Area with ownership and governance of the Bank of England undertaken on a shareholder basis.

Choice of currency arrangements

The Fiscal Commission considered the currency options for an independent Scotland. Following a detailed analysis of the various options, the Commission[111]:

"commends to the Scottish Government retaining Sterling as part of a formal monetary union, and believes that this provides a strong overarching framework for Scotland post-independence."

Analysis highlights a number of key reasons why this would be in both Scotland and the UK's interests immediately post-independence[112]:

1. the UK is Scotland's principal trading partner accounting for 2/3 of exports in 2011, whilst figures cited by HM Treasury suggest that Scotland is the UK's second largest trading partner with exports to Scotland greater than to Brazil, South Africa, Russia, India, China and Japan put together

2. there is clear evidence of companies operating in Scotland and the UK with complex cross-border supply chains

3. a high degree of labour mobility – helped by transport links, culture and language

4. on key measurements of an optimal currency area, the Scottish and UK economies score well – for example, similar levels of productivity

5. evidence of economic cycles shows that while there have been periods of temporary divergence, there is a relatively high degree of synchronicity in short-term economic trends

It would, of course, be open to people in Scotland to choose a different arrangement in the future. However, we believe that this proposal is the right one for Scotland and that it reflects the modern partnership that we seek between the nations of these isles following independence.

A shared successful monetary union needs to have an adequately designed framework for financial stability and fiscal sustainability. These are areas which have also been examined in detail and reflected in the recommendations and advice of the Fiscal Commission.

Financial stability and financial regulation

The financial crisis showed that many countries, including the UK, had allowed flawed models of regulation to develop. It also demonstrated that regulation can only be effective if it takes account of the global nature of financial institutions. That's why we have seen an increasing emphasis on international collaboration in recent years.

With independence, Scotland will become a full member of the EU and, as highlighted above, will retain Sterling.

Membership of the EU and the increasingly integrated single market for financial services will be central to Scotland's continuing success as a leading financial centre. We will adopt EU initiatives, just as the UK does at present. The only implication for the rest of Europe, or for multinational companies, is that such rules, regulations and directives will be implemented in 29 countries instead of 28.

Financial products and services (including deposits, mortgages, and pensions) will remain denominated in the same currency. Moreover, as part of the same single market, firms will, in the main, continue to provide products and services to consumers across Scotland and the UK no matter where they are based.

There are two main areas of financial regulation.

Firstly, there are regulations that relate to the safety and soundness of financial institutions and the overall financial system as a whole.

Secondly, there are regulations relating to the conduct and behaviour of financial institutions and how they interact with their customers.

An independent Scotland will establish our own regulator, as is the case in all other EU countries.

For the first aspect of financial regulation – financial stability – in light of reforms to improve the resilience of the global financial sector, the clear trend toward cross-border co-ordination and with significant financial firms operating across Scotland and the UK, financial stability policy will be conducted on a consistent basis across the Sterling Area. This is in line with the proposal of the Fiscal Commission[113]. It is also consistent with international trends, which includes the creation of a European Banking Union with the European Central Bank taking responsibility for regulating the largest Euro Area banks.

There are a number of practical arrangements for how this could be achieved.

The Fiscal Commission set out that the Bank of England Financial Policy Committee will continue to set macroprudential policy and identify systemic risks across the whole of the Sterling Area. There could be a shared Sterling Area prudential regulatory authority for deposit takers, insurance companies and investment firms. Alternatively this could be undertaken by the regulatory arm of a Scottish Monetary Institute working alongside the equivalent UK authority on a consistent and harmonised basis.

The Bank of England, accountable to both countries, will continue to provide lender of last resort facilities and retain its role in dealing with financial institutions which posed a systemic risk.

Where financial resource was required to secure financial stability, there will be shared contributions from both the Scottish and Westminster Governments based on the principle that financial stability is of mutual benefit to consumers in both countries.

This will reflect the fact that financial institutions both in Scotland and the UK operate – and will continue to operate – with customers in Scotland, England, Wales and Northern Ireland and their stability will benefit all concerned.

Scotland will play our full part in protecting the financial system on these isles, taking responsibility for activity within Scotland as part of joint action across the Sterling Area.

Such a framework is consistent with the clear trend toward greater international co-operation on financial stability. An additional key lesson from the recent financial crisis was the need for more robust frameworks to monitor financial risks across borders and to establish frameworks so that financial institutions cannot be 'too big to fail'. Our approach is consistent with this.

Financial products, financial regulation and protecting consumers

The second aspect of financial regulation covers the monitoring of the conduct and behaviour of firms in local markets, to ensure that financial markets function well, with choice and competition, whilst protecting consumers. It is proposed that this aspect of financial regulation will be discharged by a Scottish regulator which will assume the key responsibilities of the UK Financial Conduct Authority in Scotland.

It will work on a closely harmonised basis with the UK regulators, delivering an aligned conduct regulatory framework, to retain a broadly integrated market across the Sterling Area. The regulatory approach will include the application of single rulebooks and supervisory handbooks.

This framework will mean that firms will be able to continue to provide financial products and services no matter where they are based (for example, banks based in the UK will continue to provide services to customers in Scotland and vice versa).

An independent Scotland will work with the UK and EU to continue to realise the joint benefits of an integrated market.

The market for financial products between Scotland and the UK – including bank accounts, pensions, loans and insurance – is highly integrated. Under the framework set out above, this will largely continue after independence and will be consistent with the development of the European Single Market on financial services. This ensures that consumers can choose not only from providers of financial products and services in their home market, but also providers based elsewhere in Europe.

Where there is a fully integrated market with products able to be bought across Scotland and the rest of the UK, one common Bank of England interest rate for the Sterling Area and close alignment between the two economies and regulatory structures, there is no reason for borrowing rates for consumers to be affected.

Private pension provision will also be unaffected. Existing arrangements that individuals have with private pension providers will continue and pension payments will continue to be paid in Sterling. See Chapter 4 for more information on pensions.

In an independent Scotland, this Government will continue to support existing tax-free savings products, like savings and investment ISAs. Existing schemes will be honoured in full following independence.

We will also continue to have compensation schemes in place, providing protection equivalent to that which is available in the UK, and in line with European harmonised levels of consumer protection. This includes bank deposits, which under EU harmonised rules, are protected at the equivalent of €100,000 (£85,000). Consumers in both Scotland and the rest of the UK will remain protected on a consistent basis.

Compensation schemes will be funded by a proportionate industry levy, as is currently the case. As part of the framework for financial stability proposed above, the Scottish Government sees merit in a jointly-operated or co-ordinated scheme across the Sterling Area for key aspects of compensation.

Scotland will also be responsible for our own competition and consumer protection landscape, including money advice and financial ombudsman services. Much of this landscape is fragmented at the moment, and there is significant scope to deliver this more efficiently in an independent Scotland offering a real opportunity to deliver better outcomes for consumers.

For example, many people in Scotland, including some of the most vulnerable are getting into severe financial trouble using short-term credit, such as pay day loans, which have extremely high interest rates and default charges. Payday lenders will be subject to tougher regulation in an independent Scotland. This Government plans to introduce a cap on short-term interest rates – as there is in many countries in Europe, Japan, Canada and some US states – and to regulate advertising and place restrictions on the 'rolling over' of loans, which sees those unable to pay off the initial debt saddled with a bigger loan that is more difficult to clear.

Fiscal framework

The third aspect of a robust macroeconomic framework is a sustainable fiscal framework. Scotland has sound public finances, and a relatively strong position compared to the UK as a whole.

We will introduce a robust fiscal framework, which will promote stability and provide flexibility to respond to economic shocks. This will be a key foundation of sustainable economic growth in Scotland and will be based on a system which ensures that public sector debt and borrowing are managed effectively and responsibly.

We will follow the advice of the Fiscal Commission, which has highlighted a number of features that are desirable for the fiscal framework of an independent Scotland[114]. These include:

- fiscal rules to promote fiscal discipline and help ensure that the public finances remain on a transparent and sustainable path

- the establishment of an independent Scottish Fiscal Commission to provide advice on and scrutiny of Scotland's public finances

- the creation of a sovereign wealth fund – a Scottish Energy Fund – to enhance both the Scottish Government's ability to manage short-term fluctuations in oil revenues and to promote long-term fiscal sustainability[115]

The Scottish Government recognises that a sustainable fiscal framework is important no matter the currency arrangement. However, it is particularly important in a well-functioning monetary union to avoid significant divergences in fiscal balances.

That is why such a monetary framework will require a fiscal sustainability agreement between Scotland and the rest of the UK, which will apply to both governments and cover overall net borrowing and debt. Given Scotland's healthier financial position we anticipate that Scotland will be in a strong position to deliver this.

Within this overarching framework the Scottish Government will have full autonomy to use our fiscal and wider economic independence to boost growth, address any weaknesses in the Scottish economy and take advantage of opportunities for growth. This will need to be managed responsibly.

Monetary unions allow for significant differences in fiscal and economic policies. For example, Luxembourg and Belgium have been in currency union for decades but have substantial variations in tax policies, VAT is 15 per cent in Luxembourg and 21 per cent in Belgium[116]. Corporation tax in Ireland remains at 12.5 per cent but is higher elsewhere in the Eurozone[117].

Our tax system

The choices open to us
Within the current constitutional arrangements the Scottish Parliament, even after the implementation of the Scotland Act 2012, will be responsible for only 15 per cent of Scotland's tax revenues[118]. The Scottish Parliament will have a limited ability to vary income tax rates, be responsible for Land and Buildings Transaction Tax (a new, more progressive tax replacing Stamp Duty Land Tax), and the Scottish Landfill Tax, and retain continuing responsibility for Council Tax and Business Rates.

In contrast, with independence the Scottish Parliament will have full control over taxation. It will be for the elected government and parliament of the day to decide on individual taxes in an independent Scotland.

Until such times as tax rates are changed by a future Scottish government, they will remain the same as the prevailing rate in the UK. Future Scottish governments may wish to vary tax rates and/or thresholds for a variety of reasons. However, there will be no necessity to do so to pay for current spending.

In addition to increased flexibility in relation to tax policy, independence will allow the tax system as a whole to be re-designed based on a clear set of principles and to better link to complementary areas of policy such as welfare. Independence will provide an opportunity to design a Scottish tax system based on specific Scottish circumstances and preferences[119].

The UK tax system is complex and inefficient. It is estimated that there are over 10,000 pages of tax legislation making it one of the longest tax codes in the world, and the Office of Tax Simplification (OTS) found in 2010 that there were 1,042 separate exemptions in the UK tax system. The Fiscal Commission and other commentators, such as the Institute for Fiscal Studies, has recognised the potential for Scotland to design a simpler and more efficient tax system following independence.

Unnecessary complexity in the tax system, through multiple exemptions, deductions and allowances, creates opportunities for tax avoidance. By designing a simpler tax system based on a clear set of principles with fewer reliefs and exemptions, Scotland could reduce the scope for individuals and corporations to exploit opportunities to avoid paying their fair share of taxes and so generate additional public revenues without increasing tax rates.

A more complex tax system is also costly to administer, as well as placing extra compliance costs on taxpayers. The most recent data shows that administration costs, measured as a proportion of net revenues collected, are higher in the UK than many countries. Over the last three years of data, UK administration costs were higher on average than many countries of a comparable scale to Scotland, including Denmark, Sweden and Finland[120].

Our priorities for action

Detailed policies on tax and spending will be set out in party manifestos for the 2016 election and thereafter in the first budget in an independent Scotland. There is no requirement to increase taxes to pay for the services we currently enjoy in Scotland. The approach to tax of the current Government will focus on fairness and economic growth. To reflect this, if we are elected to be the first government of an independent Scotland, our early priorities will be those set out below.

We plan to build a taxation system which stimulates the economy, builds social cohesion and sustains Scotland's public services. These priorities will mark the first steps in reforming the tax system that we will inherit upon independence. They will also pave the way for a more significant review of the tax system in the early years of independence – in order that we can realise the full benefits of a modern and efficient tax system.

This Scottish Government's priorities will be to:

Increase personal allowance and tax credits by inflation. Personal allowances, the thresholds between income tax bands and caps on National Insurance Contributions, as well as tax credits, have all been used by successive Westminster governments to adjust the burden of taxation and the tax-take. However, these approaches to taxation can be complex and not transparent to the individual taxpayers. This Government intends following independence to introduce a clear and simple tax system in an independent Scotland. We plan in the short-term to increase transparency and certainty in the current system by uprating the basic rate allowances and tax credits by inflation each year, preserving their value in real terms. Our progressive policy will help the lowest paid workers in our economy.

Reduce Air Passenger Duty (APD) by 50 per cent. A recent study by York Aviation estimated that APD will cost Scotland more than £200 million a year in lost tourism spend alone by 2016. In addition to the direct losses to the Scottish economy, a report earlier this year by PWC showed that reducing APD

would increase other tax receipts, such as VAT[121]. A reduction in APD will allow Scotland's airports to be more competitive in attracting new direct air routes and will improve our international connectivity. More direct routes will also enable Scottish travellers to avoid connections via airports such as Heathrow. As an early priority for action the Government plans to reduce APD by 50 per cent, with a view to eventual abolition of the tax when public finances allow. This tax cut will encourage business travel and reduce costs for families of holiday flights from a Scottish airport.

Set a competitive corporation tax. We can send a clear signal that Scotland is one of the most competitive and attractive economies in Europe, with tax rates designed to boost economic activity and support the fast-growing industries that already have a comparative advantage here in Scotland. Corporation tax rates remain an important tool for securing competitive advantage and for offsetting competitive advantages enjoyed by other parts of the UK, notably London.

This Government plans to set out a timescale for reducing corporation tax by up to three percentage points below the prevailing UK rate. Modelling suggests that such a cut could increase the level of output by 1.4 per cent, boost overall employment in Scotland by 1.1 per cent (equivalent to 27,000 jobs) and raise overall investment in the Scottish economy by 1.9 per cent after 20 years[122].

Ending the Westminster Government's proposals for tax allowances for some married couples. This scheme will effectively discriminate against many families where both partners work, unmarried couples, widows, widowers, single parents and women who have left abusive relationships. Under the proposed system, around two-thirds of all married couples will not benefit and analysis of the proposals suggest that couples with children are much less likely to receive the full allowance and that many low and middle income married couples are likely to have much of the tax break clawed back through the benefits system[123]. The Institute for Fiscal Studies has noted that because of the way the scheme will operate some people will be worse off after a pay rise and that even if a government wanted to reward marriage through the tax system ther are simpler ways of doing so[124]. With access to tax and benefit powers the Scottish Government will make a different choice from that made by the current Westminster Government. Our priority is to help families with children by expanding childcare provision.

Examine the case for increase in National Insurance employment allowance for small business. Across most OECD countries both employees and employers make social security contributions. This Government plans to examine the potential to increase the employment allowance for small businesses to encourage employment.

Design a more efficient tax system. The Government plans a simple and transparent tax system after independence designed to minimise the opportunities for tax avoidance – such as the Shares for Rights Scheme – that have been exposed in the UK system[125], which mean too many individual and corporate taxpayers do not pay their fair share. Over the course of the first independent parliament, the Scottish Government and Revenue Scotland will work together to simplify the tax system to reduce compliance costs, streamline reliefs and help to reduce tax avoidance, with a target revenue gain of £250 million a year by the end of the first term.

In addition, we intend the administration of the tax system in Scotland to be simpler and lower cost. In particular, this

Government will task Revenue Scotland to reduce compliance costs for small and medium sized businesses in Scotland to counter what can often be the regressive impact of such costs on small business that generate valuable employment.

As recommended by the Fiscal Commission, the Scottish Government proposes a transitional period during which the current functions of HMRC are continued in Scotland and the rest of the UK on a shared services basis[126]. Taxpayers will therefore see no immediate change to their current arrangements for paying tax on independence. However, the initial improvements to the system will be in place within the period of the first independent parliament.

We plan to develop a new tax system for Scotland to better meet key policy objectives, based on the design principles of a modern and efficient system set out by the Fiscal Commission:

- **simplicity** – tax rules and obligations are well known, easily understood and liability is clear

- **neutrality** – the negative or unintended effects of taxation should be minimised and decisions on taxes should be made on merit

- **stability** – of both tax revenue stream and tax rules and procedures, allowing predictability and certainty in the decision making and planning of individuals, businesses and government

- **flexibility** – to respond to change, particularly in a dynamic and constantly evolving global economy

A tax system based on such clear principles will minimise administration and compliance costs, maximise tax-take and boost investment and growth. We have already demonstrated our commitment to these principles in bringing forward and enacting legislation for the new Land and Buildings Transaction Tax.

The burden of taxation and the administrative compliance costs form only one – but important – factor in the overall cost and ease of undertaking business in an economy. There is therefore the opportunity to develop taxation policy in conjunction with wider economic policy to create a comprehensive and coherent framework to continue to build upon the competitive business environment in Scotland.

In our preparations for independence we will be guided by the Commission's recommendations. These are:

- the tax system should be built around Scottish circumstances and preferences to help increase productivity and economic growth while meeting the needs of the people of Scotland

- the tax and welfare systems are key levers for tackling inequality – both are strongly interlinked and should be considered as fundamentally part of the same system. Welfare and tax policy should therefore be developed in tandem to ensure policy integration and alignment

- appropriate tax rates maximise receipts by creating the optimal level of economic activity and revenue raising potential. The Scottish Government should assess the optimal balance of tax rates and bases for key taxes, such as business and employee taxes, and levels of government spending

- an open and consultative approach with industry, independent experts, employer groups, the trade unions, and the general public, should be adopted when designing and reviewing the effectiveness of tax administrative policy to ensure the system is comprehensive, inclusive and maximises compliance

Following these recommendations will allow an independent Scotland to design a modern and effective tax system that reflects Scotland's size and circumstances and is better suited to our economic needs.

Transport

Why we need a new approach
Scotland's geographical position makes strong international and cross-border transport links vital for our economic success and our social wellbeing. Connecting Scotland with the world will never be a top priority for a Westminster Government, with its

focus on the transport needs of London and the South East. It is only with independence that we can make choices based upon what is right for Scotland and our economy and what is right for communities and the quality of life of our people.

The future of high-speed rail is just one example. Current confirmed plans exclude Scotland and Northern England, with the next phases of high-speed rail only due to connect London with Birmingham in 2026 and then Leeds and Manchester by 2033. While this investment will provide capacity and bring some journey time savings between the Central Belt and London, the economic benefits to Scotland, as well as the North East and far North West of England are marginal compared to those which will accrue to other areas of the UK. Indeed, the Westminster Government's own analysis shows that Aberdeen and Dundee's economies may suffer from such a partial approach[127].

A similar failure is clear in relation to Air Passenger Duty. Westminster's refusal to devolve Air Passenger Duty to Scotland has hampered our ability to attract new direct flights to Scotland that would improve our international connectivity and could reduce the costs to people and families in Scotland of both holidays and business travel.

The Westminster Government continues to have responsibility for key aspects of transport policy and, just as importantly, takes the final decision on the size of Scotland's budget. This has included a massive reduction in the capital spending available for crucial infrastructure projects in our country. Scotland's ability to support much needed infrastructure development has been hampered by decisions taken elsewhere, both in terms of overall spending limits and in the ways in which we are allowed to spend our money as a result of Treasury rules. This has meant slower progress on vital infrastructure and transport investment than would have been the case as an independent nation.

The opportunities available to Scotland
Independence will provide Scotland with full flexibility and more choices for our transport system. We will be able to assess our capital investment needs and our forward investment based on Scotland's budgetary position, rather than within boundaries set by Westminster. We will be able to consider options such as different ownership models for the rail network, and address issues with Scotland's international connections to the global marketplace, developing our air and sea access to the most important markets.

Since 1999, successive Scottish governments have improved transport within current devolved responsibilities, illustrating the value of decision-making on Scottish priorities for transport within Scotland, and connecting investment in transport with wider policy objectives.

For example, this Government is committed to connecting communities and developing the local and national economies of Scotland through projects such as the Borders Rail link and the Air Discount Scheme.

Following the transfer of some responsibilities for our railways, two new passenger lines and six new stations have been opened and across the network we have seen a 30 per cent increase in passenger use[128]. Road Equivalent Tariff has been introduced for more island ferry routes and we have been able to take forward major road projects to improve and complete our motorway network.

These actions demonstrate what can be achieved with a limited range of responsibilities and show that Scotland is well placed to respond more effectively to our nation's strategic transport needs with the full powers of independence.

The Scotland we can create

Independence will provide future Scottish governments with the ability to make decisions that suit Scotland's particular transport needs, creating projects and policies that are based on strong evidence of economic benefit and social cohesion.

These new powers can be used to continue the improvements to our transport networks both within Scotland and linking to Scotland. They will support economic and social opportunity by strengthening the connections between urban and rural, island and mainland, national and international, and the people of Scotland and their public services.

Independence will enable us to develop a fully integrated transport system with decision-making on the key issues being taken in Scotland and for Scotland. This means we can move forward with a clear ambition to deliver:

- integration between different modes of travel and different functions

- integration between all the powers of government to support transport and wider objectives

- full integration with the global community of nations

The choices open to us

Future Scottish governments will be able to align transport policy with other policy choices to create a more comprehensive transport strategy covering both national and international connections.

For example, independence creates the opportunity to integrate the transport network fully with the other infrastructure networks that are crucial to growing the economy. We will be able to align transport policy with energy policy to achieve Scotland's ambitious decarbonisation targets. That means the electrification of rail and the development of electric vehicles can work in tandem with the expansion of renewable energy generation and the roll-out of smart grid technologies to drive down transport emissions, enabling Scotland to meet the commitment to achieve the almost complete decarbonisation of road transport by 2050.

There will be an opportunity to decide the best way to structure and support our railways, including the best ownership model for rail and track for the benefit of the people of Scotland.

The Scottish Government is currently procuring a ten-year Scotrail franchise with a five-year review and a separate Sleeper franchise. Both procurement exercises are being expertly run under existing devolved powers by Transport Scotland and have attracted healthy interest. We are confident that they will bring better services to passengers. However, the current franchise model is unnecessarily constrained by the limits imposed by UK legislation. In the future, an independent Scotland will be free to pursue legislation that enabled alternative approaches, including public-supported and not-for-profit models. Enhanced borrowing powers will also provide more options for the delivery of rail infrastructure or rolling stock supporting better value for money.

In addition, independence will give Scottish governments a role when franchises are awarded for cross-border services – currently the Scottish Government has very limited input to these decisions which are made by Westminster alone. This will ensure Scotland's interests are fully represented.

We can use the borrowing potential of an independent country to invest in the condition, reach and connectivity of our roads – achieving the long-term objective of dualling the road network between all our cities by 2030.

And, we can ensure that Scotland's Maritime institutions – such as the coastguard – are structured efficiently and meet the needs of users of Scotland's unique seas and complex coastline.

Our priorities for action
High-speed rail is a key priority. Despite a much stronger business case from a network that includes Scotland and previous calls, not just from the Scottish Government but councils in the North of England and civic and business Scotland too, it is only now that the Westminster Government has agreed to plan for high speed to go beyond Manchester and Leeds. Meanwhile we continue to plan for a high-speed compatible link between Edinburgh and Glasgow that will act as a 'launch pad' for high-speed rail services to the South as well as releasing capacity on existing lines in the Central Belt.

Through substantial investment in the Highland Mainline and the line between Aberdeen and Inverness, along with enhanced inter-city-services delivered through the next franchise, we will ensure that high-speed rail brings benefits to all of Scotland. High-speed rail will also deliver substantially improved connectivity between Scotland and the North of England. Consistent with the Borderlands initiative, an independent Scotland could work together with northern English councils to argue the case more strongly for High-speed to go further North faster. High-speed rail will also attract air travellers from Glasgow and Edinburgh to London, freeing air slots to maintain air access to Aberdeen and Inverness, which with rail improvements will maintain and enhance the connectivity of these economically vibrant cities.

A reduction in Air Passenger Duty (APD) will allow Scotland's airports to be more competitive in attracting new direct air routes and will improve our international connectivity. More direct routes will also enable Scottish travellers to avoid connections via airports such as Heathrow, reducing average household costs for summer holiday flights from Scottish airports. For these reasons, it is essential that the Scottish Government has the power to make decisions on APD in the interests of Scotland.

Ferries are an essential part of Scotland's transport network. The quality of our ferry services impacts on us all, affecting both island and mainland communities. The Scottish Government is fully committed to delivering first class sustainable ferry services to our communities, stimulating social and economic growth across Scotland. The planned improvements to Scotland's ferry services, as set out in our recently published Ferries Plan[129] will enable our rural and remote communities to thrive, and continue to make a significant contribution to Scotland's economy. With the fully integrated transport system that independence will deliver, we can ensure the best alignment between ferries and other modes of transport.

One key cost to business and consumers is the cost of fuel. Currently around 58 per cent of the cost of petrol and diesel is made up of taxes: as a percentage of pump price, the UK had the highest tax component of diesel prices and the second-highest of unleaded petrol prices of the 28 EU member states in August 2013[130]. With independence, this Scottish Government will examine the benefits of a introducing a Fuel Duty Regulator mechanism to stabilise prices for business and consumers and how this could be made to work alongside our Scottish Energy Fund.

The Scottish Government is currently responsible for our rail and trunk road networks, major public transport projects and for the national concessionary travel schemes.

In addition, current devolved responsibilities include:

- travel information service

- sustainable transport, road safety and accessibility

- local roads policy

- bus, freight and taxi policy

- ferries, ports, harbours and canals

- the Blue Badge Scheme (for disabled drivers)

After independence, these services and responsibilities will continue as now.

Other transport functions are currently reserved to the Westminster Government, and delivered by 13 UK- or GB-wide specialist transport organisations. For a period after independence, the Scottish Government proposes that these organisations continue to provide their services in Scotland under arrangements with the Scottish Government. These arrangements, some of which will be transitional, will form part of agreements reached with Westminster.

The people of Scotland have contributed to the funding and development of these institutions over many years, and continued use of these institutions, for varying periods of time, following independence – with appropriate financial contributions to their administration, along with an equally appropriate say in their governance – is the sensible approach to ensuring continuity of service immediately following independence.

These include the Motoring Services agencies: the Driver and Vehicle Licensing Agency, Driving Standards Agency, Vehicle and Operator Standards Agency, and the Vehicle Certification Agency. These will initially continue to provide vehicle and driver licensing and testing services to the people of Scotland. However, independence will allow a Scottish parliament to determine the best way to deliver these services in the future. The Scottish Government plans to create a new, streamlined

Scottish Motor Services Agency, which will bring together the functions of DVLA, DSA, VOSA, and VCA. By the end of the first term of an independent parliament, we will have completed the design and development work, with a view to the Agency going live early in the second Parliament.

The Maritime and Coastguard Agency and the Northern Lighthouse Board will continue to provide their services for the safety of mariners.

NATS is the air navigation service provider for the UK. It is a public-private partnership, and is 49 per cent owned by the Westminster Government, 42 per cent by the Airline Group (a consortium of seven airlines), five per cent by its employees and four per cent by Heathrow Airport Holdings[131]. NATS owns and operates a large facility at Prestwick. On independence, NATS will continue its services for Scotland. The Scottish Government will negotiate an appropriate share for Scotland of the Westminster Government's stake in NATS.

The present regulatory authorities for transport are the Office of Rail Regulation (ORR) and the Civil Aviation Authority (CAA). On independence, these bodies will continue to operate in Scotland while the options for regulation are examined further, although the combined economic regulator will cover aspects of ORR's functions[132]. The same approach will be adopted in relation to the rail passenger group, Passenger Focus. This will ensure there is no disruption to the operations and safety of either rail or air services. Similarly the accident investigation branches, covering rail, aviation and maritime, will continue their operations on independence.

This approach means that drivers, hauliers, airlines and their passengers, rail operators and their passengers, and mariners experience a smooth transition as powers begin to be executed by an independent Scotland or jointly with the rest of the UK, through existing institutions.

As a full member state of the EU, we will be increasingly active in international co-operation in transport policy and regulation, as well as in international transport bodies such as the International Civil Aviation Organisation and the International Maritime Organisation.

CHAPTER

4

HEALTH,
WELLBEING
AND SOCIAL
PROTECTION

- Independence will provide the opportunity to create a fairer, more equal society, built around the needs of citizens

- Spending on social protection which includes pensions and welfare is more affordable in Scotland. We spend a smaller proportion of our national wealth and tax revenues on the provision of social protection than the UK as a whole

- There will be continuity of payments for pension and benefit recipients

- This Government proposes a series of improvements to the State Pension and to the benefits system that will:

  - extend the triple-lock on state pensions so they increase by either inflation, earnings or 2.5 per cent, whichever is higher

  - introduce the new single-tier pension and set it at £160 in 2016

  - abolish the "bedroom tax", assisting 82,500 households in Scotland – including 63,500 households with a disabled adult and 15,500 households with children – to save an average of £50 per month

  - halt the further rollout of Universal Credit (UC) and Personal Independence Payment (PIP) in Scotland

  - change elements of UK pension and welfare rules to better protect the position of women in work and on retirement

- The NHS will remain in public hands, free at the point of need, delivering high-quality, safe care for the people of Scotland

Why we need a new approach
Scotland is a prosperous country, but too many people and communities are trapped in poverty and prevented from realising their full potential.

In 2011/12, 710,000 people (14 per cent of the population) were living in relative poverty in Scotland[133]. This total is made up of 420,000 people of working age, 150,000 children, and 140,000 pensioners[134]. This Government believes it is unacceptable, in a nation with the wealth and resources of Scotland, that one in seven of us still lives in poverty.

The current Westminster approach is making the situation worse. The Institute of Fiscal Studies has estimated that the child poverty rate in Scotland will increase to 22.7 per cent by 2020[135]. This means that an additional 50,000 children will be living in poverty as a direct result of Westminster welfare changes. This will reverse improvements made over the last decade and return the child poverty rate to the level it was 10 years ago.

The UK is already one of the developed world's most unequal societies. The UK is now one of ten least equal countries in the OECD – it ranks 28th out of 34 on a measure of overall inequality. OECD analysis shows that, since 1975, income inequality among working age people has increased faster than any other country in the organisation.

Academic analysis comparing the earnings of the worst off and best off has found that the UK was the fourth most unequal nation amongst the world's richest countries[136].

These inequalities are also seen strongly in health outcomes. Life expectancy in Scotland is lower than in the rest of the UK. In 2010, life expectancy at age 65 was 1.2 years higher in the UK than in Scotland for both men and women[137]. Men born in the most deprived areas of Scotland can expect to live 10.9 years less than those in the more affluent areas – and their healthy life expectancy is only 50[138]. These statistics are a human tragedy, and they also hold us back both economically and as a society. Life expectancy in Scotland is now lower than in all other Western European countries[139]. Compared to similar countries, Scotland has a greater incidence of cancer and of premature deaths from all causes including heart disease, chronic liver disease and cirrhosis[140].

With devolution, the Scottish Parliament has been able to deliver some improvement. For some indicators, such as deaths from coronary heart disease, health inequalities have decreased, but for others, such as healthy life expectancy, mental health, smoking and alcohol and drug misuse, they remain significantly worse in the most deprived parts of Scotland[141].

Responsibility for delivering health services to our population is not enough. To tackle these major challenges, we also need responsibility for our society's wellbeing and welfare. The solution to ill-health is not in the hands of the NHS alone – it depends on breaking the cycle of poverty, educational under-attainment, worklessness, poor mental wellbeing, and, through these, preventable ill-health[142].

Westminster's changes to our welfare system make the need for a new approach more urgent. Their plans could potentially remove over £4.5 billion from Scottish households[143]. The one per cent cap on welfare benefit increases will impose real terms cuts on one million low income working age households amounting to £210 million in the five years to 2014/15[144]. Real terms cuts to child benefit will remove £1,100 from families with two children[145]. The "bedroom tax" will result in Westminster saving £50 million per year in Scotland but it will cost the Scottish economy around £50 million per year. There will also be one-off losses of around £29 million in Scotland[146]. Seventy-nine per cent of households affected by the "bedroom tax" in Scotland contain a disabled adult and the policy will impact on 15,500 families with children[147]. In Scotland's rural areas, the "bedroom tax", when combined with other factors such as expensive travel costs and the low-wage job market, will have a particularly severe impact.

The Scottish Government has been able to mitigate the impact of some of these changes, with agreement reached with Scotland's councils to protect 560,000 people from cuts in Council Tax Benefit and up to £20 million has been committed in both 2013/14 and 2014/15 to support those most severely affected by the "bedroom tax"[148]. Frontline advice and support services have a critical role in helping people to understand and respond to the Westminster's changes, which is why an additional £7.9 million for advice and support services is being provided over three years from 2012/13[149].

A new £33 million Scottish Welfare Fund is also in place[150]. This is a national scheme delivered through local authorities. It helps people facing a financial crisis and in need of short-term help and those who require essential household items to set up, or stay in, their own homes.

However, mitigation is not enough. Independence will allow the Scottish Parliament to: make decisions on welfare; reverse the most damaging of the Westminster changes; and ensure that we have a social security system for the future that meets our needs and objectives.

As well as implementing damaging welfare cuts, Westminster has also contributed, over many years, to what many people acknowledge to be a crisis in pensions provision. The State Pension lost value following the decision in 1979 to abolish the link between the state pension and earnings. It has never recovered its previous level relative to earnings[151]. In 2011, the UK State Pension ranked second worst of 27 EU member states relative to gross average pre-retirement earnings[152]. The UK pension system is also one of the most complex in the world[153].

The 1983 Conservative Government removed tax exemptions from payments by employers to their pension schemes in apparent surplus. Many employers then took "pension holidays" on contributions to their pension schemes[154]. In 1997, the then Labour Government removed Advanced Corporation Tax Relief from dividends for pension schemes, reducing pension scheme income from dividend payments by 20 per cent, causing estimated losses of up to £100 billion for pension funds across the UK[155].

Collectively, these and other decisions have helped create a UK pensions landscape where:

- 13.2 million people of working age in the UK are under-saving for retirement[156]

- private pension scheme membership has fallen: in 2011, membership of occupational pension schemes in the UK reached its lowest level since 1953[157]

- the number of people contributing to a personal pension has fallen over the last decade[158]

- access to quality pension schemes has reduced: in 1993, all the FTSE 100 leading companies in the UK had a defined benefits final salary scheme open to new members; in October 2012, there was only one[159]

The Scottish Parliament has a record of using the powers available to it to benefit older people in Scotland. With responsibility for pensions, it can also ensure that Scottish pensioners receive a state pension that reflects Scottish needs and circumstances.

Pensions

The opportunities available to Scotland
The goal of an effective pensions system is to provide the financial underpinning to support people to enjoy a full and active retirement. However, the Westminster Government has mismanaged the pensions system over many years, to the extent that an estimated 13.2 million people in the UK are now under-saving for retirement[160], while 140,000 Scottish pensioners are living in relative poverty[161].

Independence offers a unique opportunity to do better, establishing pensions on a responsible and sustainable basis for the future.

The Scotland we can create
An independent Scotland will have the powers to deliver an affordable, fair and efficient pensions system, one that rewards hard work and incentivises saving, while also tackling pensioner poverty[162]. An independent Scotland will have the

ability to protect and improve state pensions and ensure that private pensions are secure and saving for retirement is actively encouraged. An independent Scotland will be able to set the State Pension Age at a level appropriate to Scottish circumstances.

Scotland has strong foundations on which to build such a pensions system. The amount spent in Scotland on social protection, which includes pensions and other welfare spending, is lower as a share of GDP than in the UK. In 2011/12, a lower proportion of Scottish tax revenues was spent on social protection than in the UK as a whole[163]. Scotland can afford a high-quality pensions service.

The choices open to us
Scotland has the people and infrastructure needed to manage and to pay pensions. The Pension Centres, located in Motherwell and Dundee and currently part of the Department for Work and Pensions, currently administer State Pension and Pension Credit claims for everyone living in Scotland. This Government proposes they will continue to do so on independence.

The Scottish Public Pensions Agency and local authority teams already manage Scottish public sector pensions. This Government proposes that an independent Scotland will take on responsibility for the pensions of staff within the civil service, armed forces and others who work in Scotland's public service, as well as existing pensioners and deferred members. For current UK-wide public service pension schemes, the Scottish Government proposes taking our fair share of pension liabilities based on responsibilities for meeting the pension entitlements of pensioners who live in Scotland. In short, Scotland can deliver high-quality state and public sector pensions, and future Scottish governments will be able to ensure that we have efficient systems in place to deliver pensions to those who rely on them.

Scotland also has the track record – via successive Scottish governments – of delivering real benefits to older people, as exemplified by free personal and nursing care and concessionary travel. The current Scottish Government has retained these in the face of current spending pressures, and plans to continue them with independence. These initiatives, taken forward using the powers of devolution, give a clear signal of our priorities and our commitment to our older citizens. With independence, future Scottish governments will have the choice to extend this approach to securing dignity in old age into all aspects of the services and benefits we provide.

The longer-term demographic challenge of an ageing population affects every western country, including Scotland and the UK as a whole. The particular challenge Scotland faces is projected lower growth in our working age population. The Government Economic Strategy sets out a target:

> to match average European (EU-15) population growth over the period from 2007 to 2017, supported by increased healthy life expectancy in Scotland over this period

The longer-term target must be to grow our working age population in line with the projected increase in those dependent on it – pensioners and young people under 16. What is clear is that this challenge is best addressed in an independent Scotland. An independent Scotland can address population growth by creating new opportunities for young people to build their careers and families within Scotland, and through action to attract the right people with the right skills to Scotland – either Scots who have moved away or new migrants.

Our Priorities for Action

The State Pension

The general principle of this Scottish Government, in planning for pensions in an independent Scotland, is to keep the best of the current State Pensions system, while making improvements where it is sensible to do so. On independence, our approach means:

■ current pensioners will receive their pensions as now, on time and in full. Accrued rights will be honoured and protected

- planned reforms will be rolled out from 2016, including the introduction of the single-tier pension

Our priorities, if we form the government of an independent Scotland, will be to:

- establish an independent commission to advise on the state pension age for Scotland, taking into account Scottish circumstances

- ensure that around one million pensioners in Scotland benefit each year from the uprating of the State Pension by the triple-lock, initially for the first term of an independent parliament. This would protect the value of the State Pension over time against increases in prices or earnings, providing a minimum annual increase of 2.5 per cent. The triple-lock would apply to the Basic State Pension, the single-tier pension, and Guarantee Credit[164]

- set the single-tier pension at the rate of £160 per week in 2016 – £1.10 a week higher than the rate currently expected for the UK

- retain Savings Credit (the full Savings Credit payment is currently £18 per week for a single person)[165], benefiting around 9,000 low income pensioners

State Pension Age

The State Pension Age (SPA) for women across the UK is in the process of increasing from 60 to 65 between 2010 and 2018. An increase to 66 for both men and women is to be fully implemented by October 2020. A further phased increase in the State Pension Age to 67 is planned between 2026 and 2028.

The Scottish Government accepts that State Pension Age should rise to 66 in line with the existing timetable. The rapid move to 67 is a concern, however, as it is a significantly faster timetable than that announced by the previous Westminster government. Lower average life expectancy in Scotland compared to the UK means that Scots currently enjoy fewer years in receipt of the State Pensions.

In an independent Scotland, this Scottish Government will reserve judgement on the increase to 67 between 2026 and 2028. We propose that an Independent Commission on the State Pension Age is established and tasked with considering the appropriate rate of increase of the State Pension Age for Scotland over the long term. This Government plans that the Commission will report to parliament within the first two years of independence with a view to its recommendations being implemented promptly thereafter.

Current pension arrangements
On independence, everyone currently in receipt of the Basic State Pension, Graduated Retirement Benefit, State Earnings Related Pension Scheme or the State Second Pension will receive these pensions as now, on time and in full. This Scottish Government plans to uprate the Basic State Pension by the triple-lock from 2016. This provides protection for the value of pensions over time, meaning that pensions increase by average earnings, CPI inflation, or 2.5 per cent – whichever of these is highest.

This Government's commitment will be in place initially for the first term of an independent Scottish parliament. The Westminster Government has only made a commitment to the triple-lock until 2015.

This Government also proposes that the Guarantee Credit element of Pension Credit, which tops up pensioners' weekly income to a minimum level set by government, is uprated using the triple-lock from 2016. This provides an improved safeguard for low-income pensioners in Scotland compared to their counterparts in the rest of the UK where the only requirement is for Guarantee Credit to be uprated in line with earnings. This Government proposes that the Savings Credit element of Pension Credit is retained as additional support for those with low incomes and increased in line with earnings. This element provides a credit for those aged 65 or over who have made some financial provision for their retirement but are on a low income.

The new Single-Tier Pension
From 6 April 2016, new pensioners will receive a Scottish single-tier pension, similar to that proposed by the Westminster Government, but with important improvements. The main features of the pension are:

- the single-tier pension will be paid in full to everyone who reaches State Pension Age after the introduction date and has 35 qualifying years of National Insurance (NI) Contributions or NI credits

- there will be a qualifying requirement of 7 to 10 years of contributions

- all Additional State Pension rights accrued prior to April 2016 will be retained and paid to individuals on retirement

- as a result of the abolition of the state second pension, contracting out of NI contributions for those currently in defined benefit pension schemes will cease

In addition we propose to make a number of improvements to current Westminster Government plans:

- within the first year of independence, the single-tier pension will be set at a level of £160 per week (£8,320 per annum); in the unlikely event that the rest of the UK rate for the single-tier pension is set at a higher level, the Scottish single-tier pension will match the higher figure

- the rate of the single-tier pension will be increased on an annual basis in line with the triple-lock. The triple-lock provides protection for the value of pensions and is based on whichever is highest: average earnings, CPI inflation, or 2.5 per cent. This commitment will initially be in place for the period of the first Parliament of an independent Scotland. The Westminster Government, by contrast, has only committed to uprate the single-tier pension by earnings

- Provision will be maintained for those expecting to receive a State Pension based on their spouse's contributions for 15 years after the introduction of the single-tier pension, unlike in the rest of the UK

- Savings Credit will be retained for new pensioners who are on low incomes and increased in line with earnings. This will ensure that those pensioners approaching retirement who would have received Savings Credit are not disadvantaged by the move to the single-tier pension. The Westminster Government is to abolish Savings Credit for those reaching State Pension Age after April 2016

State Pension entitlement in an independent Scotland
The key points of the Scottish Government's proposals for State Pension entitlement are:

- for those people living in Scotland in receipt of the UK State Pension at the time of independence, the responsibility for the payment of that pension will transfer to the Scottish Government

- for those people of working age who are living and working in Scotland at the time of independence, the UK pension entitlement they have accrued prior to independence will form part of their Scottish State Pension entitlement. Any pension entitlement accrued in Scotland after independence would also form part of that Scottish State Pension. On reaching the State Pension Age, their Scottish State Pension would be paid by the Scottish Government

- for future pensioners who have accrued rights to the Scottish State Pension but who retire outside Scotland, the Scottish State Pension will be paid either via a Scottish equivalent of the International Pensions Centre (IPC) or by the pensions institution in the country of residence, depending on their circumstances. The Scottish IPC will be established following a transitional period of shared service provision

■ for people who build up entitlement to a range of State Pensions – in Scotland, in the rest of the UK, in Europe, or elsewhere – the current situation will continue. The only difference will be that, from independence, pension entitlement accrued from working in Scotland will be to the Scottish State Pension, rather than to the UK State Pension

Boosting the working age population
A key factor in the planning of future state pensions is the projected structure of the population. 'Dependency ratios' are used to help consider this, comparing the numbers of people of working age against the number of 'dependents' (people of pensionable age and/or children). Scotland's total dependency ratio[166], that is the number of children and pensioners for every 1,000 persons of working age, is projected to remain below that of the UK for the next 15 years[167]. This dependency ratio is a useful indicator of wider fiscal sustainability, as it includes all dependents. Beyond the late 2020s, current projections[168] suggest that, without action to increase the working age population, the total dependency ratio in Scotland and the rest of the UK will converge and from 2033 onwards will be marginally higher in Scotland than in the UK as a whole.

Taking a narrower view, the 'pensioner dependency ratio' compares the population of people of working age in Scotland with the population of state pension age. This ratio is projected to be higher than the UK as a whole over the next 20 years.

Whichever dependency ratio is used, the key issue in terms of broader Scottish population pressures, relative to the UK, is the lower projected growth in the working age population in Scotland (four per cent compared with 12 per cent), not higher growth in the pensioner population. In fact, pensioner numbers are projected to grow at a faster rate in the UK than in Scotland in the longer term. Between 2012 and 2037 the number of people of state pension age in Scotland is projected to increase by 27 per cent, lower than the projected increase in the UK of 31 per cent[169]. The difference between the two rates is projected to widen still further beyond this point, although projections this far ahead are subject to considerable uncertainty. The longer-term target must be to grow our working-age population in line with the projected increase in those dependent on it – pensioners and young people under 16.

Addressing the issue of the working-age population in the long term requires sustainable economic growth. Independence will allow Scotland to develop our own economic policy, which means we can improve productivity and participation in the Scottish economy through targeting growth sectors and coherent welfare and skills policies. Independence will also allow Scotland to address population growth by: creating new opportunities for young people to build their careers and families within Scotland; action to attract people back to Scotland; and steps to encourage skilled migrants to move to Scotland. These matters are currently reserved to Westminster, which has different priorities for the UK economy and migration. Without independence, Scotland will not have the mechanisms to address our projected demographic issues.

Occupational and personal pensions
Occupational and personal pension rights and accrued benefits will not be affected by Scotland becoming independent. An individual's occupational or personal pension will already set out the retirement benefits which will be granted under the particular scheme and under which conditions.

Currently only around half of Scottish employees contribute to a private pension (that is, to a personal or an occupational pension in the public or private sector)[170]. Helping people save for a better retirement will be one of the key focuses for this Government in an independent Scotland. This Government's proposals are to:

■ continue with the roll-out of automatic enrolment, introduced last year, to help address the historic decline in private pension saving

- continue to support tax-free savings, through products like savings and investment ISAs

- establish as soon as possible following independence a Scottish equivalent of the National Employment Savings Trust (NEST). The Scottish Employment Savings Trust (SEST) will provide a workplace pension scheme focused on people with low to moderate earnings, which will accept any employer wishing to use it

- launch a Financial Capability Strategy to build skills, knowledge and understanding about personal finance. This could include, for example, improving access to financial advice about purchasing an annuity on retirement. Recent comparisons of example annuity rates have suggested that, without good advice, the value of the annuity provided can be highly variable

Future Scottish governments could also explore ways to improve incentives to save, including through the tax system, and work with the pensions industry, employers and other stakeholders on the development of innovative pension and savings products.

Pensions regulation
The Scottish Government proposes that the structure and activities of the regulatory framework in an independent Scotland should be closely aligned with that in the rest of the UK.

We propose to establish a Scottish Pensions Regulator, which would work closely with the UK Pensions Regulator and the Financial Conduct Authority (FCA) to maintain a pan-UK approach to the regulation of private pensions. We will consider whether to include responsibilities for the regulation of pensions as part of a wider financial services regulatory body.

We consider that the current arrangements for the protection of individuals' pensions by the Pension Protection Fund (including its responsibility for the Financial Assistance Scheme and the Fraud Compensation Fund) should continue, with Scotland playing our full part. However, it will also be possible for the Scottish Government to establish a Scottish equivalent to the

Pension Protection Fund. Individuals will have the same level of protection as they do now.

This Scottish Government will ensure that arrangements for an effective compensation scheme are established, mirroring the level of protection provided in the UK Financial Services Compensation Scheme.

Cross-border pension schemes
The EU's Institutions for Occupational Retirement Provision (IORP) Directive places specific requirements on pension schemes operating across the borders of two or more EU member states.

Pension schemes that wish to accept contributions from an employer located in another EU member state must be fully funded at all times; schemes must have prior authorisation and approval from the relevant competent authority; and must comply with the social and labour laws of the host member state. These requirements would apply to those schemes that currently operate in Scotland and the rest of the UK if they continued to operate, on independence, on a cross-border basis.

The Scottish Government considers that discussions should start immediately to agree appropriate transitional arrangements to address the impact on funding arrangements for schemes that would become cross-border on independence. The case for such transitional arrangements is strong:

■ regulatory requirements for schemes operating within an integrated financial services market, as proposed for an independent Scotland, are quite different from the general case on which the IORP Directive was based

■ transitional arrangements would be strongly in the interests of the Scottish and Westminster Governments, the European Commission, employers and their employees. Indeed, the European Commission's aim in bringing forward the Directive was precisely to promote greater cross-border occupational pension provision

- member states already interpret the cross-border requirements flexibly in order to protect pension schemes. Member states have interpreted the requirement for cross-border schemes to be 'fully funded at all times' differently. For example, the period allowed for cross-border schemes in Ireland to regain full funding is decided by the Irish Pensions Board on a case-by-case basis

We will agree arrangements which will provide sufficient flexibility for employers, whilst ensuring that members and beneficiaries are protected in the way intended by the Directive.

Transitional arrangements of this kind have been implemented previously. On the introduction of the Directive, the Westminster Government's implementing legislation provided for a three year grace period for existing UK/Ireland cross-border schemes to reach full funding levels. We consider that transitional arrangements for independence should allow a scheme with an existing recovery plan to be allowed to implement that plan in accordance with the period originally set for it.

This is an issue for Westminster as much as it is for the Scottish Government. And there is no reason that this issue should not be capable of sensible and practical resolution.

Public Service Pensions
The Scottish Government is fully committed to providing a fair, affordable and sustainable pension and reward package to public sector employees.

In an independent Scotland, all public service pension rights and entitlements which have been accrued for fully or executively devolved or reserved schemes will be fully protected and accessible. There will be no difference to how much people pay for their pensions or the level of benefits they receive as a result of the move to independence.

Scotland already has the people and the infrastructure in place to deliver high-quality public service pensions. The Scottish Public Pensions Agency has unrivalled first-hand knowledge and experience of both designing and delivering occupational pensions policy for the public sector. We propose that the

Scottish Public Pensions Agency will, therefore, form the basis for delivering the additional responsibilities for public sector pensions that will be required in an independent Scotland.

In the past, public sector pensions policy has been imposed on Scotland with insufficient engagement and consultation. In an independent Scotland, this Government plans that the approach to negotiations about any future changes to public sector pensions will be positive and inclusive, rather than confrontational.

In the first term of an independent parliament, this Government will establish an independent commission to review and make recommendations on policy for an appropriate State Pension Age for Scotland. Within the first parliamentary term, this Government will also consider the Commission's findings when reviewing the impact State Pension Age policy has on the working and retirement patterns of Scotland's public servants. This Government is also committed to reviewing the pension terms of all "uniformed" services, including whether or not they should all have access to their occupational pension at a consistent age or whether this should better reflect the role they carry out and the physical impact of their service.

Scotland's social protection system

The opportunities available to Scotland
Scotland has the wealth it needs to be a fairer nation. The experience of other comparable countries across the world shows that this is more than achievable. While the UK is joint 26th on the UN Human Development Index, small countries make up a majority of the top 20 positions in the Index[171]. There is no reason why Scotland cannot match such successful small countries. Each country is different, but there are key lessons we can learn, such as the importance of social capital, trust, and a sense of national purpose[172].

In taking on independent responsibility for our social protection system, we will be building on strong financial foundations, with spending on social protection currently more affordable in Scotland than in the UK as a whole:

- in 2011/12, the most recent year for which statistics are available, 38 per cent of Scottish tax revenues were spent on social protection[173], compared with 42 per cent for the UK as a whole[174]

- expenditure on social protection as a share of economic output (GDP) has also been lower in Scotland than in the UK in each of the past five years[175]

- on an internationally comparable basis, spending on social protection in Scotland, as a share of economic output, is estimated to be lower than in the majority of EU-15 members[176]

With independence, therefore, we can afford to choose a different path for Scotland, with an approach to social justice that is based on our view of what a healthy and flourishing society should be. This is an opportunity for us to create a new Scotland.

Social justice is about wellbeing and opportunity for all and, with independence, the Scottish Parliament and Government can improve the quality of life for most people in Scotland, as well as securing the wellbeing of the most vulnerable. We can do more to promote the cohesiveness of society, to enable equality of opportunity and respect and build the intrinsic dignity of individuals and communities.

This highlights a key difference in the approach between governments in Scotland and at Westminster. Scottish administrations have sought to tackle social inclusion and cohesion, and to address equality issues. By contrast, the Westminster Government has conceded that 200,000 more children across the UK will be pushed into relative poverty by 2016 as a result of a 1 per cent cap on increases to benefit payments[177]. This equates to around 15,000 children in Scotland[178].Scottish Government analysis[179] shows that many women in Scotland will be worse off due to Westminster's changes to the benefits system. Mothers in particular are more likely to lose out financially as they are often the main carers of children and because certain benefits are typically paid to women.

Social justice and equality are objectives that should be pursued for their own sake in a civilised country. They are also important aspects of improved economic performance[180], which in turn provides for a happier, safer, healthier and fairer society. As the Fiscal Commission reported:

> Scotland is also currently part of a UK economic model and society which is one of the most unequal in the OECD. Inequality within the UK has increased in recent decades. Such patterns of inequality will continue to have a negative impact on growth and prosperity over the long-term[181].

We see the evidence in other nations, such as Norway and Sweden. They have demonstrated that fairness and prosperity are part of a virtuous circle, reinforcing each other and delivering a range of benefits for society as a whole.

Making the right choices on social justice will deliver greater equality, will deliver benefits across our society, and will be an important part of building the more prosperous and successful nation we all want Scotland to be.

The Scotland we can create

The record of successive Scottish administrations shows "the commitment to social justice which lies at the heart of political and civic life in Scotland"[182]. However, an independent Scotland will have all the necessary means to deliver a coherent approach to social justice and to tackle inequality by, for example:

- building a welfare system, based on clear principles and values that: supports people who work; provides support for people who cannot work; and fosters a climate of social solidarity

- integrating tax and benefit policy, embodying key principles of fairness and dignity

- taking a distinctive approach to providing public services, built on the principle of improving the lives of people and communities

- building on our pioneering approach of preventing problems arising, rather than relying on crisis interventions. In an independent Scotland, this can be extended and integrated with currently reserved services, such as welfare and employment

There will be immediate gains from independence, such as the abolition of the "bedroom tax", alongside benefits that can develop over time. We propose early co-ordinated action to grow the economy and employment, and increase wages, for example through the promotion of a Scottish living wage and a commitment to increase the minimum wage in line with inflation. This will improve the lives of people in Scotland. Investment in childcare and social housing can also have longer-term, positive impacts for individuals and communities, reducing the need for expensive interventions through the justice and health systems later in life. This approach can create savings for the long-term that can be reinvested for the benefit of people in Scotland in the future, and provide sustained benefits to individuals and communities.

We can also choose to protect key elements of our commitments to social justice in a written constitution. This approach is adopted in many other European nations. These rights could include a Youth Guarantee to employment, education or training, and rights to welfare support and health care. This would provide explicit guidance to future governments, of whatever political persuasion, about the needs and aspirations the people of Scotland expect to see prioritised. Social rights embedded in a constitution will put questions of social justice at the forefront of the work of Scotland's Parliament, government and public institutions.

The choices open to us
The right welfare system, working with tax and economic policy, is a powerful mechanism to address poverty and inequality.

In 2016/17, benefit expenditure (including benefits for pensioners) in Scotland is expected to be almost £19 billion per year[183]. The Scottish Government and Scottish local authorities also provide other wider welfare services, for example through social work and social care services, at an additional cost of approximately £5 billion per year[184].

BENEFITS FOR OUT OF WORK PEOPLE

INCOME SUPPORT, IN WORK CREDIT & **RETURN** TO WORK CREDIT, **JOB GRANT & JOBSEEKER'S ALLOWANCE**

BENEFITS FOR OLDER PEOPLE

STATE PENSION, **PENSION CREDIT,** TV LICENCES & WINTER FUEL PAYMENTS

BENEFITS FOR FAMILIES WITH CHILDREN

CHILD BENEFIT, CHILD TAX CREDIT, MATERNITY ALLOWANCE & **STATUTORY** MATERNITY PAY

BENEFITS FOR PEOPLE WHO ARE ILL OR DISABLED

ATTENDANCE ALLOWANCE, **CARER'S** ALLOWANCE, EMPLOYMENT & SUPPORT **ALLOWANCE,** INDUSTRIAL INJURIES, SEVERE DISABLEMENT **ALLOWANCE & STATUTORY SICK PAY**

BENEFITS FOR PEOPLE ON LOW INCOMES

WORKING TAX CREDIT, **HOUSING BENEFIT,** COUNCIL TAX BENEFIT/ COUNCIL TAX REDUCTION, **DISCRETIONARY HOUSING PAYMENTS, SCOTTISH** WELFARE FUND, SOCIAL FUND (REGULATED)

With independence, we can decide how best to allocate these resources to deliver a welfare system that meets our needs.

UK welfare changes

With independence, it will be for the Scottish Parliament and future Scottish governments to determine the future direction of the welfare system in Scotland.

Under the current system, the Westminster Government is taking forward a series of changes to the welfare system, at the heart of which is the introduction of Universal Credit (UC), a new single payment for working-age adults who are looking for work or who are in work but on a low income. UC is due to be fully implemented by 2017, but is currently beset by problems and delays.

Other major changes include:

■ the change from Disability Living Allowance to Personal Independence Payment (PIP) for people aged 16 to 64. Some people currently receiving Disability Living Allowance will not be awarded PIP because it uses different criteria for the award

■ the "bedroom tax" which reduces housing benefit by 14 per cent if the tenant is deemed to be under-occupying by one bedroom, or 25 per cent if under-occupation is by two or more bedrooms

■ an overall benefit cap, limiting the total amount of benefit a household can receive at the national average income (approximately £26,000 per year)

The Westminster Government's equality impact assessments show that the majority of the changes have negative impacts on particular groups of people[185], while the Scottish Government's recent analysis concludes that women will also lose out because of how the UC system in particular is structured[186].

We do not accept Westminster's approach to welfare. We believe that it is possible to design an efficient and fair welfare system that meets the needs of those who depend on it, and treats them with dignity and respect while supporting those who can into work.

However, it is only with the powers of independence that we will be able to build such a system.

Principles for a welfare system in an independent Scotland
There are some key principles for a welfare system which the Scottish Government has identified to inform our approach. The Expert Working Group on Welfare[187] is looking at these and other principles as part of its call for evidence. Among the principles that would underpin this Government's approach to welfare in an independent Scotland are:

- Scotland's benefits and tax credits system and employment support services should protect our people from poverty and help them fulfil their potential, in work and in life

- over the course of our lives, we should contribute to the welfare system when we can. In return, we should be able to access that system when we need to

- the benefits system should be fair, transparent and sympathetic to the challenges faced by people receiving them, respecting personal dignity, equality and human rights

- the benefits, tax credits and employment support systems should work in harmony to ensure that people who lose their job do not face extreme financial uncertainty

- for those who cannot undertake paid work, benefits should not relegate them to a life of financial uncertainty and poverty. Benefits must support a standard of living that ensures dignity and enables participation in society

- the administration of benefits and tax credits should be swift, streamlined and responsive to individual circumstances

The Expert Working Group is exploring how the benefits system should enable people who can work to move into employment, and how it can support people who can't work to participate in society as fully as possible. The recommendations of the Expert Working Group will be available well in advance of the referendum in order to further inform the debate.

The tax system and welfare

Tax and welfare are two of the most powerful means that governments have to address poverty and income inequality. Recently published evidence[188] shows the overall regressive nature of Westminster's changes to taxation and benefits in recent years. Levels of income inequality have been made worse by decisions of Westminster[189]. It would be open to an independent Scotland to choose to alter this balance.

In its *Principles for a Modern and Efficient Tax System in an Independent Scotland*[190], the Fiscal Commission recognised that, along with welfare policy, taxation is the main means to consider the distribution of income and wealth across society. Taxation is also important in supporting efforts to reduce inequality and boost economic opportunities. The commission also recognised the opportunity for Scotland from an integrated policy framework for tax and welfare:

> The tax and welfare systems are key levers in tackling inequality – both are strongly interlinked and should be considered as fundamentally part of the same system. Welfare and tax policy should therefore be developed in tandem to ensure policy integration and alignment[191].

This Scottish Government has already demonstrated our commitment to enhancing the progressive nature of the taxation system in our approach to implementing the limited taxation powers devolved by the Scotland Act 2012[192].

We have also demonstrated a commitment to fairness and tackling inequality by ensuring public sector workers in government and its agencies are paid the Scottish living wage of £7.45 per hour, rising to £7.65 from April 2014 (minimum wage is £6.31 per hour for those aged 21 and over). We have encouraged other public, private and Third Sector bodies to follow suit. The living wage can help provide certainty for households who are already dealing with pressures on family budgets caused by rising food and fuel prices and, with independence, it will be open to future governments to extend the reach and scope of the living wage. This Government has also indicated that, following independence, the minimum wage should be increased by at least the rate of inflation (see Chapter 3).

Our priorities for action

The UK welfare system is now too complicated, and is in need of fundamental reform. We disagree with the approach being taken by Westminster to achieving these aims. The welfare system of an independent Scotland will reflect the principles we believe that are at the heart of Scotland's approach to social justice, including fairness, respect and dignity.

Immediate priorities for action
The Scottish Government considers that the immediate priorities following independence must be to reverse the most damaging and counterproductive of the UK welfare changes. Action in these areas will enable us to relieve the hardship being caused to some of the most vulnerable people in Scotland. It will also free up money in the Scottish budget that is currently directed towards mitigating the worst effects of Westminster's changes.

- **abolish the "bedroom tax" within the first year of the first independent Scottish parliament.** This will save 82,500 households in Scotland – including 63,500 households with a disabled adult and 15,500 households with children – an average of £50 per month[193]. The cost of abolishing the "bedroom tax" at around £50 million per annum is estimated to be less than the overall harm it does directly to the Scottish economy (£50 million per annum plus one-off losses of £29 million). As such, there is a clear case in monetary terms for its abolition even before the wider social costs are taken into account

- **halt the further rollout of Universal Credit and Personal Independence Payment in Scotland** allowing the first government of an independent Scotland to take forward reforms to the welfare system that meet Scotland's needs and reflect our priorities. This Government plans to ensure that those already in receipt of Universal Credit by May 2016 are no worse off than anyone else in the following ways. We will:

    - remove housing benefit from the single payment, restore it as a separate benefit and maintain direct payments to social landlords. This Government plans to also maintain housing benefit as a separate payment in any longer term reform. This will provide protection for some of our most vulnerable citizens

- restore the ability of claimants to receive individual support rather than single household payments. We will maintain such an approach in taking forward any longer term reforms. It is estimated that this will benefit 880,000 individuals, many of them women[194]

- equalise the earnings disregard between first and second earners and continue such an approach into any longer term reforms. It is estimated that this would benefit as many as 70,000 people by as much as £1,200 a year and will be of particular benefit to women who are most often the second earner in a household[195]

- **ensure that benefits and tax credits increase in line with inflation** to avoid the poorest families falling further into poverty

These priorities enjoyed widespread support amongst those who gave evidence to the Expert Working Group on Welfare, as well as reflecting the views of stakeholders more widely[196].

Alongside our priorities for immediate improvements we also plan to maintain access to passported benefits, such as free school meals. This will support 130,000 children in Scotland[197].

A further early priority for this Government will be to launch an urgent review of the conditionality and sanctions regime, to establish an approach that is proportionate and ethical, and that avoids excessive or blanket measures which penalise those looking for work. We will also conduct an urgent review of the system of assessments for disability benefits.

We will follow the recommendation of the Fiscal Commission and develop the tax and welfare systems in tandem to ensure policy integration and alignment[198].

Future welfare in an independent Scotland

With independence, there will be the opportunity for longer term welfare reform in Scotland, built on the principles set out above. The recommendations of the Expert Working Group – which is due to report in spring 2014 – will help to inform the approach of this Government to longer-term reforms.

Our overarching aim will be that benefits work hand-in-hand with programmes designed to help people find work. We want to help people move into sustained employment and, with independence, we will have the opportunity to develop our public services in a way that aligns welfare with other public services such as health, housing and social care. In this way, people can look forward to a more personalised package of support than at present. And when people's circumstances change through ill health, unemployment or retirement, they will know what levels of support they are entitled to and can plan for the longer term with certainty.

In considering our approach to welfare in the longer term, a priority will be to live within our financial resources, just as we have done throughout our period in office since 2007. However, we will not allow changes to the welfare system to be driven by short-term cuts to budgets, but by what is best in the long-term interests of the people of Scotland.

Social investment

In the longer term, this Scottish Government will pursue policies which conform with the idea that welfare is a "social investment" – an investment across a person's life that is designed at all stages to promote equality, fairness and social cohesion. This is an idea that has been discussed by the Expert Working Group on Welfare and is part of its call for evidence[199]. It defines welfare as all of the services and benefits that we receive from the state rather than just cash transfers.

A social investment approach starts from the premise that the delivery of welfare services should not be seen as simply a safety net for individuals who cannot support themselves. Instead they should be seen as an opportunity for positive investment in people throughout their lives. Social investments are designed to produce specific returns, such as learning and development in early years, employment and health gains in adult life, and for older people, increased independence and ability to be active in their communities. This investment is repaid through better outcomes for people, families and communities, and through increased contributions to society, whether that is through taxation or other means. This approach is designed to create a shared responsibility amongst citizens, helping to establish a social partnership between them and the state, where high-quality public services are provided in return for people participating in society through work where this is possible or making other positive contributions where this is not.

So, for example, ensuring that there is high-quality readily available childcare supports parents to find sustained employment, but it is also an investment in children to give them the best start in life. And, as a result of this early investment, when those children go on to achieve their full potential, they will repay that investment through their productivity and creativity as active members of a more cohesive society.

Another example of social investment will be the use of active labour market policies to get people into good quality sustainable work. This can ensure that our young people, for example, are supported to develop their skills and experience. DWP research into the early stages of the Work Programme suggests that, at the moment, many providers are prioritising more "job-ready" participants for support, ahead of those who are assessed as having more complex/substantial barriers to employment[200]. Our social investment approach would not encourage focus on short-term gains. With independence, we could develop more targeted labour market policies suited to Scottish circumstances, matching demand – in growth areas like engineering, renewables, oil and gas and life sciences – with young people seeking to develop their skills, expertise and experience.

The Nordic countries have shown that effective social protection systems, based on the social investment principle, can help to reduce unemployment, increase earnings and spending power as economies grow.

The social investment model recognises that people require lifelong investments, made at different times in their lives. When these investments are made through the delivery of high-quality services, enjoyed by all members of society regardless of income or background, the life chances of all members of society are improved. The social investment model fosters a culture in society that is more inclusive, more respectful and more equal. It also places the cash transfers that people traditionally think of as welfare – such as out of work benefits and tax credits – in a wider, more cost-effective and socially beneficial context when viewed over the longer-term. Investments in childcare, education, health and active labour market policies will reduce reliance on, and also the costs of the cash transfer parts of the welfare system.

A social investment approach will reap benefits for the whole of Scotland in the medium and long-term. Scotland already practises this model of investment in the areas over which the Scottish Government already has powers – in our approach to early years and the prioritisation of youth employment for example. We now want to extend that approach into the crucial areas of welfare, employment and childcare – all currently reserved to Westminster.

The social investment approach creates a framework of guiding principles that will underpin the development of welfare policies, but in order to deliver it, Scotland must have control of the full range of powers, and responsibility for all government revenues and expenditure. It offers an alternative approach to that being pursued by Westminster.

Halt the further rollout of Universal Credit and Personal Independence Payment
As well as the recommendations of the Expert Working Group, our precise proposals for longer term welfare reform will also depend on the state of the system inherited by Scotland on independence.

Universal Credit rollout has been affected by significant controversy delay. The National Audit Office[201] has concluded that it has not achieved value for money and the Department for Work and Pensions has no detailed view of how UC is meant to

work. The NAO also notes that rollout across the UK has been scaled back considerably and the DWP does not yet know to what extent its new IT systems will support national roll-out. Their report goes on to say that the Department has not yet been able to assess the value of the systems it spent over £300 million to develop.

The rollout of Personal Independence Payment (PIP) has also been difficult and created significant anxiety amongst recipients of Disability Living Allowance (DLA) and those people and organisations that support them.

Any change to disability benefits requires the medical re-assessment of recipients of disability benefits. We know that recipients of disability benefits, and the organisations that support them, have lost faith in the reassessment process. The work capability assessment which considers whether those in receipt of Incapacity Benefit should instead receive Employment and Support Allowance has already been reviewed four times and, in the eyes of many, has lost all credibility. The roll out of PIP using the same process will cause even greater hardship for the most vulnerable members of our society.

Westminster has been forced to delay the introduction of PIP twice. The latest delay means that current DLA cases will not begin to be migrated to the new PIP until 2015, well after the referendum.

It is, at this time, not possible to predict precisely how many people in Scotland will be in receipt of UC or PIP in an independent Scotland in early 2016. By the time of the referendum, however, the number of people receiving UC or PIP will be very small.

The current Scottish Government considers that the continued roll out of UC and PIP is not in the best interests of Scotland. Halting these changes will give an independent Scotland the opportunity to design and implement a welfare system suited to our needs. In the event of a vote for independence in the referendum, the Scottish Government will ask Westminster not to proceed any further with the roll-out in Scotland of UC and PIP, in order to give the Scottish Government elected in 2016 maximum flexibility to begin to reform the welfare system in line with its priorities. This Scottish Government will not proceed with UC and PIP if we form that government. For those not already in receipt of UC and PIP, the existing welfare arrangements will remain in place (changed by our immediate priorities such as abolishing the "bedroom tax"), until longer-term reforms are introduced in Scotland.

Tackling in-work poverty
The current welfare system has failed to tackle in-work poverty. It will be a priority of this Government to do so in taking forward welfare reform in an independent Scotland.

Despite periods of time when overall poverty has reduced, in-work poverty levels have remained stubbornly consistent from one year to the next, meaning that over time, in-work poverty has accounted for a greater proportion of the overall number of households in poverty in the UK. Two thirds of children who live in poverty in the UK have at least one parent in paid work[202].

Critical to this is that much of the work available to families is low-paid, low-skilled, insecure and underpinned by a minimum wage that has failed to keep up with the cost of living.

Our proposals on childcare, and the establishment of a Fair Work Commission to ensure the minimum wage, matches inflation are designed to address these issues.

Importantly, from a social investment perspective, investments in early years childcare, and ensuring that benefits and tax credits keep pace with inflation, will help to reduce the potentially damaging consequences that affect children who are raised in homes living below the poverty line. In other words, they can reduce costs in the longer-term. That is why the social investment principle will guide the action of the current Government as we reform welfare in the future.

Delivery of benefits in an independent Scotland
We accept the Expert Working Group on Welfare's recommendation in its first report that there should be a transitional period of shared administration for delivery of benefit payments[203]. As highlighted by the Group, this makes sense in the short term, not least because it ensures continuity of payments for millions of benefit recipients elsewhere in the UK. However, we propose that such a system of shared administration will last only until 2018 and be organised in such a way that will:

- allow the first government of an independent Scotland to introduce its priorities for change from 2016

- allow that government to begin the work towards creating a welfare system that better reflects Scotland's priorities

We will therefore work to ensure the transitional period is as short as possible, with a target for it to end in 2018.

As we look towards our own system of administration for welfare and pensions, we will benefit from the fact that much of the infrastructure for making such payments already exists in Scotland. As the Expert Working Group on Welfare reported:

Scotland delivers almost all parts of the current UK benefits system to people living in Scotland from locations within Scotland[204].

Delivery of benefits to people in Scotland is carried out mainly by the Department for Work and Pensions (DWP), with HM Revenue and Customs (HMRC) responsible for the administration of Child Benefit and Tax Credits. Currently all claims for Jobseekers Allowance, Employment and Support Allowance, Income Support and Incapacity Benefit made by people living in Scotland are processed in Scotland.

All claims for State Pensions and Pension Credit in Scotland are also processed in Scotland, as are all applications to the Child Maintenance Service from Scotland.

There are four HMRC Contact Centres in Scotland and 28 Enquiry Centres that deal with all revenue matters, including claims for Child Benefit, Working Tax Credit, and Child Tax Credit, which are administered by HMRC. In addition, as at April 2011, 1,800 local authority staff in Scotland provided combined Housing Benefit and Council Tax Benefit services[205]. This substantial infrastructure that already exists in Scotland will provide us with the required capacity to ensure the effective and efficient payment of benefits. Added to that will be our agreed transitional arrangements, which will form a solid, and sensible, platform from which to develop both medium and longer-term options. We will seek agreement with the Westminster Government in the transitional period to cover:

- the term of the agreement and arrangements for varying that term

- the services each government will provide to citizens

- the financial arrangements for providing those services

- data sharing and record keeping

- contracts, leases and all third party arrangements

We also envisage that our system of delivering benefits in the future – including health assessments – will be in the public sector. In designing the most appropriate future delivery arrangements, therefore, we will work in partnership with local government, the Third Sector and others. We will ensure that the people most directly affected by the system of welfare support, those in receipt of benefits, will play a central role in its design.

Housing and communities

The Scotland we can create

Building strong communities has been central to the Scottish Parliament's approach to social justice since devolution, but we remain a nation of unequal outcomes, with some places and groups suffering profound disadvantage and inequality[206]. Under the current settlement, we are limited by the powers available to us. As an independent country, we can do more to put our communities at the heart of policy-making in areas currently reserved to Westminster, creating new opportunities to make different and better choices.

Just as we believe that the people of Scotland are best placed to make decisions in the best interests of all in Scotland, so we believe that local people will also secure the best outcomes for their communities. Successful regeneration is dependent on a wide range of organisations, including the public, private and Third Sectors, working together alongside communities themselves. In Scotland, the importance of local decision making is already being recognised, not least in the proposed Community Empowerment Bill, and with new responsibilities we can see this approach extended across all aspects of government.

The choices open to us

Decisions made at Westminster undermine our efforts to create resilience in communities. For example, the "bedroom tax" risks forcing people away from the communities that support them.

The housing challenges facing Scotland are very different from those in England. Social housing remains an essential part of our housing system, catering for 23 per cent of households[207]. The harsher Scottish climate and the challenges of heating remote homes call for an ambitious approach to energy efficiency and carbon emissions reduction.

Successive Scottish Governments have taken a distinctively Scottish approach, which prioritises the sustainability of communities. However, there is more that can be achieved. Full flexibility over our budgets will enable future Scottish Governments to broaden action to make more affordable

housing available to meet housing need and tackle fuel poverty. Removing constraints placed on us by the Westminster Government will open up opportunities for action to further improve the quality of housing, for example in the social rented sector, and allow governments to introduce different ways of supporting first-time buyers.

Our priorities for action

The current devolution settlement places significant constraints on the Scottish Government's freedom to invest in housing supply. The Institute of Fiscal Studies observed that "under the present devolution settlement, the Scottish Government is bearing the cost of greater investment in social housing and lower rents, whilst some of the benefits of that spending accrue to Westminster in the form of lower housing benefit payments"[208]. This Government, therefore, will ensure greater integration between our policies on housing supply and housing benefit support.

Recently the Scottish Government has also pioneered innovative financing approaches for affordable housing. At least 1900 new affordable homes are currently being delivered in communities across Scotland using new mechanisms. These measures have had to conform to UK Treasury rules, which are often not designed for Scotland's needs or circumstances.

With independence, we will make use of our increased flexibility to deliver a more appropriate financial framework to support housing investment in new and innovative ways.

Similar restrictions are in place in other aspects of housing finance. For example, when the Westminster Government invests in loans and equity stakes to support market housing, the consequential resources for Scotland must also be used to provide loans or equity stakes. While the current Scottish Government has chosen to invest these resources in a range of housing initiatives, especially shared equity, other options, such as increased investment in social housing, have not been possible. With independence, this Government will ensure these limitations are removed so that the most effective investment choices can be made.

Independence will allow a joined-up system in which future Scottish governments can take strategic decisions about up-front investment in housing supply, to best support our communities and our house building sector, based on the full-life costs and benefits of that investment.

Fuel poverty is another very real problem for far too many of our people, putting at risk the very young and older people. Scotland is an energy-rich nation, but currently only has control over one of the contributing factors to fuel poverty – the energy efficiency of Scottish dwellings.

The current UK regulatory model has proved to be ineffective in providing meaningful incentives for improved energy efficiency of Scotland's homes. It has done little to increase households' ability to access low cost "dual fuel" tariffs. Around nine per cent of households in Scotland are without mains gas and 43 per cent[209] of these households live in fuel poverty[210]. Independence will enable a regulatory approach that is tailored to specific Scottish conditions that influence the costs of keeping homes warm, such as our climate, our mix of urban, rural and remote communities and our distinctive housing stock.

In addition, the Energy Expert Commission will advise on ways in which an independent Scotland can promote fairer, more affordable energy prices, and meet the need to address fuel poverty and deliver measures to improve energy efficiency. The Government has already announced our intention to save households money by funding from central resources the existing Energy Company Obligation and Warm Homes Discount (see Chapter 8), and give full weight to the Expert Commission's findings.

Health, social care and the NHS

The Scotland we can create

The provision of health and social care services is one of the major responsibilities of the Scottish Parliament and Government. Since 1999, successive Scottish governments have made steady improvements to Scotland's health and the quality of healthcare, while protecting the NHS as a free, truly public service, consistent with the values of the NHS and the priorities of people in Scotland.

Responsibility for the health service in Scotland has allowed us to show what can be achieved with the full powers of independence. Scotland has taken a very different approach to health and social care from that taken by Westminster governments over the years. We have maintained a commitment to the NHS as a public service and, in delivering free personal care, we have demonstrated that Scotland can provide support for older people in a way that looks after them, maintains their dignity, and respects the contribution they have made to society.

Without devolution, NHS Scotland – like its counterpart in England – would have been repeatedly re-organised by the Westminster Government of the day, regardless of the needs of the health service in Scotland. It would now be exposed to private competition and an unfair system of social care. We would be experiencing today the consequences of Westminster decisions on our health service in the same way as we are seeing the impact of Westminster's welfare choices on our most vulnerable fellow citizens.

CHILDREN BORN
IN THE POOREST PARTS
OF OUR COUNTRY CAN
EXPECT TO LIVE
11 YRS LESS*
THAN THOSE IN THE
WEALTHIER AREAS

AND CANCER
MORTALITY
76%**
HIGHER
FOR
THOSE
IN
DEPRIVED AREAS

*SOURCE: SCOTPHO **SOURCE: NHSSCOTLAND

Under devolution, NHS Scotland has been reshaped and modernised – but to reflect our requirements and the opportunities for a health service in a country the size of Scotland. Currently this Government and our partners in health boards and local authorities are taking radical steps to join up health and social care, ensuring that organisational barriers do not prevent people receiving the care they need in the setting they prefer, for example, at home.

With independence we can address directly inequalities in Scotland, which are the root cause of many of the country's remaining health issues. If in government after the 2016 election, we will adopt a government-wide approach to the health and wellbeing of our nation with confidence that the actions we take, and their success, will be down to our own efforts and our own decisions. The alternative is for Westminster to continue to control the overall level of Scotland's budget, and to make decisions that directly affect poverty and wellbeing through the tax and benefits systems.

In an independent Scotland, we will continue to provide high-quality, world-leading health and social care to the Scottish people in a way that reflects the founding principles of the NHS and our social care services. Independence will not affect the day-to-day management of the NHS in Scotland or how people access NHS services. However, it has the potential to transform the environment within which our NHS operates. Similarly, it will not mean ending current cross-border arrangements with health services in the rest of the UK, which have continued even though the NHS in Scotland already operates independently.

The choices open to us

With independence, we can build on the gains of devolution for our health and social care services to enhance the health and wellbeing of people across society.

Since the Scottish Parliament was established in 1999, we have had full operational responsibility for the National Health Service in Scotland, and for health and social care policy. Scotland has chosen a different way forward for our NHS compared to successive Westminster Governments. There is no competition, or internal market, in Scotland. GPs refer patients to a treatment centre within their own health board area, and they will be referred elsewhere if the required service is not provided locally. One of the strengths of the integrated model in Scotland is greater consistency of approach and clear responsibility for NHS Boards to deliver safe, effective and person-centred services, for which they are held to account through annual accountability reviews, held in public.

Successive Scottish governments have ruled out the disruptive and costly structural reforms and upheaval that have taken place in NHS England. Avoiding these multiple and costly reorganisations, and privatisation, has allowed us to focus on improving safety and quality of care.

The Scottish Parliament has used its responsibilities to introduce free personal care and protect the National Health Service. Major achievements of the health and care services in Scotland under devolution, which we can build on with independence, include:

- introduction of the smoking ban in public places

- our world-leading patient safety programme with major reductions in levels of hospital healthcare associated infections (a programme which has been endorsed by Don Berwick, adviser on healthcare issues to Barack Obama)

- significant reductions in premature mortality from cancer, heart disease and stroke

- reduced waiting times and delayed discharge from hospital

- the removal of prescription charges and introduction of free eye tests

- the highest level of dementia diagnosis in the UK

- a focus on the importance of the early years as a foundation for long term health and wellbeing through initiatives such as Family Nurse Partnership and the Early Years Collaborative

- protection of the frontline NHS budget

- a single vision for sustainable quality across health and social care services

- agreement to the integration of adult health and social care services

- unique workforce partnership arrangements

Our priorities for action

This Scottish Government plans to continue with current arrangements for the management of the NHS in Scotland, focussing on sustainable quality and for the integration of adult health and social care services. Services will be accessed in the same way as under the devolution settlement.

Despite efforts to address the challenge of health inequalities in Scotland over recent years, health inequalities persist and demonstrate that the "fundamental causes" of health inequalities – the socio-economic inequalities in society – are the most important.

Recent research shows the strong correlation between poor health and poverty[211]. It suggests that the reason for Britain's high health inequalities is the failure of successive Westminster governments to choose to reduce inequality.

Independence will also allow us to do more to tackle major causes of ill-health, which disproportionately affect poorer communities. In March 2006, Scotland was the first country in the UK to enact a ban on smoking in public places. This has resulted in a dramatic reduction in smoking related diseases[212]. We have also led the way in developing ambitious proposals to tackle harmful drinking by legislating for a minimum unit price for alcohol.

We have maintained our commitment to strong action to tackle smoking and alcohol misuse with all the powers available to us. In contrast, the Westminster Government has chosen to put on hold proposals for plain packaging for cigarettes, and abandon plans for minimum pricing for alcohol.

With independence, we will have greater scope and clearer powers to regulate alcohol and tobacco, including through taxation – reducing the opportunities for legal challenge which have held up several of our initiatives to date.

We are already taking a distinctive approach to food standards[213]. Independence will allow this to be linked to tax policy and advertising regulation – allowing a coherent and concerted approach to issues of obesity and poor diet, which disproportionately affect poorer communities.

A major advantage of independence for health and wellbeing in Scotland is therefore to have the ability to use the full range of levers to promote good health. It is matched by the opportunity to grow Scotland's economy for the benefit of all and address inequalities in Scottish society that have not been, and will not be, addressed under Westminster.

After independence, Scotland will maintain a very strong relationship with the other countries of the UK. Scotland will continue to work with other parts of the UK to provide services where this provides access to the highest quality of care and delivers the best outcomes. There are already effective cross-border working arrangements in place, which will provide a strong foundation for continued co-operation, just as there is with Ireland. Partnership arrangements are also in place with a number of European countries, including, for example, Sweden.

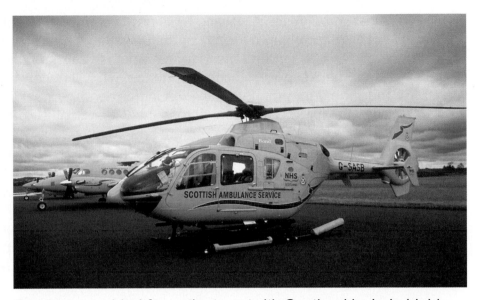

Services provided for patients outwith Scotland include highly specialised care for people with rare diseases or conditions, and certain types of transplantation. The rare cases of transplants being conducted outwith Scotland are for lung, small bowel and paediatric transplants. Because there is a relatively small number of these procedures, contracting these services from clinical specialists offers the best health outcomes for Scotland's patients. These arrangements will continue exactly as they are at present after independence.

On independence, Scotland will continue the current arrangements for organ donation across the UK, maintaining one donor register and sharing donated organs. This will ensure that all organs are placed with the best matched patient. The Irish Health Service Executive also co-operates on organ transplantation with NHS Blood and Transplant (NHSBT), who co-ordinate transplant services across the UK. This reflects international best practice in transplantation where groups of countries work together, for example Eurotransplant in mainland Europe (Austria, Belgium, Croatia, Germany, Luxembourg, Netherlands and Slovenia), and Scandiatransplant in the Scandinavian countries (Denmark, Finland, Iceland, Norway and Sweden).

Arrangements for reviewing NHS pay are already devolved but NHS Scotland currently operates within UK structures and modifies UK agreements to reflect Scottish circumstances where necessary. With independence, we will review the machinery for pay determination in partnership, including the potential for improvement across the wider Scottish public sector. The Scottish Government has developed a Scottish GP contract in partnership with the BMA, and with independence we will continue to work with them, and all relevant partners, to ensure that GP contracts are developed to meet the needs and circumstances of the people of Scotland. Similarly, for hospital based doctors and dentists, the Scottish Government will work with all relevant partners in Scotland, and seek to co-operate with Westminster where appropriate, to negotiate pay, terms and conditions.

Scotland is already responsible for the regulation of some health professions – those who came to be regulated after the establishment of the Scottish Parliament. After independence, we will become responsible for all regulation. We will seek to co-operate with Westminster, and the devolved administrations, to ensure that health professional regulation is maintained in the best interests of patient safety and the consistent treatment of healthcare professionals. We will also maintain the existing professional healthcare regulatory bodies, which are funded by fees from registrants, and will continue to operate in Scotland after independence.

Sport

The Scotland we can create

Scots are passionate about sport and our country has a long and proud sporting tradition. Tens of thousands of Scots already realise the benefits to be gained from participating in physical activity and we want more people to get active. We believe that by looking at physical activity and sport together will we harness that passion and tradition to make positive changes in our country – improving health, reducing anti-social behaviour and making our society fairer.

Scotland already competes as a nation in our own right in international competition with 11 governing bodies of sports directly affiliated to their International Federation[214]. Scotland competes very successfully and, since 1998, the **sport**scotland Institute of Sport has helped prepare many of Scotland's best athletes to perform on the world stage.

In 2014, Scotland has the privilege of hosting two of the world's greatest sporting events – the 20th Commonwealth Games in Glasgow and the Ryder Cup in Gleneagles. These events present a wonderful opportunity for us to realise our ambition of helping Scots to become more active. The Games coming to Scotland provide an exceptional opportunity to make our nation healthier, and to celebrate our modern and vibrant culture both at home and on the world stage.

Since 2007, over £73 million has been invested in sports facilities across Scotland. This substantial investment has enhanced the sporting infrastructure of our local, regional and national sporting assets in the following ways:

- development of world-class facilities such as the new indoor sports arena and Sir Chris Hoy Velodrome in Glasgow

- a network of new high-quality regional multi-sport facilities including the Aberdeen Sports Village and Ravenscraig and Toryglen centres of sport

- development of 23 football pitches and 12 new and upgraded swimming pools in communities throughout Scotland

- a new £25 million National Performance Centre for Sport to be developed at Heriot Watt University that will provide Scotland's first ever dedicated performance centre available to all of Scottish sport. It will offer our elite athletes the facilities and services to train and prepare for competing at international level

In addition, substantial progress has been made to encourage and support the growth of local participation in sports and physical activity. This has included:

- £80 million investment through Active Schools offering over five million opportunities for Scottish children in over 100 different sports this year

■ an additional £8.5 million of funding to ensure PE is delivered in all schools

■ the establishment of 114 Community Sports Hubs bringing local people together and providing a home for local clubs and sports organisations

■ a £10 million Active Places Fund that will create and improve places in local communities where people can become active

■ £24 million through the CashBack for Communities scheme to improve facilities and provide over 750,000 opportunities for local communities to participate in sport and physical activity

■ £5 million invested in clubgolf since 2003 which has provided 260,000 children in Scotland with an opportunity to try out golf

At an elite level, our athletes are supported by the **sport**scotland Institute of Sport with training, support and advice which helps them produce world class performances and, through Coaching Scotland, we have a framework which will lead us to a vibrant, highly skilled coaching system that is world renowned.

In an independent Scotland, we will build on this record to grow a world class sporting system at all levels, with real strength in schools, clubs and high performance sport.

Our priorities for action
An expert Working Group on Scottish Sport is considering how sport can develop and take advantage of the opportunities presented by independence.

Membership of the Working Group has been drawn from a broad cross section of interests in sport, physical education, health, education, business and the Third Sector to fully represent all the opportunities sport presents. The early work of the Group has focused on ensuring Scotland can be successful in future Olympic and Paralympic Games. From its work so far, the group has concluded that "….there is no reason that securing National Olympic and Paralympic Committee status should not be a relatively straightforward process for an independent Scotland, recognising that the final decision-making powers and the timescales involved are a matter for the relevant international bodies". The work of the group will conclude in spring 2014 with a final report on how independence can improve Scotland's sporting credentials.

Based on the Group's work and the recent experience of newly independent states, the Government does not envisage any significant barriers to Scotland achieving Olympic and Paralympic accreditation and being able to participate at Rio 2016. For example, Montenegro and the Balkan States received recognition within one year of independence, while Croatia and Slovenia were accredited before securing UN membership.

Independence will mean that more Scottish sportswomen and sportsmen will have the opportunity to compete at the highest level of international competition. It will also mean that the key decisions on athlete development will be taken in Scotland with the needs of the athlete at the centre. This will help many more of our sports-people reach their full potential.

A successful sporting nation, alongside the considerable
investment this Government is already making in Scottish
sport, has the power to inspire all ages and abilities in all areas
of Scotland to get even more active. This will have enormous
benefits for Scotland's health and wellbeing.

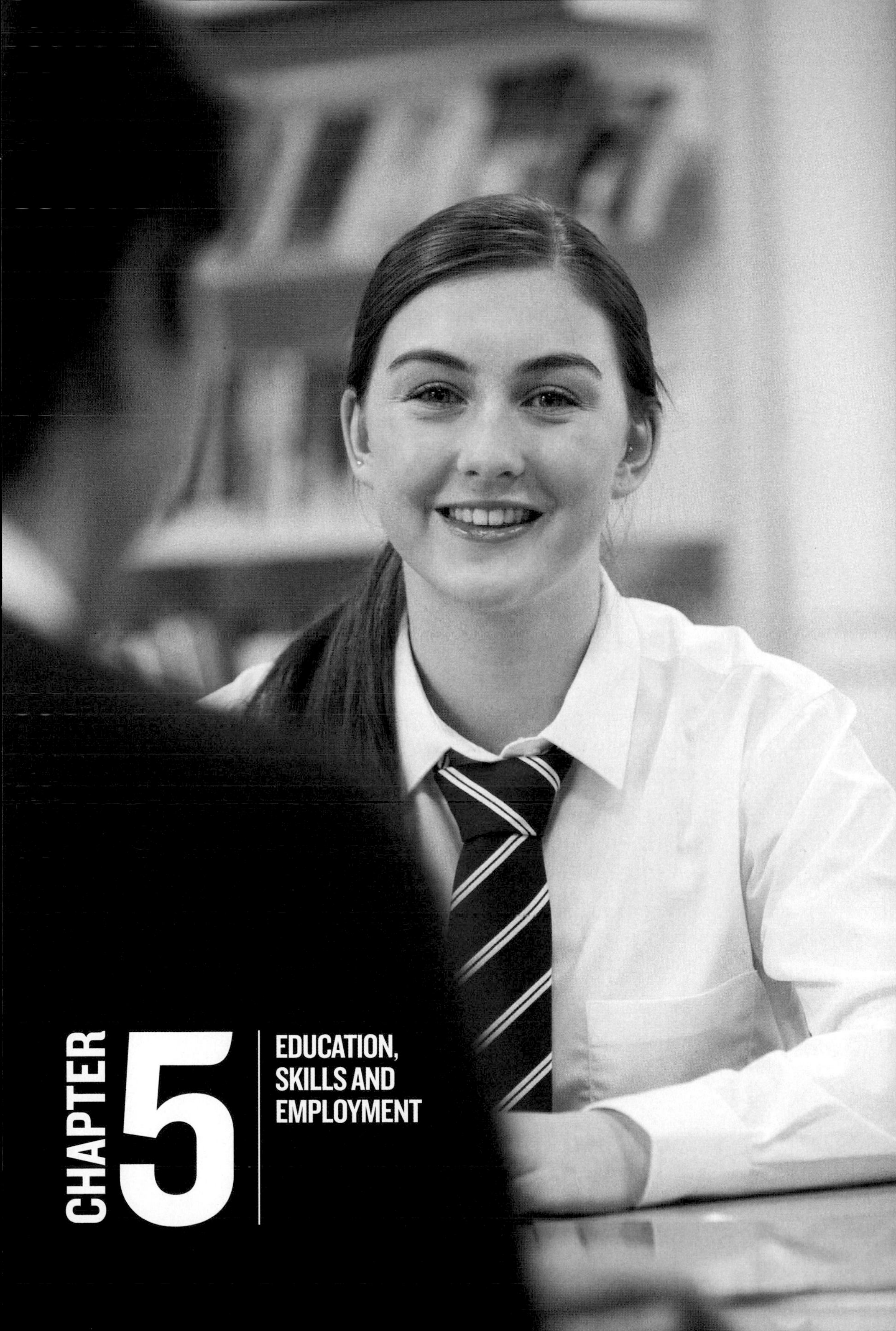

CHAPTER 5

EDUCATION, SKILLS AND EMPLOYMENT

- This Government plans a transformation in childcare provision for every child between age one and school age. By the end of the first independent Scottish Parliament all three and four years olds, and vulnerable two years olds, will be entitled to childcare equivalent to the time spent at primary school

- With independence benefits, taxes and employment services will work with the education system in raising attainment amongst our most disadvantaged young people

- Access to higher education will be based on ability, not wealth; this Government will protect free tuition fees for Scottish students and continue to provide appropriate support for living costs

- This Government will provide levels of public investment in university research that will enable our researchers and universities to remain internationally competitive

- Education and employment rights could be made part of the written constitution of an independent Scotland, including a youth guarantee to employment, education or training

Why we need a new approach

Education represents an investment, not just in our children, but in our culture, society and economy. Quality education helps young people be successful learners and grow into confident individuals, responsible citizens and effective contributors to society. A highly skilled population leads to higher wages, better jobs and economic growth, and benefits the health and wellbeing of each of us. Investment in the people of Scotland through excellent education and high skills greatly enhances our likelihood of employment.

However making this a reality for each and every one of our young people is the work of more than just our nurseries, schools, colleges and universities.

A child in poverty is a child that has yet one more barrier to learning. A child whose home life is chaotic, or who is hungry, cannot do their best. And a child who worries about the future of their family, is a child who is distracted from fulfilling their potential.

This simple reality has seen generations suffer the lack of equality of attainment in our schools. Pupils from the most disadvantaged 20 per cent of areas leave school with significantly lower qualifications than those in the most affluent 20 per cent. That gap is greater than most of the developed nations against which we measure ourselves[215].

The main tools for tackling poverty – and for tackling the attainment gap – lie in the tax and benefits system and employment services. All need to play their part in a coherent system that delivers for children, allows parents to work, and boosts family income.

Currently these critical powers are under the control of Westminster, which is not using those tools to tackle poverty or promote work in Scotland – but to cut welfare. Over the five years to 2015, these cuts will potentially remove over £4.5 billion from Scottish households, £1 billion of it affecting children directly[216]. Indeed a further 15,000 Scottish children will be pushed into poverty as a result of just one of those welfare cuts – capping the rise in working-age benefits[217].

Poverty plays a huge role in attainment. We need to join up our action to improve education with our action to eradicate poverty – and to do that, Scotland needs to take control of the tax and welfare system and the powers that influence the labour market.

Social work and Scotland's approach to children in trouble or at risk is unique. Next year will mark 50 years since the landmark Kilbrandon Report that established the Children's Hearing's system; Scotland has a proud tradition of a progressive approach. We have strong social work services and dedicated staff, but the reality is that their work – and the lives of the children they are trying to help – are inevitably tied to decisions on tax and welfare taken elsewhere.

Even where we have some powers already, too often decisions taken by Westminster impact on our ability to make the progress Scotland needs.

For example, decisions by Westminster on student visas have restricted access for international students, posing a direct threat to Scotland's universities and colleges. Not only do some prospective students find it difficult to obtain a visa to come and benefit from a Scottish education, but they are unable to use this education for the benefit of Scotland by remaining after graduation and playing an active part in the economy and culture of Scotland.

As a result of this, Universities Scotland have said in relation to Westminster's visa policy that "it is hard to see a bigger risk, or a more poisonous gun pointed at our collective success"[218].

Of perhaps even greater damage is the impact on post-graduate international students. Westminster's policy ignores the needs of Scotland and the universities resulting in the Scottish Council for Development and Industry (SCDI) describing it as its "biggest source of concern" in relation to Scotland's universities[219].

Independence will provide the ability for Scotland to develop our own immigration system ensuring that we benefit from the skills and enthusiasm of those highly educated people who wish to make Scotland their home.

As long as we rely on funding decisions at Westminster, we will bear the consequences of decisions that Scotland does not support. On universities, for example, the introduction of top-up fees in England substantially reduced government investment in higher education south of the border, and therefore reduced the size of Scotland's allocated budget – although universities and their funding are devolved to Scotland.

Progressive policies will tackle poverty, support jobs, and protect family incomes. Independence will give Scotland the powers to free children from poverty and enable them to meet their potential. Independence will also break the link to Westminster policies that Scotland neither wants nor needs.

The opportunities available to Scotland

Scotland has a proud tradition of commitment to excellent education for all our citizens. We have long enjoyed an international reputation as the first nation in the world to introduce a democratic system of schooling, open to both boys and girls, as early as the 17th century.

Our strengths and successes in education and employment have built on all that is best in that tradition and come from choices made in Scotland under devolution.

The pre-school sector, schools, and colleges and universities have all benefited from decisions of successive Scottish Governments, including massive expansion of nursery places, a radical overhaul of schools through the new Curriculum for Excellence (CfE), reform of the college sector, free university tuition and support for Scotland's world-class universities.

Excellence and high achievement can be found throughout our education system – in our nurseries, schools, colleges and universities. Scottish education is good but we believe it can once again be great.

Nursery and childcare

Our approach begins with giving every child the best start in life. That is why we have increased the provision of pre-school places for three and four year olds. In 2007 this stood at 412.5 hours a year. We have already expanded this to 475 hours and, with our new Children's Bill currently before Parliament, this will expand to 600 hours – around 15 hours per week – from August next year.

Nursery education benefits the child but it also makes it easier for parents – particularly mothers – to work. This helps family finances, both by saving them the equivalent of up to £707 in childcare costs every year[220] and by boosting income from work, benefiting the whole family. Our new Children's Bill does not just expand the number of hours, but also gives more flexibility so that parents have more choice over how they use the nursery hours to best fit in with family life and maximise the opportunity of finding work.

With independence – and the powers over the tax and benefits system – we can go even further. We want to extend the support we give to our youngest children and their parents, to expand childcare provision and deliver additional rights and opportunities for parents, so that Scotland matches the very best in Europe.

Primary and secondary schools

The substantial investment in Scotland's schools has seen secondary school attainment levels increase year-on-year. In 2011/12, school-leaver destinations – the numbers getting a job,

going on to college or university, or undertaking training such as a Modern Apprenticeship – were the best on record[221]. Building on this, 2012/13 saw the highest pass rates for Highers (77.4 per cent) and Advanced Highers (82.1 per cent)[222]. In 2012/13, 89 per cent of school leavers were in positive destinations – positive and sustained learning, training or work – the highest proportion ever[223].

This strong record of achievement means Scotland is well-placed for the next step now under way in our country's education history: Curriculum for Excellence (CfE).

CfE is the radical renewal of the way Scotland's schools teach. It focuses on achieving the highest possible levels of literacy and numeracy, developing skills for learning, skills for life and skills for work. But it goes further and delivers knowledge and understanding of society, the world and Scotland's place in it. And, because education is also about who we are as a nation, it helps pupils develop well-informed views and act responsibly.

All of this comes against a background of reduced class sizes in the early years of primary school and substantial investment programmes in new school buildings, halving the number of children being taught in substandard buildings[224].

Higher and further education

Higher education is one of Scotland's major strengths with more universities in the *Times Top 200 world universities* per head of population than any other nation[225]. This Government has restored free access to higher education to Scottish domiciled undergraduate students, maintained the number of places available at our universities and provided additional funded places in support of widening access.

Scottish universities are internationally renowned for the quality of their research. Around half of Scotland's research has been assessed as world-leading or internationally excellent[226] and Scotland ranks third in the world (after Switzerland and the Netherlands) and ahead of all the G8 countries in terms of citations per researcher[227]. The excellence of research in Scotland's universities contributes to Scotland's international reputation for research and innovation. Investment in Research and Development (R&D) activity is a key component of driving innovation and supporting improved long-term economic performance. Currently, Scotland has over 620 organisations in the science and innovation sector employing over 30,000 staff[228]. The continued expansion of this sector, after independence, will be vital to achieving sustainable economic growth.

Scottish universities are highly attractive to overseas students[229]. In 2011/12 Scottish institutions received an income of £337 million from non-EU student course fees alone[230] as well as benefiting from the wider contribution that international students make to Scotland's economy and society, and the longer term contribution that international alumni make to extending the reach of Scottish universities overseas.

This Government's reforms to colleges reflect our ambition for the sector to realise its potential. We have created institutions that are better able to work with other learning partners, and deliver the provision that learners need to get a job, and that employers need to become more competitive – including nearly one-fifth of higher education provision in Scotland. Our colleges will lead in making real some of the ideas from the Commission for Developing Scotland's Young Workforce, in creating new partnerships between school and colleges to deliver a still

broader range of vocational opportunities, further enriching the senior phase of CfE. This is supported by our funding floor for colleges of £522 million this and next year, rising to £526 million 2015/16, and by record levels of further education student support.

Employability
The education initiatives for those aged over 16 are complemented by the training opportunities provided through Skills Development Scotland, including in excess of 25,000 Modern Apprenticeship places in 2012/13. To further boost the opportunities for young people seeking to enter the labour market, Scotland is the only European country with a dedicated Youth Employment Minister, who is responsible for a range of initiatives and activities to maximize the chances of Scotland's young people.

Employment services and training for employability will be significantly improved by independence. At the moment, the financial benefits of successful employment initiatives by the Scottish Government – such as Modern Apprenticeships, Higher and Further Education funding and other training programmes – go to the Westminster Government in the form of reduced welfare payments and increased tax revenues. With independence we will retain these benefits in Scotland and can re-invest them in our people by funding more employment programmes.

The education sector has already successfully shown the potential for joining up policies across a range of areas, both in the early years, through the *Early Years Collaborative*, and for post 16 training and education opportunities[231]. Independence will provide the mechanisms to extend this coherent approach to government, connecting education to other services such as the benefits system and the immigration system.

Scottish policy is working for our young people, and provides a substantial foundation upon which an independent Scotland can build. *Opportunities for All* is our guarantee of employment, apprenticeship or training for all young people aged 16 to 19. This commitment is especially important for those who, for whatever reason, are furthest from the labour market. For many in this group our support is offered through Activity Agreements. This approach is grounded in the reality of an individual's personal circumstances and offers tailored help to move towards employment.

In an independent Scotland we will build on the success of collaborative working, with individuals of all ages, to support their journey towards and into sustainable employment. In doing so we will truly create opportunities for all. By integrating employment and skills policy and delivery, independence can ensure the most appropriate support for those looking for work and those preparing to enter or re-enter the labour market.

Improvements to the Scottish education system have been the result of extensive work within Scotland, with stakeholders, professionals and users of the services, including employers. Scottish education policy has looked around the world for inspiration and incorporated lessons from elsewhere into existing structures, building on the best in Scotland with innovations from elsewhere. This record shows how self-government in Scotland successfully delivers new and effective policies to improve society and achievement in Scotland, and provides a model and example for Scotland following independence.

The Scotland we can create
Scottish education is poised to take advantage of the powers of independence to make Scotland the best place to grow up.

Independence will provide the ability to join up policy, tackling head-on the issues that have blighted generations. We can create opportunities for the whole education system, in particular allowing us to:

■ invest in the early years of childhood by transforming the childcare system to match the best in Europe

■ integrate our approach to education with wider social policies, such as taxation and benefits, and to address the child poverty that can adversely affect the ability of young people to learn and to develop

■ focus on employment issues and a person centred approach to supporting those who want to work, with action on a living wage and the minimum wage so that more Scots get a fair reward for their hard work (see Chapter 3)

■ support our university sector, promote it internationally and encourage both academic staff and students from around the world to study and settle in Scotland and to contribute to our economy and society

Poverty causes problems for Scottish education which cannot be fixed by improvements in our schools alone, even though the CfE and the wide range of innovative work can try and limit the effects of deprivation on our children's education.

Currently Westminster controls tax, benefits and labour market policy, and Scotland controls education policy. One may undermine the other, as when changes to welfare increase child poverty.

The Scottish Government agrees with the conclusion of the OECD that "education systems don't have to choose between equity and opportunity and high performance"[232]. With independence, a welfare system aligned with our education system can address child poverty and educational under-achievement in Scotland. We believe that poverty is not, and must not be accepted as, inevitable in Scotland.

This approach is true to our proud educational heritage in Scotland. To build on this legacy, the written constitution of an independent Scotland could also enshrine the right to education for the benefit of individuals and society as a whole.

Early learning and childcare

The choices open to us

We know that investment in the early years can bring huge rewards in later life, both at an individual level, and for society as a whole. If we want to make the most of Scotland's people, our greatest asset, and support them to flourish in a vibrant society and economy, then it is essential to focus on their development at the earliest stages. Improving opportunities for young Scots, therefore, is one of the most important reasons for choosing independence.

Extensive provision of early learning and childcare for all families is a hallmark of some of the most advanced and successful countries today. There is a wide range of evidence indicating the potential benefits of high quality, funded early learning and childcare, with all social groups benefiting from high quality pre-school provision and children from the poorest families gaining most from universal provision[233].

Clearly, the principal aim of providing this support is to give children the best start in life and the greatest chance to succeed as they grow and develop into adults. However, it brings with it other important benefits for society as a whole.

Childcare has important benefits for children and it also provides a key support to participation in the labour market, particularly for women. For example, in Denmark, which has extensive childcare provision, 79 per cent of mothers with children under six work, whereas in the UK the comparable figure is 59 per cent[234]. Of mothers citing childcare as a barrier to working full-time, over 70 per cent say it is because of the costs[235]. Under the devolution settlement, the tax revenues and benefits savings arising from increased labour market participation by mothers would flow to the Westminster Government. With independence, these benefits would accrue over time to the Scottish Government, substantially bolstering the financial case for a transformational change in childcare provision.

Under the Westminster system, families in Scotland have waited too long for the provision of adequate and fair childcare provision. Independence will give us the powers to make that ambition a reality, and become a modern, successful, socially just country that cares for our most vulnerable and provides opportunities for each and every child who lives here. With independence we can develop a distinctive system, built round the needs of our children and their families.

The goal of this Scottish Government, therefore, is to deliver a transformation in the provision of high quality, early learning and childcare throughout Scotland. We are taking the first steps on that journey with the Children and Young People Bill, currently before the Parliament, introducing a significant enhancement of the early learning and childcare offered to all families. The legislation increases provision for each three and four year old and our most vulnerable two year olds to a minimum of 600 hours, up from the current 475 hours, and also introduces flexibility to meet parents' needs fully and properly.

These changes, bringing with them a required increase in capacity, and a growing skilled workforce, will be introduced without compromising on quality. Our view, however, is that only independence will allow us to unlock the resources to support a much more ambitious transformation in the care we give to our children in the first years of their lives.

Our priorities for action

Parents in the UK face some of the highest childcare costs in Europe[236]. Although these costs are currently lower in Scotland than in England – £94.35 per week compared with £106.52 for two, three and four year olds – parents in Scotland still spend around 27 per cent of household income on childcare, compared to the OECD average of 12 per cent[237].

Independence will give us the opportunity to invest more in the supply of services, rather than subsidising demand. This is the approach adopted in the most successful countries and will ensure resources are spent most effectively, and that childcare becomes more affordable.

In an independent Scotland, this Government would develop a universal system of high quality early learning and childcare for children from the age of one to when they enter school.

We will:

- in our first budget: provide 600 hours of childcare to around half of Scotland's two year olds. Those whose parents receive working tax credit or child tax credit will benefit

- by the end of the first Parliament: ensure that all three and four year olds and vulnerable two year olds will be entitled to 1,140 hours of childcare a year (the same amount of time as children spend in primary school)

- by the end of the second Parliament: ensure that all children from one to school age will be entitled to 1,140 hours of childcare per year

This transformational change to childcare in Scotland will allow parents, in particular women, to choose to work without worrying about the cost of looking after their children. With independence the benefits of their work – in economic growth and tax revenues – will stay in Scotland, contributing to meeting the cost of this childcare provision.

Such a transformational extension in the provision of early learning and childcare will need to be introduced on a phased basis, in a way that is manageable and sustainable. This approach will need to be managed carefully and agreed with delivery partners.

It will be essential to maintain the highest quality provision in order to support child wellbeing and development; alongside providing significant support to families and sustainable employment opportunities. The universal provision will give children an entitlement to a minimum number of hours and, as now, parents will be able to access or purchase additional hours to support working patterns.

In Scotland we already invest significant resources in early learning and childcare, equal to many of our European neighbours. However the outcomes we achieve from this investment do not match those of our most successful neighbours. We therefore plan to undertake a review of our cost structure, based on international examples, to ensure that our future investment in early learning and childcare achieves the best possible outcomes.

Capital investments will be required to build up the estate, both in terms of expansion of the current estate and new build, for stand-alone (nursery or daycare) provision to meet the needs of children before school, so that our children learn and are nurtured in high quality environments.

Investment will also be required in training and to substantially increase the workforce. The expansion of childcare will provide around 35,000 new jobs. Investment will also cover regulation, inspection and ensure the quality of expanded provision through the functions of Education Scotland, the Care Inspectorate and the Scottish Social Services Council.

Funded early learning and childcare will be part of a high quality universal system, with local authorities delivering and securing provision to ensure that education and quality are protected and improved. Building local authority provision, along with expansion within the third and private sectors, will contribute to the delivery of the highest quality provision.

Supporting Scotland's universities

The choices open to us
There will be major direct gains in an independent Scotland for Scotland's universities. Scotland has been an educational leader since the early part of the 15th century. It is home to some of the world's oldest and most prestigious universities as well as some of the finest specialist vocational and modern institutions.

Scotland's high quality education, research and innovation attracts scholars and researchers from across the globe, who in turn draw on their positive experiences to promote Scotland's academic opportunities and welcoming culture; a British Council survey suggests that 86 per cent of students said they would recommend the Scottish experience to others and 91 per cent said Scotland was a good place to be[238].

The Scottish Government already supports this international exchange by funding student mobility initiatives such as the Outward Mobility Fund, Erasmus and the Fulbright, Commonwealth and Saltire Scholarship schemes, which provide 200 awards of £2,000 to undergraduate and postgraduate students from China, India, and North America. Scotland is an active partner in Erasmus and the Bologna Process – which launched the European Higher Education

WE HAVE MORE UNIVERSITIES IN THE GLOBAL PREMIER LEAGUE PER HEAD OF POPULATION THAN ANY OTHER NATION

SCOTLAND WELCOMES MORE THAN

40,000

INTERNATIONAL STUDENTS EACH YEAR

SOURCE: HIGHER EDUCATION STATISTICS AGENCY

Area in 2010 and supports student mobility across Europe. The Scottish Government also recently launched a pilot project offering funding for up to 250 Scottish domiciled students undertaking their undergraduate degree in the EU. This means for the first time Scottish students studying in Europe will be entitled to the same support with living costs as students studying at home. Independence will provide the opportunity to do even more, and will give Scotland a clear platform to engage in international arenas and a stronger voice in Europe as a full member state.

The Scottish university sector is developing international relationships and promoting Scotland's commitment to educational excellence, for example through collaborative research projects and campuses based abroad. We can make the international promotion of the higher education sector in Scotland, as the educational and research destination of choice, a priority in an independent Scotland, through our own overseas diplomatic and trade network.

Our priorities for action
Free access to higher education
The university sector is one of the main drivers of the Scottish economy and ensuring a supply of trained graduates to contribute to our economy is one of its significant outputs.

In 2011/12, there were 167,365 full-time students in Scottish Higher Education Institutions[239] and Scottish students accepted by our universities rose to a record number this year with 27,990 students accepted to study in 2013/14, an increase in 2 per cent compared with the same stage last year[240].

On independence, Scottish domiciled students will continue to have free access to higher education. This guarantee will save Scottish students up to £9,000 a year compared with the cost of studying in England.

Free education for those able to benefit from it is a core part of Scotland's educational tradition and the values that underpin our educational system. One of the major achievements of devolved government in Scotland has been to restore this right to Scottish domiciled undergraduate students.

In contrast, the Westminster Government has pursued an increasingly market-driven approach to higher education, increasing tuition fees for undergraduate students to up to £9,000 a year. This divergence in funding policy between Scotland and England, and resulting disparity in the cost of securing a university education, creates a huge financial incentive for students from England to study in Scotland. In that context, and to ensure Scottish students remain able to study at Scottish higher education institutions, this Government had little option but to allow Scottish institutions to set their own tuition fees for students from the rest of the UK at a rate no higher than the maximum annual tuition fee rate charged to such students by universities elsewhere in the UK.

This policy has not prevented students from the rest of the UK accessing Scottish universities. In 2012/13, the first year of the new arrangements, 4,800 students from the rest of the UK were accepted through UCAS to study at Scottish universities, an increase of 180 acceptances (4 per cent) on the previous academic year[241].

Following independence, the Scottish Government proposes to maintain the *status quo* by continuing our current policy of charging fees to students from the rest of the UK to study at Scottish higher education institutions.

This policy, based on residence, recognises the need to maintain the current mix of students from different parts of the UK in Scottish universities in order to ensure that Scottish domiciled students have the opportunity to study in Scotland, and that Scotland secures the graduate skills it requires, while ensuring that the universities also benefit from the contribution of students from the rest of the UK and beyond.

The Government believes that continuing to charge students from other parts of the UK is the best way to achieve this balance, recognising that there is a long history of substantial numbers of students from elsewhere in the UK coming to Scottish universities to take advantage of our high quality education, our common language and the parallel system of educational qualifications that make Scotland an attractive place for them to study. These students would pay substantial fees if studying in their own countries.

We believe that in an independent Scotland it will be possible for an objective justification for this charging regime to be established. On that basis, we consider that retention of tuition fees for students, based on residence in the rest of the UK, is an appropriate and necessary measure to ensure Scottish domiciled students continue to have access to higher education opportunities. If the Westminster Government change their policy and return to a higher education system where access to university is based on the ability to learn, not the ability to pay, we would also review our charging policy.

Our policy is based on the unique and exceptional position of Scotland in relation to other parts of the UK, on the relative size of the rest of the UK, on the fee differential, on our shared land border and common language, on the qualification structure, on the quality of our university sector and on the high demand for places. We believe that these distinctive characteristics will enable us to justify objectively the continuation of our current policy in a way which is consistent with the principles of free movement across the EU as a whole and which is compatible with EU requirements.

With independence, we will continue to support access to higher education in Scotland for students from elsewhere in the EU in accordance with our support for student mobility across Europe.

Research
Higher education research in Scotland is internationally recognised and respected for its quality and its innovative and collaborative nature. The excellence of our universities and strength of the research base is reflected in Scotland's success in successfully competing for funding within the UK and internationally.

In 2011/12, Scottish universities attracted £905 million[242] in research funding from a wide range of sources, including government, business, charities and the EU.

This Government has shown our commitment to university research by increasing investment in research and knowledge exchange activities by 38 per cent since 2007 and supporting global excellence, through investment of £13.8 million in 2013/14 for world-leading research[243].

While funding is important, a strong research base also requires an environment in which research is respected and valued and where government, businesses and our universities work in partnership to grow our economy and improve our society.

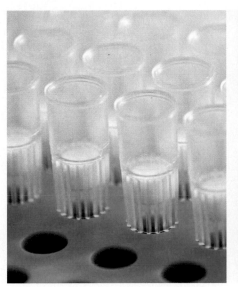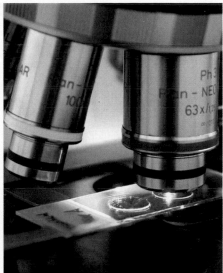

This Government has been instrumental in supporting the development of such an environment – advancing novel ideas such as the internationalisation of our research pools and, more recently, the establishment of a network of innovation centres which have the potential to transform the scale and nature of university-business relationships and collaborations.

The best research operates across boundaries, be they disciplinary, institutional or nation state. We recognise and will continue to support collaborations at a range of spatial scales – continuing to participate in existing collaborations that work well while seeking to extend our global reach as an independent country.

The UK operates as a 'common research area', ensuring no barriers to collaborative research and access to facilities for researchers throughout the UK. We recognise the benefits – for the academic community, business and research charities – of maintaining long-term stability in research funding and systems that support initiatives of scale and researchers working together across boundaries. It is clearly in the interests of both Scotland and the rest of the UK to maintain a common research area including shared research councils, access to facilities and peer review.

While the rest of the UK will remain an important research partner, we will also extend our global reach. Scotland can already point to notable successes in working across European boundaries with international research centres increasingly attracted to Scotland by the quality of our research base including the Fraunhofer Institute for Applied Photonics – the first Fraunhofer Institute to be located in the UK – and the European Lead Factory, a Europe-wide platform for drug discovery supported by the Innovative Medicines Initiative.

We want to build on these successes. Horizon 2020 – the EU's new programme for research and innovation – in particular offers a significant opportunity for Scotland's universities to build these partnerships and access the considerable research funding available[244]. We are also following with interest the wider progress of the European Research Area, with its focus on strengthening transnational co-operation and enabling researchers and scientific knowledge to circulate freely.

Our universities are already active players on the world stage extending their world-class teaching offering and forming partnerships and research collaborations across the globe. We are keen to further develop these collaborations. With independence, Scotland and our universities will be in a stronger position, as a sovereign nation state, to promote Scottish higher education overseas with a dedicated overseas diplomatic and trade network enhancing Scotland's visibility on the international stage.

Research funding

Public funding for university research in Scotland and across the UK is currently delivered by a dual support system comprising:

- a block grant given by the funding council of each country (funded from devolved budgets) and

- competitively awarded grants from the UK-wide Research Councils (funded through the tax base)

These two sources make up the majority of university research income. In 2011/12 Scottish universities received a third of their research income from the Scottish Funding Council and won a further quarter in competitive funding from the Research Councils and National Academies[245].

The UK and other funders benefit from the quality of the research undertaken in Scotland, our centres of excellence and infrastructure, and the lack of barriers to research collaboration. After independence this Government will seek to continue the current arrangements for a common research area and funding through established UK Research Councils, as we believe this would benefit both Scotland and the rest of the UK in supporting collaboration.

Scotland already contributes to the funding of the Research Councils through the UK tax system. With independence, we would intend to negotiate with the Westminster Government a fair funding formula for Scotland's contribution based on population share but taking reasonable account of the fact that the amount of research funding received by Scottish institutions from the Research Councils may reflect higher or lower levels of funding.

Providing a direct contribution from the Scottish Government budget in this way would create more transparency and clearer accountability around our investment, enabling Scottish interests to be better and more consistently reflected in the identification of Research Council priorities.

This Government plans to ensure that levels of public investment in university research are sufficient to enable our researchers and universities to remain internationally competitive with current levels of government investment in university research (though the Scottish Funding Council and the Research Councils) at least maintained as part of wider and longer term plans to harness increased funding from the private sector and other sources including Horizon 2020.

An independent Scotland will have the opportunity to internationally enhance the profile of our institutions, and will have new responsibilities for immigration policy, following independence, to attract leading research talent from around the world to study and settle in Scotland.

CHAPTER **6** | INTERNATIONAL RELATIONS AND DEFENCE

- For the first time, Scotland's national interests will be directly represented on the international stage

- Under our plans, Scotland's foreign, security and defence policies will be grounded in a clear framework of **participating** in rules-based international co-operation to secure shared interests, **protecting** Scotland's people and resources and **promoting** sustainable economic growth

- We will continue to be a member of the EU and will have a seat at the top table to represent Scotland's interests more effectively; we will not be at risk of leaving the EU against the wishes of the Scottish people

- An overseas network of 70 to 90 international offices is planned, built on Scotland's existing capacity and our share of the UK's international assets

- Scotland will recognise and act on its responsibilities, as one of the wealthiest nations on the planet, to international development

- Our defence plans focus on a strong conventional defence footprint in and around Scotland and the removal of nuclear weapons, delivering a £500 million defence and security dividend in 2016/17

- Scotland's security will be guaranteed as a non-nuclear member of NATO, with Scotland contributing excellent conventional capabilities to the alliance

Scotland's international relations

Why we need a new approach

Scotland has always been an outward facing nation, exporting goods, people and ideas around the world and welcoming ideas and people from other countries into our national culture. The current Scottish Government's ambition for an independent Scotland has deep internationalist roots and is based on a firm belief that, as an independent country, we will have a distinct and valuable contribution to make to world affairs. Scotland will be a committed and active participant in the global community of nations.

In the conduct of international affairs no country operates in isolation. The global and regional context creates the conditions and defines the range of choices and options that each state must address. Globalisation enables not only the greater movement of goods, people and ideas, but also the transmission of threats across borders, presenting an ever-shifting set of challenges and opportunities. In particular, demand for resources will increase over the next 20 years putting Scotland, a country with abundant fresh water, major oil and gas supplies and the potential to become a renewable energy powerhouse, at the forefront of global discussions.

An independent Scotland would be no different from any other independent country. Governments plan and act to ensure that their societies can capitalise on opportunities while adapting to face longer-term challenges, and reacting to more acute threats and emergencies, whether natural or man-made. An independent Scotland will perform these functions.

The impact of world events has increasingly important implications for both domestic and foreign policy. An international outlook has never been so necessary. As recent financial events have demonstrated, no economy is isolated from global economic conditions and every nation is increasingly dependent, to a greater or lesser degree, on the flow of international trade and investment and its relationships with others. The development of a coherent set of polices surrounding an independent Scotland's position on foreign affairs, defence and security will therefore be essential.

An independent Scotland would not need to replicate the structure of the Westminster Government or adopt its processes. Scotland's smaller size and specific national interests mean that we can adopt a more focused approach to the design and delivery of foreign and defence policies.

Under our plans, an independent Scotland's foreign, security and defence policies would be grounded in a clear framework:

- participation in rules-based international co-operation to secure shared interests. Scotland will be an active member of global institutions and will be party to fair and reciprocal agreements which respect human rights. Scotland will also be an active participant in international development, in line with the UN Millennium Development Goals and other relevant international agreements. Given Scotland's place in the western world and our history of friendship with a broad range of other nations, our interests will largely coincide with many others in the international community. It is therefore in Scotland's national interest to be a member of multilateral institutions alongside partners and friends with common interests and to co-operate with other nations in pursuit of common concerns and promotion of common values

- protection of Scotland, our people and our resources. This encompasses the role of defence and security capabilities in ensuring the safety of Scotland's territory, citizens, institutions, values and systems against factors which could undermine prosperity, wellbeing and freedom. It also includes the role of the Government's overseas services in protecting Scots abroad

- promotion of sustainable economic growth. Using Scotland's place in the world and our approach to global affairs to develop Scotland's economy is key to ensuring the continued and increased prosperity of the nation. Promotion of the many other positive aspects of Scottish life will also be a significant component of this work ranging from highlighting Scotland's world-class universities, to capitalising on our cultural and environmental profile, building on our already impressive international reputation

Today, Scotland has no formal voice on the international stage. Instead, we are represented by a Westminster Government that has based its actions, too often, on different international priorities. We see that most clearly in matters of war and peace and in our relationship with the EU.

As the government of an independent country, the primary purpose of our international engagement would be the promotion and protection of Scotland's national interests. Currently these can only be a part of the UK's considerations and Westminster's policies will rarely be fully aligned with what is right for Scotland.

Where Scotland's interests coincide with the interests of the rest of the UK, together we will form a more powerful voice for action. When Scotland has a distinct view, we will have a new ability to build alliances and make our case, ensuring that what is right for the people of Scotland is heard.

This independence advantage will be of greatest benefit in our relationship with the EU. This Government sees close engagement with the EU as an opportunity for Scotland, rather than the threat it seems to be for some in the UK. In 40 years of UK and Scottish membership of the EU, Scotland has not had direct representation at Europe's top table, and the price has been paid by important Scottish industries, including our fishing and agriculture sectors. On these issues, Westminster's approach has too often been to the detriment of Scottish jobs and prosperity.

Distrust and disengagement has dominated Westminster's attitude to the EU for too many years. A new threat is now emerging: the growing possibility that, if we remain part of the UK, a referendum on future British membership of the EU could see Scotland taken out of the EU against the wishes of the people of Scotland, with deeply damaging consequences for our citizens and our economy.

While the UK seeks an ability to project global power, an independent Scotland can choose a different approach. If in government, we will direct our international efforts, first and foremost, into deepening and consolidating relationships with friends and partners, new and old, across the world and, through this, expanding opportunities for people and businesses in Scotland.

Our bywords will be co-operation, development and trade. Our clear priorities will be commerce and partnership, not conflict. Scotland will be a champion for international justice and peace.

Independence will provide a step change for Scotland internationally. We will no longer be in the shadow of Westminster, with its increasingly insular and isolationist elements. Instead we can bring a new and distinct accent and approach to world affairs.

The opportunities available to Scotland
Scotland starts with an enviable reputation and a strong international identity. Our international brand is one of our most important assets as a country.

Even without independent status, Scotland's international brand value already ranks 15th out of 50 nations according to international comparisons published in 2012. Scotland has continually scored highly and is ranked similarly to – and often ahead of – other comparably-sized, high income, democracies such as Denmark, Finland, Ireland and New Zealand[246]. This provides an excellent starting point and the move to independence will, in itself, deliver a boost to Scotland's international recognition. We can use this important moment in our history as an opportunity to extend a welcome to the world and an invitation to engage more fully with our newly independent nation.

As an independent country, we can choose to build on these strengths, with an overseas network that works better for Scotland, and an overseas presence at the heart of our strategy to generate new economic opportunities for our nation.

Scotland will be entitled to a fair share of the UK's extensive overseas properties (or a share of their value) allowing us to use existing premises for some overseas posts. For example, the Foreign Office owns or leases almost 5,000 properties overseas[247]. The estimated value of this estate is around £1.9 billion. Based on a population share (our actual share will be a matter for negotiation) Scotland would be entitled to around £150 million allowing us to establish ourselves quickly and for little initial cost in our priority countries.

We will have the opportunity to design our overseas footprint based not on an imperial past or a desire for global power, but on what works for Scotland in the modern world. That means we can choose to put investment into practical advantages for the people of Scotland rather than the UK's priorities.

We are fortunate to have extensive domestic expertise to provide a firm base to build our international service. The current Department for International Development staff and offices in East Kilbride and Scottish Development International (SDI) staff in Glasgow will provide a strong institutional foundation.

Future Scottish governments will also have the opportunity to access the full range of expertise that has been developed in our universities. For example, Scotland is home to internationally recognised schools and institutes of international relations at the universities of Aberdeen, Edinburgh, Glasgow and St Andrews.

The Scotland we can create

On independence, Scotland will be clearly positioned as a country which observes international law and respects and promotes human rights, democratic values, equality and good governance. We have unique advantages and experience to offer in the field of climate change and energy. We have shown that we can innovate through our approach to international development and aid. We also have world leading expertise to offer in education, health improvement and research. This is an exceptionally strong starting position and shows clearly the contribution an independent Scotland can make internationally.

Scotland therefore has much to offer the world and much to gain from direct participation, in our own name, in the global community.

Independence gives us the ability to advance Scotland's interests in our immediate neighbourhood and through engagement – for example, with our extended family, the Scottish diaspora. Our existing network of Global Scots, made up of leading Scottish business people and experts with an affinity for Scotland, will continue to ensure Scottish companies develop, expand and thrive locally in a competitive international market.

With our immediate neighbours in the British Isles and Northern Europe, independence will create opportunities for co-operation, with future governments able to engage as equals in partnerships that enhance Scotland's position in relation to important policy areas including energy, tourism, security and culture.

In the EU, an independent Scotland will be able to engage early and directly across the range of the Union's activities, ensuring Scottish interests are considered. Scottish governments will be able to promote our priorities in a system based on consensus and alliance building, where Scotland's votes will bring direct influence with the Commission and within the Council of Ministers. Being at the top table will transform Scotland's place in Europe.

Scotland has much to offer international development. With the limited powers of devolution, we have developed a highly successful programme of international development work, supporting projects in our seven priority countries for development – Malawi, Zambia, Rwanda, Tanzania, India, Pakistan and Sri Lanka. We have also offered humanitarian and other specific support to a small number of other countries.

With independence we will have the ability, and determination, to extend these efforts significantly and can ensure that Scottish development investment complies with international best practice. Our ambition is for Scotland to be a global leader in this field. We can ensure that international development is a central part of our international responsibilities and overseas engagement, underpinning the actions of the Scottish Government at home and abroad.

Scotland's foreign policy and international relations will take place within three overlapping and interacting spheres that will be the cornerstones of Scotland's foreign policy:

- our partnership with the other nations of these islands

- our regional role as an active member of the EU with strong links to the Nordic countries and the Arctic

- the global context: our independent role in international and multilateral organisations, including the UN and NATO

Scotland in the British Isles

The choices open to us
Devolution has shown the strengths of having different political systems in Scotland and the rest of the UK for both countries. Since 1999 many areas of Scottish life, including health, justice and education, have to all intents and purposes been independent.

The Scottish approach to these issues – for example, banning smoking in public places, protecting free education and pushing for a minimum price for alcohol – has challenged the rest of the UK to consider different approaches to address challenges common to both countries. We have also been able to consider the Westminster approach to policy issues, sometimes rejecting those that are not suitable for Scotland or that have no support here. With independence we can change the nature of our co-operation and extend these policy conversations across the

Independence will allow Scotland and the rest of the UK to work together on matters of common interest, as nations do across the world. This will include current cross-border arrangements on health treatments, combating serious and organised crime and terrorism and administrative arrangements to deliver services to the people of Scotland and the rest of the UK when this makes sense. To suggest otherwise is to believe that the Westminster Government would act against the express interests of people and businesses in the rest of the UK.

Scotland's most important diplomatic relationships will be with the rest of the UK and Ireland, reflecting cultural history and family ties, shared interests in trade, security and common travel. The current Scottish Government plans a substantial diplomatic presence in both London and Dublin and will be active participants in the British-Irish Council, the secretariat of which is already based in Edinburgh.

Scotland and the rest of the UK will have a very close and constructive relationship on many foreign policy issues; it is natural that the values and interests of such close neighbours will often be aligned. The current Scottish Government would intend to support the rest of the UK in maintaining its seat on the UN Security Council. However, there will be issues on which a fundamentally different approach is right for Scotland and only independence gives us the opportunity to take that different path.

Scotland in the European Union

The choices open to us

We believe that Scotland's natural position is as an active participant in the EU, which provides us with unparalleled access to a market of over 500 million people.

We believe that an independent government, acting to protect Scotland's national interests within the EU, can restore some of the ground lost in recent decades when key Scottish industries have not been a priority for Westminster in EU negotiations. The debate over Scotland's relationship with the EU is, however, one that will almost certainly feature in future Scottish election campaigns, with some arguing for a looser form of partnership.

The advantage of independence is that the people of Scotland will have the sole and final say. We will not be taken out of the EU against our wishes as may turn out to be the case if we are not independent.

Within the EU there will be important opportunities for future Scottish governments to determine priorities and maximise the benefits of our membership. These include:

- **Scotland's democratic voice in the EU:** the EU has considerable influence over Scotland's economic and social welfare, from the single market to its common policies on a wide range of social and cultural matters. Independent membership of the EU would ensure that the Scottish Government is able, for the first time, to participate at every level in the EU legislative and policy process. With independence the Scottish Parliament will have an enhanced role in EU issues, holding the Scottish Government to account for positions taken in the EU, and ratifying reforms to the EU treaties

- **prioritising interests and partnerships:** as an independent member state, Scotland will be in a much better position to advance our interests than as part of the UK. In practice the EU seeks consensus – solutions acceptable to all member states. To reach unanimity, all countries whatever their size have an equal say, and can advance their arguments and interests. On the rare occasions in which a consensus cannot be reached, a formal vote is held to settle the common position. Scotland would have our own votes on these occasions, and would align our votes with those member states whose interests best match Scotland's. An independent Scotland can therefore never find itself in a less favourable position than now – when we do not have our own voice – in representing Scotland's interests in the EU. Indeed, smaller EU member states tend to be relatively more successful in negotiations than are the large member states[249]

- a partnership approach to freedom, security and justice: engaging with EU partners against organised crime, terrorism, drug and people trafficking and money laundering

- the opportunity to play a full role in the EU's common foreign and security policy, including co-operation to enhance Europe's defence capability and enhancing Scotland's contribution to international development and environment goals, such as the Millennium Development Goals

With independence, Scotland will take its proper place as a full member within the structures of the EU, giving us the ability to effectively represent Scottish interests within the EU.

Following a vote for independence the Scottish Government will immediately seek discussions with the Westminster Government, with member states and with the institutions of the EU to agree the process whereby a smooth transition to independent EU membership can take place on the day Scotland becomes an independent country.

The discussions will be held during the period in which Scotland remains part of the UK and by extension, part of the EU. This will allow the transition to independent EU membership to proceed without disrupting the continuity of Scotland's current position inside the EU single market or the rights and interests of EU citizens and businesses in Scotland. The Scottish Government believes that ensuring a seamless transition to independent EU membership will be in the best interests of Scotland, all member states and the EU in general, as well as those individual EU citizens and businesses who would be affected by any alternative approach.

The Scottish Government has proposed an 18-month period between the referendum and independence, which we believe is realistic for the terms of Scotland's independent membership of the EU to be agreed and all the necessary processes completed. It also provides sufficient time for the Scottish Government to undertake the necessary legal and institutional preparations for independent EU membership.

The Scottish situation is *sui generis*. There is no specific provision within the EU Treaties for the situation where, by a consensual and lawful constitutional process, the democratically determined majority view in part of the territory of an existing member state is that it should become an independent country.

Article 49 of the Treaty of the European Union provides the legal basis, and defines the procedure, for a conventional enlargement where the candidate country is seeking membership from outside the EU. As Scotland joined the EU in 1973 this is not the starting position from which the Scottish Government will be pursuing independent EU membership. Article 49 does not appear to be the appropriate legal base on which to facilitate Scotland's transition to full EU membership.

The alternative to an Article 49 procedure, and a legal basis that the Scottish Government considers is appropriate to the prospective circumstances, is that Scotland's transition to full membership is secured under the general provisions of Article 48. Article 48 provides for a Treaty amendment to be agreed by common accord on the part of the representatives of the governments of the member states.

Article 48 is therefore a suitable legal route to facilitate the transition process, by allowing the EU Treaties to be amended through ordinary revision procedure before Scotland becomes independent, to enable it to become a member state at the point of independence.

The Scottish Government recognises it will be for the EU member states, meeting under the auspices of the Council, to take forward the most appropriate procedure under which an independent Scotland will become a signatory to the EU Treaties at the point at which it becomes independent, taking into account Scotland's status as an EU jurisdiction of 40 years standing. The European Parliament will also play its role in Scotland's transition.

The Scottish Government will approach EU membership negotiations on the principle of *continuity of effect*: that is, a transition to independent membership that is based on the EU Treaty obligations and provisions that currently apply to

Scotland under our present status as part of the UK, and without disruption to Scotland's current fully integrated standing within the legal, economic, institutional, political and social framework of the EU.

We recognise that specific provisions will need to be included in the EU Treaties as part of the amendment process to ensure the principle of continuity of effect with respect to the terms and conditions of Scotland's independent EU membership, including detailed considerations around current opt-outs, in particular the rebate, Eurozone, Justice and Home Affairs and the Schengen travel area.

Scotland is likely to be a net financial contributor to the EU, subject to negotiation on issues such as the rebate and Scottish take up of EU funding programmes. The EU budget has been agreed until 2020. We see no reason for re-opening current budgetary agreements. Prior to 2020, we consider that the division of the share of the UK rebate would be a matter for negotiation between the Scottish and Westminster Governments.

Our intention to retain Sterling as the currency of an independent Scotland is based on an analysis of the potential impact of the alternative currency options on Scottish people and businesses, including the ease with which they can conduct their business with people and companies across the rest of the UK and beyond. While the Scottish Government recognises the political and economic objectives of the Eurozone, an independent Scotland will not seek, nor will we qualify for, membership of the Eurozone. Scotland's participation in the Sterling Area will not conflict with wider obligations under the EU treaties.

As Article 140 of the Treaty on the Functioning of the European Union (TFEU) makes clear, an EU member state is only permitted to join the Eurozone and adopt the Euro as its currency if the "convergence criteria" have been met. These convergence criteria include:

- inflation rate: the applicant country's inflation rate to be no more than 1.5 percentage points higher than the three lowest inflation member states of the EU

- government finance: the applicant country ratio of annual deficit to GDP to be less than 3 per cent and ratio of gross debt to GDP to be less than 60 per cent

- exchange rate: applicant countries must have been a member of the Exchange Rate Mechanism II (ERM II) for two consecutive years and should not have devalued its currency during that period

- long-term interest rates: the applicant country's nominal long-term interest rate must not be more than two percentage points higher than in the three lowest inflation member states

Under the TFEU a member state that fails any of these four tests will not be permitted to join the Eurozone.

It is important to note that the decision as to when, or if, to include a currency in the ERM II – a pre-condition for Eurozone membership – rests entirely with individual EU member states. The UK (and thus Scotland) is not a member of ERM II. If a national government decides not to join the ERM, as it is entitled to do, then by definition it cannot become eligible for membership of the Eurozone. Sweden is an example of an EU member state in this position – despite being an EU member since 1995, Sweden is not in the ERM II.

This Government will not seek membership of the Schengen area either. Instead, an independent Scotland will remain an integral part of the broader social union of close economic, social and cultural ties across the nations of the UK (including the Isle of Man and the Channel Islands) and Ireland. An essential part of this social union, and one that will be fully maintained with independence, is the free movement of nationals between Scotland and the rest of the UK and Ireland. There are no circumstances in which the Scottish Government would countenance any measure being taken that jeopardized the ability of citizens across the rest of the UK and Ireland to move freely across our borders as they are presently able to do. It is for this reason that following independence Scotland will remain part of the Common Travel Area (CTA), which dates back to the 1920s.

There are absolutely no grounds to believe that the EU would challenge Scotland remaining part of the CTA rather than joining the Schengen area. The EU has spent all of its 50 or so years of existence seeking to remove borders across the EU. The EU Treaties recognise that membership of the Common Travel Area is not compatible with membership of the Schengen area.

The current CTA between the UK and Ireland is based on administrative agreements, rather than binding treaty obligations to which an independent Scotland would succeed. These arrangements are reflected in the UK's immigration laws (and those of the Republic of Ireland) and could be replicated by an independent Scotland in due course. Within the CTA, an independent Scotland will work with the Westminster and Irish Governments to ensure that visa and immigration controls and practice meet certain shared standards. The detail of this would require negotiation but full harmonisation is not required; Ireland and the UK already operate different immigration systems within the Common Travel Area.

More generally, the Scottish Government will seek to retain the current flexibility to opt into new measures on Justice and Home Affairs. An independent Scotland will seek to participate wherever possible in new proposals, which can bring significant benefits to Scotland and the whole of the EU.

International policy

The choices open to us

An independent Scotland can emulate comparable countries with the most effective approach to international affairs: soundly based policies which enable the country to engage seriously and competitively in the world; rigorous priorities for our international focus; and the right external relationships to advance and protect our interests.

Countries of comparable size to Scotland take lead roles in international organisations. Sweden, New Zealand, Switzerland and Finland have all made significant global contributions to security, peace and reconciliation initiatives: New Zealand, for example, played a key role in the Oslo Process that banned cluster bombs and similar weapons. These nations capitalise on their soft power and build coalitions – normally informal and related to specific issues – to advance their objectives. The effectiveness of a coalition lies less in the sheer numbers involved and more in their ability to develop strong and sound arguments for negotiations.

There are inherent advantages in being a smaller, well-governed, independent state in a rapidly-changing world, with the ability to respond to developments and with the scale to bring national institutions and civic society together quickly if need be. By focusing our diplomatic efforts flexibly on key national priorities, Scotland will not require the same scale of diplomatic service as the UK currently maintains.

Focusing on issues and areas to achieve most impact will be fundamental to the success of Scotland's role on the international stage. In the fields of international development, human rights, climate change and climate justice, Scotland already has a well-established international reputation and a contribution to make that would be enhanced significantly with independence.

Our priorities for action

In an independent Scotland, this government would develop strong bilateral relations and play a full role in the international organisations that set the standards for trade, finance, health, labour relations and other key issues and support an international legal system that is a foundation for Scottish prosperity and security.

The main multilateral organisations such as the UN, WTO and OECD provide frameworks for negotiations which give nations a voice in decisions that are agreed and implemented internationally. International organisations provide strategic, political, economic and societal platforms for smaller countries[252].

Bilateral, or state-to-state, arrangements also continue to play their part in shaping a nation's foreign affairs. The UK's bilateral treaties cover a range of important matters such as mutual legal assistance in criminal matters or international conventions on terrorism.

Following a vote for independence Scotland will declare and notify our intention to assume responsibility for the UK's multilateral and bilateral treaties, where it is in Scotland's interest to do so. The Scottish Government expects that other parties to these treaties will welcome Scotland's intention to sign up to, and continue, these obligations. The UK itself has shown how entire treaty issues with newly independent states can be readily and speedily resolved. On the day of independence of the Czech Republic and Slovakia (1 January 1993) the UK wrote to both countries stating that the UK would regard all the bilateral UK – Czechoslovakia treaties as now continuing between the UK and the Czech Republic on the one hand and the UK and Slovakia on the other, with the substantive treaty provisions continuing to operate with both successor states as they had done previously with the predecessor state.

Scotland's membership of the EU will represent a key element of an independent Scotland's international relations and foreign and security policies. The EU provides a forum for discussions and agreement between member states on specific foreign policy questions, and collective action through the development of a Common Foreign and Security Policy, the Common Security and Defence Policy, and the European External Action Service established under the Lisbon Treaty.

This Government plans that Scotland will be an active and committed participant in the Common Foreign and Security Policy. The EU's external policies support stability, promote human rights and democracy, seek to spread prosperity, and support the enforcement of the rule of law and good governance, complementing the foreign policy efforts of individual states. Scotland would benefit from this Europe-wide approach which is broadly aligned with Scotland's values.

Scotland will take its place as a member of the United Nations, working with like-minded countries to promote global issues of importance to the Scottish people, such as human rights and tackling climate change and to advance global development, including support to those countries most in need. The UN continues to form the basis for international co-operation,

51 INDEPENDENT UN MEMBERS IN **1945** ⟩ **193** NOW

committed as it is to maintaining international peace and security, developing friendly relations among nations and promoting social progress, better living standards and human rights.

Scotland will also join NATO, which is the basis of security for the North Atlantic area. NATO membership is in Scotland's interests, and the interests of our neighbours, because it underpins effective conventional defence and security co-operation.

Other key multi-national organisations Scotland will participate in include:

- Council of Europe: best known for the European Court of Human Rights and the European Convention for the Protection of Human Rights and Fundamental Freedoms (ECHR)

- the Organisation for Security and Cooperation in Europe (OSCE)

- the Organisation for Economic Co-operation and Development (OECD)

- World Trade Organisation (WTO)

- the Commonwealth

Each of these organisations has its own procedure for membership. Scotland is already a member of them through the UK, and so already meets the essential requirements. Following a vote for independence, the Scottish Government will initiate steps to ensure Scotland's membership as an independent country as swiftly as possible.

This Government intends that Scotland will also seek a closer relationship with the Nordic Council of Ministers. Scotland has key shared interests with our geographical neighbours in the North Atlantic, such as Iceland and Norway, and a common interest in the Arctic and High North.

We plan to establish a network of overseas offices to represent Scotland's interests internationally, with a particular focus on promoting sustainable economic growth, participating in rules-based international co-operation and protecting Scotland's people and resources.

Scottish embassies will have five core functions:

- **commercial:** to maximise commercial benefits for Scottish businesses, including an expansion of export and investment, and to assess strategic economic opportunities for Scotland and our economy

- **governmental:** to ensure effective engagement with governments and other public institutions within the host state and to promote Scottish interests

- **cultural:** to promote Scottish culture internationally and to engage with members of the Scottish diaspora

- **development:** to ensure Scotland's international development priorities and commitments are being delivered

- **consular:** to provide appropriate support for Scottish citizens, and where relevant other EU citizens, and deal with issues such as visa applications

There will be variation in the range and scale of services available in different locations. Some embassies will fulfil primarily a political or governmental function, for example our permanent representation within the EU, ScotRep.

The most significant investment of resources will be devoted to the development of commercial opportunities for Scotland in key markets overseas. Co-ordinated teams of trade experts and diplomats will represent Scottish interests, opening up markets and assisting Scottish businesses to expand internationally. Our world-class range of cultural activities will also support our activities in promoting Scotland.

The existing SDI network of 27 overseas offices provides a firm foundation for independent Scottish international representation. Over the past five years, SDI has increased Scotland's presence in emerging markets in the Middle East and Asia. This Government plans that the existing SDI network remains following independence, co-locating with the new diplomatic and consular services. Where SDI is currently located in a country but not in its capital city, a Scottish embassy or political mission would be established to supplement and complement the work of the trade offices.

Our planned initial locations will include: London; Beijing; Berlin; Brasilia; Canberra; Delhi; Dublin; Islamabad; Madrid; Moscow; Paris; Pretoria; Seoul; Tokyo; Warsaw; Washington and in view of the close historical and co-operation ties with Malawi, Lilongwe. Additional sites in Asia, the Middle East, South America, Africa and Europe will be identified.

Scotland's network of embassies will be supported in some countries, including the United States, Canada and China, by consulates. We will also appoint members of the Scottish diaspora and prominent local people as honorary consuls to represent Scottish interests in nations where there is no direct Scottish representation.

Our representation in the EU will be built on existing Scottish Government representation in Brussels. We will establish Scottish permanent representation to the UN and other multilateral organisations. By way of comparison, Ireland maintains permanent representation at the Council of Europe (Strasbourg), the OECD and UNESCO (served by the same office in Paris), the OSCE (Vienna), the UN (Geneva and New York), NATO Partnership for Peace (Brussels) and the EU (Brussels). Similar representation is maintained by Denmark and Finland.

Similar countries to Scotland (such as Denmark, Ireland, Finland, Slovakia and New Zealand) have between 50 and 100 overseas missions, and 1,100 to 2,700 staff. The Government estimates the running costs of our initial proposed network of 70 to 90 overseas offices at £90 million to £120 million. This is expected to be below Scotland's population share of the UK's total expenditure on overseas representation in 2016/17 giving opportunities for savings. Scotland would also be entitled to a fair share of the UK's assets.

Scotland will be willing to co-locate diplomatic missions with other nations, including, and in particular, with the rest of the UK in current premises. This is common practice internationally. The UK has arrangements with Canada under a Memorandum of Understanding and with other nations. Ireland and Denmark also use this approach successfully to provide support to their citizens overseas. For example, the Helsinki Treaty of Co-operation between Denmark, Finland, Iceland, Norway and Sweden provides for consular assistance[253]. Other nations also share some consular services, such as Australia and Canada.

In addition, an EU citizen has the right to request the consular or diplomatic protection of any other EU member state when in a non-EU country where his/her own member state is not represented by a permanent consular post or diplomatic mission.

International development

Our priorities for action
With a focus on working in partnership and achieving real and tangible outcomes on the ground, the Scottish Government's international development policy seeks to build upon the historical and contemporary relationships that exist between Scotland and the developing world. Scotland will seek to be a global leader in the field of international development, championing best practice and innovation. Being a global leader in international development is not necessarily just about the size of aid given in absolute monetary terms, but the impact that can be made across government policy. The provision of aid is one tool within international development and an independent Scotland would enshrine a legislative commitment to spending 0.7 per cent of Gross National Income on Official Development Assistance.

Delivering a coherent approach to international development across all Scottish Government policies – crucially trade, environment, defence and finance – would be the key to success and global impact. The Scottish Government therefore has several key propositions that will guide our approach to development. They are:

- **More and better aid:** The Scottish Government would meet from the point of independence, and thereafter maintain, the 0.7 per cent target, with an aspiration towards one per cent over time and ensure Scotland's aid is of high quality, including through appropriate geographical and thematic focus. The Government plans to introduce a legislative basis to ensure adherence to the 0.7 per cent target as a binding, statutory commitment

- **Debt relief:** The Scottish Government will give careful consideration to the question of "unjust" debts; will work to ensure that Scottish export policies do not create new unjust debts; and support moves to establish Scotland as an international centre for debt arbitration

- **Gender equality:** Gender equality and the empowerment of women are Millennium Development Goals in their own right. They are also critical to the delivery of other key development goals including in education and health. An independent Scotland will put gender equality at the heart of our development work

- **Do No Harm** – ensuring policy coherence: As an expression of the values driving our foreign policy, this Government will ensure that other Scottish Government policies do no harm to developing countries, do not undermine international development aims and ideally contribute to international development success – through a rigorous approach to policy coherence for development. A key example of this approach is that our Climate Justice Fund and our International Development Fund are being developed and implemented within and across Government, providing a streamlined approach to both international development and climate change

Scotland's international development programme will be delivered as part of an integrated approach to international relations. However, we will not allow commercial or other considerations, including military considerations, to influence our approach improperly.

Development sections within Scottish overseas offices will ensure effective delivery of programmes supported by the people of Scotland and will work closely with Scotland's private and third sectors, and our civil society partners, to maximise the impact of both governmental and non-governmental efforts.

The Scottish Government intends under independence to work with the UK's Department for International Development (DFID) to ensure that there is a smooth transition phase for programmes on the ground in developing countries. There will be continued support, where appropriate, to those DFID programmes which span the independence period to avoid any sudden disruption to those programmes and their recipients. International development is just one of the areas where future Scottish and Westminster governments can choose to work together to complement each other's activity. Scotland is also likely to be a significant donor to multilateral organisations reflecting similar priorities as the UK in this area.

Defence

Why we need a new approach

Improving the way defence is delivered in and for Scotland is one of the most pressing reasons for independence.

For decades we have been part of a Westminster system that has sought to project global power, giving Britain the capacity to engage in overseas military interventions and to deploy nuclear weapons.

Scotland has been home to one of the largest concentrations of nuclear weapons anywhere in the world, despite consistent and clear opposition from across civic Scotland, our churches, trade unions and a clear majority of our elected politicians[254]. Billions of pounds have been wasted to date on weapons that must never be used and, unless we act now, we risk wasting a further £100 billion, over its lifetime, on a new nuclear weapons system. Trident is an affront to basic decency with its indiscriminate and inhumane destructive power.

Westminster's commitment to nuclear weapons leaves other aspects of our defence weakened. Costs for the successor to Trident are to be met from within the defence budget, taking money from conventional equipment and levels of service personnel. The Royal Navy will have two new aircraft carriers years before it has the aircraft to put on them. Cost overruns are endemic and major projects have been significantly delayed. Scotland can do better.

In Scotland, the adverse consequences of Westminster's defence policies have been felt in many ways.

- the latest figure for defence spending in Scotland (2007/08)[255] is £1.4 billion less than Scotland's current contribution of £3.3 billion to UK defence and security budgets[256]. With independence Scotland's defence spending will not only provide Scotland's security, but will increase economic benefits and employment on which Scotland currently misses out

- in March 2013 the Westminster Government announced that only 600 more Armed Forces personnel would be based in Scotland by 2020[257] – a fraction of the significant increase promised by the MOD in July 2011[258]

- the RAF base at Leuchars will cease flying operations in autumn 2014. Craigiehall, outside Edinburgh, the former Army Headquarters in Scotland, has been earmarked for disposal, and Forthside in Stirling and Redford Barracks in Edinburgh will at least partially close

- Scotland is a maritime nation and yet the UK has no maritime patrol aircraft and no major surface ships are based in Scotland. There is greater risk to safety and security in Scotland's airspace and waters as a result

- Ministry of Defence employment – civilian and service – in Scotland has fallen from 24,680 in 2000 to 15,340 in 2013, a proportionately larger fall than across the UK as a whole. Consequently, Scotland's share of UK-based Ministry of Defence personnel has fallen from 9.2 per cent to 7.5 per cent over this period[259]

The Westminster Government suggests that we need Britain for our defence, but the reality is very different. Scotland has been failed by decades of poor decisions. So we now have weapons that we do not need – like Trident – and lack assets that we do need – like maritime patrol aircraft.

An independent Scotland can follow the path of similar independent nations and make our own contribution to collective defence arrangements which, as part of NATO, far surpass any security that is offered by Britain alone.

The opportunities available to Scotland

An independent Scotland will have the opportunity to decide our own defence priorities to ensure our security, in partnership with our allies and within the wider international community. It will be the people of Scotland, through our Parliament, who will decide whether or not our young men and women are sent to war and we can choose, through our written constitution, to put in place safeguards to ensure that Scottish forces will only ever participate in military activity that is internationally recognised as lawful and in accordance with the principles of the UN Charter.

The flexibility that being a small state can bring will mean that Scotland can take an integrated approach to national security, with our defence capabilities playing a role alongside other areas of government.

We have in existing naval, army and air force bases the underpinning infrastructure we need to meet our defence needs and regional defence responsibilities. We also have sufficient expertise, built up over years of service and Scotland's proud military tradition, with Scots who have served at all levels of Britain's armed forces and at senior levels in the Ministry of Defence and NATO.

We will inherit a share of existing UK defence assets, giving us most of the equipment we need to establish Scotland's defence forces in the immediate post-independence period. The division of assets and liabilities will of course need to be negotiated. However, by way of indication, in 2007 the Ministry of Defence estimated the total value of its assets and investments[260] at just under £93 billion. A Scottish share based on population would be around £7.8 billion.

By making different choices on nuclear weapons and global reach we can save a substantial proportion of Scotland's current defence contribution to the UK, while still having levels of defence spending that allow us to deliver the capabilities we need. Within this budget allocation will be significant investment in procurement, which can support key Scottish industries including the shipbuilding industry.

A new and more appropriate level of defence spending will also free up valuable resources for investment in other national priorities. It will give Scotland an independence defence dividend that can be used to improve our approach in areas of social policy.

The Scotland we can create

With independence, therefore, we can create the most appropriate domestic defence for Scotland, one that sees us fulfilling both our international responsibilities and the commitment we have to the security and safety of people living in Scotland. We can create an approach to defence that positions us as partners for peace in the wider world.

With independence, future governments can choose to equip Scotland with specific, specialist capabilities, allowing us to develop particular expertise that adds value for our allies: for example allowing Scotland to take on a role in internationally sanctioned peace-keeping or peace-making operations.

While the UK approach has left significant gaps in our defence capabilities, in particular in relation to maritime protection and reconnaissance, with independence we can, once again, make an effective contribution to regional defence in recognition of our important strategic position in the North Atlantic.

The choices open to us

Defence capability will be an important part of the mix of responses available to an independent Scotland in addressing opportunities, threat and risks. At the point of independence the Scottish Government proposes that there will be core Scottish defence capabilities to contribute to this task and fully protect Scotland and our people. Priorities for the further development of Scotland's defence and security capabilities should be refined following the strategic review of security undertaken by the first elected parliament and government of an independent Scotland.

The Scottish Government believes that these key roles for Scotland defence forces, working closely with partners and other parts of government, should be considered in depth in the security review:

- securing Scotland's borders, land, airspace and sea, deterring attacks and protecting our citizens and assets from threat

- protecting Scotland's national interests and economic wellbeing, alongside the key values and underlying principles that support Scottish society and our way of life. This task would include supporting other parts of government, for example in natural disasters or other emergencies

- contributing to the protection and promotion of human rights, the rule of law, democratic values, international peace and security, building on Scotland's national interests by being a progressive voice in the world

Our priorities for action

Scotland's defence and security policy will be a key part of wider international policy, protecting Scotland's interests through a strategic approach to national security, and providing military capability to defend our national interest. We will take our own decisions about involvement in military action, while continuing to make a full contribution to our own defence and that of our allies.

Scotland will be part of collective defence arrangements, giving the people of Scotland the same security guarantees that they enjoy today. Within this framework of mutual defence we will be able to deliver a more responsible defence posture better suited to Scotland's strategic needs and interests. Improved parliamentary oversight of defence and long-term, consensus-based arrangements for strategic planning can mean that spending is based on sound decisions. Our approach will mean substantial savings on defence spending, continued investment in Scotland's defence industries and the basing of Scottish service personnel closer to their families and homes.

The current Scottish Government has identified five defence priorities for an independent Scotland:

- maintaining the commitment to a budget for defence and security in an independent Scotland of £2.5 billion

- securing the speediest safe withdrawal of nuclear weapons from Scotland

- building a focus on maritime capabilities, such as air and sea-based patrol, and specialist forces able to operate around our coasts, protecting Scotland's maritime assets and contributing to collective security in the North Atlantic

- progressively building to a total of 15,000 regular and 5,000 reserve personnel over the 10 years following independence

- reconfiguring the defence estate inherited at the point of independence to meet Scotland's needs, including the transition of Faslane to a conventional naval base and joint headquarters of Scottish defence forces

This Scottish Government envisages a phased approach to reaching the level of Scottish defence forces set out above. This will be achieved through a staged process involving 7,500 regular and 2,000 reserve personnel at the point of independence, rising to around 10,000 regulars and 3,500 reserves by the end of the five years following independence, subject to consideration in the strategic defence review. The final force levels will provide capacity for Scotland to make enhanced contributions to international partnership operations.

The units of the Scottish Army will carry on the names, identities and traditions of Scotland's regiments, including those lost in the defence reorganisation of 2006.

This level of defence capability will require the continued operation of all current major military bases in Scotland. In particular Faslane will become the main operating base for the Scottish Navy, and the headquarters for the Scottish defence forces as a whole.

Following a vote for independence, the Scottish Government will immediately start to put in place defence capabilities to meet Scotland's needs on independence, and to provide the foundations to develop these capabilities in line with the outcome of the strategic review. The priorities in the period between the referendum and independence day, will include:

- establishing a military staff to advise the Scottish Government in the transition and the development of appropriate defence capabilities

- putting in place joint arrangements with the Westminster Government to identify and transfer units and personnel wishing to serve in Scottish defence forces

- identifying, in negotiation with the rest of the UK, a first tranche of defence assets and bases to transfer to Scottish defence forces, pending wider agreement

Effective joint agreements will be of particular importance to both Scotland and the rest of the UK in the transitional period following independence. It will be in the interests of both countries to ensure arrangements are taken forward in an orderly and secure manner. This approach will retain for the transitional period some integrated services for the security of Scotland and the rest of the UK.

By independence day, the Scottish Government will have in place a core set of military capabilities from which it will then build. That will include a number of military units (air, land and sea-based) under Scottish Government control.

The process of transition will be based on negotiated agreement between the Scottish Government and the Westminster Government. The Scottish Government expects that both governments will act responsibly and that over time the number of personnel from the rest of the UK based in Scotland will decline while Scottish personnel numbers rise.

Scotland's defence forces

The Scottish Government has carried out an initial assessment of forces levels in the years following independence[261].

Defence capabilities at the point of independence

Maritime forces

One naval squadron to secure Scotland's maritime interests and Exclusive Economic Zone (EEZ) and contribute to joint capability with partners in Scotland's geographical neighbourhood, consisting of:

■ two frigates from the Royal Navy's current fleet

■ a command platform for naval operations and development of specialist marine capabilities (from the Royal Navy's current fleet, following adaptation)

■ four mine counter measure vessels from the Royal Navy's current fleet

■ two offshore patrol vessels (OPVs) to provide security for the 200 nautical mile Exclusive Economic Zone (EEZ). However, as the Royal Navy only has four OPVs currently[262], a longer lead time for procurement might be necessary

■ four to six patrol boats from the Royal Navy's current fleet, capable of operating in coastal waters, providing fleet protection and also contributing to securing borders

■ auxiliary support ships (providing support to vessels on operations), which could be secured on a shared basis initially with the rest of the UK

These arrangements will require around 2,000 regular and at least 200 reserve personnel.

Land forces

An army HQ function and an all-arms brigade, with three infantry/marine units, equipped initially from a negotiated share of current UK assets, and supported by:

- a deployable Brigade HQ

- two light armoured reconnaissance units

- two light artillery units

- one engineer unit deploying a range of equipment for bridging, mine clearance and engineering functions

- one aviation unit operating six helicopters for reconnaissance and liaison

- two communication units

- one transport unit

- one logistics unit

- one medical unit

Special forces, explosives and ordnance disposal teams will bring the total to around 3,500 regular and at least 1,200 reserve personnel.

Air forces

Key elements of air forces in place at independence, equipped initially from a negotiated share of current UK assets, will secure core tasks, principally the ability to police Scotland's airspace, within NATO.

- an Air Force HQ function (with staff embedded within NATO structures)

- Scotland will remain part of NATO's integrated Air Command and Control (AC2) system, initially through agreement with allies to maintain the current arrangements while Scotland establishes and develops our own AC2 personnel and facility within Scotland within five years of independence

- a Quick Reaction Alert (QRA) squadron incorporating a minimum of 12 Typhoon jets based at Lossiemouth

- a tactical air transport squadron, including around six Hercules C130J aircraft, and a helicopter squadron

- flight training through joint arrangements with allies

In total this would require around 2,000 regular personnel and around 300 reserve personnel.

Civilian support
In addition to military capability following a vote for independence, the Scottish Government will establish core government capacity for defence functions, such as strategic planning, oversight and policy functions for defence and security. Given the importance of ongoing shared security interests between Scotland and the rest of the UK, we will ensure a partnership approach during the period of transition to independence.

Following a vote for independence, priorities for the Scottish Government capacity dealing with defence will be planning for the strategic security review to be carried out by the first Scottish Parliament following independence, based on the most recent UK National Risk Assessment and input from Scottish experts and academic institutions.

Defence capabilities five years after independence
Further development of Scotland's defence and security capabilities will be decided following the strategic review of security undertaken by the first elected Parliament and government of an independent Scotland.

However the current Scottish Government believes that the following elements should be prioritised for delivery as early as possible in the first five years following independence, building on the forces in place at independence:

Maritime forces
A second naval squadron to contribute to NATO and other operations outside home waters, incorporating the naval command platform, and a further two frigates with tanker and support ship capacity.

Overall the model would involve around 2,400 regular and at least 270 reserve personnel. While most of the personnel would be required by the five year point, this model envisages increases continuing through the first ten years following independence (due to procurement of new Scottish naval vessels).

Land forces

Developing the All Arms brigade's capabilities to include:

- increases to strengths of the three infantry battalions (to a combined total of 1,500 regular and 300 reserve personnel)

- upgrading of the light armour, artillery, aviation and medical units

- increasing the strength of the special forces unit

- increasing the number of personnel deployed to conflict prevention, disarmament and defence diplomacy

Overall, this would entail an increase in numbers, over the years following independence, to around 4,700 regular and at least 1,110 reserve personnel.

Air forces

Increasing the fast jet fleet of Typhoons potentially up to 16 aircraft which would enable Scotland to contribute to alliance operations overseas.

Increasing the Scottish contribution to capabilities for air defence, as part of an integrated system within NATO.

At present, the UK has no maritime patrol aircraft. During this period options for procurement will be taken forward and airborne maritime patrol capability delivered. A detailed specification of requirement will be developed as a priority and final numbers of aircraft required will depend on this. However, the numbers maintained by comparable nations suggests a potential fleet of four.

Development across all of those areas would entail an overall increase in numbers to around 3,250 regular and at least 300 reserve personnel.

Defence capabilities after 10 years
This Government plans that, 10 years after independence, Scotland will have a total of 15,000 regular and 5,000 reserve personnel across land, air and maritime forces.

Service personnel and veterans

The Scottish Government respects the service of current personnel. We will ensure that all current service personnel will be eligible for a post in the Scottish defence forces, though they will not need to take it up.

All service personnel will have the reassurance that they will not face compulsory redundancy during their service contract. This Scottish Government would examine how the terms and conditions of service personnel could be improved, for example through the official representation of service personnel.

Where whole or part of units are identified for transfer to Scottish defence forces, the Scottish Government will ensure that all current UK service personnel within those units can remain with them for at least a transitional period, where they wish to do so. A similar approach will be followed for reserve personnel and the important role of cadet forces will also be maintained.

The aim will be a phased and responsible approach to the position of those currently serving in the UK armed forces who might wish to transfer to Scottish defence forces. Some may transfer immediately, while others would continue in their current role. It is our intention that terms and conditions remain harmonised through this period. Any sensible approach would recognise that, at the end of that process, it is highly likely that citizens from the rest of the UK, Ireland and from other Commonwealth countries would be serving in an independent Scotland's defence forces. Though it would ultimately be a decision for the rest of the UK, we also expect that Scottish citizens will continue to serve in UK forces if they wish to, as citizens of Ireland and the Commonwealth do.

Reserve personnel make a valuable contribution to defence capability and will do so in an independent Scotland. Our proposals include a baseline requirement for around 1,700 reserve personnel at the point of independence. However as there are currently an estimated 2,200 trained reserve personnel in Scotland[263], it would be both feasible and desirable to increase numbers beyond the baseline that requirement suggests, in order to build flexibility and enhance capability. In the longer term the Government envisages the reserve force building to 5,000 personnel after 10 years.

Scotland and the rest of the UK will also continue to owe the same debt of gratitude to veterans who have served in the past. The Scottish Government will build on our existing strong record in this area to ensure that veterans continue to access the services and benefits that they are entitled to. This will include full service pensions and pension entitlement, following agreement with the Westminster Government.

Defence infrastructure
The transitional period will also include continued arrangements for the use of defence infrastructure in Scotland by UK forces and vice versa. The Scottish Government will protect the bases inherited at the point of independence and we expect that, over time, the main military facilities in Scotland will be used by Scottish defence forces. This transitional period would allow for appropriate planning, including for the continuation of shared basing into the longer term where that was in the best interests of both Scotland and the rest of the UK.

While details will be negotiated with the rest of the UK, the Scottish Government currently envisages that:

- current and envisaged major army facilities will continue to be needed at Kinloss, Leuchars, Glencorse, Fort George, Dreghorn and the elements of Redford to be retained by the UK Ministry of Defence

- in addition there will be a need to consider where additional air assets, not currently located in Scotland, might operate from. Given the retention of the runway at Leuchars, the Scottish Government would envisage air operations being reinstated there, alongside an army presence

- Faslane will be retained as the main naval base for an independent Scotland. In addition it will be the location for the joint headquarters of the Scottish defence forces. Options will be considered for re-instating Rosyth as a supporting naval base, alongside its current industrial uses

- given that the transfer of Typhoons from Leuchars will have been largely completed before the referendum, Lossiemouth will continue to be a main operating base for fast jet aircraft and Scotland's air policing capability. The Scottish Government will negotiate with the Westminster Government to establish the joint facilities it would be in the interests of both countries to maintain there

The transition of Faslane from a submarine base to Scotland's main naval base and joint force headquarters will be managed gradually: personnel and equipment will be brought into the Scottish defence forces and infrastructure will be developed, while the personnel and equipment remaining within the Royal Navy are relocated by the Ministry of Defence.

The Scottish Government intends the transition to be complete within ten years[264]. The transitional arrangements will support both the day to day operations and the workforce levels at the base. We will retain the capacity for shared arrangements with the rest of the UK and other allies, recognising Faslane's excellent deep water facilities and its geographical position.

There are currently 6,700 military and civilian jobs at HMNB Clyde[265]. Through its role as a main conventional naval base and Joint Forces HQ, this Scottish Government expects that, at the conclusion of transitional arrangements, the number of Scottish military personnel at Faslane will approximately match military numbers there currently. Those military personnel will be supported by a significant number of civilian personnel. During the transitional period large numbers of personnel from the rest of the UK will also be based there. In addition, work to reconfigure Faslane as a conventional naval base is expected to involve major construction activity, and related jobs, in the area.

There are a range of other defence facilities around Scotland used by NATO and the UK, such as the weapon ranges in the Hebrides and the training area around Cape Wrath. The Scottish Government expects these to continue to be used after independence, following discussions with the rest of the UK and allies.

The negotiation of shared arrangements as a transitional measure would not preclude such arrangements being carried forward into the longer term, where both the rest of the UK and Scotland considered them the most effective means of delivering defence capabilities.

Negotiations on the maintenance of shared capabilities would not include nuclear weapons. This Scottish Government would make early agreement on the speediest safe removal of nuclear weapons a priority. This would be with a view to the removal of Trident within the first term of the Scottish Parliament following independence.

The detailed process and timetable for removal would be a priority for negotiation between the Scottish Government and the Westminster Government. However we have noted the work undertaken by the Scottish Campaign for Nuclear Disarmament (CND), which suggests that Trident could be dismantled within two years[266].

The Scottish Government plans to explore the potential for Scotland's defence industry capabilities to diversify into other activities. For example, in a report in 2007 the STUC and CND noted that "many of the skills currently used to maintain Trident would be directly relevant to renewables[267]" and the report highlighted the advantages the Lower Clyde area offers such activity. The Scottish Government's work will therefore focus on the potential offered by energy, particularly marine renewables, although it will also examine other aspects of defence diversification, for example those relevant to the shipbuilding industry. The research and development capacity of Scotland's defence industries offers the opportunity to boost Scotland's business R&D. Other comparable countries have much higher levels of R&D activity (a key driver of economic growth). Finland, for example, uses an innovation agency as its primary tool for R&D activity. Defence diversification could play an important role in Scotland's future industrial strategy.

Scotland's defence industries
Scotland's defence industries are an important source of employment and provide high quality defence products to

the UK armed forces and more widely. If in government in an independent Scotland the Scottish Government will work with defence industries to support their continued growth and to meet Scotland's own defence needs.

Scotland will ensure our defence budget is utilised to:

■ support the procurement of equipment and services in Scotland, where consistent with European procurement rules

■ support defence-related R&D, innovation and design

■ support small and medium enterprises in particular to expand their marketing effort internationally

■ develop a clear role for each government department and agency in areas such as licensing, accreditation and dual-use

This Scottish Government expects that the proportion of the budget allocated for procurement of single use military equipment[268] will be at least equivalent to that currently allocated by the Westminster Government (14 per cent in 2012/13). In the first term of the independent Scottish Parliament we expect personnel numbers in Scottish defence forces to be steadily increasing. Therefore during this period personnel costs would initially be lower and it would be possible to boost the proportion of the budget allocated to procurement over the first part of that period.

The Scottish Government regards support for our shipbuilding industry as a priority given our focus on maritime defence capabilities. Whilst keeping within EU procurement requirements, the Scottish Government will protect the future of Scotland's shipyards and maintain capabilities important to our long-term interests.

This Scottish Government will take forward the procurement of four new frigates, to be built on the Clyde, preferably through joint procurement with the rest of the UK. Two of these will be ordered in the first parliamentary term of independence and, when built, will bring the number of frigates in the Scottish navy to four (the two new frigates as well as the inherited Type 23s). The Scottish Government believes that is the appropriate number of frigates in the longer term, and will order the further two frigates in time to replace the Type 23s when they are retired from service.

Recent Westminster decisions have demonstrated the importance of Scotland's shipbuilding industry to the Royal Navy. The Ministry of Defence has also shown that it is keen to develop opportunities for joint procurement and there are strong reasons why both the Scottish and Westminster Governments would want to explore the potential for joint procurement of future naval vessels.

We also plan to prioritise procurement within the first five years of maritime patrol aircraft, based on a detailed specification of need (the numbers maintained by comparable nations suggests a potential fleet of four). Depending on negotiation with the rest of the UK on division of assets, further procurement needs will have to be addressed, including for offshore patrol vessels.

In an independent Scotland, we will, where appropriate, work with the Scottish defence industry to deliver identified Scottish defence capability requirements. Scotland would seek to work in partnership, build the necessary alliances and align our defence requirements with the collective needs and priorities of NATO allies, including the rest of the UK.

Joint procurement is in the interests of Scotland and the rest of the UK[269], preserving the strengths of defence industries around the whole of the UK. Joint orders would maintain the expected numbers of jobs in the defence industries sector, including shipbuilding, and support companies as they seek to expand their business internationally.

The EU Defence Procurement Directive aims to open up the defence equipment market to competition and to contribute towards the development of an efficient European market for defence equipment. Whilst EU law allows an exemption from the requirement for open competition in certain, very limited, circumstances related to national security, it should be the exception not the norm.

Outwith Europe, Scotland will also build bilateral defence and security relationships with a range of key partners and on a range of security issues. These countries will also provide potential markets for Scotland's defence industries.

International partnerships

As the government of an independent Scotland we will be committed to working in partnership and through alliances. Scotland will be a part of key defence organisations, such as NATO, OSCE and the EU. The defence and security relationship with the rest of the UK will be fundamentally important, both for the rest of the UK and for Scotland.

Scotland will also explore flexible, shared arrangements for delivery of defence and security with our neighbours and partners. Again, the rest of the UK would be an essential, but not exclusive, element in this.

Following a Yes vote in 2014, the Scottish Government will notify NATO of our intention to join the alliance and will negotiate our transition from being a NATO member as part of the UK to becoming an independent member of the alliance.

The basic premise of NATO is that all members must make an active commitment to the alliance and Scotland would recognise and play our full part in building collective security and capability. Scotland's geographical position and strong national interest in being able to robustly monitor and protect our maritime environment will be a key part in the contribution we make to the alliance. Scotland also provides an important range of training areas and other facilities that are actively used by NATO members.

Membership of NATO will be in the interests of Scotland, the rest of the UK and other NATO members. Scotland occupies an important place in regional security arrangements that NATO members enjoy. While recognising that Scotland's membership requires discussion and agreement by NATO members, it will be in the interests of Scotland and other members of the alliance to secure an independent Scotland's membership in the period between the referendum and independence. Most importantly for Scotland and our neighbours, failure to reach an agreement would leave a gap in existing NATO security arrangements in north west Europe.

Scotland would take its place as one of the many non-nuclear members of NATO. The Scottish Government is committed to securing the complete withdrawal of Trident from an independent Scotland as quickly as can be both safely and responsibly achieved.

Constitutional guarantees

Only independence will enable Scotland to play a full role working within and alongside the international community in creating the conditions for nuclear disarmament. The development of a written constitution for Scotland would also provide the opportunity to include a constitutional ban on nuclear weapons being based in Scotland.

Many countries around the world place constitutional controls on the use of military power. Our view is that Scotland's constitution should include a 'triple lock' on military deployments, based on the principles that military action would need to be:

- in accordance with the principles of the UN Charter

- properly agreed by the Scottish Government

- approved by the Scottish Parliament

This will not conflict with the right to act immediately and legitimately in self-defence in extraordinary circumstances, such as when attacked, as recognised in the UN Charter. This position is consistent with NATO's Article 5 commitment to collective defence.

CHAPTER **7**

JUSTICE,
SECURITY AND
HOME AFFAIRS

- With independence, Scotland will have the full range of powers needed to keep our people and communities safe, to further reduce crime, to take a coherent approach to tackling crime and to create stronger and cohesive communities

- A security and intelligence agency will ensure the safety and security of Scotland's citizens, the first responsibility of any government, within strict legal controls determined by the Scottish Parliament

- We plan a controlled points-based system to support the migration of skilled workers for the benefit of Scotland's economy

- An independent Scotland will have an inclusive approach to citizenship and a humane approach to asylum seekers and refugees

Why we need a new approach

Key powers needed to make our communities safer, stronger and more secure are currently controlled by Westminster, including decisions about drugs, firearms, gambling, road safety and the proceeds of drug trafficking. To tackle the underlying causes of inequality in our society, we need to take decisions about welfare benefits, incentives to employment and overall levels of public expenditure. This will ensure that our distinctive Scottish approach to justice, in its broadest sense, can be fully realised.

Whilst the Scottish Government and Parliament are making a positive difference with the powers we have, there is still much work to be done to ensure the justice system works effectively, particularly for those communities most blighted by crime.

A key element of the Scottish Government's approach to tackling crime has been to use funds seized from criminals to invest in our communities and provide positive opportunities for young people. The Cashback for Communities programme, established in 2007, has invested over £50 million recovered under the Proceeds of Crime Act (2002) to fund activities and facilities in communities across Scotland[270]. However, the total amount that Scotland is able to retain and reinvest from the proceeds of crime is capped by the Westminster Government at £30 million a year. Westminster has refused requests for the cap to be removed to allow more resources seized from criminals in Scotland to be invested in our communities.

Whilst the Scotland Act 2012 provided Scotland with some limited additional powers, for example to set a different drink driving limit from the rest of the UK and to license air weapons, Westminster has refused to devolve further powers necessary to help make our roads and communities safer.

With decisions on immigration taken in Scotland we can adopt an approach that works better for Scotland's economy and society. In particular, we can reverse some of the decisions taken by Westminster which are damaging the ability of Scotland's colleges and universities to attract high-quality international students. It is also difficult to conceive of a Scottish government that would ever adopt the crude "go home" approach tried by the current Westminster Government.

The opportunities available to Scotland

The existing independence of Scotland's legal and justice systems ensures a strong starting point for our independent country. Successive Scottish governments have legislated to ensure that we keep up-to-date with the requirements of a modern justice system. These reforms demonstrate the value of taking decisions here in Scotland, as well as highlighting the barriers that exist as part of the current constitutional arrangements.

With devolution, Scotland has benefited from taking decisions for itself across a wide range of justice issues. The Scottish Government has introduced a series of improvements to modernise our justice system and ensure that it can meet the needs of our citizens in the 21st century. Through our focus on prevention, crime in Scotland is falling and people feel safer in their communities[271]. Recorded crime is at a 39-year low[272] with homicides at their lowest level since 1976[273] and the crime clear-up rate is the highest in over 35 years[274].

Despite budget cuts imposed by Westminster, the Scottish Government has continued to invest in front-line policing. The establishment of Police Scotland has ensured that local policing is maintained, but with access to specialist expertise and equipment whenever necessary. Scotland is maintaining police numbers at over 1,000 extra officers compared with 2007[275] and the Scottish Government has rejected other changes to policing proposed by Westminster which would, for example, allow people without relevant policing experience direct entry to senior police roles.

Scotland has led the way in tackling crime and in promoting preventative approaches. Scotland's Serious and Organised Crime Strategy[276] and new Scottish Crime Campus at Gartcosh will ensure that agencies work together to share intelligence and deal effectively with organised criminals. However, some measures needed to deal with organised crime, such as the control of firearms and decisions on the proceeds of drug trafficking, are currently reserved to Westminster.

With independence, we can ensure that security and intelligence functions are focused on defending our democratic values and securing our fundamental rights and freedoms. These functions will be carried out under democratic control in Scotland. The right balance must be struck between the rights enshrined in the new Scottish written constitution, including key human rights such as the right to privacy and to freedom of expression, and the need to keep us safe and secure from serious threats such as terrorism. Our security and intelligence agency will be subject to legislation which protects human rights and sets out clearly the powers and responsibilities of, and controls over, the agency. These will be in line with international standards, including ensuring that there is expert and democratic control of the agency[277].

The Scotland we can create
Justice is one of the fundamental responsibilities of government: to provide safety, security and fairness to the citizens of the country. Our justice system provides the foundation for delivering the kind of nation Scotland should be – a thriving and successful European country, reflecting shared values of fairness and opportunity, and promoting prosperity and social cohesion. Our existing responsibilities combined with new powers, will enable us to build a Scotland that is more prosperous, communities that are safer and a society that is more comfortable with itself.

A primary function of government is to ensure the security of its citizens, and to protect them, their property and way of life against threats. An independent Scotland will have national security arrangements that reflect Scotland's specific needs and values, recognising the risks and threats we face, based on a full review of security requirements and on a regular assessment of threats.

An independent Scotland will also be responsible for immigration and citizenship, with the opportunity to develop an immigration policy that sensibly meets Scotland's population and economic needs, while enriching our society.

The justice system

The choices open to us

An independent Scotland will have control over policy on welfare, employment and public expenditure. It is our more deprived communities that suffer most from the impact of crime and are most vulnerable to the influence of organised crime. By providing our young people with positive opportunities, through employment and education, we can help them to participate fully in society and create stronger and more cohesive communities. We also know that access to employment, housing and other services are key to reducing re-offending[278]. Issues arising from debt, housing and welfare problems also place demands on our courts. Rather than just dealing with the consequences of crime and disadvantage through our devolved justice system, an independent Scotland will be able to use the full range of powers available to government to make our communities safer, stronger and more secure.

There are also some specific issues that will become the responsibility of the Scottish Parliament on independence. Responsibility for these will allow Scotland to take an integrated approach to issues that affect our communities like drugs and gun crime. The priorities of the current Scottish Government in an independent Scotland would be:

Firearms: building on current work to improve control of airguns in Scotland, firearms legislation could be simplified, making it easier for the public to understand and easier to enforce.

Road traffic offences and drink driving: building on current proposals for a new drink drive limit, Scotland's roads could be made safer through more appropriate penalties for drink driving, and powers for the police to conduct random breath tests any time, anywhere[279].

Gambling: it is estimated there are 30,500 problem gamblers in Scotland[280]. With independence, Scotland will have the powers to better tackle problem gambling through effective regulation of the industry, in contrast to Westminster's approach of greater deregulation[281].

Drugs: since 2008, Scotland's drug strategy, *The Road to Recovery*, has led the UK in tackling drugs issues and has received international acclaim for its focus on care, treatment and recovery. Drug taking in the general population is falling[282] and drug taking among young people is at its lowest level for a decade[283]. Whilst drugs policy is currently devolved, drugs classification remains reserved to Westminster. Independence will allow decisions on drugs policy and drug classification to be taken together in a coherent way.

Our priorities for action
Independence will provide the Scottish Parliament and Scottish Government with the opportunity to address significant justice issues that will help define the nature of society in an independent Scotland. For example, a new written constitution will protect and enshrine our distinctive justice and legal systems to support the rule of law, human rights and a strong democracy.

Following independence, existing laws, whether passed by the Westminster or the Scottish Parliament, will continue to apply until they are amended by the independent Scottish Parliament. Human rights will continue to be protected, as they are for devolved matters under the Scotland Act 1998. The independence of Scotland's judiciary and prosecutors will be maintained. Our police, courts, prisons, community justice and fire and rescue services will continue to operate. Police, fire and other public sector pensions will be paid and accrued rights will be protected.

Existing well-established arrangements to ensure effective cross-border co-operation between Scotland's justice agencies and those in the remainder of the UK will continue, including, for example, cross-border policing and arrest, and prisoner transfers.

The Inner House of the Court of Session and the High Court of Justiciary sitting as the Court of Criminal Appeal will collectively be Scotland's Supreme Court. Our courts will continue to collect income from fines imposed on offenders. However, rather than transferring more than 75 per cent of this income out of Scotland to the UK Treasury, Scotland will retain the full value, providing approximately £7 million in additional income to invest in our communities. The Westminster Government's cap on income which Scotland can retain under proceeds of crime legislation, currently set at £30 million each year, will be removed.

Following independence, Scotland will continue as a member of the EU and other international organisations concerned with justice, including the Hague Conference on Private International Law and the Council of Europe, which covers the European Convention on Human Rights and a range of criminal law issues. Scottish courts will still refer points of EU law to the European Court of Justice in Luxembourg and people will continue to be able to make an application to the European Court of Human Rights in Strasbourg.

An independent Scotland will maintain current arrangements for extradition, including participation in the European Arrest Warrant scheme and seeking agreements to ensure that criminals can be pursued and brought to justice across international borders. Scotland will work with other EU member states to protect the public and tackle cross-border crime, including through participation in co-operative institutions such as Europol and Eurojust. However, an independent

Scotland would not rely solely on the European Arrest Warrant procedures for arrests that take place between Scotland and the rest of the UK. It will be in the interests of an independent Scotland and the rest of the UK to agree arrangements for cross-border arrests that are as efficient and effective as the current arrangements. Such a bilateral arrangement is explicitly allowed under European legislation.

An independent Scotland will also play an active and committed role in the EU's Common Foreign and Security Policy (CFSP), which enables EU members to co-operate to enhance Europe's security.

Security and intelligence

The choices open to us

An independent Scotland will be able to take a strategic approach to national security, underpinned by effective planning and investment across government. There will be contributions from the police, a new Scottish security and intelligence agency, the military and others, to ensure appropriate responses to a range of identified threats and risks, including terrorism, cyber security threats and national emergencies.

As part of that, Scotland will need an independent security and intelligence capacity to ensure our security. Independence offers an opportunity to build a new model for such work, which is fit for the 21st century and which provides a proportionate means of ensuring Scotland's national security. We have studied a range of international comparators[284] in preparing our proposals[285].

Our priorities for action

The current Scottish Government plans to set up a single security and intelligence agency for Scotland on independence. The purpose of the agency will be set out in legislation, and will include the requirement to work with partners to ensure Scotland's national security.

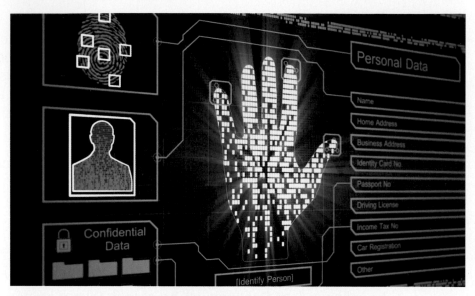

This will be a modern and fit-for-purpose security and intelligence agency. By day one of independence, it will be responsible for and capable of functions including:

- investigation of threats

- liaison: with Police Scotland and others in Scotland; with the rest of the UK; and internationally

- intelligence gathering, receipt and handling

- production of open-source intelligence material

- assessment and analysis

- production of risk and threat assessments

- protection of Scotland's critical infrastructure

- cyber security functions

In carrying out these functions it will build on expertise which exists in Scotland in the gathering and analysis of information and intelligence.

Initially, we will draw on expertise (such as training and IT) from other countries, primarily, given our long joint history, from the rest of the UK. Such joint working in the early period after independence will deliver a seamless transition ensuring that the security of both countries is continuously maintained. The

UK has, in the past, provided such support for the creation or development of security services in other countries[286].

Setting up a new agency will allow us to do things differently, unconstrained by historical structures and precedent, and avoiding any barriers between different agencies. As well as traditional covert capability, we will invest in the means to analyse the vast amount of information which is openly available, and to develop our capacity for strategic assessment.

A Scottish security and intelligence agency will play a leading role in ensuring the resilience of our critical infrastructure. Scotland is the only country in the UK to have published a critical infrastructure strategy, *Secure and Resilient*[287], which provides a framework for improving the resilience and protection of Scotland's critical assets. Following independence, we will further develop our own capability and our particular focus on a wide range of critical assets, while collaborating closely with the rest of the UK. This collaboration will be crucial, given the UK dependence on critical Scottish assets (particularly energy).

We will invest in cyber security, both in terms of protective measures and to attract and retain the right skills in Scotland. Our strategy will be to secure Scotland from attack, and also protect our citizens and strengthen our economy. Delivery of some aspects of the Scottish Government's cyber security strategy will be undertaken by the Scottish security and intelligence agency, but other partners such as our universities and businesses will also be involved in our joint effort against cyber threats.

We will continue to work with the rest of the UK on cyber security. This will be in the mutual interests of Scotland and the rest of the UK. During the initial period the focus will be on maintaining our levels of cyber security and ensuring a seamless transition. We expect that the independence settlement will include appropriate recognition of Scottish taxpayers' proportionate contribution to the UK's current Cyber Security Programme (a programme of UK-wide investment scheduled to finish before Scotland becomes independent in 2016).

Relationship with the Scottish criminal justice system
In line with good practice, a new security and intelligence agency will be independent of, but work extremely closely with, Scotland's single police service, Police Scotland. There is already a long track record of close co-operation between the UK security services and the police in Scotland. The agency will build on that history and make the relationship even more effective, while ensuring that there is very clear separation in terms of responsibilities, tasking, governance and accountability.

Detention and arrests will continue to be a matter for Police Scotland and prosecution will continue to be a matter for the Lord Advocate.

Working with partners
The rest of the UK will be our closest neighbour and our most important friend and ally. There is no doubt that intelligence-sharing will be in the best interests of the people of Scotland and of the rest of the UK. The Scottish and Westminster Governments will engage closely as equal and co-operative allies in tackling issues of joint interest such as terrorism and serious organised crime. It will be a strong relationship of sovereign equals.

Existing agencies already work closely together. For example, Scotland plays an active part in the UK Counter Terrorism Strategy and, given that responsibility for policing and justice is already devolved to the Scottish Parliament, there is extensive cross-border co-operation on security. The effectiveness of these arrangements was seen in the co-operation between Scottish police forces, the Security Service and the Metropolitan Police Service after the Glasgow Airport bombing. It will be in the mutual interests of Scotland and the rest of the UK to ensure that this cross-border co-operation continues following independence, supported by Police Scotland and a Scottish security and intelligence agency.

Some commentators have questioned whether the UK would choose to share intelligence with Scotland. However, as the Westminster Government's *Scotland Analysis: Security* paper of October 2013 made clear: "It is clearly in the UK's interests to be surrounded by secure and resilient neighbouring countries, including – in the event of a Yes vote – an independent Scottish state"[288].

A new security and intelligence agency will have the appropriate security arrangements necessary to give assurance to international partners that it can receive and handle intelligence safely and securely. There is already significant experience and expertise within both the Scottish Government and Police Scotland in handling sensitive, classified information, and the necessary procedures for doing so are well understood. The new agency will also liaise closely with international partners on operational matters, building from the basis of existing relationships.

An independent Scotland will explore the benefits of developing closer relationships with the primary EU agencies already engaged in cyber security: the NATO Cooperative Cyber Defence Centre of Excellence; the European Network Information Security Agency; and the European CyberCrime Centre.

Legislation, governance and oversight
Early legislation will set out the purpose, duties and powers of a Scottish security and intelligence agency and the controls that will exist on the use of these powers.

Under independence, Scottish citizens will enjoy written constitutional rights for the first time. Striking the right balance between maintaining the constitutional and human rights of our citizens and the need for national security will be vital. In order to protect the safety of others, some of the work undertaken by security and intelligence agencies means, by necessity, interference with the privacy of specific individuals. Such work can and does save lives, but it needs to be done in a proportionate and managed way.

There has been extensive public debate about surveillance and the collection of information, especially in relation to online communications. In an independent Scotland, legislation will set out clear arrangements for investigatory powers, building on – and updating where necessary – the Regulation of Investigatory Powers Act 2000 and the Regulation of Investigatory Powers (Scotland) Act 2000[289]. Our planned legislation will ensure that law enforcement agencies have the powers that they need to do their job and keep Scotland safe, while also clarifying the limit of those powers and the extent of the controls over them.

The controls put in place will be wide-ranging and comprehensive. The planned legislation will bring democratic control of our national security to Scotland for the first time. Scottish Ministers will be accountable to the Scottish Parliament for what a Scottish security and intelligence agency does in their name. The Scottish Parliament and the Scottish equivalent of the relevant Commissioners[290] will scrutinise and challenge the work of the agency, including its covert work. They will be given clear legislative powers to support their work, including the power to require documents to be provided and to require the senior management of the agency to give evidence. There will also be detailed budget scrutiny from the Auditor General for Scotland, and the top-level budget will be scrutinised by the Scottish Parliament as part of the Budget Bill.

This scrutiny will ensure that the agency is acting properly, legally, efficiently and effectively, in line with international principles for intelligence service oversight[291]. These processes must take transparency as their starting point. But in so doing, they will appropriately and rigorously protect aspects of the agency's work that cannot be made public, and will respect the control principle[292] at all times.

Resources
Ensuring that Scotland is secure will be the primary responsibility of the Scottish Government, and the investment made in the agency will reflect that. The exact size and cost of a security and intelligence agency will be determined by the risks and threats that Scotland face. The UK agencies cost around £2 billion per year; based on population, Scotland contributed £206 million last year[293]. We anticipate maintaining a comparable level of spending under independence.

In the early years we will make a significant level of investment in setting up the agency. Scotland, of course, already has a substantial existing capital stake, from our investment in UK

intelligence infrastructure. We will expect investment to be recognised in the arrangements that are agreed with the UK as part of the independence settlement.

Immigration

The choices open to us

One of the major gains from independence for Scotland will be responsibility for our own immigration policy. Currently immigration is a reserved matter, and the Westminster Government's policy for the whole of the UK is heavily influenced by conditions in the south east of England. Westminster has also adopted an aggressive approach to immigration, asylum seekers and refugees, culminating in the recent controversy over advertisements to tell people to leave the UK and "go home".

Scotland has a different need for immigration than other parts of the UK. Healthy population growth is important for Scotland's economy. One of the main contributors to Scotland's population growth is migrants who choose to make Scotland their home. In future our enhanced economic strategy will also do more to encourage young people to build their lives and careers within Scotland and to attract people to live in Scotland.

Scotland's differing demographic and migration needs mean that the current UK immigration system has not supported Scotland's migration priorities. The current Westminster approach is strongly focused on reducing the overall number of migrants and introducing caps for certain categories of skilled individuals. In April 2012, the Westminster Government stopped the post-study work visa, which allowed recent graduates to work or set up a business in the UK for 24 months thus retaining skilled and educated graduates as part of the UK labour force. Westminster has also set financial maintenance thresholds for most migrants at a standard level across the UK despite variations in average earnings. With independence, each of these decisions will be for Scottish governments, with policy choices made on the basis of Scotland's needs and priorities.

Historically Scotland's population has grown at a lower rate compared to the rest of the UK. The latest population projections suggest that Scotland's workforce will not grow as rapidly as the UK as a whole[294]. Scotland's population needs are therefore different to the rest of the UK and Scotland has a clear economic rationale for growing our population – in particular our working age population. The Government Economic Strategy sets out a target "to match average European (EU-15) population growth over the period from 2007 to 2017, supported by increased healthy life expectancy in Scotland over this period".

Scotland is not well served by Westminster's decisions on immigration and, given our specific circumstances, finding the right approach for Scotland's economy and society is an important part of ensuring a more sustainable future for our nation.

An independent Scotland, as a modern democracy, will meet our international obligations and play a responsible role on the world stage. We will demonstrate our respect for international law, human rights and social justice in offering asylum to those seeking a place of refuge from persecution, war, natural disaster or other major crises. Scotland already plays its part in efforts to provide a home for refugees as part of the UK and will do so as an independent country.

The asylum process in an independent Scotland must be underpinned by an emphasis on robust, fair, socially-responsible and thorough decision-making, with clear adherence to human rights and equality principles and to the rule of law.

Our priorities for action
Migrants have played an important part throughout Scottish history in enriching and renewing our culture and boosting the economy of the country. We will welcome people who want to come to work and live in Scotland.

We plan to continue in the current Common Travel Area with the rest of the UK and Ireland so there will be no need for border checks between an independent Scotland and England. The Common Travel Area already allows for different and independent systems within Ireland and the UK, the Isle of Man and the Channel Islands. This flexibility in the Common Travel Area will enable us to implement our own design for a controlled and more flexible immigration system.

As a full member of the EU, Scottish borders will remain open to EU nationals exercising their treaty rights, just as Scots are free now to move throughout the EU.

For non-EU nationals, independence will enable us to develop and operate a controlled, transparent and efficient immigration

system. This Government will take forward a points-based approach targeted at particular Scottish requirements. The system will enable us to meet the needs of Scottish society with greater flexibility, for example by providing incentives to migrants who move to live and work in more remote geographical areas, assisting with community sustainability, or adding new categories of skills.

We plan to lower the current financial maintenance thresholds and minimum salary levels for entry, to better align them with Scottish average wages and cost of living. This will open up greater opportunities for key skilled individuals from overseas who could play important roles in our society and economy and fill vital vacancies in individual businesses.

A particular issue for Scotland is the post-study work visa. There are over 30,000 international students from more than 150 countries in Scotland; over 11 per cent of all students studying in Scotland are drawn from elsewhere in the EU and about 10 per cent are from the rest of the world[295]. This Government plans to reintroduce the post-study work visa. This visa will encourage more talented people from around the world to further their education in Scotland, providing income for Scotland's education institutions and contributing to the local economy and community diversity.

An independent Scotland will have the opportunity for a new model of asylum services separate from immigration. We propose that a Scottish Asylum Agency should oversee asylum applications. The process will be both robust and humane, and we will continue Scotland's present approach of promoting the integration of refugees and asylum seekers from the day they arrive, not just once leave to remain has been granted (as is the case in the rest of the UK). In an independent Scotland, we will close Dungavel, end the practice of dawn raids and inhumane treatment of those who have exercised their legitimate right to seek asylum. If a failed asylum seeker is a risk to the public, secure accommodation will be sought whilst steps are taken to remove them. If there is a need for forcible removals, these will be undertaken with respect for human rights. Independence will also afford the opportunity to address asylum seekers' access to employment, education and accommodation.

Citizenship

The choices open to us
Deciding who is a citizen is a defining characteristic of an independent state and future Scottish governments will have the power to determine rules on citizenship and nationality.

Our priorities for action
At the point of independence, this Government proposes an inclusive model of citizenship for people whether or not they define themselves as primarily or exclusively Scottish or wish to become a Scottish passport holder. People in Scotland are accustomed to multiple identities, be they national, regional, ethnic, linguistic or religious, and a commitment to a multi-cultural Scotland will be a cornerstone of the nation on independence.

We plan that British citizens *habitually resident*[296] in Scotland on independence will be considered Scottish citizens. This will include British citizens who hold dual citizenship with another country. Scottish born British citizens currently living outside of Scotland will also be considered Scottish citizens.

Following independence, other people will be able to apply for Scottish citizenship. For example, citizenship by descent

will be available to those who have a parent or grandparent who qualifies for Scottish citizenship. Those who have a demonstrable connection to Scotland and have spent at least ten years living here at some stage, whether as a child or an adult, will also have the opportunity to apply for citizenship. Migrants on qualifying visas will also have the option of applying for naturalisation as a Scottish citizen.

The UK allows dual or multiple citizenship for British citizens. If a British citizen acquires citizenship and a passport of another country, this does not affect their British citizenship, right to hold a British passport or right to live in the UK. The Scottish Government will also allow dual citizenship. It will be for the rest of the UK to decide whether it allows dual UK/Scottish citizenship, but we expect the normal rules to extend to Scottish citizens.

Passports

Inherent to citizenship is the right to hold a passport. In an independent Scotland all British citizens born or habitually resident in Scotland on day one of independence will have the right to acquire a Scottish passport, although, as in most countries, there will be no requirement to hold one. A Scottish passport will also be available to anyone who acquires Scottish citizenship through naturalisation. It is envisaged that passport lengths will continue to be five years for children and 10 years for adults and will carry a fee comparable to that presently required for a UK passport which will be used to cover the administrative and production costs of the passport. As a member of the EU, Scottish passports will follow the EU passport model and therefore will broadly follow the current look of UK passports in colour, size, and layout, but will be identified as a Scottish passport on the front cover. They will be designed to meet the standard requirements for all EU passports and will be valid for international travel in the same way UK passports are at present. The Scottish Government will continue to recognise any currently valid UK passports until their expiry date.

CURRENT STATUS	SCOTTISH CITIZENSHIP?
AT THE DATE OF INDEPENDENCE	
British citizen habitually resident in Scotland on day one of independence	**Yes, automatically** a Scottish citizen
British citizens born in Scotland but living outside of Scotland on day one of independence	**Yes, automatically** a Scottish citizen
AFTER THE DATE OF INDEPENDENCE	
Child born in Scotland to at least one parent who has Scottish citizenship or indefinite leave to remain at the time of their birth	**Yes, automatically** a Scottish citizen
Child born outside Scotland to at least one parent who has Scottish citizenship	**Yes, automatically** a Scottish citizen (the birth must be registered in Scotland to take effect)
British national living outside Scotland with at least one parent who qualifies for Scottish citizenship	Can **register** as a Scottish citizen (will need to provide evidence to substantiate)
Citizens of any country, who have a parent or grandparent who qualifies for Scottish citizenship	Can **register** as a Scottish citizen (will need to provide evidence to substantiate)
Migrants in Scotland legally	May **apply** for naturalisation as a Scottish citizen (subject to meeting good character, residency and any other requirements set out under Scottish immigration law)
Citizens of any country who have spent at least ten years living in Scotland at any time and have an ongoing connection with Scotland	May **apply** for naturalisation as a Scottish citizen (subject to meeting good character and other requirements set out under Scottish immigration law)

CHAPTER **8**

ENVIRONMENT,
RURAL SCOTLAND,
ENERGY AND RESOURCES

- Direct representation in Europe will allow an independent Scotland a full voice in negotiations affecting key Scottish sectors, including agriculture, fisheries and aquaculture, to reflect Scottish priorities and benefit rural and coastal communities

- In recent negotiations Scotland would, as an EU member state, have had the opportunity for substantial uplift in agriculture and rural development funding via the Common Agricultural Policy. An independent Scottish Government will be able to negotiate directly to ensure Scotland does not lose out in the future

- Fishing quotas will be retained in Scotland as a national asset for the benefit of future generations

- An independent Scotland will have the platform to champion action on climate change at the global level

- An independent Scottish Parliament will have the opportunity to enshrine protection of the environment in a written constitution, ensuring its protection for future generations

- The government of an independent Scotland will have the powers to properly prioritise the needs of rural Scotland in relation to telecommunications, postal services, fuel and energy policy

- The principles of stability and certainty this Scottish Government is committed to will guarantee new investment in energy: we have no plans to increase the overall tax burden on the oil industry and no changes will be made to the fiscal regime without consultation

- Under our proposals, a single GB-wide market for electricity and gas will continue, with the current market trading arrangements, provided that they meet Scottish requirements for energy security supply

- We propose to establish a Scottish Energy Fund to provide investment for future generations and to smooth receipts from oil revenues

Scotland is blessed with an abundance of natural resources that can bring prosperity and ensure our nation meets the global challenges of the 21st century, such as food and energy security, and climate change. Independence will provide the powers to ensure that everybody in our society enjoys the benefits of our natural resources and that these are harnessed in line with Scotland's needs and priorities.

Recent assessments of the cost of living in rural Scotland highlight the many issues that are currently reserved to Westminster where the approaches taken by Westminster governments are hindering rural development and making life challenging for families, communities and businesses in rural Scotland[297].

Independence can empower our rural communities, and ensure that appropriate regulation of vital issues such as digital connectivity, postal and parcel deliveries, and energy reflects the needs of rural Scotland.

Agriculture

Why we need a new approach
Scotland's agriculture sector underpins the rural economy and our successful food and drink sector. Our farmers and crofters, in their stewardship of Scotland's land, contribute greatly to our natural heritage, and support our environment and successful tourism sector.

Scotland's diverse agriculture ranges from small crofting enterprises to large intensive livestock and arable farms. Agriculture is also comparatively more important to the Scottish economy than to the UK's as a whole, and it is distinctive. For instance, about 85 per cent of our land has "less favoured area" status compared with 15 per cent in England[298]. Scotland is also home to more than one quarter of the UK's beef herd[299].

However, Scotland's farmers and crofters have been repeatedly let down by Westminster governments which have failed to prioritise Scottish farming in domestic policies and, in European negotiations, and have argued and acted against Scotland's interests.

The record of UK representation of Scottish Agriculture in Europe

The interests of rural Scotland have been repeatedly traded off against other UK priorities in European Union (EU) negotiations where Scotland has no direct voice.

Successive Westminster governments have argued for a significant reduction in agricultural support payments, despite Scotland's already low share of funding and need for support given our geographical and climatic challenges. These payments are vital to ensure our farmers and crofters continue to produce food, deliver environmental benefits and sustain our rural communities.

As a result of Westminster not sharing Scottish priorities, Scotland has the third lowest average direct payment per hectare in Europe[300]. Indeed, in the newly negotiated agricultural subsidies for 2014 to 2020 (Pillar 1 of the Common Agricultural Policy), Scotland will have a lower average rate per hectare than any other member state in Europe and than the rest of the UK[301].

In November 2013, the Westminster Government chose to disadvantage Scotland further by deciding, despite cross-party opposition in the Scottish Parliament, to distribute across all the countries of the UK over €220 million of agricultural subsidy uplift, received from the EU to promote convergence. The uplift is a direct consequence of Scotland's lower payments, and should have been used to benefit Scottish farmers who have the lowest per hectare rates.

The position is similar when it comes to support for rural development. As part of the UK, Scotland currently receives the lowest average payment rate per hectare of rural development funding in Europe (under Pillar 2 of the Common Agricultural Policy)[302]. This is because the Westminster Government does not prioritise this support in its negotiations in Europe, despite pressure from the Scottish Government to do so. The UK chose not to join 16 other countries in securing additional rural development funding. This could have provided vital funding for environmental schemes, rural facilities, food businesses and tourism projects, amongst others[303].

Not only has Westminster failed to negotiate a better deal for Scotland, but our position is getting comparatively worse[304]. This is something an independent Scottish Government can tackle directly as part of the next CAP negotiations, likely to commence around 2018.

There is also the prospect of agricultural support being cut completely if Scotland remains in the UK. Scotland faces the possibility of leaving the EU because of Westminster's planned in/out European referendum. If there is a vote to leave the EU, Scottish agriculture and our rural industries will no longer be part of the CAP and will be in the hands of a Westminster government with a stated policy of drastically reducing or even ending farm payments.

The record of the Westminster Government on domestic agriculture policy

Scottish farming not only suffers from poor representation in Europe, but also from Westminster's failure to prioritise its interests in domestic policy in the areas where Westminster retains control.

For example, levy income from livestock reared in Scotland but slaughtered south of the border is used to promote beef, lamb and pork from elsewhere, not Scottish beef, lamb and pork.

The Westminster Government also has a poor record on responding to the needs of Scottish rural industries during times of crisis. For example, during spells of severe weather, or in relation to other animal welfare concerns, the UK Department of Transport required extensive and time-consuming lobbying by the industry and the Scottish Government before it agreed to relax rules on drivers' hours.

The Scotland we can create

With the powers of independence, and direct representation in Europe, we can secure and grow Scottish agriculture's place in our society and economy for the future. It is in our national interest that we retain the skills and capacity to produce food on our own land. Scotland's priorities will be reflected by the actions of our negotiators in Europe, greatly improving our opportunities for funding and to ensure that EU policies are tailored to Scottish circumstances. Ministers in an independent Scotland will also be able to ensure that every department of government works to support rural Scotland when required. In areas where we agree with the Westminster Government, Scotland will be its ally in agriculture negotiations, increasing our combined negotiating strength, both in terms of votes and representation at the negotiating table.

With independence, farmers and crofters will continue to receive CAP payments because the budget is already set until 2020. But, crucially, with independence Scotland will qualify for future member state funding increases.

The choices open to us

As an independent member state of the EU, Scotland will be able to promote directly our economic and social interests and protect our citizens by participating on equal terms with all other member states in EU affairs.

Scottish Ministers will also gain direct access to their counterparts in other member states through bilateral meetings, which Westminster currently does not allow for agriculture. As a member state we will have the authority to deal directly with all European institutions and be treated as an equal partner.

Common agricultural policy

Direct Farming Support (Pillar 1 of CAP): If Scotland had been independent when the latest CAP budget was being decided, we would have benefited from a principle that by 2020 no member state would receive less than an average of €196 per hectare. This would have brought Scotland an extra €1 billion between 2014 and 2020.

Rural Development Support (Pillar 2 of CAP): With independence, Scotland will be able to negotiate fairer allocations for rural development – similar to those achieved by many other member states. For example, despite having an area of agricultural land equal to around 25 per cent of that of the UK[305], Ireland negotiated an allocation of almost €2 billion for rural development – almost 85 per cent of the total allocation for the UK[306]. Finland negotiated a €600 million uplift[307]. This demonstrates what independent countries similar in size to Scotland can achieve within EU negotiations when they are able to reflect their own needs and priorities.

Our priorities for action

The Scottish Government firmly believes that the only government capable of properly representing Scotland's interests in the EU decision-making process is a government elected by, and directly accountable to, the people of Scotland. If we form that government we will:

- **provide a direct voice for Scotland's farmers in Europe,** and Scotland's agriculture sector will be a priority for Scotland's engagement with the EU. In the next round of CAP negotiations, Scotland's interests will be directly represented. An independent Scotland can negotiate the best possible deal for Scotland's farmers, crofters and rural communities.

- **use Scotland's farming levies to promote Scottish produce.** With independence, all levies for livestock raised in Scotland can be used to promote Scottish agriculture, not the produce of our competitors.

■ **reduce the burden of European livestock regulations.**
We will argue that Europe's regulatory burden should be
reduced in recognition of Scotland's good animal health
record and disease-free status.

■ **support new entrants into agriculture.** We will investigate
how we can use fiscal measures to provide opportunities for
new entrants to agriculture.

Fisheries

Why we need a new approach

The Scottish fishing industry has much to gain from
independence. Supporting our fishing communities and seafood
sector will always be a priority for Scottish governments.

In 2012, Scotland accounted for 87 per cent of the total value of
UK landings of key stocks, representing 37 per cent of the Total
Allowable Catch (TAC) of these stocks available to the EU[308].
However, Scotland receives just 41 per cent of the European
Fisheries Fund allocation to the UK, despite having a far higher
share of both the UK sea fishery and aquaculture sectors. As
a result of being a low priority for the UK in EU negotiations,
Scotland receives just 1.1 per cent[309] of European fisheries
funding despite landing 7 per cent of the European Union's wild-
caught fish[310] and accounting for more than 12 per cent of EU
aquaculture production[311]. Scotland is the world's third largest
salmon producer with 83 per cent of UK aquaculture production
by volume[312].

Our fishermen need a voice at the top table in Europe. Despite
two thirds of the UK industry being based in Scotland, Scottish
Ministers have not been allowed to speak on behalf of the UK
in Europe, even on occasions where the interest is almost
exclusively Scottish. This means that Scotland's representatives
– who are closest to the needs of the Scottish fishing sector –
are not able to ensure that their voice is properly heard.

Only independence can safeguard the future of Scotland's
fishing communities and seafood sectors and prevent our
fishing quotas – the industry's lifeblood – from being transferred
outside Scotland or being top-sliced by the Westminster
Government.

The Scotland we can create

The fishing industry has a strong heritage in Scotland, and continues to make a key contribution to our economy while supporting many fragile coastal communities.

With independence, for the first time, Scotland will have a direct say in European fisheries negotiations. An independent Scottish Government will have the power to always prioritise Scotland's needs. In areas where we have agreement with the Westminster Government, Scotland will be an ally in fisheries negotiations – increasing our combined negotiating strength both in terms of votes and representation at the negotiating table.

Independence will give Scotland's fishermen their own distinct voice in Europe, with Scotland participating at every level in the EU policy process.

As an independent member state of the EU, Scotland will be negotiating as one of the foremost and most respected fishing nations in Europe. This status will give Scotland the opportunity to take a leadership role in reforming the Common Fisheries Policy to deliver fisheries management at regional and member state level. This will involve negotiating management of fishing opportunities and securing funding for diversification of economic opportunities in our coastal communities.

The choices open to us

An independent Scotland will be able to negotiate directly for Scottish priorities without them being compromised in favour of wider UK objectives, bringing a new certainty for Scotland's fishing communities that their fishing rights will be protected. As an independent

SCOTLAND IS THE WORLD'S THIRD LARGEST

SALMON PRODUCER*

83%*
OF UK FISH FARMING PRODUCTION

IT LANDS

87%**
OF THE TOTAL VALUE OF UK LANDINGS OF KEY STOCKS

37%**
OF THE TOTAL ALLOWABLE CATCH IN THE EU

*SOURCE: DEPARTMENT FOR ENVIRONMENT, FOOD AND RURAL AFFAIRS
**SOURCE: SCOTTISH GOVERNMENT

member state in our own right, Scotland can keep Scottish fishing quotas in Scotland.

Independence is not merely about completing the current powers of the Scottish Parliament in relation to Scotland's fisheries. It is about devoting our energies to playing a full and leading role in Europe as a key fishing nation, with the authority of being a member state rather than being limited to lobbying UK Ministers and European Commission officials.

Our priorities for action

If in power after the 2016 election we will:

- **prioritise the needs of the Scottish fishing industry and aquaculture** in European negotiations

- **protect Scotland's fishing quotas**, preventing fishing quota being permanently transferred outside Scotland and safeguarding Scotland's fishing rights for future generations

- **use Scotland's fishing levies to promote Scottish seafood**. In an independent Scotland the industry's levies will remain in Scotland to support the Scottish industry's objectives and priorities for our catching, onshore and wider seafood sectors

Food and drink

Why we need a new approach

Scotland's food and drink sector has been extremely successful in recent years. Despite the global recession, our exports[313] are up 52 per cent since 2007[314] and our £4 billion whisky industry exports 40 bottles overseas each and every second[315]. Our food and drink sector turned over £13.1 billion in 2011[316], breaking initial growth targets six years early.

As international demand for our produce continues to increase, the Scottish Government has already been working closely with industry to support sustainable growth and identify and secure access to new export markets. For example, growth in demand for Scottish farmed salmon across Asia is an important opportunity to strengthen the economies of fragile

rural communities. Scotland's food and drink industry does an excellent job promoting the Scottish brand, but Scotland is constrained by the current constitutional settlement, which prevents it from directly engaging on a level footing with other countries.

The UK's planned in/out referendum on EU membership threatens our food and drink industry's current access to Europe's single market of 500 million citizens and 20 million businesses. There is also a real concern, particularly for the whisky industry, that if the Westminster Government takes Scotland out of the EU, we will lose the backing of the EU's trade negotiations with countries like India, the United States and China.

The Scotland we can create

Scotland's food and drink sector contributes 18 per cent of Scotland's overseas exports[317], but less than 1.5 per cent of the overseas exports of the UK as a whole. There are therefore clear benefits to Scotland having more direct control over our own priorities.

Independence will boost Scotland's international profile, delivering new opportunities for food and drink exports, as well as attracting new visitors to our country to enjoy our produce. An independent Scotland will have the opportunity to promote itself effectively in the UK and domestic markets. Just as the rest of the UK is already a significant market for other food-exporting nations such as Ireland, so it will remain Scotland's biggest and closest market.

The choices open to us

Food and drink exports will continue to be a priority area for our international trade efforts. With independence and our own more effective overseas representation, we can promote our products to the world, and tackle barriers to trade that the Westminster Government does not prioritise, such as the export of Scotch beef to the growing markets of Asia. An independent Scotland will have the opportunity to market Scotland's food and drink on an integrated basis, rather than having some marketing bodies with a Scottish focus and others responsible for the UK.

An independent Scotland will be able to engage directly in the EU and participate in key negotiations surrounding third party trade agreements and access to international markets. As a member state we will have a say in any legislation that allowed the banning or restriction of Genetically Modified Crops.

Scotland is already well-regarded internationally for the quality of its food and drink. With independence, our profile can only rise and producers across the country will benefit as a result.

Our priorities for action

We plan to:

■ **promote food and drink overseas**. Using Scotland's overseas representation we will extend promotion of the Scottish brand and our world-class produce. In addition, the global publicity generated by the independence process itself will be an important platform for our food and drink exports

■ **properly resource Export Certification**, which can open new markets to Scottish produce. This work will be a priority for an independent Scottish Government

- **use Scotland's levy to promote Scotland's produce.**
  In an independent Scotland, income from our food sectors
  will be retained in Scotland to promote our produce, with
  opportunities to continue co-operation with the rest of the
  UK on research and other issues

Rural communities

Why we need a new approach
Scotland's rural and island communities are a significant and
prominent part of our nation, culture and economy. Just over
£32 billion was produced in the rural regions of Scotland in
2011, which is approximately 30 per cent of total output from the
Scottish economy (excluding North Sea oil and gas)[318]. Rural
Scotland is a significant part of Scotland's economy as a whole
and intrinsic to Scotland's identity, and to our appeal as a visitor
destination.

Many of the functions necessary to the rural economy and
the health of rural and island communities are currently
administered by the Westminster Government, which means
that insufficient weight is given to the needs of rural Scotland.

Successive Westminster governments have failed to deliver
the economic opportunity that rural Scotland should expect.
Too many of our communities remain marginalised. It is time
for our natural wealth to work better for these communities and
for people in all parts of our nation.

Other countries have taken a different approach. For example,
in the early 2000s, while countries such as Sweden auctioned
3G telephony licences in a way that sought to maximise
coverage across the country, the UK approach sought to
promote "economic and efficient management and use of the
spectrum". The result was a patchy network which left large
parts of rural Scotland without coverage (see Chapter 9).

But it is not just the digital divide that is affecting development
in rural Scotland. In the 1990s the Westminster Government
opened up competition in the parcel sector without requiring
private sector operators to deliver services to all parts of the UK.

The result has been average mark-ups on standard delivery prices of 195 per cent in the Highlands and 508 per cent in the Scottish Islands[319].

Scotland's rural areas also face higher average costs of car travel and road haulage, due to longer average travel times and relatively higher fuel prices. This increases the costs for goods and services and travel more generally.

The Scotland we can create

Scotland's rich natural resources are central to our identity as a country and as a people. They underpin the growth of a thriving rural economy, and the industries of tourism, farming, fishing, forestry and food and drink, as well as new opportunities in renewable energy.

This Government's vision for an independent Scotland is a nation where opportunity exists across all of Scotland: empowering communities; protecting the environment; and giving all our industries a stronger voice in the international decisions that affect them. We seek to create a Scotland where our people benefit from rural economic development, and where we reverse rural depopulation in those areas it continues to impact upon.

The choices open to us

With independence, future Scottish governments will be able to fully support Scotland's rural communities with all the functions of government and within the EU, rather than relying on Westminster, where priorities are often different.

With independence, this Scottish Government will have the opportunity to negotiate for additional allocations of European rural development funding to lift Scotland off the bottom of the EU league table. Sixteen countries were able to secure increases in rural development funding at the recent CAP negotiations. This demonstrates what independent countries, several of which are similar in size to Scotland, can achieve within EU negotiations when they are able to reflect their own needs and priorities.

With similar funding increases we could: invest in rural tourism and environmental protection; ensure more investment in broadband and renewables; and fund start-up assistance for young farmers.

Our priorities for action

Our plans include:

- **postal delivery services and Royal Mail**. With independence, the regulation of mail in Scotland will be in the hands of the Scottish Parliament, providing an opportunity to address the way the market functions to deliver fairer prices across all of Scotland in rural and remote areas, especially for parcel services. The Scottish Government disagrees with the recent privatisation of Royal Mail. It presents a threat to the Universal Service Obligation which is of vital importance to rural communities. This Scottish Government plans to bring the Royal Mail back into public ownership in an independent Scotland (see Chapter 9).

- **rural broadband and mobile services**. In an independent Scotland, the Scottish Government will have direct control over the way in which spectrum licences are issued, ensuring maximum availability of mobile telephony and broadband throughout Scotland as a whole, including our rural areas

Scotland's target of a reduction of greenhouse gas emissions of at least 42 per cent by 2020 compares to the UK's 34 per cent target, is more than double the EU's 20 per cent target, and, distinctively, also includes our share of international aviation and shipping emissions. We are committed to a minimum of 80 per cent emissions reduction by 2050 and our recent, second *Report on Proposals and Policies*[325] sets out a strategy for Scotland to deliver a 57.8 per cent reduction in emissions by 2027.

The Scotland we can create

With independence, Scotland can play a crucial role in the international debate on climate change. With an independent seat in the EU, adding our voice to those of other nations with high ambitions on climate change, we can present evidence of effective action within Scotland and argue directly for our European neighbours and other developed nations to share Scotland's ambition of reducing greenhouse gas emissions. We can also show that other nations can share the economic benefits of making an early transition to a low carbon economy.

With experience of addressing global issues such as: climate change; restoring natural habitats; improving the quality of rivers and lochs; managing fragile marine areas; and minimising waste, Scotland has an important global contribution to make.

The choices open to us

An independent Scotland will have its own voice among important international institutions like the United Nations, the EU and EU energy forums, supporting further EU climate and energy targets to 2030. This Government supports a legally-binding EU greenhouse gas emissions reduction target for 2030 and reform of the EU Emissions Trading System to deliver greater pre-2020 ambition to cut emissions.

With independence, Scotland will be able to negotiate fairer EU funding allocations for rural development, with some of these funds targeted for environmental protection and accelerated delivery of our commitments on reducing greenhouse gas emissions.

Our priorities for action

If we form the government of an independent Scotland we will:

- **seek to enshrine environmental protection in the constitution.** With independence we will have the opportunity to enshrine protection of our environment in the proposed written constitution for Scotland

- **show international leadership in tackling climate change.** An independent Scotland will champion tackling climate change in international forums including the UN and the EU – encouraging and supporting others to share Scotland's ambition

- **negotiate increased European funding for environmental protection.** This Government will seek a better deal on Pillar 2 of the Common Agricultural Policy in the next CAP negotiations, allowing increased funding for environmental protection and emissions reduction measures

Scotland's energy market

Why we need a new approach
The operation of our energy market and its regulation is currently the responsibility of Westminster. Over many years, successive Westminster governments have lacked a coherent approach to energy. In a country of Scotland's energy wealth, it is unacceptable that consumers now face rising prices, increased fuel poverty and the risk that our renewable energy ambitions are not fulfilled.

A well-functioning energy market, delivering the best outcome for consumers in the long-term, is a prerequisite for a flourishing economy and society. By this standard, Westminster has failed.

SCOTLAND ALREADY GENERATES 1/3 OF ITS ELECTRICITY NEEDS FROM RENEWABLES AND IS WORLD LEADER IN THE FAST GROWING GREEN TECHNOLOGY SECTOR

SOURCE: DEPARTMENT OF ENERGY AND CLIMATE CHANGE

Underinvestment in energy generation over decades has led to a looming security of supply crisis. Spare generating capacity throughout the UK is now at its lowest level for a generation, and Ofgem forecasts that it will contract even further[326].

The Westminster Government's proposals to reform the electricity market are intended to address these concerns, but they present major risks. Scotland's ability to provide for our own long-term energy requirements may be compromised – and our status as a provider of reliable supplies to the rest of the UK is now endangered.

This situation should not have transpired. Scotland's substantial energy resources and balanced generation mix can provide secure long-term supplies of energy at home and substantial cross-border exports, helping to maintain a comfortable generating capacity margin throughout the GB grid. Scotland's surplus energy can help to prevent energy shortages and price spikes across these islands.

The Scotland we can create

Scotland is already a net exporter of electricity, with huge recent growth in the deployment of renewable generation. Between January 2010 and April 2013, industry has announced £13.1 billion of investment with an associated 9,100 jobs[327]. Currently, more wave and tidal power devices are being tested in the waters off Scotland than in any other country in the world, with Europe's largest tidal array having recently been consented in the Pentland Firth.

Independence for Scotland is the opportunity to maximise the benefits of our energy wealth, including:

- enhancing security of supply for Scottish consumers

- promoting decarbonisation of electricity generation, supporting Scotland's climate change ambitions, maintaining Scotland's non-nuclear stance, and delivering greater long-term stability in energy prices for consumers

- growing a thriving Scottish energy sector, specialising in areas of competitive advantage and creating new jobs

- tackling fuel poverty in Scotland more effectively, addressing the specific needs of Scottish consumers

- developing new models of community ownership and community benefit from energy generation and delivering real community empowerment

The choices open to us

Achieving security of supply for Scottish consumers will be the central priority for an independent Scotland. This Government proposes that, provided this is not jeopardised, Scotland will continue to participate in the GB-wide market for electricity and gas, reflecting the integrated transmission networks between Scotland and the rest of the UK. There is a common interest in sharing our energy resources with our neighbours: Scotland can continue to provide safe and secure supplies of electricity and gas and can assist the rest of the UK in meeting its renewable energy targets. Our continued participation in a single GB-wide energy market is also in line with the trend for increasing integration of energy markets across Europe.

However, as a substantial supplier to the rest of the UK, an independent Scotland will require a far greater degree of oversight of the market arrangements for energy and firmer safeguards over Scottish energy security. The Scottish Government plans to establish an Energy Partnership with the Westminster Government, ensuring that we jointly steer the approach to the energy market and that Scotland's long-term interests are better served. An independent Scotland can ensure that there are market incentives to deliver a mix of generation, as set out in the *Scottish Government's Electricity Generation Policy Statement*[328], combining renewable and thermal forms of generation. Through this partnership, the Scottish Government will ensure that new investment in Scottish generation is not compromised by the Westminster Government's proposals to overhaul the structure of the electricity market and enter into expensive, long-term contracts for new nuclear generation.

Under these proposals, the current market trading arrangements for electricity and gas will continue, with the aim of maintaining a competitive market for energy throughout these islands. This meets the legitimate expectation of consumers, suppliers and generators of energy across Scotland and the rest of the UK.

This Government proposes that a single Transmission Operator will continue to balance supply and demand across Scotland and the rest of the UK.

Following independence, Scottish renewable energy will continue to represent the most cost-effective means for the rest of the UK to meet its renewable ambitions. The continuation of a system of shared support for renewables and capital costs of transmission among consumers in Scotland and the rest of the UK is a reasonable consideration for meeting the UK's ongoing green commitments. Regardless of its source, Scottish generation is now essential to ensuring the lights stay on across these islands: without Scottish generation and Scottish renewable energy, the spare capacity margin across the GB grid would already be in negative figures.

The characteristics of Scotland's energy generation, supply and use are unique in their geography and peripheral nature – requiring a distinctive regulatory regime. An independent Scotland will designate a new independent National Regulatory

Authority for Energy, operating in co-operation with the electricity and gas market regulator in the rest of the UK. This model of regulatory co-operation is in line with the increasing levels of co-operation throughout Europe.

An independent Scotland will be an important voice in EU institutions in support of greater levels of integration and interconnection. This will require stronger representation in Europe.

With independence, control of offshore licensing and leases will create new opportunities to deliver community benefits from offshore development while giving due regard to the diverse marine environment.

Our priorities for action

Energy bills

Recent energy price increases highlight more than ever the need to use all the powers available to us to help people with their energy bills. An independent Scotland will be free to design a new means of funding and delivering energy efficiency improvements to Scottish homes that is fairer and better suited to our needs.

The current Westminster scheme to address fuel poverty and improve energy efficiency is operated through energy companies. The costs of programmes like the Energy Company Obligation (ECO) and Warm Homes Discount are met by householders through their energy bills irrespective of income.

We plan to transfer responsibility for these measures from energy companies to the Scottish Government – and to meet the costs from central resources. By passing on these cost reductions to their consumers, energy companies will be able to reduce bills by around five per cent, or approximately £70 every year.

This change will be made at an appropriate point to ensure continuity of work for Scottish businesses in the energy efficiency provider sector and for households and landlords arranging for improvement works.

Under these proposals, we will retain the statutory target to eradicate fuel poverty. The reduction of emissions from housing would also continue to play a key role in meeting our climate change targets.

This Scottish Government will also continue the overall levels of support for ECO and the Warm Homes Discount.

The urgent need to reduce the cost of energy for consumers is now an active area of debate and discussion. The Scottish Government will remain responsive to any further proposals that may emerge from Westminster over the coming months.

Energy Regulation

Regulation of energy was considered in the Scottish Government's paper *Economic and Competition Regulation in an Independent Scotland*[329]. Following independence, this Government plans to simplify the regulatory landscape to one that is more appropriate for a country of Scotland's size, bringing together economic regulatory functions in the vital sectors of communications, energy, transport, and water into one combined economic regulator. Consumers will benefit from having a more powerful regulator acting on their behalf, with strong powers to ensure that markets are working efficiently in Scotland. Industry will benefit from dealing with fewer regulatory bodies and from greater stability and consistency in regulatory decisions.

The energy arm of the Scottish regulator could, in principle, be based at the Scottish offices of Ofgem. It will work in partnership with the energy regulator in England and Wales in a model of shared regulation of the integrated GB-wide market. The Scottish Government's Expert Commission on Energy Regulation[330] is currently assessing evidence on models of co-operation between regulators and national governments under these arrangements – it will report to the Scottish Government in spring 2014.

Under the Government's proposals, the Scottish regulator will ensure that the regulation of energy delivers reliable supply, a fair outcome for Scottish consumers, the continued decarbonisation of energy generation, and the conditions for the continued sustainable growth of the energy industry in Scotland. This model rests upon open and competitive energy markets, and the adequate supply of energy to meet demand and deliver a comfortable capacity margin.

Renewable energy and reducing energy demand

Scotland's energy future, in common with the rest of the world, lies in renewable energy. It is the responsibility of countries that have benefited from the production of hydrocarbons to lead the way in investing in a low carbon future. In the long term, renewable energy represents a safer, more cost-effective means of electricity generation than the expensive nuclear plants that the Westminster Government favours. The transition to renewable energy reduces our dependence on carbon-intensive fuels, and brings long-term stability to energy prices for consumers.

As part of the planned Energy Partnership, the Scottish and Westminster Governments will have a shared objective to increase the deployment of renewable generation, requiring the continued support of consumers throughout these islands, as renewable energy competes with more established, higher carbon, forms of generation. The planned continuation of a GB-wide market will ensure that Scotland's renewable energy resources continue to support the low carbon ambitions of the rest of the UK – supplied at the cost-effective prices that Scottish renewables can offer.

Following independence, this Government will also introduce a leasing system for offshore and foreshore renewables, designed to increase investment and production while benefiting local communities, particularly in our island areas, replacing the Crown Estate Commissioners. We will continue to support research and development on renewables and low carbon technologies.

Measures on energy production will be complemented by incentives for greater energy efficiency, through minimising energy demand and reducing energy bills, and through water efficiency, material and resource efficiency, reducing wastes and increasing productivity.

Oil and gas

Why we need a new approach

Successive Westminster Governments have failed to provide effective stewardship of Scotland's oil and gas resources. Operators place a premium on operating under a stable and predictable tax regime so that the post-tax returns from investments can be appropriately evaluated. In recent years, the UK North Sea fiscal regime has not provided this certainty, and investment in the oil and gas sector has suffered. Over the past decade there have been 16 substantive changes to the fiscal regime. These frequent changes, often without prior consultation, have earned the UK a reputation for fiscal instability, inhibiting new investment, decreasing the life-span of some fields and damaging the Scottish economy.

Sir Ian Wood commented on the issue of fiscal instability within the interim report to his *UKCS Maximising Recovery Review*, saying that "clear views were expressed that fiscal instability has been a significant factor in basin under-performance". We welcome this report, which also makes clear that the current structure of having the regulatory body situated within the Department for Energy and Climate Change, is "no longer adequate to meet the challenges of managing an increasingly complex basin". The evidence gathered by Sir Ian showed unanimously that the existing regulator is "significantly under-resourced and under-powered"[331].

The Westminster Government has also cut funding and staffing for the Coastguard, an essential public service which helps to protect those who work offshore.

Westminster governments have also failed to re-invest the proceeds of the North Sea to provide a long-term benefit to future generations. Stabilisation funds and sovereign wealth funds are common among oil and gas producing countries, with the UK being a notable exception[332]. Norway's oil fund, for example, was established in 1990 and is now worth around £470 billion, equivalent to £90,000 per head in Norway, making it the largest sovereign wealth fund in the world. In contrast, successive Westminster governments have accumulated debts which are now worth in excess of £1 trillion.

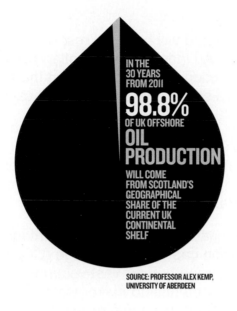

IN THE
30 YEARS
FROM 2011
98.8%
OF UK OFFSHORE
**OIL
PRODUCTION**
WILL COME
FROM SCOTLAND'S
GEOGRAPHICAL
SHARE OF THE
CURRENT UK
CONTINENTAL
SHELF

SOURCE: PROFESSOR ALEX KEMP,
UNIVERSITY OF ABERDEEN

The Scotland we can create
The oil and gas sector has been a major part of the economy of Scotland since the 1970s. Oil and gas production is estimated to have contributed around £22 billion to Scottish GDP in 2012[333]. Through the success of the last five decades, Aberdeen has become an international oil and gas centre of excellence, home to an industry that is leading the world in many areas, supported by strong academic research in Scotland's universities. In 2013, oil and gas was the largest single sector in the FTSE 100 Index of leading companies[334], and a sector in which Scottish firms are leading global players.

Scotland now has a second opportunity to steward our oil and gas assets for the benefit of the nation, as well as supporting the growth of an industry that in many areas is the best in the world.

Overall, Scotland has the vast bulk of the UK's offshore oil and gas reserves, which are estimated to have a wholesale value of £1.5 trillion. Record investment in 2013 points to a bright and lengthy future for oil and gas production in Scotland. As well as the substantial reserves in the North Sea, there are now major developments taking place to the west of Scotland, especially west of Shetland[335]. Scotland is estimated to have the largest conventional oil reserves in the EU – around 60 per cent of the EU total. Scotland is also estimated to have the second largest volume of proven gas reserves in the EU after the Netherlands[336].

For the sake of future generations living and bringing up their families in Scotland, we must not lose out on the opportunity that these remaining reserves provide.

The choices open to us

With independence, Scotland will have full responsibility for our oil and gas reserves. An independent Scotland will aim to maximise the safe production of oil and gas from the fields off Scotland's shores, with a stable and predictable fiscal regime.

With independence, we can ensure that the huge wealth generated by Scotland's natural resources benefits all of our people. An independent Scotland could also use our position as a major hydrocarbon producer to drive the most ambitious low carbon economic transformation of any country.

Scotland also has many natural competitive advantages for the development of carbon capture and storage (CCS). The North Sea is a natural storage hub for vast volumes of carbon dioxide. There is also the potential to make use of the existing infrastructure from the oil and gas industry, and there are a range of commercial opportunities to capture carbon in the central belt of Scotland. Only independence provides Scotland with the autonomy to make the necessary strategic investments that will support the growth of CCS.

Our priorities for action

An Expert Commission has been established to consider an appropriate fiscal and regulatory regime for oil and gas in an independent Scotland. The Expert Commission is considering options for the implementation of the key principles set out in the Scottish Government's paper *Maximising the return from Oil and Gas in an Independent Scotland*[337]. The Expert Commission will publish its report in spring 2014.

The Scottish Government welcomes the contribution that Sir Ian Wood's interim report makes to the debate. Particularly welcome is the proposal to create a new regulator. This will provide the necessary skills, knowledge and authority to ensure that we maximise the potential of the wealth of resources remaining. The Scottish Government's Expert Commission will consider Sir Ian Wood's report in full.

Health and safety

Safety in the oil and gas industry is of paramount importance. The Scottish Government will work with all interested parties to ensure safety is further enhanced, building on the existing health and safety regime to develop a modern, rigorous and well-funded Scottish regime. This will include working with all agencies to ensure that safety remains the first priority for those who service the oil and gas industry. Increasingly, the spread of best practice on safety is itself an area of commercial growth. Scottish businesses lead in many aspects of safe practices worldwide – the Scottish approach to health and safety will enhance this export strength.

There will be a presumption in favour of adopting all existing aspects of current health and safety standards. Scotland will also have a well-resourced coastguard to protect and save lives.

Fiscal and regulatory certainty

The taxation regime for oil and gas extraction is an important factor in maximising investment and production. It is in Scotland's interests to develop an oil and gas tax regime that balances revenues, environmental objectives, and incentives for continued development and exploration.

With independence, this Government will develop a tax regime with three overarching aims:

- to support and incentivise production

- to provide long-term stability and certainty, including a commitment to formal consultation on future reforms

- to provide efficient fiscal incentives that encourage exploration and help maximise economic recovery rates

The Scottish fiscal regime will recognise factors central to offshore operations, including:

- exploration periods with long time-lags and significant up-front costs

- highly capital-intensive development requirements

- significant geological, technical and economic risks

- sophisticated business structures and specialised technology

- costs of decommissioning

Encouraging exploration activity will be a key objective. In Norway, for example, measures to reimburse the tax value of exploration costs for companies not in a tax-paying position have contributed to a substantial increase in the number of exploration licences awarded in Norwegian waters.

We have no plans to increase the overall tax burden on the industry on independence, and are clear that no changes will be made to the fiscal regime without consultation.

The current licensing and regulatory regimes in operation will continue, and existing energy licences will continue to be in force in an independent Scotland. This will provide operators and investors with certainty about the fiscal and regulatory regime on independence, whilst ensuring that the industry continues to make a fair and proper contribution to Scotland's public finances.

Decommissioning

The Scottish Government is committed to providing certainty and stability on the long-term treatment of decommissioning tax relief. It will continue to engage with the industry on future reforms.

Post-independence decommissioning relief will be provided in the manner and at the rate currently provided through the current fiscal regime.

Responsibility for decommissioning tax relief will be the subject of a negotiation between the Westminster and Scottish Governments. Successive Westminster governments have accrued around £300 billion in tax receipts (2012/13 prices) from oil and gas production. The Scottish Government will seek a commensurate contribution to meeting the costs of decommissioning from Westminster.

However, the outcome of these negotiations will have no impact on the value of relief received by operators. The

Scottish Government will also seek to maximise the economic benefits to Scotland of the decommissioning process, including maximising the substantial opportunities for our supply chain overseas.

Scottish Energy Fund

This Government will make the creation of a Scottish Energy Fund an early priority. If we form the government of an independent Scotland we will invest revenues from oil and gas production for two purposes:

- to provide investment for future generations from a natural resource that can only be extracted once

- to provide income that can smooth receipts from oil revenues, recognising that these vary from year to year (as all tax receipts do)

Stabilisation funds and sovereign wealth funds are common among oil and gas producing countries, with the UK being a notable exception. The Fiscal Commission's report on savings and stabilisation funds for Scotland[338] concluded that there is clear merit in Scotland establishing both a short-term stabilisation fund and a long-term savings fund on independence.

Immediately following independence, we will establish a stabilisation fund to manage year on year changes in oil and gas tax revenue. To embed the fund into the management of the public finances of an independent Scotland, we will plan Scotland's public finances and borrowing requirement on the basis of a cautious forecast for oil and gas revenue, transferring any surplus to the stabilisation fund, and withdrawing resources should out-turn oil and gas receipts come in below forecasts. The mechanisms for forecasting oil and gas revenue, and the role of the fund in managing public finances, will be transparent and credible and subject to independent scrutiny.

A long-term savings fund will invest a proportion of the wealth from Scottish oil and gas production in financial assets. The fund's operation will be a key factor in the management of Scottish public finances, helping to lock in a strategy of prudent financial management, and strengthening Scotland's credibility in international financial markets.

Investments into the savings fund will not require Scotland to be in budget surplus, but will be started once Scotland's overall budget deficit is reduced to below the level of long-run economic growth and when debt is on a downward trajectory. The Scottish Government proposes to start making modest investments into the savings fund when the Scottish economy has achieved this position. The Office of Budget Responsibility has forecast that the UK will reach this point around 2017/18.

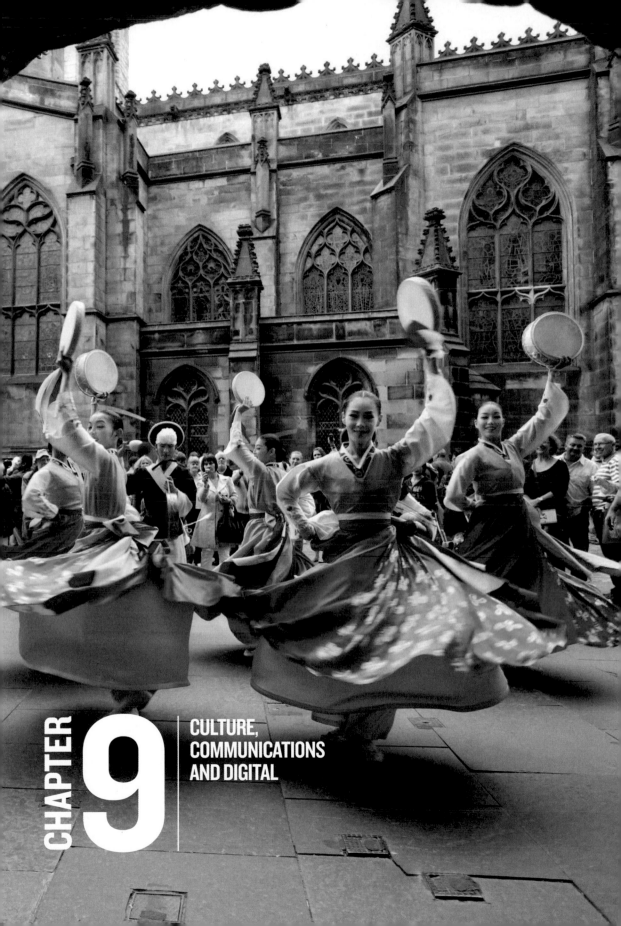

CHAPTER **9** CULTURE,
COMMUNICATIONS
AND DIGITAL

■ Under independence, this Government will promote and support culture and heritage, both for their intrinsic value and for the benefits they contribute to Scotland

■ Under our proposals, a Scottish Broadcasting Service, providing TV, radio and online services, will be established as a publicly funded public service broadcaster, working with the BBC in a joint venture

■ On independence, the licence fee will be the same as in the rest of the UK, and all current licence fee payment exemptions and concessions will be retained

■ Existing licences for broadcasters in Scotland will be fully honoured

■ If this Government is re-elected in 2016, the Royal Mail will be brought back into public ownership in Scotland, with a commitment to existing service levels including the Universal Service Obligation

■ In telecommunications policy, our approach will give greater priority to improving geographic coverage, particularly in remote rural areas

■ Under our plans, the National Lottery will continue in Scotland, with Camelot retaining its licence as operator

Why we need a new approach

Scotland's strong and vibrant culture is one of our most enduring and powerful national assets. Our rich heritage gives Scotland its sense of place and underpins our understanding of our past, our present and our future. Scotland's creative communities – our artists, writers, poets, dancers, directors, musicians and designers – provide new insights and drive forward new ideas. They help us see ourselves in new ways and present Scotland in its many dimensions to the wider world.

Culture and heritage are already the responsibility of the Scottish Parliament, and this Scottish Government has focused on promoting Scotland's culture, creative industries and historic environment at home and internationally. For example, we have sought to protect these sectors from the level of cuts made in England by Westminster. This Government does not measure the worth of culture and heritage solely in money – we value culture and heritage precisely because they embody our heart and soul, and our essence.

Under independence, Scotland's cultural strengths will be extended to other areas currently reserved to Westminster, including broadcasting. The BBC is one of the few bodies explicitly reserved in the Scotland Act 1998. However, despite the professionalism of BBC Scotland staff and management, survey evidence suggests that Scottish viewers and listeners register – at less than 50 per cent – the lowest level of satisfaction with BBC services recorded anywhere in the UK[339]. Evidence also suggests that people in Scotland want more Scottish programming alongside access to the best from the rest of the UK and the wider world[340].

Broadcasting is a critical part of our creative industries, a key economic sector that is growing rapidly. In 2012, UK television exports are estimated to have grown by 4 per cent compared to the previous year, to £1.224 billion[341]. It is an industry that provides skilled, well-paid employment with indirect benefits felt widely across our economy. The Scottish Government believes that much more can be achieved to boost the creative economy of Scotland.

Scotland currently stands far behind countries and regions of similar size in terms of the hours of original television production and employment by our national broadcaster. The Scottish Government has successfully pressed for increased production in Scotland: in particular, the share of BBC network production made in Scotland rose from 3 per cent in 2007 to 9 per cent in 2011, slipping slightly to 7.6 per cent in 2012. However, the money we contribute in licence fees should be doing more to service Scottish audiences, and to deliver jobs and opportunities here in Scotland for those involved in our creative sector and creative industries.

In 2011/12, BBC Scotland's total expenditure was just over £200 million on all of its activities, compared to a contribution to licence fee income of £320 million from Scotland. BBC spending in Scotland is likely to fall to around £175 million by 2016 through the 'Delivering Quality First' programme.

The creation of BBC Alba in 2008, and its availability on digital television since 2011, marked a step change in Gaelic broadcasting. Its weekly audience figures of 637,000 demonstrate an appeal considerably beyond the Gaelic-speaking community, showing the benefit of the Scottish Government's investment in the service[342].

In 2008, the Scottish Broadcasting Commission recommended the establishment of a Scottish Digital Network funded from licence fee resources. A greater level of Scottish public sector broadcasting would increase production in Scotland, reflect Scotland to itself, and increase plurality in publicly-funded public service broadcasting. The Westminster Government has not agreed to this proposal, and within the current constitutional settlement the Scottish Government has not been able to enhance Scottish public sector broadcasting.

Communications – telecommunications and mail services – are currently the responsibility of Westminster. As a result, the Westminster Government has gone ahead with plans to privatise the Royal Mail, despite the overwhelming opposition of Scotland's MPs and calls by the Scottish Government to postpone any sell-off until after the people of Scotland have had their say in next year's referendum. This Westminster decision poses a direct threat to postal services in Scotland.

We have also felt the impact of other decisions in communications policy that did not take account of Scotland's circumstances. When 3G mobile licences were auctioned in 2000, an initial coverage target of 80 per cent of the UK population was set. This was increased to 90 per cent of the UK population in December 2010. Despite the efforts of the Scottish Government, a distinct Scottish target was not set. Currently, 3G coverage in Scotland is the lowest of the four UK nations, reaching only 96 per cent on the most optimistic estimates. Furthermore, there is a disparity between urban and rural Scotland. Coverage in rural Scotland drops to as low as 92 per cent[343], demonstrating that there will always be poorer coverage in rural areas unless these areas are given priority in allocating licences.

An independent Scottish Government would have been able to do more to deliver improved coverage for people across Scotland.

The opportunities available to Scotland

Scotland's beauty, historic attractions and hospitality are famed across the world, and Scotland's commitment to our culture and heritage enjoys international recognition, notably from the United Nations Educational, Scientific and Cultural Organization (UNESCO)[344].

The inspiration and significance we draw from our culture and heritage, including Gaelic and Scots, are fundamental to shaping our communities and the places in which we live. Culture and heritage make our communities attractive places to live, work, invest and visit. They are powerful forces for both renewal and regeneration. Through their contribution to our social fabric, community cohesion and economic wellbeing, culture and the arts support better outcomes for healthier, safer and more resilient communities.

Scotland hosts more than 200 cultural festivals a year. The 2012 Global Culture Summit, held in Edinburgh and attended by 33 nations from across the world, demonstrated that Scotland can facilitate and shape international cultural dialogue. Scotland is home to five internationally celebrated World Heritage Sites. Sixty per cent of visitors to our best known attractions are from outside the UK. The Forth Bridge has been nominated as Scotland's sixth World Heritage Site, a tribute to Scotland's engineering and industrial legacy which is renowned around the world. Historic Scotland's "Scottish Ten" laser-scanning project[345] is promoting present-day Scottish heritage and technology on an international stage.

In 2014 Scotland will welcome the world for the Commonwealth Games, the Ryder Cup and the second year of Homecoming Scotland. Staging these major events demonstrates that Scotland is an international cultural and sporting centre and promotes our world-class facilities and attractions.

Scotland's culture and heritage also make a valuable contribution to our economic and social wellbeing. For example, in 2011 creative industries generated £2.8 billion in gross value added for Scotland's economy[346].

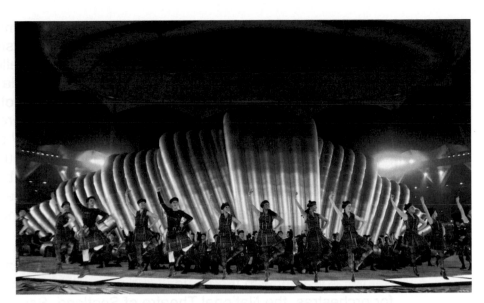

Our historic environment has been estimated to contribute £2.3 billion to our economy, supporting 60,000 jobs in the tourism and construction industries[347].

Scotland's 360 museums and galleries attract approximately 25 million visitors a year and generate approximately £80 million for our economy whilst sustaining more than 4,400 jobs[348]. A study of Edinburgh's festivals in 2011 showed that they contributed over a quarter of a billion pounds to Scotland's economy, supporting more than 5,000 jobs[349].

An independent Scotland will enable culture and heritage to flourish as a driver in our continued development and as an aspect of our everyday lives. The expression, celebration and development of our traditional and distinct Scottish culture will be given further impetus with independence. These strengths will also provide an independent Scotland with unique selling points as we look to promote Scotland internationally.

The Scotland we can create
The present Scottish Government has produced an ambitious cultural programme. We know that public funding of the arts is a fundamental good, and independence will provide the opportunity to take this to new heights. And with independence our cultural and creative life will flourish.

Independence will directly affect broadcasting, which is currently reserved to Westminster. The BBC's current charter runs to 31 December 2016, after the planned date for independence in March 2016. Channel 3 and Channel 5 licences are being renewed to 2025. The Channel 4 licence is also likely to be renewed to 2025 in the near future. As part of the Channel 4 renewal process, the Scottish Government is pressing for increased production from Scotland more in line with our population share.

Scotland's cultural life and heritage take many different forms, as diverse as the land, peoples and places of our country. Already they are being stimulated by the prospect of independence. As a nation we have the unique opportunity to build a society that nurtures and is nourished by songs, poems, stories, drama, dance, paintings and sculpture, and that welcomes people from all over the world to come, to inspire and to be inspired, to innovate and to create.

Our priorities for action

This Government's immediate priority for broadcasting on independence will be to develop a broadcasting policy for Scotland based on three principles:

- there should be an increase in production opportunities for Scottish producers, and an increase in productions that reflect life in Scotland and of Scots

- Scottish viewers and listeners should continue to have access to all their current channels

- there should be no additional cost to viewers and listeners as a consequence of independence

Existing arrangements will therefore form the starting point for broadcasting services in Scotland. The licence fee payable in Scotland at the point of independence will be the same as the licence fee payable in the rest of the UK. All current licence fee payment exemptions and concessions, including those for people aged over 75 and for people who are sight-impaired, will be retained.

This Government will also respect existing charters and licences to broadcast when Scotland becomes independent.

We believe that Scotland's publicly-funded public service broadcaster should strengthen our democracy and foster cultural production and participation. It should be a trusted, reliable, impartial source of information. It should reflect the diversity of the nation and our world to the people of Scotland, and should seek opportunities to collaborate beyond our borders to pioneer innovation in entertainment, education and journalism.

To deliver on these ambitions under independence, we plan to create a new public service broadcaster, the Scottish Broadcasting Service (SBS). The new broadcaster will initially be founded on the staff and assets of BBC Scotland, and will broadcast on TV, radio and online.

The SBS will offer a wide range of programming and content on TV, radio and online. It will reflect the variety of our nation in terms of geography, ethnicity, language, belief, lifestyle and taste. The SBS will be independent of government, impartial in its editorial view and given creative freedom in production. An expert panel will devise the SBS charter and propose governance arrangements to ensure that the SBS focuses on quality, serves the interests of the people of Scotland, and works in partnership with staff. These principles will subsequently be enshrined in legislation.

The SBS will inherit a proportionate share of the BBC's commercial ventures, including BBC Worldwide Ltd, BBC Studios and Productions Ltd and BBC News Ltd, and of their associated ongoing profits. Scotland's population share of those profits ranges from around £13 million to £19 million per year[353].

The SBS will receive licence fee revenue from Scotland, which is of the order of £320 million; £13 million from BBC commercial profits; and around £12 million from the Scottish Government for Gaelic broadcasting – a combined total for publicly-funded public service broadcasting in Scotland of £345 million. By comparison RTÉ in Ireland spends approximately £286 million on providing full TV, radio and online services. The level of funding for public service broadcasting in Scotland means that there will be no necessity for the SBS to raise revenue from advertising. In addition, as the BBC's spend in Scotland in 2016/17 is estimated to be only around £175 million, independence will mean almost doubling the level of public spending on public service broadcasting and production in Scotland.

The SBS will start broadcasting when the current BBC charter comes to an end on 31 December 2016. On TV, the SBS will begin with a new TV channel and take on the responsibility for BBC Alba. On radio, the SBS will begin with a new radio station in addition to taking on responsibility for Radio Scotland and Radio nan Gàidheal. The SBS will also provide online services, including a catch-up player and news website. Over time, the SBS will develop its services to reflect the broad interests and outlook of the people of Scotland.

Currently, BBC Scotland delivers a range of original programming for the BBC network. We propose that the SBS should enter into a new formal relationship with the BBC as a joint venture, where the SBS will continue to supply the BBC network with the same level of programming, in return for ongoing access to BBC services in Scotland[354]. Through this new relationship between the SBS and the BBC, existing BBC services will continue, with the SBS having the right to opt-out of BBC 1 and BBC 2 – when appropriate – as BBC Scotland can already. Current programming like *EastEnders*, *Doctor Who*, and *Strictly Come Dancing* and channels like CBeebies, will still be available in Scotland.

The SBS will continue to co-commission, co-produce and co-operate with the BBC network. The SBS will commission or produce a share of BBC network original productions reflecting the Scottish population share, in terms of both hours and spending. These arrangements will shift commissioning power and resources from the BBC to Scotland, while providing continuity for the BBC, consistent with its recent moves to decentralise from London.

The SBS will be encouraged to explore the opportunities with other broadcasters for co-production and co-commissioning, beyond the joint venture agreement with the BBC, to build on the strengths that the Scottish production sector has in comedy, drama, natural history and factual entertainment programming.

BBC charters are generally set for 10 years, with the new charter due to begin on 1 January 2017. SBS co-operation on this basis with the BBC will be predicated upon there being a Westminster government that shares our commitment to publicly-funded public service broadcasting. Should it become clear in the future, potentially after the 2015 UK General Election, that there is a risk to the licence fee at Westminster, then the Scottish Government would establish a contractual agreement with BBC Worldwide Ltd to secure continued access to BBC Services for the people of Scotland. BBC channels are already broadcast live in Ireland, the Netherlands and Switzerland through contractual arrangements with BBC Worldwide.

Channel 4 is also a public service broadcaster, similar to the BBC although on a much smaller scale, but it is funded from privately raised funds from commercial exploitation of assets, as well as from advertising and sponsorship. Channel 4 currently commissions around 3 per cent of its original output from Scotland[355]. Ofcom is currently consulting on Channel 4's quota of programmes produced outside England, with a proposal that the volume could increase over time to a minimum of 9 per cent of original production by 2020[356].

Although on independence Channel 4 will have a licence extending to the end of 2024, this Government will work to ensure that a structure is in place by 2016 that recognises the need for an appropriate minimum level of original production, in terms of both value and hours, that reflects Scotland's population size.

In Europe, there are examples of channels that operate across different countries, including those with public service obligations. For example, ARTE operates in Germany and France, with two shareholders, ARTE Deutschland and ARTE France, who each have a 50 per cent share of the group and provide 50 per cent of the content. One possible long-term model for Channel 4 might be a company part-owned by a Channel 4 Scotland which controls a shareholding proportion matching Scotland's population share, with the number of hours and proportion of spend also matching this level.

We will also encourage inward investment in film and television production in Scotland, and use our new overseas network to promote Scotland as a location for film and television production. We plan to continue the existing fiscal incentives for such production, and, within the first term of an independent Scottish parliament, we propose to look at ways to encourage further development in the sector, through incentives, infrastructural investment and support for development, skills and training.

Regulation of broadcasting is currently carried out by Ofcom, which also regulates telecommunications and postal services. The Scottish Government proposes that the economic regulatory functions of Ofcom should be included in a combined economic regulator[357]. Appropriate measures would also be put in place to recognise the cultural significance of broadcasting within Scotland's new regulatory arrangements. An independent Scotland will also co-operate with the rest of the UK on managing the spectrum, just as Ofcom and Ireland's ComReg co-operate at present.

The National Lottery

On independence the National Lottery will continue to operate in Scotland. People will still be able to play National Lottery games, and the infrastructure enabling them to do so will remain in place. At present the licence to run the National Lottery is held by Camelot Group plc, and is in place until 2023.

We will ensure that Scotland continues to receive our fair share of funding from the National Lottery. At present the Big Lottery Fund, **sport**scotland, Creative Scotland and the Heritage Lottery Fund distribute good cause money across Scotland. However, many decisions are still made at a UK-wide level. In an independent Scotland, all decisions about the distribution of good cause money will be made in Scotland to ensure that the needs of local communities are met.

Communications

The choices open to us

Independence provides the opportunity to deliver the Scottish Government's vision of a strong, stable and modern digital economy within a regulatory framework that meets best practice, delivering benefits for citizens, communities and the economy, and reducing the digital divide. Providing continuity of service to citizens, clarity for industry and stability for investment will also be a key aspect of the Scottish Government's approach to telecommunications policy in an independent Scotland.

Currently, telecommunications policy and regulation are reserved to the Westminster Government, and mobile and broadband initiatives are fragmented at a UK level. For example, the Westminster Government is currently delivering a number of programmes: a £530 million rural broadband fund (with a further £250 million on which they recently consulted); a £150 million super-connected cities fund; and a £150 million mobile infrastructure fund. All of these projects are being administered separately – they have different aims and objectives and are not fully aligned with each other. The overall investment made by Westminster is not being utilised to maximum impact. With independence, we will have the opportunity to direct these resources more effectively within Scotland to achieve good connectivity across Scotland.

In an independent Scotland, governments will have the ability to align policy, taxation and regulation to deliver a coherent overall approach, and design broadband and mobile initiatives more effectively and specifically targeted at the needs of Scotland. Independence would also provide the opportunity for the Scottish Government to look at options for bringing telecommunications and broadcasting regulation closer together to deliver a more integrated market.

Our priorities for action

The Scottish Government is already building the foundation for world-class digital infrastructure in Scotland. We are making a significant investment in the Step Change programme which will see investment of over £410 million, from a range of funding sources[358], to make available fixed fibre broadband to 85 per cent of Scottish properties by the end of 2015 and around 95 per cent by the end of 2017. This will significantly enhance digital connectivity and is essential for bridging the digital divide in coverage that exists today between urban and rural areas. Under our proposals, this initiative will continue after independence.

Future wireless and mobile technologies will also play a key role and have the potential to provide high-speed broadband to rural areas at a more affordable cost. Forthcoming spectrum releases, such as the 700 MHz band, could offer significant benefits for mobile broadband coverage, in particular in rural areas. After independence, our approach will be to ensure new spectrum licences in Scotland deliver maximum availability of mobile services throughout Scotland as a whole – not just our urban areas.

Roll-out of 3G in Scotland has been slow, particularly in comparison to European counterparts such as Sweden. 3G services were introduced in both the UK and Sweden in 2003. By 2004, coverage in Sweden was around 85 per cent[359] – while in Scotland, according to figures published by Ofcom[360], even by 2010 3G coverage was only at 66 per cent. Rural 3G coverage in Sweden today is 98 per cent, and 99 per cent overall[361].

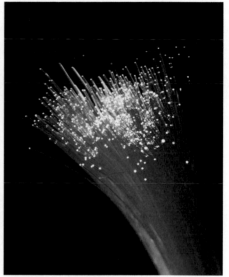

A recently published report from Ofcom states that outdoor 3G coverage in Scotland is at 96.6 per cent[362], but there is still a disparity between urban and rural areas, and these high figures do not reflect the reality of the user experience in rural areas. Recent research into mobile performance commissioned by the Scottish Government confirms that the user experience of 3G services across rural areas does not always reflect the headline coverage figures reported[363]. For example, research indicates that for the Highland Council region, around 84 per cent of the geographical area is without a 3G signal, compared to Ofcom data (using data underpinning Ofcom's 2013 UK infrastructure report[364]) which indicated that only 63.6 per cent is without a 3G signal. Other local authority areas with large discrepancies include Scottish Borders (58.5 per cent compared to 39.7 per cent) and Perth and Kinross (60.2 per cent compared to 42.6 per cent). Factors such as poor in-building coverage – even in urban locations – contribute to this finding as 3G signals typically revert to 2G when signals are poor, worsening the user experience.

The recent auction for 4G mobile services requires one licensee, Telefónica UK Ltd, to provide 95 per cent indoor coverage across Scotland, which is likely to provide 98-99 per cent outdoor coverage. However, parts of rural Scotland are still likely to endure poor 4G coverage. The target date for fulfilment of the 95 per cent Scottish coverage target is 2017, and it is likely that the more rural areas will be left to the end. In contrast, 4G coverage in Sweden is already at over 90 per cent.

It is clear that auction design is critical in countries with large geographical areas with sparse populations, to give consumers access to service and choice. The auction design and allocation of licences is currently outwith our control in Scotland.

With independence, we can learn from the regulatory and policy regimes of countries like Sweden to achieve greater coverage targets. We will explore the feasibility of setting higher obligations – such as at local authority level – as was our request during the 4G consultation process.

The optimum regulatory framework to support the delivery of world-class digital services is particularly important in the context of the geographical challenges faced by Scotland. This will be a priority for this government on independence. Regulation of telecommunications was considered in the Scottish Government's paper *Economic and Competition Regulation in an Independent Scotland*[365]. The paper recognises that it is vital that the design and delivery of regulation is effective and efficient, and meets the principles of better regulation: that it is simple, transparent, proportionate, consistent, accountable and targeted only where needed. It must generate confidence among investors and customers, and offer stability to the market, recognising the long-term investments that are made, and offering certainty to the market that investors will get return on their investment.

A Scottish telecommunications policy will be designed with these principles in mind, and will continue to comply with the responsibilities of all EU member states.

Providing continuity of service to citizens, clarity for industry and stability for investment is central to the Scottish Government's vision for telecommunications services. Telecommunications markets currently operate on a GB-wide basis, and will continue to do so. We will put in place arrangements consistent with EU rules to deliver continuity for regulation, telecommunications

infrastructure and services in the short-term. This will ensure a seamless transition to independence and will give confidence to customers and investors. Any changes to the current regulatory framework will be fully considered and discussed with stakeholders, and designed in the best interests of citizens, industry and the economy.

One specific issue that has been raised by the Westminster Government is roaming charges for mobile telephone users after independence[366]. Roaming charges are currently applied at the discretion of companies and up to specific European limits. The European Commission (EC) limits have already cut charges for voice calls, texts and internet access by 75 per cent since 2007.

There is no reason, in a competitive integrated market, for companies to frustrate customers on both sides of the border by introducing roaming charges after independence. The EC recently published an ambitious package for telecommunications market reform[367]. When approved, the proposals will ban incoming call charges while travelling in the EU from 1 July 2014, and abolish all other mobile roaming charges by 2016. There is therefore no question of mobile phone users in an independent Scotland facing such charges.

For similar reasons, there is also no question of calls from land-lines in Scotland to other parts of the UK being subject to international call rates, as the EC has also proposed to make international fixed-line calls the same price as domestic calls.

Postal Delivery Services and Royal Mail

Postal services are of great importance in Scotland. Over recent years, under successive Westminster governments, there has been a reduction in the number of post offices, increases in the price of postage, and high parcel delivery charges in rural areas.

On independence, responsibility for regulating postal services, such as the Royal Mail will transfer from Ofcom to a Scottish regulator. This will provide the opportunity to ensure a universal postal service is in place which suits Scotland's needs, in particular the needs of our remote and rural communities.

The EU requires postal deliveries and collections to be made five days per week in a member state. In an independent Scotland, there will be a service to match, as a minimum, the level of service provision inherited from the UK on independence, which is currently a six days per week service for mail.

Regulating postal services will also allow an independent Scottish government to take steps to address the high cost of parcel delivery in remote and rural areas.

Royal Mail

The Scottish Government and the majority of Scottish MPs at Westminster opposed the privatisation of the Royal Mail. The Royal Mail was a shared asset that belonged to all parts of the UK. The refusal of the Westminster Government to delay privatisation or to reconsider in light of Scotland's opposition to privatisation demonstrates the importance of Scotland having responsibility for services in Scotland.

A privatised Royal Mail threatens the quality of service and risks further increasing the price of postage. On independence, the Scottish Government will begin the process of renationalising the Royal Mail in Scotland. Our approach to renationalisation will be considered in the light of circumstances at the point of independence, including the prevailing structure of the Royal Mail. At present, the Royal Mail is predominantly in private ownership, with around 10 per cent owned by employees and around a third remaining in public ownership. Bringing the Royal Mail into public ownership will require negotiation with the UK on Scotland's share of the government stake, and establishing a new publicly-owned postal service in Scotland. Costs arising from this process will also require negotiations with Westminster, recognising that it proceeded with the sale of Royal Mail after the Scottish Government had made clear our intention to bring the mail service in an independent Scotland into public ownership.

Post Office
On independence, Scotland will inherit our share of the state-owned Post Office Ltd, which provides a range of services through crown offices and sub-postmasters. Westminster has been responsible for the separation of the post office network from Royal Mail, thereby risking the long-term future of post offices if Royal Mail chooses not to renew the inter-business agreement with Post Office Ltd once the current contract expires in 2022.

Sub-postmasters operate as independent businesses: many receive a subsidy to ensure a network of post offices in remote and rural locations. The Scottish Government has also invested in the post office network through the Post Office Diversification Fund and the Rural Rate Relief Scheme.

Independence will allow post office services to focus on what is best for communities and businesses across Scotland, including:

- greater use of post offices for delivery of government services, increasing footfall and income for sub-postmasters and providing improved and more efficient public services to individuals and communities

- redirecting resources within the Post Office to support local post offices which deliver frontline services, particularly in the context of post offices which are community hubs

- enhancing the link between a publicly owned Royal Mail and post offices in Scotland

PART 4

CHAPTER **10** | BUILDING
A MODERN
DEMOCRACY

- Independence will ensure that Scotland always gets the governments that the Scottish people elect

- Independence will enable Scotland to build a modern, European democracy, founded on a written constitution, enshrining the fundamental rights and values that underpin our society and based on the principle of the sovereignty of the people of Scotland

- The Scottish and Westminster Governments are already committed under the Edinburgh Agreement to work together constructively in light of the outcome of the referendum in the best interests of the people of Scotland and the rest of the UK

- Following a Yes vote, the Scottish Government will negotiate to ensure that Scotland can become an independent country within the EU, with a fair allocation of assets and liabilities between Scotland and the rest of the UK and arrangements to ensure public services continue to be delivered in the interests of the people of both countries

- We propose that Scotland's independence day should be on 24 March 2016. The first election in an independent Scotland will then take place on 5 May 2016

- Between the referendum and independence, we will put in place the initial constitutional platform for independence and the arrangements for the transfer of powers to Scotland

- The legislation on independence will place a duty on the Scottish Parliament elected in 2016 to establish a constitutional convention to prepare the permanent written constitution of Scotland

- An independent Scotland will safeguard and strengthen Scotland's equality and human rights framework, and maintain our existing strong commitment to the European Convention on Human Rights

- We will support greater subsidiarity and local decision-making and work with local councils to embed the position of local government within a written constitution

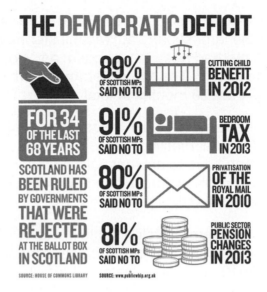

THE DEMOCRATIC DEFICIT

89% OF SCOTTISH MPs SAID NO TO — CUTTING CHILD BENEFIT IN 2012

91% OF SCOTTISH MPs SAID NO TO — BEDROOM TAX IN 2013

80% OF SCOTTISH MPs SAID NO TO — PRIVATISATION OF THE ROYAL MAIL IN 2010

81% OF SCOTTISH MPs SAID NO TO — PUBLIC SECTOR PENSION CHANGES IN 2013

FOR 34 OF THE LAST 68 YEARS SCOTLAND HAS BEEN RULED BY GOVERNMENTS **THAT WERE REJECTED** AT THE BALLOT BOX IN SCOTLAND

SOURCE: HOUSE OF COMMONS LIBRARY   SOURCE: www.publicwhip.org.uk

Why we need a new approach

The Scottish Government's vision is of a Scotland, fit for the 21st century and beyond, which is founded on the fundamental principles of equality and human rights and characterised by our economic success and social justice and the ability of our people to have control over the decisions which affect them: the opportunity for all Scotland's people to play a part in our future.

The Scottish Parliament, re-established in 1999, was the result of widespread dissatisfaction in Scotland at the "democratic deficit" – decisions being made for Scotland by successive Westminster Governments without popular support here. However devolution, for all its successes, has been only a partial solution to the democratic deficit. The responsibilities of the Scottish Parliament are limited and are decided by Westminster. They exclude key reserved powers, such as welfare, pensions, taxation, energy, international relations, the EU and defence.

With independence, Scotland will always get the governments we vote for. The trend of Scotland voting for one government and getting another has become more stark since 1945[368]. For 34 of the 68 years since 1945, Scotland has been ruled by governments that were elected by fewer than half of Scottish constituencies. Constituency results for Scotland rarely affect the outcome of UK General Elections. Indeed, in only two of the 18 elections since 1945 (October 1964 and February 1974) would the largest party at Westminster have been different if Scotland had been independent and not returned MPs to Westminster[369]. The two governments which were elected lasted for less than 26 months in total.

This means that Scottish votes play a limited role in the results of UK General Elections. To win elections at Westminster, the UK parties have to present policies that appeal to voters in other parts of the UK, where voting patterns now differ markedly from those in Scotland.

These long-term developments in voting patterns in Scotland have created an unstable and unsustainable political system. Since 2010, the Westminster Government has been led by the Conservative Party. That party has only one Scottish MP and won either none or only a single seat in the preceding three UK General Elections. Conservative and Conservative-led Westminster governments attract the support of a small minority in Scotland[370]. Nevertheless, those governments have responsibility for important areas of national and international policy for Scotland.

Independence for Scotland is the only solution that can eliminate this democratic deficit and remove these fundamental instabilities from the heart of the current political system in the UK. Only independence, completing the powers of the Scottish Parliament, can secure for Scotland the government and policy choices in reserved areas that the people of Scotland support.

With independence, Scotland will have the full range of responsibilities of a normal independent country and our parliament and government will receive their powers from the people. Independence will also enable Scotland to build a modern democracy.

A key responsibility of the first parliament of an independent Scotland will be to put in place a written constitution to underpin the democratic gains of independence. A written constitution will be a significant step forward for an independent Scotland. It will replace the central principle of the UK constitution – the absolute sovereignty of the Westminster Parliament – with the sovereignty of the people of Scotland, which has been the central principle in the Scottish constitutional tradition.

Is further devolution an alternative?

The devolution arrangements under the Scotland Act 1998 allow adjustments to the devolved powers of the Scottish Parliament. In practice, other than changes under the Scotland Act 2012[371] (which introduced a limited extension of the Parliament's responsibilities for taxation due to come into force over the next few years), only minor powers have been transferred to Scotland since the creation of the Scottish Parliament in 1999. Even when the 2012 Act powers are in force, the Parliament will be responsible for raising only 15 per cent of tax receipts in Scotland.

With the agreement of Westminster, devolution could be extended within the UK to cover all domestic and economic matters and to provide full fiscal responsibility for Scotland. This would mean that Scotland would collect our own taxes and make a payment to Westminster for common services such as defence. Such a system operates in the Basque country and Navarra in Spain.

However, all the indications are that the Westminster Government believes that further devolution of taxes should be strictly limited. It is also unlikely that any significant elements of the welfare system will be devolved. Without further devolution in these key areas, Scotland will not have the powers needed to grow our economy or to deliver a fair society that meets the aspirations of the Scottish people.

Even full devolution within the UK would leave important matters of foreign affairs in the hands of Westminster. In particular, Scotland would not have independent representation in the EU, and would be subject to the decision on the UK's membership of the EU taken across the UK as a whole in the referendum promised by the current Prime Minister. This could result in Scotland being taken out of the EU against the wishes of the people of Scotland and contrary to our interests.

Westminster would continue to take decisions on defence matters and Scotland would remain the base for the Trident nuclear weapon system and its successor.

Westminster would also maintain its claim of sovereignty over Scotland in all matters. Although by convention the Westminster Parliament does not legislate for matters that are the responsibility of the Scottish Parliament, it retains the ultimate power to do so and could unilaterally change the powers of the Scottish Parliament, or indeed abolish the Parliament entirely.

So under devolution Westminster decisions on reserved matters – welfare and tax – have a direct effect on wide areas of Scottish life and the Scottish Parliament's responsibilities. Westminster decisions on funding for England of services devolved to Scotland also have a direct impact on the Scottish budget through the Barnett funding formula.

The possibility of full devolution of economic and domestic matters is not on the table. It is not being offered by the Westminster Government or the main UK political parties.

Independence, in contrast, is guaranteed to deliver all the powers Scotland needs if we are to make the most of our potential as a nation. Only independence will ensure Scotland's international position and full membership of the EU. It is the only option that enables Scotland to be a full and equal partner on these islands. Only independence will remove the residual power of the Westminster Parliament to legislate in devolved matters.

The Scottish Government therefore believes that independence is the optimum model for the government of Scotland and the one that will best serve the interests of the people of Scotland. It is by far preferable to the range of devolution alternatives that might be proposed.

The Scotland we can create

An independent Scotland will recognise the importance of empowering our communities, valuing the diversity of talents, skills and contributions of our people and the importance of ensuring that all are treated with dignity and respect. Independence would enable us to harness all of Scotland's resources, voices and energy to meet our current challenges head on – working with creativity and resourcefulness to shape the kind of society and economy we want for Scotland. Devolution has only taken us so far.

An independent Scotland will build on existing, robust and well-established foundations to develop our governance and a modern participative democracy.

The Scottish Parliament and Scottish Government have demonstrated their competence to govern Scotland. Scotland's independent judiciary is based on a historical tradition that predates the Treaty of Union, as is Scotland's distinct legal system.

Scotland also has well-established institutions for other functions of state governance: the police, local authorities and an active civic society and media. The basic building blocks of the nation are therefore in place and, in many respects, we are the best placed of any nation in modern times for a move to independent statehood.

The creation of a written constitution will be an important development for Scotland. A written constitution is more than a legal document. It is a statement of intent for the nation. The process of coming together to develop, draft and approve such a document is an important part of defining the sort of nation we wish Scotland to be.

Only with independence will Scotland have this opportunity to modernise and guarantee our democracy and protect, promote and extend the rights of our people, embedding them in our constitution, law and policy.

The transition to independence

Our priorities for action
The Edinburgh Agreement[372] committed the Scottish and Westminster Governments to work together constructively in light of the outcome of the referendum in the best interests of the people of Scotland and the rest of the UK.

In the period between a vote for independence in the referendum on 18 September 2014 and independence day on 24 March 2016, agreements will be reached with the rest of the UK, represented by the Westminster Government, and with the EU and other international partners and organisations, on the issues set out in this guide. We are planning for independence in March 2016 to allow a realistic time for preparations and for the Scottish Parliament to take on the necessary powers.

The Scottish Government will enter this process in a spirit of constructive co-operation and friendship and will look to these agreements to provide the basis for a continuing close and fruitful relationship between Scotland and the rest of the UK, and to ensure the continued provision of services to the people of Scotland and the rest of the UK.

Constitutional platform for independence
Existing constitutional arrangements in Scotland will provide the basis for the transition to independent statehood, with additional powers transferred as soon as possible after the referendum, giving the Scottish Parliament the ability to declare independent statehood for Scotland in the name of the sovereign people of Scotland.

The key legislative steps towards independence will then be taken by the Scottish Parliament, following the initial transfer of responsibilities. As with the referendum, independence will be made in Scotland. Some parallel legislation, dealing with matters relating to the rest of the UK, will be taken forward at Westminster.

This early transfer will also enable the Scottish Parliament to extend the devolved competences of the Scottish Parliament and Scottish Government into all policy areas, including those currently reserved to Westminster, for the purpose of making preparations for independence.

The transitional period will also see the necessary foundations laid for Scotland's engagement with the international community. This will include the transition from membership of the EU as part of the UK to independent membership. It will also enable Scotland to move to a position of full participation in the

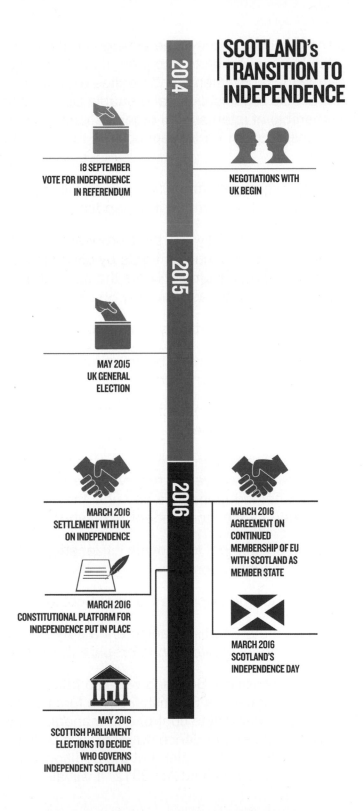

SCOTLAND's TRANSITION TO INDEPENDENCE

2014

18 SEPTEMBER
VOTE FOR INDEPENDENCE
IN REFERENDUM

NEGOTIATIONS WITH
UK BEGIN

2015

MAY 2015
UK GENERAL
ELECTION

2016

MARCH 2016
SETTLEMENT WITH UK
ON INDEPENDENCE

MARCH 2016
AGREEMENT ON
CONTINUED
MEMBERSHIP OF EU
WITH SCOTLAND AS
MEMBER STATE

MARCH 2016
CONSTITUTIONAL PLATFORM FOR
INDEPENDENCE PUT IN PLACE

MARCH 2016
SCOTLAND'S
INDEPENDENCE DAY

MAY 2016
SCOTTISH PARLIAMENT
ELECTIONS TO DECIDE
WHO GOVERNS
INDEPENDENT SCOTLAND

international community. The arrangements will provide for the continuing application to Scotland of multilateral and bilateral international agreements and treaties with other countries and international organisations and enable Scotland to negotiate membership of international organisations. This will include giving the Scottish Parliament powers to ratify international treaties.

Legislation during the transition period will put in place a constitutional platform for independence. It will:

- bring Scotland fully into the European mainstream on the protection of human rights by giving the European Convention on Human Rights the same legal force for reserved matters as it already has for devolved matters

- provide for the continuity of the monarchy in Scotland

- implement agreements between the Scottish and Westminster Governments

- provide for a transparent and democratic system for ratification of treaties

- provide for the "continuity of laws": all current laws, whether in currently devolved or reserved areas, will continue in force after independence day until they are specifically changed by the independent Scottish Parliament

- define entitlement to Scottish citizenship on independence day and subsequently

- provide for the Supreme Court of Scotland

- place on the Scottish Parliament a duty to establish a constitutional convention to prepare the written constitution

During the transition, Scotland will also take on the powers it needs to establish a Scottish finance function enabling the Scottish Government to control and manage Scotland's public finances from independence day. This will build on the work already under way to implement the additional fiscal powers devolved by the Scotland Act 2012. It will also ensure that an appropriate macroeconomic framework for an independent Scotland is agreed, put in place and ready to operate effectively from independence day, in line with advice from Scotland's Fiscal Commission[373].

The Scotland Act 1998 will also be updated to apply in the context of independence, so that the correct legal framework is in place for the Scottish Government and Parliament on independence day. The constitutional platform, along with the refreshed Scotland Act, will be the founding legislation of an independent Scotland and will not be subject to significant alteration pending the preparation of a permanent constitution by the constitutional convention.

Agreements and negotiations
Negotiations with the rest of the UK will cover a range of issues. These will include the arrangements for the Sterling Area (see Chapter 3), the role and governance arrangements of the Bank of England, a fiscal stability pact and Scotland's share of the UK's £1267 billion[374] of net assets. This would include physical assets in Scotland, such as Jobcentre Plus, DWP and HMRC offices, the Crown Estate and the defence estate. It will also include assets outside Scotland in which Scotland nevertheless has an interest as part of the UK, such as the overseas missions of the Foreign and Commonwealth Office.

Agreements will also cover other national assets and institutions (for example official reserves, the BBC and its archives, and UK and GB-wide systems for administering welfare and taxation, wherever located). Scotland's share of UK assets will be realised in a combination of ways – through physical assets, cash transfer and continued use of assets through shared service agreements.

Discussion will also cover the allocation of liabilities, including apportionment of the national debt, the current and future liabilities on public sector pensions, civil nuclear decommissioning and social security benefits.

In addition, agreement will be sought on issues including:

- the continued delivery of services across GB and the rest of the UK where this is in the interests of service users and the two governments, either for a transitional period or in the longer term

- operational agreements for cross-border services (for example, for health treatment, for intelligence sharing, for mutual aid between police forces and health services) based on existing arrangements where appropriate

- the position of staff in reserved areas of public service, including the options for those in the armed forces, the diplomatic service and home civil service. Transitional arrangements for these organisations and staff will be developed with the current employers and trade unions

- the transition and management of contracts for goods and services

At the beginning of such a process of negotiation, it will make sense to agree a process for resolving any disputes in a way that both governments see as fair and equitable. Some matters will also continue to be discussed following independence, as was the case in the dissolution of Czechoslovakia in 1992.

The outcome will be an overall agreement between the Westminster Government and the Scottish Government, ratified at both Westminster and Holyrood.

Agreements will also be reached in relation to the terms of Scotland's continuing membership of the EU, and membership of other international bodies, including the United Nations, NATO, the Organisation for Security and Co-operation in Europe, the International Monetary Fund, the World Bank Group and the World Trade Organisation. Both the Scottish and Westminster Governments will be involved in these negotiations with our international partners.

Preparations will be required for Scotland to inherit the bilateral treaty obligations to which it is currently party as part of the UK. Relevant treaties will be continued on independence (for example on extradition, double taxation and mutual aid). Through this process Scotland will maintain and build upon our bilateral relations with major overseas partners. In line with established procedures, the Scottish Government will notify the UN and other states of Scotland's intention to succeed to the UK's existing international treaties.

Benefits and costs of establishing an independent Scotland
The Scottish Government is already responsible for the delivery of many public services in Scotland. After independence, the remaining functions of government – some of which, such as benefits administration, are already located in Scotland – will also become the responsibility of the Scottish Government.

The transition to independence is a major opportunity to improve service delivery. It is an opportunity for Scotland to create more effective and efficient public services designed to meet the needs of Scotland's people. We will not simply replicate existing UK approaches, which may sometimes reflect the past more than current needs and opportunities.

Examples of the opportunities include:

- better, simpler systems for tax that will reduce future operating costs for government and reduce compliance costs for taxpayers

- more streamlined systems for paying welfare that will keep costs down and which are easy to understand and access by everyone who needs them

- better targeted overseas representation in places of particular importance to Scotland in terms of business opportunities

Independence is also an opportunity to invest in providing public services and employment based in Scotland. This investment will deliver a longer term economic gain, with roles previously paid for by Scottish taxpayers elsewhere in the UK being located in Scotland. Employment of public servants in Scotland will contribute to the Scottish economy, thus offsetting on a continuing basis any one-off costs from establishing new government functions on independence.

Key functions that will transfer include welfare policy and administration, defence, international representation and international development, citizenship, nationality and borders, and fiscal policy, including tax policy and administration. An important element of the move to independence will be planning and carrying out the transfer of these functions in a way that gives the Scottish Parliament and people control of key decisions as quickly as possible, ensures continuity of services to the public with maximum assurance, delivers efficiencies, and keeps any one-off costs for the transition to a minimum.

Negotiations with Westminster to agree the shared service delivery mechanism will provide continuity of services during the transition, and will clarify the continued roles for UK civil servants working in Scotland in these areas. Additional roles will be created in Scotland to deliver some of the new services.

The forecasts of Scotland's fiscal position provided in Part 2 of this guide already include a proportion of the costs of delivering UK-wide services in Scotland. These forecasts include an element for the costs to Scotland of, for example, running Her Majesty's Revenue Customs and the Department of Work and Pensions, the Armed Forces, and the costs of other UK departments like the Treasury and Foreign and Commonwealth Office. Scotland's taxes, of course, already contribute to the costs of running these programmes and have helped to pay for major projects and assets such as computer systems.

A number of factors will influence the size of the one-off investment that Scotland will make in the transition to independence. These include the negotiations that will take place between the two governments on apportioning assets and securing public services in Scotland and the options chosen for improving systems and providing more modern and responsive public services for people in Scotland over the period following independence.

It will be for the Scottish Government, under the scrutiny of the Scottish Parliament, to decide whether, and how quickly, to introduce new systems, and therefore the scale of these one-off costs and whether they are spread over a shorter or longer period. The investment in systems and processes will be a small proportion of an independent Scotland's total budget, and will be offset by decisions taken in Scotland to deliver future services or projects differently from the rest of the UK. This investment will secure for Scotland a modern and efficient system of government, as well as additional public sector employment which is currently paid for by us but delivered from elsewhere.

Transfer of assets
Following a vote for independence, the Scottish Government will negotiate with Westminster to agree a sharing of assets and liabilities that is fair, equitable and reflects Scottish needs and those of the rest of the UK. Assets already used to deliver devolved public services in Scotland, such as schools, hospitals and roads, would remain in Scottish hands. Physical assets located in Scotland and needed to deliver currently reserved services, such as defence bases and equipment, and buildings to support administration of welfare, tax and immigration, will transfer to the Scottish Government.

Defence and overseas assets transferred as part of these negotiations will form a basis for Scotland's defence forces and overseas representation following independence.

The negotiations will also agree how best to share assets such as bespoke IT software used to deliver reserved services. Scotland has shared the costs of the development of these systems and so it would be reasonable to expect that access to these systems would be available for the transition period as needed.

Assets located elsewhere in the UK will also have to be included in negotiations, as Scotland has contributed to their value over a long period of time. For physical assets like these, the equitable outcome may be to provide Scotland with an appropriate cash share of their value. On a similar basis Scotland would be entitled to a copy of software and other systems to run currently reserved services and functions.

Assets that are not related directly to particular services, such as the UK's public shareholdings in banks, will also be part of negotiations. Scotland would expect to receive a population share of these assets, or their value in cash.

In some cases, the transfer of reserved assets to Scotland might take place over a period of time – for example, where it is agreed that services would be shared for a transitional period – or the value of the asset might be offset against the share of the inherited UK national debt that Scotland agrees to finance.

Transfer of liabilities

Negotiations would also agree how to apportion liabilities. Again, equity would be a guiding principle in the negotiations. The biggest UK public liabilities include pensions for public sector employees, the costs of nuclear decommissioning, and the national debt.

The Scottish Government already meets the cost of most public service pensions (NHS staff, teachers, police and fire-fighters) in Scotland, and Scottish local authorities are responsible for the costs of the funded pension schemes of which their employees are members. These arrangements will continue and no changes will be required following independence.

The Scottish Government has set out how responsibility for meeting the future costs of public sector pension schemes currently administered by to the Westminster Government could be apportioned[375], based around which government each pension scheme member works for immediately after the date of independence. The same paper also proposes a simple and fair approach to apportioning responsibility for paying the state retirement pension, depending on country of residence at independence.

The Scottish Government will ensure that the costs of civil nuclear decommissioning in Scotland are met in future. Costs relating to nuclear decommissioning arising outside Scotland would be for the government of the rest of UK to meet. Costs which Scotland would be responsible for relate to the three civil nuclear installations in public ownership in Scotland. Meeting the costs of decommissioning the two operational civil nuclear sites in Scotland (Hunterston B and Torness) will be a matter for the owners, as now.

The national debt

The apportionment of the UK national debt – expected to peak at 86 per cent of UK GDP, almost £1.6 trillion, in 2016/17 – will be negotiated and agreed as part of the overall settlement on assets and liabilities.

The precise apportionment of national debt will be a matter for agreement. Under any realistic scenario, Scotland's projected share of the UK debt as a percentage of Scotland's GDP will be less than the debt of the rest of the UK expressed in the same terms.

The national debt could be apportioned by reference to the historical contribution made to the UK's public finances by Scotland. Using 1980 as the base year, Scotland's historical share of the UK national debt in 2016/17 is projected to be approximately £100 billion. This is equivalent to 55 per cent of Scottish GDP, compared to UK public sector net debt of £1.6 trillion (86 per cent of GDP) in 2016/17 (see Chapter 2).

Other methods for dividing responsibility for the national debts would produce different results. For example the Fiscal Commission's first report looked at an apportionment based on population. On this basis, Scotland's notional share of UK debt in 2016/17 is projected to be around £130 billion, equivalent to 75 per cent of GDP – still less than that of the UK total of £1.6 trillion (86 per cent of GDP).

The Scottish Government will service the share of the national debt allocated to Scotland. Scotland currently contributes to the servicing of the national debt through the taxes paid to the Treasury from people and businesses in Scotland. Scotland's overall fiscal position is currently healthier than the UK's, enabling us to meet the cost of debt servicing.

The Fiscal Commission looked in detail at options for transferring debt to Scotland[376]. Following that consideration, the Scottish Government does not envisage that a proportion of UK debt would be legally transferred to Scotland on independence, since this is likely to require the agreement of lenders and would introduce unnecessary complexity.

Instead, the Scottish Government envisages that the two governments, once Scotland's share of the UK debt has been set, will establish arrangements under which the servicing costs of this share is met by the Scottish Government.

The average maturity of UK debt at present is about 15 years. The longest dated UK debt is for 60 years. It will be for the governments to agree the maturity profile of UK debt so that the Scottish Government refinances our agreed share of the UK debt as it matures, based on the overall maturity profile of UK debt, as part of a planned programme of borrowing. Over time, therefore, the full amount of UK debt apportioned to Scotland will become the responsibility of the Scottish Government. At that point, Scotland will cease financing UK debt.

During this transitional period, the debt servicing costs payable by Scotland to the rest of the UK will reduce until the full amount of inherited debt is refinanced. From that point, Scotland will be responsible for managing all debt servicing costs directly, through interest payments to lenders.

Such a transitional process will provide continuity and certainty for lenders, and keep borrowing costs down for both governments. The process, including the amount of debt refinancing and associated timescales, will be planned and agreed in advance, allowing markets to satisfy themselves that it is transparent, predictable, well-ordered and low-risk.

Management of debt
To manage future debt and borrowing, Scotland will establish a debt management function. This will be an early priority following a vote for independence and Scotland will be operationally ready to borrow from the markets from independence day.

The debt management function will plan and undertake the management of the debt stock, refinancing of inherited debt, and the placing of new debt. This function is carried out at present for the UK as a whole by the UK Treasury's Debt Management Office (DMO). The Scottish Government will seek to establish links with the UK DMO, and also with other DMOs in the EU and among Commonwealth countries to assist in the set-up phase.

We will recruit skilled and experienced staff to ensure credibility in the sovereign bond markets. We will also develop an institutional framework for sovereign borrowing and establish relationships with market makers.

The Scottish debt management service will also operate a sub-lending function. At present, Scottish local authorities borrow from the Westminster Government's public works loan board. Following independence, borrowing facilities would instead be provided from within the Scottish debt management service.

Independent Scottish governments, like those of other countries, would have the option of borrowing from Scottish citizens and others through a Scottish national savings and investment function. However, with low rates of interest prevailing in the sovereign markets, this is unlikely to be an early priority. The government will be able to meet all of our borrowing requirements from sovereign debt markets.

Interest rates paid on new Scottish bonds will be determined by the markets, based on an assessment of risk, and the demand in the market for sovereign bonds. This assessment takes into account fundamental factors such as the degree of control that the borrowing government has habitually demonstrated over its borrowing, accuracy of economic and fiscal forecasts, liquidity, transparency and credibility of economic and fiscal plans, as well as key ratios such as that of debt stock to GDP and the annual deficit-to-GDP ratio and their future outlook. Markets also take account of credit agencies' ratings. The agencies themselves use the same broad indicators of credit-worthiness.

The Scottish Government is determined to sustain and build on Scotland's existing reputation for fiscal prudence so that Scottish bonds are seen as high quality, safe investments. The Scottish Government expects Scottish bonds to become firmly established as a low risk, gilt-edged investment backed by Scotland's substantial oil reserves and a stable, high-skilled economy trading successfully within the EU with few uncertainties. Borrowing costs should match the very low levels enjoyed by other comparable states such as Norway, Finland and Sweden.

Constitution, government and citizens

The choices open to us

Independence will enable Scotland to be a modern, democratic European country with independent government institutions that build on the existing Scottish Parliament, Scottish Government, autonomous legal system and independent judiciary. The Scottish Parliament and Government will be democratically accountable to the people of Scotland for the full range of government activity, removing the continuing democratic deficit which affects Scotland in areas currently the responsibility of Westminster.

Central to this will be a written constitution setting out and protecting the rights of the people of Scotland. The constitution of a country defines who makes decisions on behalf of its people and how the people choose those decision-makers and influence their decisions. A constitution is the basis of everyday life, not separate from it. It sets out the rights of citizens and the role of government. It defines how decisions are made about spending on health and welfare, about the laws of the land and about peace and war.

A written constitution should also set out the aspirations we have for our country and our vision for the future.

One of the first and most fundamental tasks of the parliament of an independent Scotland will be to establish the process for preparing Scotland's first written constitution through an open, participative and inclusive constitutional convention. A written constitution should be designed by the people of Scotland, for the people of Scotland.

The process by which Scotland adopts a written constitution is as important as its content. The process will ensure that it reflects the fundamental constitutional truth – that the people, rather than politicians or state institutions, are the sovereign authority in Scotland.

The pre-independence legislation will place on the Scottish Parliament a duty to convene an independent constitutional convention to debate and draft the written constitution.

A constitutional convention will ensure a participative and inclusive process where the people of Scotland, as well as politicians, civic society organisations, business interests, trade unions, local authorities and others, will have a direct role in shaping the constitution.

In taking this path, Scotland will be following in the footsteps of many other countries, not least the United States of America, whose constitutional convention in 1787 drafted the Constitution of the United States.

International best practice and the practical experience of other countries and territories should be considered and taken into account in advance of the determination of the process for the constitutional convention. In the last decade, citizen-led assemblies and constitutional conventions have been convened in British Columbia (2004), the Netherlands (2006), Ontario (2007) and Iceland (2010). Since 2012, Ireland has been holding a citizen-led constitutional convention to review various constitutional issues.

Our priorities for action

Many voices will contribute to the debate and help shape the content of Scotland's written constitution. Key equality and human rights principles, including the requirements of the

European Convention on Human Rights (ECHR), would be embedded in the written constitution. Beyond those there are certain provisions that the present Scottish Government will propose for consideration by the constitutional convention:

- equality of opportunity and entitlement to live free of discrimination and prejudice

- entitlement to public services and to a standard of living that, as a minimum, secures dignity and self-respect and provides the opportunity for people to realise their full potential both as individuals and as members of wider society

- protection of the environment and the sustainable use of Scotland's natural resources to embed Scotland's commitment to sustainable development and tackling climate change

- a ban on nuclear weapons being based in Scotland

- controls on the use of military force and a role for an independent Scottish Parliament in approving and monitoring its use

- the existence and status of local government

- rights in relation to healthcare, welfare and pensions

- children's rights

- rights concerning other social and economic matters, such as the right to education and a Youth Guarantee on employment, education or training

The Monarchy and the Crown

On independence Scotland will be a constitutional monarchy, continuing the Union of the Crowns that dates back to 1603, pre-dating the Union of the Parliaments by over one hundred years. The position of Her Majesty The Queen and head of state will form an intrinsic part of the constitutional platform in place for independence in 2016.

For two independent states to share the same monarch is not a novel or unique situation. Indeed amongst the 53 member States of the Commonwealth (including Australia, Canada, New Zealand and Jamaica) have the Queen as their Head of State – an independent Scotland will become the 17th member of that family of nations.

Earlier this year the rules on succession to the Crown were amended (for Scotland and elsewhere) to remove outdated gender discrimination[377]. An independent Scottish Government will promote, and support amongst the Commonwealth States with the Queen as Head of State, a similar measure to remove religious discrimination from the succession rules.

Parliament and Government
Scotland already has many of the institutions that a modern independent state requires: a parliament elected by the people, a government accountable to that parliament, an impartial civil service, an independent judiciary and an autonomous legal system. These institutions will continue on independence, underpinned by new constitutional arrangements reflecting Scotland's new constitutional status. They will be based on the sovereignty of the Scottish people, rather than the sovereignty of Westminster.

The existing Scottish Parliament and Scottish Government provide a robust framework for the governmental arrangements of an independent Scotland. The parliament and government structures have demonstrated since devolution in 1999 their competence in managing and delivering the necessary executive and legislative functions for Scotland in important devolved areas, such as health, education and justice.

On independence, the Scottish Government will acquire new responsibilities in currently reserved areas, especially the economy, welfare, defence and international relations. The Government has already developed the capacity to formulate policy in these areas, and this will continue in preparation for independence.

The Scottish Parliament
Scotland already has a modern, accessible parliament, elected on a proportional representation system. It will remain the parliament of an independent Scotland.

The Scottish Parliament has set an example within the UK on how a modern legislature should operate. In line with its founding principles of power sharing, accountability, access and participation, and equal opportunity, the Parliament has successfully put into practice the principles on which it was founded:

- the petitions system makes the Parliament accessible and improves accountability

- the legislative process gives civil society and individuals significant opportunities to participate before and during the formal Parliamentary processes

- parliamentary committees and, since 2008, the Scottish Cabinet take the process of government to all parts of the country – during the summer of 2013 alone, for example, the Cabinet has convened in Lerwick, Hawick, Campbeltown and Fraserburgh

■ participation and engagement is built into the work of government, parliament, local government and the wider public sector

Equality and human rights

The choices open to us

An independent Scotland will have at its heart the respect, protection and promotion of equality and human rights.

This will be enshrined in a written constitution to bind the institutions of the state and protect individuals and communities from abuses of power.

As a modern independent state, Scotland will play a full role by living up to our international obligations on equality and human rights and framing these through the constitution, legislation and policy as a basis for protecting rights, and securing fairness and equality for our people. It has been common in modern democratic states for equality and human rights to be treated as distinct and different spheres of concern by national governments, international institutions and civil society. While we recognise this, we also see the right to equality and protection from discrimination as integral parts of human rights in a modern society, and human rights as a fundamental part of a truly democratic state.

Scotland has a strong history in protecting the rights and freedoms of everyone living in our country and has used our limited powers to their maximum extent to promote a fair and more equal society. The European Convention on Human Rights is an intrinsic part of the Scotland Act 1998 and, since devolution, the promotion of equality has also framed the work of the Scottish Parliament, evident in the establishment of an Equal Opportunities Committee and across Scottish legislation.

While Scotland's current equality and human rights framework is strong, that framework's future cannot be guaranteed under current constitutional arrangements[378].

Our priorities for action

Safeguarding equality and human rights in a written constitution

On independence, all the rights and protections which people currently have under existing equality and human rights legislation will continue. In addition, we will seek to secure equality and human rights for everyone in society by embedding them in a written constitution.

As well as allowing us to ensure that the rights in the European Convention on Human Rights are enshrined in a written constitution, independence gives Scotland the ability to consider whether other rights, such as those in the United Nations Convention on the Rights of the Child, should also be enshrined.

The principles written into the constitution will form an integral part of the structure of the country and will shape the development of future Scottish policy and systems – including those areas Scotland will inherit under independence such as welfare, employment and taxation – to deliver greater equality and social justice. This could, for example, create new ways to help families strike the right balance between paid work and care for older or younger people and potentially encourage more women into the workforce.

Strengthening legislation, support and enforcement

From day one of an independent Scotland, equality and human rights legislation and infrastructure will continue to protect and promote equality and human rights for the benefit of Scotland's people.

Following independence, full powers also offer Scotland scope to consider strengthening or extending equality and human rights legislation and to develop an enforcement and promotion infrastructure which considers the appropriate alignment of equality and human rights. As a government we would develop any future changes in full consultation with the people of Scotland, including with the Third Sector, public authorities, businesses, trade unions and equality communities. Our approach would be designed to reflect internationally recognised principles which guarantee independence from government and provide the power and resources to operate effectively. Scotland has, and will continue to have, our own UN-accredited national human rights body.

Strengthening Scotland's influence on the international stage
This Government believes that human rights and protection from discrimination should not be restricted to those fortunate enough to live in Scotland or other progressive modern states.

Scotland currently meets the requirements of a range of international equality and human rights treaties[379]. On independence, Scotland will sign up as an independent country to these treaties and strengthen our international voice to shape the legislation and frameworks that flow from them, contributing to the wider goals of promoting international stability and democracy in other world regions.

An independent Scotland, as a full member of the international community of nations, could lead by example by demonstrating our own commitment to best practice in the fields of equality and human rights. In doing so, Scotland will be building on the strong foundations of work already being undertaken in fields such as international development and climate justice.

Equality in public life
Scotland has made significant advances in increasing the diversity of representation in public life, but many groups – such as women, disabled people and ethnic minorities – are still not participating fully in the decision making of our country. We are missing talent and perspectives across our institutions and

businesses. Increased diversity is good for business and good for the quality of decision-making.

The Scottish Government's ambition is that appointments for which we are responsible should broadly reflect the wider population. We will continue our work to improve representation for all groups, and maintain our focus on improving the gender balance of public boards within current legislation.

If in government in an independent Scotland we will ensure that Scotland's institutions have equality and diversity at the heart of their governance. We will expect public and private institutions to improve the diversity and gender balance of their governance. We will also consult on a target for women's representation on company and public boards and, if necessary, we will legislate as appropriate.

Better government – Scotland's public services

As a country, we place a high value on our public services. We recognise the power that they hold in transforming lives and communities, supporting economic development and well being, and opening up opportunities for us all to participate in the benefits that Scotland has to offer. However, there are currently pressures on our public services from economic circumstances, and there will be future pressures from the changing shape of our society.

Scotland has already adopted a distinctive approach in our public services, focused on improving outcomes and building the assets and resilience of people and communities, through prevention and early intervention. It values collaboration by those involved – by people and communities, Third Sector, public providers and businesses. Our approach crucially recognises the importance of designing services with, and for, the people they are there to serve, and of building on our strengths.

With independence, we can go further by joining together those services that are currently under UK control with those currently delivered by Scottish organisations. We can build on our strong record of valuing the public service workforce by creating good employment opportunities. We can explore new ways of working across public services that mean people get what they need in the way that best suits them – being creative and innovative and being shaped by the rights and principles we have placed at the heart of our constitution.

The present Scottish Government has made major reforms to public services in Scotland to protect front-line delivery in the face of Westminster cuts. For example, we have reduced the number of police forces while maintaining 1,000 extra officers. We have reduced bureaucracy by cutting the number of public bodies from 199 to 113, a reduction of 43 per cent[380]. Our proposals for UK public bodies on independence show how we can further streamline the public sector by integrating the functions of a large number of UK bodies into the public sector in Scotland.

The choices open to us

Independence will ensure that decisions about policies and services will be made in Scotland in line with the views and needs of the people of Scotland.

Scotland's scale is an advantage. The UK tax and welfare system is so big it has proven difficult to reform. The National Audit Office has found that there were significant problems in managing the implementation of Universal Credit. We can do things on a more manageable scale in Scotland. Stakeholders in Scotland tell us of the benefits of being able to get all the key decision-makers in one room. We will be able to do that in currently reserved areas too and improve policy and delivery through better engagement with service users and interest groups.

Existing devolved public services are spread broadly across Scotland. The largest public sector employers like the NHS, local authorities and Police Scotland already have a major presence in communities across Scotland – NHS Scotland employs 156,600 people; Scottish Local Government employs 247,900; and the Scottish police and fire and rescue services employ 30,200[381].

The Scottish Government has policy functions concentrated in Edinburgh and Glasgow, but delivery functions and public

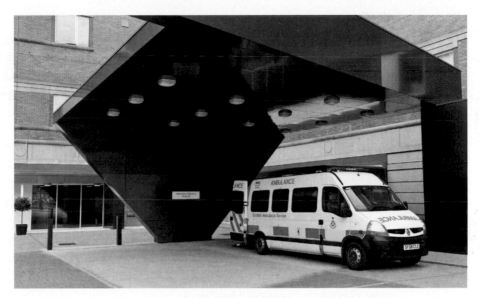

bodies have a much wider geographical footprint. Under independence Scotland can continue to spread the benefits of public sector employment as we take on new functions from Westminster Government bodies. We can improve services by joining up those that are currently under UK control with those delivered by the Scottish Government.

This will enable us to:

- focus the entire public sector in Scotland more clearly on delivering outcomes that matter for the people of Scotland

- further integrate public services and rationalise the complex public body landscape, ensuring that public services are delivered in a way that supports our overall approach to improving outcomes for people and communities in Scotland

- streamline the cluttered UK public sector landscape by incorporating the functions of a number of UK public bodies into existing Scottish bodies

- create high quality jobs in the Scottish Government and the wider public sector in Scotland that drive service improvement

- make faster progress in preventing problems arising rather than just treating them when they do occur

Public services on independence

On independence, the Scottish Government will take on responsibility for making decisions for Scotland across the full range of policy issues that affect people in Scotland. This means that the Scottish Parliament will control all areas of policy that are currently reserved to the Westminster.

In preparing for independence, the Scottish Government will build on Scotland's existing devolved public services. Scotland already has, as well as our own judicial system, an independent National Health Service, the Scottish police and fire and rescue services and local authorities with responsibilities for schools, transport, housing, leisure and social work services amongst others. There are also many Scottish public bodies such as Scottish Enterprise, the Scottish Environment Protection Agency and Scottish Natural Heritage.

On independence, the Scottish Government will maintain our current, unified structure and not create different, fragmented departments like those of the Westminster Government. This structure has been successful in delivering joined-up thinking and co-operation and provides a firm basis for taking on the full range of policy and functions of an independent national government.

On independence, Scotland will have:

- an independent fiscal policy function, making decisions on taxes and spending in Scotland

- an external affairs capability supporting an independent foreign policy, including distinct overseas representation and a Scottish international development function

- a welfare policy capability, meaning decisions about welfare and pensions can start to be made in Scotland

- a debt management function to support an independent fiscal regime

- a new security and intelligence agency, working closely with Police Scotland, focused on threats to Scotland like cyber crime

- an expanded Revenue Scotland, ready to progressively take on additional responsibilities for tax and excise collection/credits

- Scottish representation at the EU, NATO, the UN and a range of other international organisations

- a Scottish Defence Headquarters and an initial independent armed forces capability

- a new single economic regulator, the functions of which will be progressively expanded

- a shared service agreement with HM Passport Office

- a new Scottish Civil Service Commission

We will also move swiftly to begin the process of establishing a Scottish postal service in public ownership.

Around 300 public bodies currently act for Scotland at the UK level. As well as proposing new public bodies, we have developed proposals for sharing arrangements with the Westminster Government. In summary, our proposals on public bodies mean:

- around 60 per cent will transfer their functions to a new or existing body in Scotland either for independence day or after a transitional period

- around 30 per cent are proposed to continue to be based on a shared services approach, but with shared accountability to Scotland and the rest of the UK. Around 40 per cent of such bodies are small advisory or technical committees in highly specialised areas

- the remainder, almost 10 per cent of UK bodies with functions relating to Scotland, do not need to be replicated in Scotland (for a variety of reasons)

Development of public services after independence

The structure of public services under independence will be for future Scottish governments and parliaments to decide. The current Scottish Government's plans for the Parliamentary term beginning in May 2016 would be to:

- take on responsibility for administering benefits and the state pension, with staff transferring from the Westminster Government to the Scottish Government

- establish a citizen-focused personal tax system, with staff transferring from HMRC to provide the necessary skills and capacity within Revenue Scotland

- set up a Scottish Border and Migration Service

- establish a Scottish Passport Agency

- develop the Scottish Tribunal Service to include tribunals dealing with employment and other matters previously reserved to Westminster

- establish a new industrial relations body (similar to ACAS) and a Scottish Health and Safety body

We plan to maintain shared services in areas where it makes sense to do so, and where it is in the interests of both Scotland and the rest of the UK, such as:

- NHS Blood and Transplant

- the Royal Mint

- the Research Councils

- Air and Maritime Accidents Investigation

- some expert and technical advisory groups, for example the Committee on Radioactive Waste Management

- the Green Investment Bank

- the Hydrographic Office

Where functions continue on a shared services basis, there will need to be adjustments to the governance of these bodies to ensure there is appropriate accountability to the Scottish Government and Scottish Parliament. These can build on arrangements already in place for cross-border bodies dealing with devolved matters.

Workforce

Good quality public services require well-motivated and fairly rewarded workforces with a genuine sense of service to their community. Public sector employment brings economic benefits to Scotland, as well as providing the vital public services on which we all depend. The Scottish Government is therefore proud of our partnership working across public services which, in a period of sustained fiscal consolidation by the Westminster Government, has seen the employment of 1,000 extra police officers[382], 1,000 extra qualified nurses and midwives and over 1,500 additional doctors[383]. The Scottish Government has, in addition, opposed the Westminster Government's damaging reductions to pensions and conditions of service, and sustained a policy of no compulsory redundancies in central government and across the NHS in Scotland.

Under independence, responsibility for a wide range of currently reserved services and functions will be transferred to the Scottish Government. The Westminster Government employs nearly 30,000 civil servants in Scotland at present and many will transfer to the employment of the Scottish Government and its agencies[384]. An independent Scottish Government will also employ additional staff to deliver our new functions on matters such as taxation, defence and employment. Where it makes sense for Scotland, some services will continue to be delivered jointly with the rest of the UK, for either a time-limited period of transition or on a continuing basis.

The detail of these arrangements, including those for staff transfers, will be negotiated with the Westminster Government. We will work with the Westminster Government to preserve continuity of employment for all staff, either by transfer to the

Scottish Government or through continued employment by the Westminster Government, where it continues to require their skills. We will seek to ensure that all staff who wish to continue in service are able to do so. The pension entitlements and other terms and conditions of employment of civil servants transferring from the Westminster Government will be fully honoured. They will join a skilled and diverse workforce in the civil service in Scotland, based on the principles of honesty, integrity, objectivity and impartiality, committed to good employment practice and with a continued commitment to no compulsory redundancies.

Local government

The choices open to us

Independence gives us an opportunity to renew democracy at all levels in Scotland. Independence is about people and communities as much as it is about parliaments or governments. The extension of the powers of the Scottish Parliament through independence creates a new opportunity to consider the right level for decisions to be made across Scottish society and gives us the powers we need to deliver necessary reforms.

Local government is an integral and essential element of the overall good governance of Scotland. It assesses and responds to local circumstances and aspirations to deliver a range of services, from education and care to transport and planning, that form the bedrock of our society.

Scottish local government has benefited under devolution from a closer working relationship with central government. Local government has been equipped with stronger powers, adopted a new, more proportionate electoral system, has spearheaded the vital move towards community planning of local services and embraced an improved and performance-focused audit regime.

The Scottish Government and local government have worked in partnership to deal with and mitigate the actions of successive Westminster administrations – exemplified currently by the joint response to replacing Council Tax Benefit and wider welfare reforms. This sends a very powerful signal of the sort of partnership approach that we can develop as new powers come to Scotland after independence.

The Scottish Government and local authorities are now implementing and building on the legacy of the Christie Commission[385], to reform and improve Scotland's public services. This shared journey towards a vision of strengthened community planning, involvement and empowerment has been set out in the Government's response to the Christie Commission, in the joint Statement of Ambition with local government, and in our consultation on the forthcoming Community Empowerment Bill. This shared purpose will continue beyond the referendum and into an independent Scotland, capitalising on the benefits that independence brings.

Our priorities for action
On independence, the responsibilities and services of local government will continue as normal, as councils' statutory basis, funding, contracts and workforce will remain in place.

The Scottish Government will consider in partnership the appropriate responsibilities for local government and local communities, to realise strong local democracy, in line with the Lerwick Declaration[386] made by the First Minister on 25 July 2013:

We believe that the people who live and work in Scotland are best placed to make decisions about our future – the essence of self-determination. Therefore we support subsidiarity and local decision making.

For example, Scotland's island communities have challenges and opportunities that differ from those in other parts of the country. That is why the Scottish Government has established the Islands Areas Ministerial Working Group, to engage in discussions with Orkney, Shetland and Comhairle nan Eilean Siar about the opportunities that are important for our island communities in the context of the referendum and independence. We have committed to separate discussions for any issues of interest to mainland councils with islands. The Group is covering issues such as energy, the Crown Estate and transport. With independence, an Islands Bill to implement conclusions of this work will be one of the current Scottish Government's priorities for the Scottish Parliament elected in 2016. Similarly, we are working as part of the Scottish Cities Alliance, comprising the seven local authorities with cities within their boundaries, to consider how issues specific to Scotland's cities can be best tackled in the future.

Independence will also provide the platform to embed the role of Scottish local authorities in a written constitution. The Scottish Government will embed the position of local government in the constitutional platform and argue for Scotland's written constitution, post-independence, to recognise the status and rights of elected local government. Such constitutional recognition is normal in developed democracies such as Germany, Denmark and Sweden, and this should also be the case in a modern, independent Scotland.

A constitutional provision such as this would enable Scotland to fully implement an important aspect of the European Charter of Local Self-Government. That Charter commits states to applying basic rules guaranteeing political, administrative and financial independence of local authorities. In particular it provides that: "The principle of local self-government shall be recognised in domestic legislation, and, where practicable, in the constitution"[387].

Given the lack of a written constitution, the UK – or a devolved Scotland within the UK – would find it impossible to provide this degree of constitutional recognition to local government. However, in the context of independence this new opportunity for local government will open up.

Civic society and Third Sector

The choices open to us
At the heart of any modern democracy should be the strong voice of its people, influencing the decisions that affect them.

Scotland's civic society has always helped define who we are as a nation. Business philanthropists, churches, co-operatives and mutuals, trade unions, charities and many other organisations and individuals have contributed significantly to the Scotland we know today. Scotland's Third Sector and civic institutions are a valued and essential part of Scotland's distinctive infrastructure. They inform and shape our public life and contribute to the development of the Government's policies. Crucially, they bring the voices of communities into the public and political arena, providing diversity, richness and perspective to debates on the big issues facing Scotland. Civic groups and voluntary groups have been particularly important in shaping Scotland's approach to major issues such as violence against women, community ownership and shifting attitudes on matters such as same sex marriage and independent living for disabled people.

The current Scottish Government is committed to supporting the development of a capable, sustainable and enterprising Third Sector. The sector plays a key role in achieving the Government's purpose by supporting Scotland's communities and in the delivery of public services. The sector has specialist expertise, the ability to engage with vulnerable groups and individuals, and a flexible and innovative approach. With independence, the current Scottish Government's vision for the sector will not change – we want to continue to work with our Third Sector partners, ensuring that everyone in Scotland has a successful and fairer future.

Our priorities for action
The regulation of charities operating and/or registered in Scotland is already devolved. There are arrangements in place between the Office of the Scottish Charity Regulator (OSCR) and the Charity Commission to regulate and monitor charities registered in England and Wales but operating in Scotland. There is a memorandum of understanding that sets out the current operational arrangements for OSCR and the Charity Commission to work together to provide better regulation and guidance for charities that operate across England, Scotland and Wales. It will be in everyone's interests for this process to continue following independence.

Many charities currently operate cross-border in the UK and Ireland. Although responsibility for the legal framework surrounding charities is already devolved, income tax and corporation tax exemptions and reliefs for charities are reserved, along with legislation covering tax relief on Gift Aid, investment income, trading profits and Capital Gains Tax.

The Scottish Parliament in an independent Scotland will control both charity law and tax matters. This will enable future Scottish governments and parliaments to consider taxation policy that would enhance opportunities for charitable giving.

Civic society, and within that the Third Sector, also represent groups across our society, giving them special perspectives about the needs of our people. These perspectives will allow them to play a key part in developing Scotland's written constitution and the legislative and policy frameworks that will shape an independent Scotland.

The Third Sector must remain a key partner, playing a major role in our economy and in the design and delivery of public services. This Government will foster the creativity and innovation that exists within Scotland's communities to enable a thriving Third Sector, a positive environment for social enterprise and to value the work of volunteers, charities and community organisations.

Scotland leads internationally in our approach to social enterprise and is recognised for the strength of our Third Sector. With the responsibilities of independence – over welfare, taxation and the economy – we can do more to assist the sector's growth, effectiveness and sustainability.

PART 5

In the section that follows, we set out the answers to 650 questions about independence that have been asked of us.

Many of these questions have straightforward, factual answers. The answers to some others will depend on the outcome of negotiations with the Westminster Government, and here we set out what we consider to be the reasonable and common sense position, based on the interests of both the rest of the UK and of Scotland. Where the answer to a question depends on the policy decisions of a future government of an independent Scotland, we give the view of the current Scottish Government.

We expect you to find the answers to your questions here. However, if there is a question not covered, please visit www.scotreferendum.com/contact for details of how to submit your own question. We will then add your question and our answer to the Question and Answer section on the scotreferendum.com website.

1. **What is the benefit of independence?**
    The referendum is a choice between two futures for Scotland.
    We can choose independence, which will put Scotland's future
    in Scotland's hands, or we can leave big decisions on
    Scotland's economy and the future shape of our society in the
    hands of Westminster. We believe independence is the right
    choice for Scotland because it is better for you and your family
    if decisions about Scotland are taken by the people who care
    most about Scotland: the people who live and work here.

    Independence means that the decisions about Scotland that are
    currently taken by governments at Westminster – often by
    governments that have been rejected by the majority of people
    in Scotland – will be taken here instead.

    The ability to take such decisions in Scotland has a direct impact
    on your life and the life of your family. With independence,
    Scotland's Parliament will be able to make sure that Scotland's
    wealth works better for the people who live here, and will mean
    a better quality of life for people in Scotland.

    There is already good evidence that taking decisions in
    Scotland works. It is because the Scottish Parliament has
    power over the health service that the NHS in Scotland is not
    following the privatisation route favoured by Westminster, and
    it is because decisions on higher education are taken by the
    Scottish Government that students are not being charged
    £9,000 a year to go to university.

    But because Westminster still controls tax and social security
    policy in Scotland, people in Scotland are subject to the
    "bedroom tax" today, just as they were to the "poll tax" in
    the 1990s.

    It is also because Westminster makes decisions for Scotland
    that Scottish taxes will go towards the estimated £100 billion
    that a new nuclear weapons system will cost in its lifetime on
    the Clyde, that postal services are being privatised, and that the
    disabled and vulnerable are bearing the brunt of cuts to the
    welfare state. Not one of these decisions has been supported
    by the majority of people or politicians in Scotland.

If these powers transfer to Scotland, we will have a guarantee that – for the first time – decisions about taxes, social security, nuclear weapons and other key areas that affect life in Scotland will only be taken with the approval of a Parliament elected entirely by people in Scotland.

The ability to build a fairer and more prosperous Scotland will be in the hands of the people of Scotland.

2. **Why is becoming independent important?**
Independence means that Scotland's future will be in Scotland's hands. It means we can make more of Scotland's wealth, talent and resources for the benefit of the people who live in Scotland – through a stronger economy, more jobs, and people getting a fairer return for their hard work and efforts.

It will allow Scottish governments to do specific things like improve childcare, make the tax system fairer, cut energy bills and scrap the "bedroom tax".

Independence is about improving the quality of life for all people across Scotland. We will be able to take decisions on our economy designed for Scotland's particular needs and based on our own priorities.

Similar countries to Scotland have seen higher levels of economic growth over the past generation. That is because they have the bonus of being independent, and are able to make the right choices for their nation and economy. If Scotland had matched the levels of growth of these other independent nations, between 1977 and 2007, GDP per head in Scotland would now be 3.8 per cent higher, equivalent to an additional £900 per head.

3. **What will independence deliver for me?**

With independence, the Scottish Parliament will have all the powers we need in Scotland to make life better for the people who live here. The present Scottish Government's policies for an independent Scotland include:

- delivering a transformational change in childcare, so that every child from age one to starting school is guaranteed 30 hours of provision for 38 weeks of the year – this will reduce costs for families and improve support for people with children to return to work (see Chapter 5)

- reducing your energy bills by an average of five per cent, by removing the costs of some environmental schemes from your energy bill and funding them from central government resources (see Chapter 8)

- protecting your state pension, with stronger guarantees that the real value of your pension will not fall (see Chapter 4)

- ensuring that the minimum wage rises in line with inflation (see Chapter 3)

- protecting the value of benefits, tax allowances and tax credits by uprating these in line with inflation (see Chapter 3)

- building a fairer Scotland by halting the roll out of Universal Credit, scrapping the "bedroom tax", and halting some of the most damaging welfare changes being introduced by the Westminster (see Chapter 4)

4. **How will we become independent?**

Scotland will become independent if the people of Scotland vote Yes in the referendum on 18 September 2014. After a vote for independence, the Scottish Government will reach agreement with Westminster and the EU on arrangements for the transition to an independent Scotland, based on our proposed date of 24 March 2016. You can find out more about the transition to independence in Chapter 10.

The Economy

5. **Can Scotland afford to be independent?**
    Yes. Scotland is one of the wealthiest nations in the world. In terms of our total economic output per head we ranked eighth out of the 34 developed countries in the OECD in 2011. We raise more tax and our public finances have been stronger than the UK as a whole over the past 30 years.

    Despite all these strengths, many families in Scotland are struggling to make ends meet. We are a wealthy country and yet the full benefit of our vast wealth is not felt by the people who live and work here. With independence, we can make sure Scotland's wealth and resources work better for the people of Scotland. To find out more about Scotland's public finances see Chapter 2.

6. **How would being independent benefit Scotland's economy?**
    The Scottish Government believes that independence is the key to economic success. Scotland needs control over economic and fiscal powers to unlock our potential, boost growth and create sustainable, fairly-rewarded jobs.

    Full control of the most effective levers of growth – such as tax, welfare and regulation – will allow Scotland to develop policies designed to deliver sustainable economic growth.

    Scotland is already a wealthy nation, but the full benefit of that wealth is not felt by people across the country. With independence, we can turn our rich country into a prosperous society, with the many strengths of our economy delivering more for the people who live and work here.

7. **Will an independent Scotland continue to use the Bank of England?**
    Yes. The Bank of England is the central bank for Scotland, as well as for England, Wales and Northern Ireland. It was formally nationalised in 1946 and is therefore an institution and asset owned both by Scotland and the rest of the UK.

For day-to-day monetary policy, the Bank of England is operationally independent of government. It currently sets monetary policy according to the economic conditions across the UK as a whole. The Scottish Government supports the Fiscal Commission proposals that, after independence, monetary policy would be set by the Bank of England according to economic conditions across the entire Sterling Area and that the Bank should be accountable to both Scotland and the rest of the UK through a shareholder agreement.

Currency

8. **What currency will an independent Scotland use?**
We propose that the pound Sterling will continue to be the currency of an independent Scotland.

9. **Will Scotland join the Euro?**
No. The current Scottish Government is clear that Sterling should continue to be the currency of an independent Scotland.

10. **Will an independent Scotland have control over fiscal policy?**
With independence, Scotland will have full control over fiscal policy, with full powers on taxes, spending and borrowing. Currently, the Scottish Parliament is responsible for just 7 per cent of taxes raised in Scotland. Even with the new tax powers of the Scotland Act, this figure will only increase to around 15 per cent. Only with independence will Scotland have full control over 100 per cent of tax revenue and fiscal policy.

11. **Will an independent Scotland have control over monetary policy?**
Day-to-day monetary policy would be decided independently of government by the Bank of England as it is now, taking account of economic conditions across the Sterling Area. The Scottish Government would seek formal input into the governance and remit of the Bank of England.

12. **Why would an independent Scotland wish to remain in a currency union with the rest of the UK?**
A shared currency is in the economic interests of both Scotland and the rest of the UK, as key trading partners. It will make it easier for people and companies to go about their business across the two countries.

13. **How can Scotland be independent if we keep the pound?**
Independent countries around the world share currencies. Countries like France, Germany, and the Netherlands do not have their own currency but are independent, and control their own resources. This approach makes sense for Scotland and the rest of the UK, because it will make it easier for us to trade with each other and will also mean that things like our mortgages and pensions will continue to be paid in pounds and pence, just as they are today. To find out more about keeping the pound, see Chapter 3.

14. **What contribution would an independent Scotland make to the Sterling Area?**
Scotland is the second largest export market for the rest of the UK. It would be damaging to jobs in England, Wales and Northern Ireland, and to the economy of the rest of the UK, if Scotland did not continue to use the pound. It is estimated that the rest of the UK exported £59 billion to Scotland in 2012 – trade that supports tens of thousands of jobs elsewhere on these islands.

Continuing to share the pound with Scotland will also be beneficial for the value of Sterling. The Sterling Area's balance of payments will be supported by Scotland's broad range of assets and exports, including North Sea oil and gas. North Sea oil and gas production boosted the UK's balance of payments by £39 billion in 2012/13.

15. **What would happen to Scottish banknotes in a Sterling Area?**
Scottish banknotes will continue to be issued as at present.

Currently Scottish banknotes are issued by three authorised commercial banks in Scotland and are fully backed by Sterling balances held at the Bank of England – meaning they are recognised and accepted as being of equal value to Bank of England notes.

Fiscal Sustainability

16. **Is Scotland a prosperous country?**
Yes. An independent Scotland would be one of the top ten richest countries in the OECD – ranking eighth amonst the 34 member countries in terms of GDP per person, compared to the UK which would rank 17th.

The Scottish Government believes in independence because we want to turn this economic strength into tangible gains for individuals and families.

Five of the seven countries that would rank above Scotland in the OECD are small independent nations, such as Norway, with many similarities to Scotland. With the skills and natural resources at our disposal we have the potential to grow faster and in a more sustainable manner.

17. **What will Scotland's share of national debt be and how will it repay it?**
The UK national debt is expected to peak at 86 per cent of UK GDP, almost £1.6 trillion in 2016/17.

The national debt could be apportioned by reference to the historic contribution made to the UK's public finances by Scotland. Using 1980 as the base year, Scotland's historic share of the UK national debt in 2016/17 is projected to be approximately £100 billion. This is equivalent to 55 per cent of Scottish GDP.

Other methods for dividing responsibility for the national debts would produce different results. For example the Fiscal Commission's first report looked at an apportionment based on population. On this basis, Scotland's notional share of UK debt in 2016/17 is projected to be approximately £130 billion, equivalent to approximately 75 per cent of GDP – still less than the UK.

Under any realistic scenario, Scotland's projected share of the UK debt as a percentage of Scotland's GDP will be less than the debt of the rest of the UK expressed in the same terms.

18. **Would an independent Scotland increase national debt in an attempt to grow the economy?**
Independence will bring the important decisions about the economy – including responsible borrowing to fund growth – to the Scottish Government and Parliament. It will allow decisions to be made in the interests of the people of Scotland and be based on Scotland's strengths and opportunities.

The most effective way to reduce national debt is by increasing sustainable economic growth, a priority of the current Scottish Government. Further details of our proposed approach are outlined in Chapter 3.

19. **How important will North Sea oil revenues be to an independent Scotland?**
Scotland is endowed with significant oil and gas reserves. The tax revenues from these, which currently go to the UK Treasury, would remain in Scotland, generating significant tax revenues for Scotland.

But Scotland's economy is not dependent on oil and gas. Oil and gas revenue makes up a smaller part of Scotland's economy than is the case for other oil producing countries. For example, over the period 2000/01 to 2011/12, oil and gas revenues accounted for 15 per cent of Scotland's overall tax income, compared to 30 per cent for Norway.

Without offshore oil activity, GDP per person in Scotland is 99 per cent of the UK average (within the UK, only London and the South East have higher levels of GDP per capita). This rises to

about 120 per cent when a geographic share of North Sea
output is included.

The position is similar for tax receipts, with estimated onshore
tax receipts per person in Scotland broadly in line with the UK,
but £1,700 per person higher than the UK average with the
inclusion of offshore revenues.

20. **Will Scotland have a sovereign wealth fund?**
We propose that, and as recommended by the Fiscal
Commission, an independent Scotland should establish a
Scottish Energy Fund to stabilise revenues in the short-term
and to ensure that a proportion of oil and gas tax receipts are
invested for the long-term benefit of the people of Scotland.

The decisions of successive Westminster governments to
spend Scottish oil revenues rather than investing a proportion
of them represent a major lost opportunity. Norway began
transferring money into its oil fund in 1996. The fund is now
worth £470 billion, equivalent to around £90,000 per person in
Norway, and is the largest sovereign wealth fund in the world.

Analysis by the Fiscal Commission concluded that, had it used
its oil wealth to establish an oil fund in 1980, Scotland could
have eliminated its share of UK public sector net debt by
1982/83. By 2011/12 Scotland could have accumulated financial
assets of between £82 billion and £116 billion. That would be
equivalent to between 55 per cent and 78 per cent of GDP.

21. **Is Scotland's economy dependent on oil?**
Not at all. Scotland has a mixed and varied economy that
supports employment right across the country. Scotland's
economy is diverse, with key strengths across a range of
sectors such as food and drink, tourism, creative industries, life
sciences, universities, financial services and manufacturing.

Oil and gas revenue makes up a smaller part of Scotland's
economy than is the case for other oil producing countries.
For example, over the period 2000/01 to 2011/12, oil and gas
revenues accounted for 15 per cent of Scotland's overall tax
income, compared to 30 per cent for Norway.

Taxes and Taxation

22.   How would an independent Scotland use tax powers?
The UK tax system is one of the most complicated in the world. With independence Scotland will have the ability to develop a simpler tax system that is better suited to our economy.

With its current powers, the Scottish Parliament has frozen council tax and delivered the most competitive business rates in the UK. The current Scottish Government has already legislated to replace UK Stamp Duty Land Tax with a new and fairer Land and Buildings Transaction Tax and has made clear its intention to use the opportunities of independence to reduce Air Passenger Duty and Corporation Tax to boost the economy.

Independence will make the Scottish Parliament responsible for its own finances and will provide access to the key economic levers, including taxation, to give Scotland the opportunity to develop policies to stimulate the economy, sustain Scotland's public services and build social cohesion. Full details of our proposed approach are set out in Chapter 3.

23.   What will tax rates be in an independent Scotland?
On independence, Scotland will inherit the tax system and the prevailing UK rates and thresholds for all taxes. Decisions on specific taxes – including tax rates, allowances and credits – will be made by the Parliament and Government of an independent Scotland. For the first time ever there will be a guarantee that taxes will be set by a government that has the support of the people of Scotland.

Independence will provide the Scottish Government and Parliament with the powers to set tax rates and thresholds which are right for Scotland, allowing Scottish Ministers to develop policies that will deliver sustainable economic growth and a fair society.

24. **Would the current rates and thresholds for personal income tax be altered or would there be any significant changes in the rates of insurance premium tax, VAT or employers' National Insurance contributions?**

Detailed policies on tax and spending will be set out in party manifestos for the 2016 election and thereafter in the first budget in an independent Scotland. There is no requirement to increase the general rate of taxation to pay for the services we currently enjoy in Scotland.

The current Scottish Government's approach to tax is focused on fairness and economic growth. In Chapter 3 of this paper we set out our early priorities for taxation, were we to form the first government of an independent Scotland.

25. **How much tax does Scotland currently pay into the UK?**

In 2011/12, Scotland contributed £56.9 billion in tax revenue to the UK including a geographic share of North Sea oil. This is the equivalent of £10,700 per person and compares to £9,000 per person in the UK as a whole.

Scotland is estimated to have paid more tax than in the UK as a whole every year since 1980/81, averaging over £1,350 a year higher over that period when adjusted for inflation.

26. **Will the way I pay tax change if Scotland becomes independent?**

Initially on independence, you will continue to pay your tax and receive tax credits in the same way as you do now. Behind the scenes, we will be working to transition the administration of the tax system to Revenue Scotland, the Scottish tax authority, with a view to making the system simpler and more efficient for the taxpayer.

27. **How would an independent Scotland improve on the UK tax system?**

Independence will enable the Scottish Parliament to set all taxes in a way which stimulates economic growth, sustains the public services of Scotland and builds social cohesion. The design of a tax system will be decided by the elected Government and Parliament of an independent Scotland.

The Scottish Government is already reforming aspects of the Scottish taxation system with the new powers devolved by the Scotland Act 2012. This process has been informed by the knowledge and participation of a range of experts and representatives of civic Scotland. The current Scottish Government plans to follow this model of collaborative tax policy development to design a simpler Scottish tax system to replace the complex UK tax code.

28. **How will tax collection be improved in an independent Scotland?**

The opportunity to create a tax system that is less cumbersome and less open to avoidance is a benefit of independence. The Scottish Government is setting up a tax authority in Scotland, Revenue Scotland, which will provide the foundations for a tax administration system for all taxes in Scotland. Revenue Scotland will be collecting devolved taxes from April 2015.

There will be a transition phase after independence where, by agreement with HM Revenue & Customs, taxes would continue to be collected through existing HMRC systems. Scotland-specific arrangements will be put in place for the collection of all taxes in Scotland as quickly as possible.

Following independence we plan to build on the recommendations of the Fiscal Commission report on tax. These include deploying modern technologies, such as online filing. Over the course of the first independent Parliament, the Scottish Government and Revenue Scotland would work together to pursue opportunities for simplification of taxes and tax collection, with the aim of collecting up to £250 million a year of additional revenues, without increasing tax rates.

29. **How long will it take to set up a distinct Scottish tax system following independence?**
The Scottish Parliament will have formal legal responsibility for all taxes upon independence. The Scottish Government will make arrangements that will maximise its discretion over the tax system while HMRC continue to collect tax revenues for a transitional phase.

After the transition, Revenue Scotland will collect all taxes in Scotland. We plan that the collection system for personal taxes in Scotland will be in place within the first term of the Scottish Parliament in an independent Scotland.

We will maintain stability of collection for business taxes while we carry out fundamental work with businesses to implement a streamlined collection system.

30. **How much will it cost Scotland to run its own tax system?**
The UK tax system is complex and costly. It is widely accepted that there is considerable room for improvement in its design and operation.

Revenue Scotland, working with Registers of Scotland and the Scottish Environment Protection Agency, will set up the necessary administrative systems for Land and Buildings Transaction Tax and Scottish Landfill Tax and cover the basic cost of administration for the first five years of operation for £16.7 million. This is 25 per cent less than HMRC estimated for the cost of setting up and operating for five years in Scotland like-for-like equivalents of Stamp Duty Land Tax and UK Landfill Tax.

Building on that, we will create a tax system in Scotland that is simpler and costs less to administer than the current UK system.

31. **Will I pay more tax after independence?**
The process of becoming independent will not, in itself, change the tax you pay. There is no requirement to increase the general rate of taxation to pay for the services we currently enjoy in Scotland.

As is the case in any country, overall tax levels will be set by the government and parliament of the day in response to the needs of the economy and the public services that the Scottish people want.

32. How will taxes be administered for businesses with headquarters in Scotland but offices in England or elsewhere?

In the interconnected global economy many companies already operate across a number of different countries without difficulty. The Scottish Government has made clear its intention to ensure an independent Scotland remains an attractive and competitive place to do business.

The Scotland Act 2012 means that by 2016, whatever the result of the referendum, there will be differences between the tax systems in Scotland and the rest of the UK. Preparations are in hand to make sure that administration is as simple as possible for businesses in Scotland and elsewhere.

Following a vote for independence, the Scottish Government will seek a double taxation agreement with the Westminster Government. It will be in the interests of both Scotland and the rest of the UK to ensure that cross-border tax affairs for companies and individuals operating in both jurisdictions are as fair and simple as possible.

33. Will Scottish taxpayers with overseas interests continue to be protected from double taxation after independence?

Yes. The Scottish Government is committed to a tax system that will ensure fairness for cross-border taxpayers, including those due to pay tax in both Scotland and the rest of the United Kingdom.

An independent Scotland will signal its intention to adhere to all international tax treaties in force between the UK and third party states, so that these treaties can continue in force between Scotland and that state. This was what happened, for example, when the Czech Republic and Slovakia adopted the double taxation agreement between the United Kingdom and Czechoslovakia in 1993.

34. **What tax relief would be available to specific sectors in an independent Scotland?**
At the moment of independence, Scotland will inherit the tax system and the prevailing UK rates and thresholds for all taxes, including tax reliefs. Thereafter decisions on the tax system and all specific taxes – including tax rates, allowances and credits – will be made by the Parliament and Government of an independent Scotland.

35. **Would the main business rates in an independent Scotland continue to match England?**
The Scottish Government has committed to match the poundage for business rates in England for the rest of this parliamentary term. The Scottish Government is also delivering the most competitive business rates regime in the UK with our support for the Small Business Bonus, which currently helps 92,000 businesses.

Our policy is that taxes in Scotland should be competitive to create an attractive business environment, while ensuring that companies pay their fair share of taxes.

36. **Would the fuel duty rate be altered following independence?**
With independence we will examine the benefits of introducing a fuel duty regulator mechanism to stabilise prices for business and consumers.

37. **Who would be liable to pay Scottish taxes?**
The Scottish Government will build on the existing definition set out in the Scotland Act 2012 and general international protocols to establish a definition of a Scottish taxpayer based on residence. In general, this means that people who live in Scotland for most of the year will pay their taxes here. Where people split their time between Scotland and other countries, including England, Wales and Northern Ireland, there will be clear rules set out in statute to determine which tax authority they pay their taxes to.

Banks

38. **What about bank bail-outs if there is another financial crisis?**
A priority of all governments is to ensure that there is no further banking crisis. Improvements to financial regulation and crisis management are taking place in the UK, the EU and globally. The emerging system reduces risk of exposure to the taxpayer. For example, in the UK, the most risky and speculative financial activities will be separated from retail and high street banking following the recommendations of the Vickers Report.

If in the future wider support from governments is required to stabilise the financial system, this would be coordinated through the governance arrangements agreed between the governments of the Sterling Area.

39. **Could an independent Scotland protect depositors on the same basis as the UK deposit guarantee scheme?**
Yes. An independent Scotland will comply with EU rules to provide a deposit guarantee of a minimum of €100,000 (£85,000).

40. **What impact will independence have on the basing of the Green Investment Bank in Edinburgh?**
The UK Green Investment Bank plc was created in 2012 as a UK funding institution to attract funds for the financing of the private sector's investments related to environmental preservation and improvement. Under our plans, the Green Investment Bank will continue to be shared between an independent Scotland and the rest of the UK and continue to be headquartered in Scotland.

Lender of Last Resort

41. **Who will be the lender of last resort to Scottish financial institutions?**
In the Sterling Area, lender of last resort arrangements for financial institutions will continue to operate on a common basis across Scotland and the rest of the UK. This will reflect the reality of our integrated financial system. The Bank of England, as the institution responsible for financial stability, will continue

to play its role in the effective functioning of the banking system using its operations under the Sterling Monetary Framework.

Banks receive lender of last resort facilities from across the world, and it is normal for countries to act in a coordinated way to secure financial stability. For example, the RBS and Barclays received significant liquidity support from the US Federal Reserve at the height of the financial crisis.

Macroeconomic Policy

42. What credit rating would an independent Scotland have?
Countries of a comparable size to Scotland, such as Norway, Finland and Sweden, currently enjoy very low levels of borrowing costs through careful management of the public finances. We expect Scotland to have the top credit rating.

To manage debt and borrowing, Scotland will establish a debt management function. Further detail on debt management is set out in Chapter 3.

43. What will the cost of government borrowing be in an independent Scotland?
The cost of government borrowing will reflect the underlying fundamentals of the economy. Scotland has a strong economy and is in a stronger fiscal position than the rest of the UK. For example, it is estimated that the total amount of tax raised per person in Scotland, including North Sea taxes, has been higher than the equivalent figure for the UK in every single year since 1980/81.

In order to keep borrowing costs low, a government must have clear and credible commitments to maintain sustainable levels of public sector debt. Scotland is well placed, therefore, to have a top credit rating and government borrowing will be undertaken in an affordable and sustainable manner.

Although the expectation would be that Scotland will receive the top credit rating, the example of the UK, which has lost its triple-A rating without a subsequent meaningful increase in borrowing costs, demonstrates that the most important factors are the fundamental strengths and assets of the Scottish economy.

44. **How will an independent Scotland boost the economy when there are pressures on public finances?**
Independence will allow Scotland to design policies on tax, spending and regulation for the particular needs of the Scottish economy, to support the growth and innovation that will deliver prosperity and jobs.

All developed economies need to address the challenges posed by changing social and economic circumstances. Scotland, with its strong asset base and skilled workforce, will be in a strong position to face these challenges.

Spending on social protection (on things like welfare benefits and pensions), as a share of GDP, has been lower in Scotland than in the UK in each of the past five years – and lower than in the majority of EU-15 countries during 2011.

45. **What deficit will an independent Scotland inherit and how would this be managed?**
Scotland's deficit is forecast to fall to between 1.6 per cent and 2.4 per cent of GDP in 2016/17 with a historic share of UK debt and to be between 2.5 per cent and 3.2 per cent of GDP if we take on a population share of UK public sector debt. The Office of Budget Responsibility forecasts that the UK will run a deficit of 3.4 per cent of GDP in the same year. The IMF estimates that the average deficit across the G7 economies will be 3.2 per cent in 2016. Based on this approach, the net fiscal balance for an independent Scotland in 2016/17 is therefore forecast to be better than for the UK as a whole.

When assessing a country's finances an important figure to consider is the current budget balance. This measures the degree to which current taxpayers meet the cost of paying for the public services they consume today and includes a contribution to debt interest payments. If a country is running near to a current budget balance or surplus it may still have to borrow to fund capital expenditure. However, such borrowing will be for long term investment which can be expected to increase the economy's productive capacity in future years. Such borrowing can therefore be part of a sustainable approach to managing public finances.

Assuming a share of debt interest payments based upon Scotland's historic contribution to the UK public finances, Scotland's Current Budget Balance is estimated to be between 0.1 per cent (i.e. a surplus) and -0.7 per cent of GDP in 2016/17. Assuming a population share of debt interest payments, Scotland's current budget balance in 2016/17 is projected to be between -0.8 per cent and -1.5 per cent of GDP. This compares to a forecast for the UK as a whole of -1.9 per cent.

Business

Support to Business

46. How can Scotland improve business growth?
With independence, the Scottish Government and Parliament will have control over the full suite of economic levers, including taxation, business regulation, infrastructure and investment.

The government of an independent Scotland will be able to create a more supportive, competitive and dynamic business environment. Full details of the current Scottish Government's proposals on this are set out in Chapter 3.

Within the powers currently available the Scottish Government is pursuing a range of actions supporting sustainable economic growth and higher quality jobs, including the Small Business Bonus Scheme, supporting Foreign Direct Investment, the Scottish Investment Bank and investment in infrastructure.

With independence, future Scottish Governments will be able to develop these policies further to enable Scotland's businesses to reach their full potential. Future Scottish governments will have the ability to make choices over tax, use measures to boost innovation and exports, promote good industrial relations and support small and medium enterprises.

For example, corporation tax rates remain an important tool for securing that competitive advantage. Following independence we will announce a timetable for a reduction in the corporation tax rate of up to three percentage points. Modelling has already suggested that such a cut could increase the level of output by 1.4 per cent, boost overall employment in Scotland by 1.1 per cent (equivalent to 27,000 jobs) and raise overall investment in the Scottish economy by 1.9 per cent over the long term.

Other key policies to support business that we plan to introduce include:

- supporting investment, including research and development

- strengthening the role of the Scottish Investment Bank

- expanding skill development, bringing together employment and skills policies and putting modern apprenticeships at the heart of our approach

- expanding manufacturing, with a particular focus on manufacturing opportunities through the development of our offshore energy potential

- targeted use of loan guarantees

- reduce Air Passenger Duty by 50 per cent to boost international connections

47. **Will Scotland still trade with the rest of the UK?**
Yes. The rest of the UK is Scotland's main trading partner and this will continue following independence.

48. **Will financial services firms still be able to operate across the UK and EU?**
Yes. Firms and institutions based in Scotland will continue to operate across UK and EU markets.

49. **Will Scotland keep its trading relationships in Europe and across the world?**
Yes. Scotland will maintain its trading relationships as an independent member of the European Union. As an EU member state Scotland will continue to benefit from participation in the World Trade Organisation and other relevant international trade organisations.

50. **Will an independent Scotland improve exports?**
Independence will enable the Scottish Government to focus investment in Scotland's overseas representation in ways that will deliver key gains for Scotland's economy, including more targeted support for companies wishing to export for the first time or increase their existing level of exporting.

51. **Will Scottish industries be promoted in the EU?**
Yes. As an independent member of the EU, Scotland will have a seat at the top table in the European Institutions. This will enable the Scottish Government to better promote our economic and social interests in EU affairs.

52. **Will companies be able to make a public share offering in an independent Scotland?**
Independence will have no impact on Scottish companies' ability to make a public share offering. Companies from any country can be listed on a stock exchange provided that they meet the criteria of that exchange.

53. **Would companies based in an independent Scotland still be able to float on the London stock exchange?**
Yes. Businesses and individuals in an independent Scotland will retain access to capital markets in the UK and globally. For example, around 2,500 companies from over 70 jurisdictions are listed on the London Stock Exchange.

54. **Will an independent Scotland need new systems for trading on international financial and stock markets?**
No. In the Sterling Area, existing domestic and global systems and infrastructure would continue to facilitate Sterling-based transactions.

Global trading activity in any stock will remain as it is now, and continue to depend on the market on which that particular company's stock was traded.

55. **How will independence help Scottish businesses to win public sector contracts?**
Under EU public procurement law, Scottish firms will continue to have access to procurement opportunities across Europe. Independence will give Scotland our own voice in the EU in order to secure improvements for business. At home we will continue the distinctive Scottish approach to generate training and employment opportunities through public procurement.

56. **What will happen to Scottish firms if other countries (such as England, Wales and Northern Ireland) begin favouring their locally domiciled companies?**
Under EU law, this is not allowed.

Employment

57. **How would independence help create jobs?**
A country's people are its greatest asset and it is vital that everyone in Scotland has the opportunity to fulfil their potential. Well rewarded and sustained employment is the best route out of poverty and to tackle inequality.

The actions outlined in Chapter 3 are designed to improve job opportunities and long-term economic resilience. With independence, we will focus on creating better work opportunities, with the aim of creating maximum employment for the entire workforce for the long-term success of Scotland's economy.

58. **What will happen as a result of independence to people in Scotland employed by companies from other parts of the UK?**
Nothing will change as a result of independence. Employers based in the rest of the UK, or further afield, will be able to continue operating in Scotland, and people employed by them will not notice any difference. Today, around 16 per cent of Scotland's private sector employees work for enterprises that are owned outside the UK.

59. **Will the national minimum wage in an independent Scotland remain aligned to the UK level?**
The minimum wage has failed to increase in line with inflation in almost a decade. In every single year since the recession of 2008 the minimum wage has failed to keep up with the cost of living. If it had, some of the lowest paid Scots would be earning the equivalent of £675 more.

We plan that the minimum wage will rise at least in line with inflation. Further information is set out in Chapter 3.

60. **Will a living wage be introduced?**

The current Scottish Government fully supports the Living Wage campaign and its principle of encouraging employers to reward their staff fairly. We have led by example by ensuring all staff covered by the public sector pay policy are paid the Scottish Living Wage. This covers the 180,000 people in Scotland working for central government, its agencies and the NHS.

This is part of the Scottish Government's "social wage" – the contract between the people of Scotland and their Government. Our commitment to support the Scottish Living Wage for the duration of this Parliament is a decisive, long-term commitment to those on the lowest incomes. However, over 400,000 people in Scotland are working for less than the living wage and the majority of these are women.

A priority for action in an independent Scotland for the current Scottish Government would be to fund the Poverty Alliance to deliver a Living Wage Accreditation Scheme to promote the living wage and increase the number of private companies that pay it to make decent pay the norm in our country. We will continue to support and promote the living wage if Scotland becomes independent.

61. **How would the labour market work more effectively in an independent Scotland?**

Our view is that in order to build a fairer and more prosperous Scotland we need to combine employment law that protects the rights of employees with a regulatory regime that encourages companies to grow and create jobs.

A partnership approach to addressing labour market challenges is important. The Scottish Government has already, within the devolved settlement, adopted a strong social partnership approach, working with the voluntary sector, unions, employer associations and employers directly. We will continue that approach after independence, for example by ensuring that there is high quality, readily available childcare supporting parents to find sustained employment and the use of active labour market policies to get people into good quality, sustainable work. This is particularly important for supporting young people into the labour market.

62. **Would laws around unfair dismissal, employment tribunals, industrial relations and trade union rules change in an independent Scotland?**
The laws that are in place immediately before independence would remain in place on independence. After that, decisions on specific laws, including in relation to employment, will be made by the Parliament and Government of an independent Scotland.

63. **What difference would independence make to laws on unfair dismissal, employment tribunals, industrial relations and trade union rules?**
While each element of employment regulation has individual impacts, taken together as a system, they need to balance the twin objectives of protecting the rights of employees and encouraging companies to grow and create good quality jobs.

The current Scottish Government would reverse recent changes introduced at Westminster which reduce key aspects of workers' rights. For example on independence we will restore a 90 days consultation period for redundancies affecting 100 or more employees. Further detail of the current Scottish Government's proposed approach in this area is set out in Chapter 3.

Employers

64. **Why should companies base their headquarters in an independent Scotland?**
Companies base their decisions on where to locate their headquarters on a range of factors. Many successful companies are already headquartered in Scotland, benefiting from our highly skilled workforce. We believe that the economic benefits that independence will bring will further enhance the attraction of Scotland.

With independence, Scotland will be able to send a clear signal that it is one of the most competitive and attractive economies in Europe, with tax rates designed to boost economic activity and support the fast-growing industries that already have a comparative advantage here in Scotland. Corporation tax rates remain an important tool for securing that competitive advantage and for offsetting competitive advantages enjoyed by

other parts of the UK, notably London. We plan to announce a
timetable for a reduction in Corporation tax rate of up to three
percentage points. Full details of this Government's proposed
approach are set out in Chapter 3.

65. **Will businesses still be able to brand their products as
'British made'?**

Yes. "Britain" is a geographical term and, as such, businesses
could choose to continue to refer to themselves as "British" if
they wished. However, "Scotland" and "Scottish" already have
strong international brand recognition associated with quality
goods and services and innovation. This has resulted in
Scotland's brand being regarded highly in measurement tools
such as the Anholt-GfK Roper Nation Brands Index (NBI).
Independence also provides us with opportunities to grow
Scotland as a brand.

66. **Will intellectual property rights be protected?**

Yes. Intellectual property will continue to be protected. As an EU
member state, Scotland will meet European regulations and
directives on IP rights protection, as well as international patent
and trademark protections.

67. **Will independence offer improved intellectual property
services?**

Yes. Independence will allow Scotland to offer a simpler,
cheaper and more business-friendly model than the current UK
one which is seen as bureaucratic and expensive, especially for
small firms. The UK is one of very few EU countries which does
not offer a "second tier", or "utility" protection scheme which
covers the basics of IP protection and is cheaper and quicker to
access. Scotland could follow, for example, the German utility
model which is more a protection of technical innovations.

Entrepreneurs and the Self Employed

68. **Would the UK Seed Enterprise Investment Scheme
continue?**

Yes. The current Scottish Government proposes that this
scheme will continue on independence. Future decisions on
the Seed Enterprise Investment Scheme will be made by the
Government of an independent Scotland.

69. **What can be done to increase Venture Capital Investment in an independent Scotland?**
Independence will allow future Scottish governments to explore new approaches to encourage higher levels of equity financing and venture capital, responding to the needs of Scottish SMEs and building on the significant private sector partners in place under the Scottish Co-investment Fund and Scottish Venture Fund.

70. **How could commercialisation of research be enhanced in an independent Scotland?**
Innovation policy alone cannot deliver a wholesale increase in innovation activity and impact. It needs to interact effectively with other policies, such as tax, business regulations and environmental policies. Independence will enable the Scottish Government to integrate approaches across public policy to provide better support for the commercialisation of research.

Consumer Protection

71. **Will an independent Scotland be able to offer consumers the same level of protection as the UK currently does?**
Yes. Scottish consumers will continue to have the same rights as they currently do, and there will continue to be organisations that offer consumers help and advice when they need it. Independence will enable the Scottish Parliament to tailor consumer protection legislation for Scotland. We have published our full proposals for consumer protection, which are laid out in the paper Consumer Protection and Representation in an Independent Scotland: Options.

72. **When consumers are harmed, will there be systems in place to help them?**
Yes. We propose that in an independent Scotland there will be:

■ a single consumer body, which would advocate for consumers' interests, as well as provide information and education for general consumer matters and regulated industries

■ local community hubs, overseen by the consumer body, where consumers could go to ask for help and receive

advice on more than just the consumer issues initially raised
– a consumer who is struggling to meet energy bills may, for
example, have related, underlying financial or employment
issues

■ a more efficient model of trading standards, so that the
same level of service exists and the same rules apply,
no matter where a consumer lives or a business operates

■ a single ombudsman for consumers to turn to when they
cannot resolve disputes with traders, so that they can
quickly and easily seek redress without going through the
courts

73. **Will steps be taken to ensure all consumers, including the
most vulnerable, will be able to access independent advice
and education when they need it?**
Yes. Under this Government's proposals, Scottish consumers
will be able to receive personalised advice by phone, online,
or face-to-face, and while we will take advantage digital
technology, we will continue to help those consumers who
cannot easily use or access such technology.

74. **How will independence help consumers in practice?**
With independence, the Scottish Government will be able to act
on issues that are of particular concern for Scottish consumers,
such as pay day lending and nuisance calls. For example, this
Government would introduce a cap on short-term interest rates,
similar to those in place in many countries in Europe, Japan,
Canada and some US states. The current Scottish Government
plans to regulate the advertising of pay day lenders and place
restrictions on the 'rolling over' of loans.

75. **After independence, would consumers who suffer damage
as a result of cross-border sales with the rest of the UK be
protected?**
Yes. As an EU member state, an independent Scotland will
continue to meet all EU consumer requirements, including those
covering cross-border transactions. The current Scottish
Government intends to set up an EU Consumer Centre, and
consumers will be able to go there for help when they have
problems with goods bought from other EU countries.

76. **Will an independent Scotland continue to protect consumers and businesses from unfair trading practices, such as price fixing?**
Yes. Scotland will continue to meet all EU rules and regulations designed to ensure competitive markets, and we will set up a competition authority to ensure these rules are applied.

Personal Finances

Financial Products and Services

77. **Will people in an independent Scotland still have access to a wide choice of financial products and services?**
Yes. The EU Single Market ensures that products can be sold across borders. Under the European Single European Market, consumers should be able to choose products and services which have been designed by companies anywhere in the EU.

78. **Will independence affect my mortgage rate?**
In an independent Scotland mortgages rates will continue to be based on the interest rate set by the Bank of England, which in a Sterling Area will be exactly the same for Scotland as for the rest of the UK, just as it is now.

79. **Will Real Estate Investment Trusts continue in an independent Scotland?**
Yes, Scotland will inherit these and similar schemes from the date of independence. Thereafter decisions on specific schemes and support structures – such as Real Estate Investment Trusts – will be made by the Parliament and Government of an independent Scotland. The current Scottish Government recognises the positive impacts of such schemes.

80. **How will my bank account be affected by independence?**
Where you have financial products with companies, like banks, these arrangements will continue. Within the Sterling Area, your current account or savings accounts, or your credit cards and mortgages, will continue to be based on the Bank of England base rate which will be the same across the Sterling Area.

81. **Will I still have access to banks and banking services based in the UK?**

Yes. In an independent Scotland business and personal customers will continue to have access to banks and banking services in the same way as they do now.

82. **Will bank deposits and other financial products still be protected?**

Yes. An independent Scotland will have effective protection for bank deposits and other financial products, maintaining the level of protection currently provided by the Financial Services Compensation Scheme. An independent Scotland will comply with EU rules to provide a deposit guarantee of a minimum of €100,000 (£85,000).

Regulation and Regulators

83. **How will services such as energy, post, telecommunications, rail and water be regulated in an independent Scotland?**

We propose that, in an independent Scotland, these industries will be regulated by a combined economic regulator.

84. **What will be the benefit of that?**

A single economic regulator will reduce the number of regulatory bodies business has to deal with in Scotland, while increasing the consistency of decision-making. It will also be a more powerful regulator, with a stronger voice to act on behalf of consumers and ensure that Scottish markets work efficiently.

85. **Does Scotland have the necessary experience to deliver economic regulation?**

Yes. Scotland already has responsibility for economic regulation in the water and sewerage sector, and we have an extremely good track record. For example:

■ the average household bill for water services in Scotland for 2013/14 is £54 cheaper than in England or Wales and standards of service are amongst the highest in the UK.

■ the Scottish Parliament, in what was a world first, introduced retail competition for non-domestic customers. Two thirds of business customers now have lower bills as a result.

86. **Will the combined economic regulator have a role to play in protecting consumers?**
Yes. We plan to task the Scottish regulator with ensuring open and competitive markets to protect the interests of Scottish consumers while ensuring a fair return on investment for business.

87. **Will independence impose burdens on businesses by making them deal with another regulator in an independent country?**
No. There are 27 independent EU countries with their own regulators, and multinational companies operate in several of them already. Industry also frequently deals with a wide range of regulatory bodies even in the same country, such as environmental, planning, and health and safety regulators.

88. **What will independence mean for the regulation of professionals – such as architects and auditors?**
The professional regulation systems in place immediately before independence will remain in place on independence. After that, decisions will be made by the government of an independent Scotland.

89. **What will independence mean for the production of official and national statistics?**
Scotland is already part of a UK-wide statistical service that meets professional requirements nationally and for the EU, so we can build on the expertise already in the Scottish statistical service. Following a vote for independence, Scotland will require a designated National Statistics Institute. We propose that the National Records of Scotland should take on that role.

90. **Will freedom of information and data protection be regulated in an independent Scotland?**
Yes. The functions of the Scottish Information Commissioner will be extended into the areas currently dealt with by the UK Information Commissioner, including data protection, from independence.

Financial Regulation

91.　**How will financial services be regulated in an independent Scotland?**
We propose that the key elements of prudential regulation will be discharged on a consistent basis across the Sterling Area.

Major financial institutions operating in the Sterling Area will therefore be subject to the same prudential supervision and oversight in both Scotland and the UK. As the Fiscal Commission Working Group made clear, such an approach is in the clear economic and financial interests of Scotland and the UK.

Macro-prudential policy and micro-prudential regulation of the most significant Sterling Area institutions will be discharged, by the Bank of England, as the shared central bank, or by the regulatory arm of the Scottish Monetary Institute in partnership with the UK body. Full details of our proposals are set out in Chapter 3.

92.　**Who would be responsible for financial stability?**
As part of the proposed Sterling Area framework, the Bank of England will retain its remit for financial stability.

93.　**Who will regulate financial conduct?**
With independence, we will ensure that all firms incorporated and authorised in Scotland comply with the highest standards expected of the financial industry. The key elements of financial conduct will be co-ordinated with the relevant UK bodies.

Independence will enable Scottish governments to act on issues that are of particular concern for Scottish consumers, such as pay day lending and nuisance calls. For example, we will introduce a cap on short-term interest rates, similar to those in place in many countries in Europe, Japan, Canada and some US states. We will also regulate the advertising of pay day lenders and place restrictions on 'rolling over' of loans which saddle those unable to pay off debt with an even bigger loan.

As is the case in all other EU countries, Scotland will be able to design its own institutional framework for financial regulation and have its own regulator. A Scottish regulator will work with the regulator for the rest of the UK to set equivalent standards, for instance where there are significant cross-border markets. Further detail is set out in Chapter 3.

Health and Safety Regulation

94. **Would the people of Scotland still be protected by strong health and safety measures?**
Yes. The legal system that is in place immediately before independence will continue on independence. Thereafter, decisions on health and safety law, including corporate homicide, will be made by the parliament and government of an independent Scotland.

Health Industry Regulation

95. **How will an independent Scotland access services from the Medicines and Healthcare products Regulatory Agency?**
The Medicines and Healthcare products Regulatory Agency (MHRA) is an Executive Agency established by the Department of Health in England. The MHRA takes forward reserved issues around the licensing, safety and efficacy of medicines and functions on a UK-wide basis. The Scottish Government plans to continue using the services of MHRA in an independent Scotland, unless and until the Scottish Parliament decided to make changes in this area.

96. **Will current legislation to regulate doctors, nurses and other health professionals continue to be in force in an independent Scotland?**
Laws which are in force in Scotland prior to independence will continue in force after independence until such times as that legislation is amended or repealed by the Parliament of an independent Scotland.

The regulation of all health professionals will become the responsibility of the Scottish Parliament on independence. The Scottish Government will seek to work in cooperation with Westminster, and the devolved administrations, to ensure that health professional regulation is maintained in the best interests of patient safety and the consistent treatment of healthcare professionals.

The Scottish Government will seek to maintain the current
professional current healthcare regulatory bodies, which are
funded by fees from registrants, which will continue to operate
in Scotland after independence.

Energy Regulation

97. **How will the energy market in an independent Scotland
be regulated?**
As an independent member of the European Union, Scotland
will be required to create a national regulatory authority for
energy. The Scottish Government's proposal of a new combined
economic regulator will bring together the economic regulatory
functions of communications, energy, transport and water. The
energy arm of the Scottish Regulator could, in principle, be
based at the Scottish offices of Ofgem. This Scottish regulator
will work in partnership with the energy regulator in England and
Wales in a model of shared regulation of the integrated GB-wide
market. Further detail of this is set out in Chapter 3.

98. **Will independence allow Scotland to have greater influence
on key regulatory matters, such as energy prices?**
Yes. Powers over key regulatory decisions, currently exercised
by Westminster, will transfer to the Scottish Parliament as a
result of independence. After that, decisions on the energy
market will be made by the Parliament and Government of
an independent Scotland.

99. **Will an independent Scotland be able to take steps to
ensure that consumers' interests are taken into account
when energy policy is set?**
Yes. The powers of independence will allow energy policy to
be designed to protect the interests of consumers and make
sure people are treated transparently and fairly. Appropriate
information on energy tariffs will help customers decide
which company to go with, and help make prices competitive.

The Scottish Government plans that, in an independent
Scotland, funding for 'green investment' would transfer from
energy bills to central government budgets. By passing on
these cost reductions to their consumers, energy companies

would be able to reduce bills by around five per cent or approximately £70 every year. Further detail on this proposal is set out in Chapter 8.

Telecommunications Regulation

100. Will there be a Scottish telecommunications regulator in an independent Scotland?

Regulation of broadcasting is currently carried out by Ofcom, which also regulates telecommunications and postal services. We propose that the economic regulatory functions of Ofcom are included in a combined economic regulator. Capacity will be developed within the new regulator to advise on the regulation of broadcasting content. We also propose that an independent Scotland co-operates with the rest of the UK on managing the spectrum, in the same way that Ofcom and Ireland's ComReg co-operate at present.

101. What approach will be taken to spectrum management and licensing and the universal service obligation in an independent Scotland?

Powers over these issues will transfer to the Scottish Parliament as a result of independence. Thereafter decisions on spectrum management and licensing and the universal service obligation will be made by the Parliament and Government of an independent Scotland.

It is the intention of the current Scottish Government that the universal service obligation will operate at least at the same level as the rest of the UK in an independent Scotland. Independence also offers the opportunity for Scotland to set higher coverage obligations on spectrum licences.

Rail Regulation

102. How will Network Rail be regulated in an independent Scotland?

We propose that, on independence, the Office of Rail Regulation will continue to operate in Scotland while the options for regulation are examined further, although the proposed combined economic regulator will cover aspects of its functions. This will ensure there is no disruption to the operations and safety of rail services.

Aviation Regulation

103. **Will an independent Scotland still be covered by the Civil Aviation Authority?**
Powers over civil aviation will transfer to the Scottish Government and Parliament as a result of independence. After that, decisions on this will be made by the Parliament and Government of an independent Scotland.

We propose to retain the current regulatory framework governing aviation on independence through a memorandum of understanding with the Civil Aviation Authority (CAA). The CAA will report to the Scottish Government on regulatory matters affecting aviation in Scotland.

Building on this initial arrangement an independent Scotland can develop its own regulatory body in due course.

104. **How will a Scottish aviation regulator be funded?**
The current Scottish Government has no plans to change the current model for the funding of aviation regulation, where the industry covers the cost of regulation.

Regulation of Outer Space Activity in an Independent Scotland

105. **Will Scotland continue to participate in international space agencies?**
Yes. Scotland will continue to work with the UK Space Agency and the European Space Agency.

106. **Will Scottish businesses be able to compete for contracts to the UK Space Agency?**
Yes. An independent Scotland will continue to be part of the European Union. In line with EU Public Procurement Law companies in Scotland will be able to compete for contracts to the UK Space Agency and the European Space Agency.

Videogame Regulation

107. **Will an independent Scotland use the UK's videogame age rating system or create its own one?**
Powers over videogame age rating system and other age rating systems will transfer to the Scottish Parliament as a result of independence. The rating system in place immediately before independence will be inherited on independence. After that, decisions on these systems will be made by the Parliament and Government of an independent Scotland.

Weights and Measures

108. **Would Scotland develop its own legislation on weights and measures, and would this be metric or imperial?**
The existing system will continue on independence.

Time

109. **What impact will independence have on the time zone that applies in Scotland?**
None. As a matter of common sense the current time zone will be retained.

Transport

Rail

110. **What will independence mean for Scotland's rail services?**
Since 2005, powers to specify and fund work on the Scottish rail network have been devolved. However, discussion about the overall structure of the rail industry remains reserved to Westminster, along with safety and standards.

Independence will not result in any immediate change to rail services. However, future governments of an independent Scotland will have greater flexibility over the budgets available to support rail services and over franchise arrangements and ownership models.

118. **Will plans for high speed rail between Scotland and England be affected by independence?**
Current confirmed Westminster plans exclude Scotland and Northern England, with the next phases of high-speed rail only due to connect London with Birmingham in 2026 and then Leeds and Manchester by 2033.

While this investment will bring some benefits between the Central Belt and London, the economic benefits to Scotland, the North East and far North West of England are marginal compared to those which will accrue to other areas of the UK. Indeed, Westminster's own analysis shows that the economies of Aberdeen and Dundee may suffer from such a partial approach.

Despite a much stronger business case from a network that includes Scotland and previous calls, not just from the Scottish Government but councils in the North of England and civic and business Scotland too, it is only now that Westminster has agreed to plan for high speed to go beyond Manchester and Leeds.

Consistent with the Borderlands initiative, an independent Scotland could work together with northern English councils to argue the case more strongly for High Speed to go further North faster. High Speed Rail will also attract air travellers from Glasgow and Edinburgh to London, freeing air slots to maintain air access to Aberdeen and Inverness, which with rail improvements will maintain and enhance the connectivity of these economically vibrant cities.

119. **What will happen to Network Rail in Scotland?**
Network Rail is a private company limited by guarantee and will continue to operate as it does now, regulated by the Office of Rail Regulation. The Scottish Government will expect to become a member of Network Rail with membership rights equivalent to those currently held by the Department for Transport to ensure it best meets its obligations with respect to an independent Scottish Government.

120. **What will happen to Network Rail's debt, which is currently guaranteed by the Westminster Government?**
An independent Scotland will continue to meet its rail financing obligations – including the servicing of regulatory debt for Scotland. This is in line with the determination made by the Office of Rail Regulation for the period 2014 to 2019. The Scottish Government will continue to meet any obligations with respect to the financing of Network Rail in Scotland, and, if required, the Scottish Government will provide its own Financial Indemnity Mechanism (FIM) to support this. Under these circumstances Network Rail would pay a fee to the Scottish Government to reflect the benefit it received from the FIM.

121. **If I buy a travel pass or season ticket before independence that continues into independence will it be valid for the whole period?**
Yes. The Scottish Government proposes no change to the ScotRail franchise, which will operate as normal. All passes and tickets will remain valid.

Roads

122. **Who will be responsible for the road network in an independent Scotland?**
The Scottish Government is already responsible for roads. This will not change with independence.

123. **Will there be road charging in an independent Scotland**
The current Scottish Government has no plans to introduce road charging.

Buses and Trams

124. **Who will be responsible for public transport, such as buses and trams, in an independent Scotland?**
Many powers relating to public transport are already devolved and in an independent Scotland decisions on them will continue to be made as they are now by the Scottish Parliament and Government.

However, some further powers will also transfer to the Scottish Parliament on independence. For example, the registration and

As an independent Member State of the EU, Scotland will continue to comply with European regulations. Implementation of EU legislation into UK law (and exercise of any aspects where there is a degree of discretion) is currently a reserved matter, however, and so this responsibility would transfer to the Scottish Parliament as a result of independence. Given the extent of EU regulation, the scope for significant change to the rules is limited but the current Scottish Government plans to achieve a healthy and sustainable freight industry in Scotland that would be able to compete effectively in the European single market.

130. **Would relevant regulations be aligned with the rest of the UK? Would a Scottish Government want to pursue a distinct course over time?**

As a member of the EU, an independent Scotland will meet its obligations under EU law with regards to the haulage industry. Regulation that is in place immediately before independence will be inherited on independence. Thereafter decisions on the regulatory framework will be made by the Parliament and government of an independent Scotland in line with Scotland's interests and to suit Scotland's circumstances.

131. **What effect would independence have on the movement of goods by road between Scotland and the rest of the UK, and between Scotland and other countries?**

Under EU regulations, all hauliers carrying out the movement of goods under 'hire and reward' between member states must have a standard international operator's licence and a community authorisation licence.

In a modern global economy many companies already operate across a number of different countries without difficulty. The Scottish Government has made clear its intention to ensure an independent Scotland remains an attractive and competitive place to do business.

Motoring Services

132. **Will an independent Scotland have its own driver and vehicle licencing and driving standards agency?**
Powers over these issues will transfer to the Scottish Parliament as a result of independence. It is the current Scottish Government's intention to continue to use the services of the Driver and Vehicle Licensing Agency, Driving Standards Agency, and Vehicle and Operator Services Agency in the immediate post-independence period. These agencies are currently self-funded through user fees. Scottish users, therefore contribute fully to the cost of providing these services.

Independence will allow the Scottish Parliament to determine the best way to deliver these services in the future. The current Scottish Government proposes the creation of a new, streamlined Scottish Motor Services Agency, which will bring together the functions of DVLA, DSA, VOSA, and Vehicle Certification Agency. By the end of the first term of an independent Parliament, the current Scottish Government would plan to have completed the design and development work, with a view to the Agency going live early in the second Parliament.

133. **Will we need to reapply for driving licences if Scotland becomes independent?**
No. The Scottish Government intends that the driver licensing regime will remain in place at the point of independence. This will ensure all licences granted by the DVLA are recognised in Scotland.

134. **Will an independent Scotland change the UK legislation for bus, coach and lorry drivers' Certificate of Professional Competence training?**
This is a decision for future elected Governments of an independent Scotland. This Government has no plans to change the present regime for Certificate of Professional Competence training.

135. **Will Scotland retain the role of Traffic Commissioner?**
Yes. The Scottish Government's intention is that an independent Scotland will retain the Traffic Commissioner's role.

Ferries

136. **How will ferry services be managed in an independent Scotland?**
Ferries are an essential part of Scotland's transport network. The quality of our ferry services impacts on us all, affecting both island and mainland communities. The Scottish Government is fully committed to delivering first class sustainable ferry services to our communities, stimulating social and economic growth across Scotland.

The planned improvements to Scotland's ferry services, as set out in our recently published Ferries Plan will enable our rural and remote communities to thrive, and continue to make a significant contribution to Scotland's economy. With the fully integrated transport system that independence will deliver, we can ensure the best alignment between ferries and other modes of transport.

Maritime

137. **How will maritime services be delivered in an independent Scotland? What will change in maritime functions with independence?**
Scotland has approximately 60 per cent of the seas and coastline of Great Britain. However, the essential maritime institutions (the Maritime and Coastguard Agency, Northern Lighthouse Board and Marine Accident Investigation Branch) are currently controlled by Westminster. The Scottish Government currently has no say in how these essential services are delivered.

Independence will let Scotland shape and develop maritime services that reflect our unique coastline and give the people who use our seas the support they need. The Scottish Government intends that the Maritime and Coastguard Agency will continue to provide its services for the safety of mariners. It also plans that the Northern Lighthouse Board and Marine Accident Investigation Branch will continue its role unchanged in an independent Scotland, funded by existing arrangements for the collection of light dues at Scottish ports through Trinity House.

It will then be for future governments of an independent Scotland to look at how these services would be provided in the years ahead. This may, if appropriate, include developing a distinct Scottish organisation to deliver some or all of these functions.

138. **Will an independent Scotland remain a member of international organisations like the International Maritime Organisation and the International Civil Aviation Organisation when independent?**
Aviation and maritime regulations will continue to apply in an independent Scotland as these activities, by their nature, are subject to international regulations. The Scottish Government intends that Scotland, as an independent state, will become a member of these organisations.

139. **Will the Royal National Lifeboat Institution continue to provide services?**
The Royal National Lifeboat Institution is totally independent of government and serves the Republic of Ireland, the Channel Islands and the Isle of Man as well as the United Kingdom. The RNLI is an integral part of the maritime search and rescue structure. Its purpose is to save lives at sea and the organisation has a proud history of providing lifeboat services and volunteer crews. Decisions about the RNLI are for the Institution itself, but we can see no obstacle to it continuing to play its vital role around the coasts of Scotland as it does around the rest of these islands.

There is a long history of maritime search and rescue being co-ordinated across borders and boundaries with all available resources and vessels deployed to assist in any incident. This will continue to be the case after independence.

140. **Will Scotland register ships?**
Yes. The present Scottish Government intends that an independent Scotland will set up a Shipping Register.

141. **Will the standards for vessels be the same as in the rest of the UK?**
Most standards for shipping and vessel safety are set by international agreement through the International Maritime Organisation and the EU and these will continue to apply in an independent Scotland as they do for the rest of the UK.

142. **Will there be any changes to the operation or structure of harbour authorities?**
All of the Statutory Harbour Authorities in Scotland operate under their own local legislation. There is no reason for this to change with independence.

Welfare

The current Scottish Government's approach to the design
of our future welfare system is set out in Chapter 4.

143. **What will happen to the welfare system in an independent
Scotland?**
Governments of an independent Scotland will be able to use
welfare powers to deliver a system that helps people into work
and protects the vulnerable.

144. **How will my benefits be paid in an independent Scotland?**
Benefits to which people are entitled will continue to be paid in
exactly the same way as they are now.

145. **What will happen to Universal Credit and the Personal
Independence Payment introduced by the Westminster
Government?**
The current Scottish Government proposes that the further
roll-out of Universal Credit and the Personal Independence
Payment should be stopped. Following a vote for
independence, we will ask Westminster to halt the roll-out of
Universal Credit and the Personal Independence Payment in
Scotland.

146. **Will I get the same benefits after independence?**
Yes. We plan that, on independence, there will be a transitional
period when the Scottish and Westminster Governments will
share the administration and delivery of benefits and State
Pensions. It is in both countries' interests that this should
happen.

Following independence, the immediate priorities will be to
reverse the most damaging and counterproductive of the UK
welfare changes. We propose to:

- abolish the "bedroom tax" within the first year of the first
independent Scottish Parliament

- halt the further rollout of Universal Credit and Personal
Independence Payments in Scotland

- ensure that benefits and tax credits increase in line with
inflation to avoid the poorest families falling further into poverty

Full details of the current Scottish Government's proposed approach are set out in Chapter 4.

147. **Will I still need to go to the Jobcentre?**
Yes. Scotland will inherit the Jobcentre structure and its functions but the Scottish Government and Parliament will have powers to look at welfare to work programmes in a different way, enabling them to develop a new approach to supporting people based on joint rights and responsibilities and a culture of respect.

148. **Will I still get my benefits on the same day of the week?**
Yes.

149. **Will I get the same amount of benefit?**
On independence our proposals mean you will continue to receive benefit payments and tax credits in the same way as you do now. Becoming independent will not, in itself, change your entitlement. However, future Scottish governments can choose to do things differently from the rest of the UK. For example, this Government will stop the damaging changes to our welfare system being introduced by Westminster, including scrapping the "bedroom tax" and stopping the roll out of Universal Credit. Full details of our proposals for a fairer welfare system are set out in Chapter 4.

150. **Will I need to apply again?**
No. We will make sure that independence does not disrupt benefits payments, and that existing claims will continue as now.

151. **Will I need to be assessed again?**
No. Scotland becoming independent will not result in a need for reassessment.

We propose that, on independence and for the transitional period, the benefits system will continue to be administered in the same way as it is now. Once Scotland establishes its own distinct system, the Scottish Government will be able to review the application process we inherit.

152. **If I am from another country and move to Scotland, will I be entitled to benefits?**
At the moment, the UK rules for benefits entitlement vary depending on which country you move from. These rules will

continue to apply in an independent Scotland until such times as the Parliament of an independent Scotland decides to change them.

153. How will I apply for benefits if Scotland is independent?
On independence and for the transitional period, the Scottish Government proposes that the administration of the benefits system will continue to work in the same way as it does now. Governments in an independent Scotland will be able to review the application process we inherit.

154. Will benefits change for disabled people?
We intend that people living in Scotland and in receipt of Disability Living Allowance will not be migrated to Personal Independence Payment.

We have also committed to abolishing the "bedroom tax", saving 82,500 households in Scotland – including 63,500 households with disabilities and 15,500 households with children – an average of £50 per month.

In addition, this Government proposes to launch an urgent review of the conditionality and sanctions regime, and review the system of assessments for disability benefits. Then, as the new independent benefits system is developed, we will work with disabled people and others with an interest in how to improve things further.

155. Will work be an important feature of welfare and benefits?
Yes. Where people can work they should work. Work is important for people's health and wellbeing, as much as for their economic position. This Government is committed to seeing an independent Scotland improve support for people that are out of work and create a welfare to work plan that is based on an individual's circumstances and on the support they need to move towards, and into, sustainable work.

156. Will the forms be the same for new benefits applicants?
During the transitional period, the benefits forms will remain the same.

When Scotland has its own welfare system, the government in an independent Scotland will be able to review the application process to make it simpler.

157. **When will the benefits system change in an independent Scotland?**

The first government of an independent Scotland can start to plan for major changes during the transitional period, with a view to implementing them after the transitional period ends, which this Scottish Government intends should be in 2018.

We set out our full proposals for early changes to the benefits system in Chapter 4.

158. **Why won't Scotland run its own benefits system from the first day of independence?**

We accept the Expert Working Group on Welfare's recommendation that there should be a transitional period of shared administration for delivery of benefit payments. As highlighted by the Group, this offers the best arrangement in the short-term. It also ensures continuity of payments for millions of benefit recipients elsewhere in the UK whose applications and payments are currently processed in Scotland. However, it is our intention that such a system of shared administration will last only until 2018 and be organised in such a way that will:

■ allow the first government of an independent Scotland to introduce its priorities for change from 2016

■ allow that government also to begin work towards creating a welfare system that better reflects Scotland's priorities and needs

159. **Can an independent Scotland afford its own welfare system?**

Yes. Scotland spends proportionally less on welfare and State Pensions than the UK as a whole. Spending on social protection as a share of overall spending is estimated to have been lower in Scotland for each year of the past five years.

Scotland's Balance Sheet demonstrates that social protection expenditure, which includes welfare payments and State Pensions, accounted for 14.4 per cent of our economic output (GDP) in Scotland compared to 15.9 per cent in the UK as a whole in 2011/12.

160. How long would the transition take to establish welfare administration in an independent Scotland?

It is our intention that a system of shared administration will last until 2018.

The Scottish Government understands people's concerns about the changes Westminster is bringing in. That is why we propose to give Westminster immediate notice, after a vote for independence, that further roll-out of Universal Credit and Personal Independence Payment should be stopped in Scotland.

161. What will change in the first years of independence, during the transitional period?

During a transitional period, Scotland will start to develop a welfare system better suited to Scottish needs and priorities. Immediate priorities for change that the current Scottish Government will pursue are set out in Chapter 4.

162. What would be different about the welfare system after the transition period?

The political parties will put forward their proposals for the people of Scotland to consider in the 2016 election. That means decisions on the future shape of our welfare state will be taken by the elected representatives of the people of Scotland.

The current Scottish Government's approach to the design of our future welfare system is set out in Chapter 4.

163. Even if welfare is more affordable now, doesn't Scotland's ageing population mean that in the long run welfare will become unaffordable?

The longer-term demographic challenge of an ageing population affects every western country, including Scotland and the UK as a whole. The particular challenge Scotland faces is projected lower growth in our working-age population, although Scotland's total dependency ratio (working age population compared to pensioners and children) is projected to be more advantageous than the UK's for at least 15 years. The Government Economic Strategy sets out a target to match average European (EU-15) population growth over the period from 2007 to 2017, supported by increased healthy life expectancy in Scotland over this period.

independent Scottish Government would be best placed to take such targeted action to meet Scotland's specific circumstances.

170. **What will happen to my existing State Pension in an independent Scotland?**

Under our proposals, pensions will continue to be paid in full and on time, as now. The current Scottish Government intends that with independence, Scotland will keep the best of the existing State Pensions system, making genuine improvements where necessary. Our approach if in government under independence will be as follows:

■ the Basic State Pension will be increased each year by the 'triple-lock' – average earnings, inflation, or 2.5 per cent – whichever of these is the highest. This protection will stay in place for at least the first term of an independent Scottish Parliament. Westminster has only committed to keeping the triple-lock until 2015.

■ Guarantee Credit, which provides pensioners with a minimum income guarantee will also be increased by the triple-lock, initially for the first term of an independent parliament. This provides extra protection for low-income pensioners in Scotland, compared to the rest of the UK.

■ Savings Credit will be retained for existing pensioners on low incomes as in the UK.

171. **I'll be retiring after 2016. What will happen to my pension on independence?**

All accrued pension rights will be protected when Scotland becomes independent.

People reaching State Pension Age from 6 April 2016 will move to a new single-tier pension. This is being introduced across the UK countries. In addition, this Scottish Government proposes that in Scotland pensioners should benefit under independence from additional protection as follows:

■ the single-tier pension will be set at £160 per week. If the rate for the single-tier pension is higher in the rest of the UK at that point, the Scottish single-tier pension will match this figure

- for the whole of the first term of an independent Scottish Parliament, the single-tier pension will be increased each year by the 'triple-lock' – that is the highest of average earnings, inflation, or 2.5 per cent. This guarantee is only in place in the rest of the UK until 2015. Guarantee Credit, which provides a minimum level of pension income, will also be increased by the triple-lock

- in addition, Scottish single-tier pensioners on low incomes will still be able to benefit from Savings Credit, which is being abolished for new pensioners from 2016 in the rest of the UK

- provision will also be maintained for those expecting to receive a State Pension based on their spouse's contributions. This protection would be in place for 15 years after the introduction of the single-tier pension, unlike in the rest of the UK

172. Will pension rights already accrued be protected in an independent Scotland?

Yes. Accrued pension rights will be protected in an independent Scotland. Our plans are as follows:

- for those people living and working in Scotland at the time of independence, the UK pension entitlement they have accrued prior to independence will become their Scottish State Pension entitlement

- any pension entitlement accrued in Scotland after independence will also form part of that Scottish State Pension

- on retirement, the Scottish State Pension will be paid by the Scottish Government

173. I've worked most of my life in England and have only moved to Scotland recently to retire. Does that affect who will pay my pension and how much I will get?

No, it will not affect how much you will get. If you are in receipt of a UK State Pension on independence and you are resident in Scotland, the responsibility for paying that pension and all associated payments will transfer to the Scottish Government.

174. **I've accrued some State Pension in England, and some overseas, but none in Scotland. I'm now living in Scotland. How will my State Pension entitlement be calculated and who will pay it?**
It will not matter where in the UK you accrued your State Pension entitlement: if you are retired and are living in Scotland on independence, the Scottish Government will be responsible for paying that pension. The amount you are entitled to will not change because of independence.

In terms of State Pension accrued outside the UK, the Westminster Government is currently not responsible for these payments. The same will be true of the Scottish Government on independence. People living in Scotland will, as is the case now, have their international pensions paid either by the country concerned or by the International Pensions Centre.

175. **I live in Scotland but I work between Edinburgh and London for different employers. What will happen to the various State Pension pots I have accrued after independence?**
All State Pension accrued up to the point of independence anywhere within the UK will count as your State Pension entitlement.

After independence, any pension entitlement gained by working in Scotland will accrue to your Scottish State Pension. Any pension entitlement from working in England, Wales or Northern Ireland will accrue to the UK State Pension and will be payable by the Westminster Government.

176. **Will it be difficult to transfer pensions to an independent Scotland?**
The Scottish Government will work with the Westminster Government to ensure an orderly transition of responsibility for pensions to an independent Scotland.

177. **How will responsibility for pensions transfer to an independent Scotland?**
The Scottish Government supports the view of the Expert Working Group on Welfare that a 'shared services agreement' for the administration of benefit payments during a transition period will be in the best interests of both the UK and Scotland.

Both during a period of transition, and in the longer term, pension payments will be administered by existing offices in Dundee and Motherwell.

State Pension Age

178. **What will happen to the State Pension Age in an independent Scotland?**
Under current Westminster Government plans, the State Pension Age is increasing to 67 for people aged between 44 and 53, over a two year period between 2026 and 2028. The Scottish Government is not persuaded that this increase is right for Scotland.

On average, Scots currently enjoy fewer years in retirement – and in receipt of State Pensions – than the UK average due to lower life expectancy. Life expectancy for both men and women in Scotland has consistently remained below the UK level, despite significant improvements over many years. In 2013, life expectancy at age 65 was 1.2 years higher in the UK than in Scotland for women; and 1.3 years higher for men.

This Scottish Government therefore reserves judgment on the Westminster Government's timetable for the State Pension Age increase to 67. Independence is the only way to ensure that the future State Pension Age in Scotland is determined according to specific Scottish circumstances.

179. **How will the decision on the State Pension Age for Scotland be taken?**
We intend if in government, to appoint an Independent Commission on the State Pension Age within the first year of independence. The Commission will have a remit to investigate and make recommendations on the appropriate rate of increase of the State Pension Age, beyond 66, that would suit Scottish circumstances. The Commission will take into account life expectancy, fairness and affordability, including implications for increased public sector pension costs.

We envisage the Commission reporting to Parliament within the first two years of independence with a view to decisions being taken promptly thereafter. Prompt implementation will allow sufficient time for longer term financial planning.

Public Sector Pensions

Full details of the Scottish Government's proposed approach
to public sector pensions are set out in Chapter 4.

180. **Could an independent Scotland afford public sector
pensions?**
Yes. Scotland's stewardship of public sector pensions can
in some areas already be argued to have delivered more
sustainable schemes than their counterparts in England
and Wales.

181. **What will independence mean for the existing rights of
members of affected public sector pension schemes?**
In an independent Scotland, all public service pension rights
and entitlements which have been accrued will continue to be
fully protected and accessible – whether they have been
accrued in schemes already executively devolved to Scotland
or those currently reserved to Westminster. Article 1 of Protocol
1 of the European Convention of Human Rights means that
pension rights are property rights under the Convention, which
governments must respect.

There will be no difference to individual contribution rates
or benefit levels as a result of independence.

On independence, the legislation and rules governing public
sector pension schemes, whether reserved or already
executively devolved to Scotland, will continue to apply (under
the "continuity of law principle"). The arrangements for these
public sector pension schemes will therefore continue to
operate as at present, bridging the period before and after
the date of Scotland's independence.

182. **Could an independent Scotland manage public sector
pensions effectively?**
Scotland already has the people and the infrastructure in place
for delivering high quality public sector pensions. In particular,
the Scottish Public Pensions Agency (SPPA) has been
responsible for administering Scotland's NHS and teachers'
pensions for over twenty years and the Scottish Government
has recently confirmed that the Agency is to administer all
police and fire-fighter pensions in Scotland from April 2015.

Alongside this delivery expertise, the SPPA is also responsible for developing policy for all of the main public sector pension schemes executively devolved to Scotland.

The SPPA's mixture of multi-scheme policy and delivery responsibilities is unique in the public service pensions landscape and is a significant asset. No other body in the UK has such first-hand knowledge and experience of both designing and delivering public service pensions policy. This includes the development of policy for, and the management of, two major sets of reforms of public service pensions in the last ten years.

183. What will independence mean for how pensions will be managed?

For scheme members and existing pensioners of Scotland's schemes, there will be no change in pension arrangements following independence. If, for example, a former NHS Scotland employee has retired, begun to draw her pension, and moves to live in England, the Scottish NHS pension scheme will continue to pay that pension, as it does at present.

For pension schemes that are currently reserved, such as civil service, armed forces and judicial pensions, the Scottish Government will work with Westminster to ensure an orderly transition of pension responsibilities to an independent Scotland. The Scottish Public Pensions Agency will form the basis for delivering the additional responsibilities for public sector pensions that will be required in an independent Scotland.

During the transitional period, pensions will continue to be paid in full and on time and pensioners will continue to benefit from safeguards, including the governance provisions of the Public Service Pensions Act 2013 and the provisions of Article 1 of Protocol 1 of the European Convention on Human Rights, which means that pension rights are property rights under the Convention which governments must respect.

For current UK-wide public service pension schemes, the Scottish Government will take its fair share of liabilities based on meeting the pensions responsibilities of pensioners who live in Scotland.

On independence, these pension schemes will continue to operate as at present. Just as today, however, it would be open to future governments to suggest changes. Independence simply means that these future decisions will be taken in Scotland rather than by Westminster.

Private Pensions

Full details of the Scottish Government's proposed approach to private pensions are set out in Chapter 4.

184. **Will my private pension benefits be protected?**
Yes. Your occupational or personal pension sets out your retirement benefits. The payment of the benefits you have built up in your existing pension will not be affected by the move to independence.

185. **What will the Scottish Government do to help people save for retirement?**
We propose following independence to:

■ continue with the roll-out of automatic enrolment into a workplace pension

■ establish a Scottish Employment Savings Trust for people with low to middle earnings

■ launch a Financial Capability Strategy to help build people's skills, knowledge and understanding about personal finance

■ work with the pensions industry in Scotland on the design of new pension products that will provide greater certainty to savers about the final value of their pensions

■ improve pension information, giving people personalised feedback on saving for their retirement

■ consider whether adjustments to tax relief arrangements would further incentivise saving

186. **Will the Scottish Government improve information and advice on private pensions?**
Yes. At present, information and advice on financial services and pensions is provided by a range of organisations, with the

result that people are often confused about where they should look for advice. This Scottish Government is proposing a new model to improve the standard of advice for consumers by providing information and advice you can access in your local area.

187. **Will automatic enrolment of employees into a workplace pension continue?**
Yes. Automatic enrolment into workplace pension schemes helps people to save for their retirement and the Scottish Government intends that this will continue.

188. **Will employees and employers continue to have access to the National Employment Savings Trust?**
The Scottish Government will work with the Westminster Government to ensure that the benefits people have built up in the National Employment Savings Trust (NEST) are accessible. This Government proposes that a Scottish equivalent of NEST should be established to help firms in Scotland enrol their employees.

189. **Will tax relief on private pensions and salary sacrifice continue in an independent Scotland?**
Yes. The current arrangements will continue at the point of independence. Scotland will inherit the tax system and the prevailing UK rates and thresholds for all taxes including tax reliefs. Decisions on specific taxes – including tax rates, allowances and credits – will be made by the Parliament and Government of an independent Scotland.

190. **Will people with pensions in the rest of the UK be affected by exchange rate fluctuations if Scotland had a different currency?**
No. With the pound Sterling as currency of an independent Scotland, pensions will be paid in pounds Sterling, as they are today.

191. **Will there be a Scottish Pensions Regulator?**
Yes. This Scottish Government proposes to establish a dedicated Scottish Pensions Regulator, to ensure the same level of protection for people's pension savings as is currently provided, and to promote an effective pensions market.

192. **Will private pensions be protected in an independent
Scotland?**
Yes. We believe it is in the best interests of all parties for the
current arrangements to continue – although we are also
prepared to make specific arrangements for Scotland – to
ensure that people will have the same level of protection as
is currently provided by the UK Pension Protection Fund, the
Financial Assistance Scheme and the Fraud Compensation
Fund.

We will also ensure that arrangements for an effective
compensation scheme are established, mirroring the level of
protection provided in the UK Financial Services Compensation
Scheme.

193. **Will consumers in Scotland have access to a pensions
ombudsman?**
Yes. Two delivery models are being considered by the current
Scottish Government. Either, a single Scottish Ombudsman
Service – a one stop shop for consumers (including in relation
to pensions) – will be established, or a specific Scottish
Financial Services Ombudsman, with responsibility for handling
complaints about pensions and financial services, will be
established.

194. **How will deficits in defined benefit private pension
schemes be addressed in an independent Scotland?**
Current deficits in defined benefit pension schemes have been
caused by the financial management of these schemes within
the UK. Many schemes are working to become fully funded and
have recovery plans in place. These will continue after
independence.

Our proposals for independence will deliver strong protection
for people's private pension savings and establish an effective
regulator system which will set the parameters for such
schemes to achieve a stable funding position.

195. **What will happen to existing UK-wide pension schemes?**
Specific requirements apply under EU law to pension schemes
that operate across different member states. However, the
cross-border rules allow member states a degree of flexibility.

Transitional arrangements were put in place by the Westminster Government and Ireland when these rules were introduced and we consider that it will be possible to agree transitional arrangements for existing UK-wide schemes. The Scottish Government is keen to start discussions with the Westminster Government and the European Commission as soon as possible, with a view to reaching agreement in the interests of employers and pension schemes across the UK.

Health and Social Care

196. What will happen to the NHS in an independent Scotland?
The NHS is already the responsibility of the Scottish Parliament. The process of becoming independent will not change the way you receive your health care. You'll still be able to visit your GP and local hospital as now.

NHS Scotland already operates independently in Scotland. NHS Scotland has been the responsibility of the Scottish Parliament since devolution in 1999.

The Scottish Government's vision for the NHS in Scotland is to maintain our publicly owned, publicly funded health service providing care free at the point of delivery.

197. Will the NHS be safe from privatisation?
Yes. Scotland has taken a very different approach from that in England. The Scottish Government has categorically ruled out the disruptive and costly structural reforms happening in NHS England. Avoiding the privatisation of services seen south of the border has allowed us to focus on improving safely and quality of care.

198. Will an independent Scotland maintain the current number of doctors and nurses in the NHS?
In Scotland's NHS, staffing decisions are made by Health Boards in line with their own local needs and circumstances. This will continue to be the case on independence. Under the current Scottish Government, NHS staffing has increased by 5 per cent overall and by 1.5 per cent in the last year. There are now over 1,000 extra qualified nurses and midwives and over 1,500 more doctors working in our health service.

199. **What will be the impact of constitutional reform on funding for medical research in Scotland?**
Medical research is a Scottish strength.

Scottish researchers win a disproportionate share of the Medical Research Council (MRC) and National Institute of Health Research (NIHR) funds for which researchers based in Scotland can apply. For example, in 2011/12, with a population share of 8.4 per cent, researchers in Scotland won 9.8 per cent of the total funds awarded by the MRC and won 14.6 per cent of the total funds awarded through the NIHR funding streams open to them.

There are clear benefits, for the whole medical research community in these islands, from Scotland remaining within a research funding system with the rest of the UK. An independent Scotland, contributing directly to the overall research council budget, will be in a strong position to influence research priority setting at a UK level.

Levels of public investment in university research will enable our researchers and universities to remain internationally competitive, with current levels of public investment in university research, through the Scottish Funding Council and Research Councils, at least maintained.

200. **How will independence affect the length of NHS waiting lists in Scotland?**
As NHS Scotland is already under the control of the Scottish Parliament, its values and priorities will continue on independence. However, with independence, the Scottish budget will no longer be constrained by decisions made at Westminster, and will therefore reflect Scottish priorities.

Our approach to transforming waiting times for patients is an example of how better results are achieved for the people of Scotland when decisions are made in Scotland. As part of the Patient Rights (Scotland) Act 2011, the Scottish Government introduced the 12 week Treatment Time Guarantee for inpatients and day cases which enshrines in law a patient's right to be treated within 12 weeks. By March 2013, 97.5 per cent of patients waited less than the 12 week standard for a first outpatient consultation. This compares with waits of six months in March 2007.

201. Will an independent Scotland still have free prescriptions?

Yes. The move to independence will not change the benefits we currently enjoy. Decisions on things like free prescriptions will form part of the policies set out by parties in their manifestos for future Scottish parliamentary elections, with the political parties each offering their own approach, just as now. The current Scottish Government's vision for the NHS in Scotland is a publicly funded health service providing care free at the point of delivery for all who need it. This includes free prescriptions.

202. What will happen to free personal care in an independent Scotland?

We have no plans to change the successful policy of Free Personal and Nursing Care in an independent Scotland. This distinctively Scottish approach is an example of how decisions made in Scotland provide better outcomes for the people of Scotland.

203. Will an independent Scotland have to put in place new arrangements for medical training and education?

No. Scotland already has five medical schools, which continue to attract high numbers of undergraduates from across Scotland and England, Wales and Northern Ireland, as well as students from overseas, who want to study medicine.

Medical education operates in a world-wide market, and Scotland continues to enjoy a well-earned reputation for providing trainee doctors with high quality training and development opportunities. Given these strengths, we see co-operation on medical training continuing on the same four-country basis as today.

204. Will medical workforce representatives participate in NHS Scotland pay negotiation processes after independence?

Yes. Responsibility for pay, terms and conditions of service for staff in NHS Scotland is already devolved.

The Scottish Government will ensure that they continue to have independent pay advice when setting pay for NHS Scotland doctors and dentists.

In recent years the Scottish Government has successfully developed a Scottish GP contract with the British Medical

Association (BMA), and with independence we will continue to work with them to ensure that GP contracts are developed to meet the needs and circumstances of the people of Scotland.

Similarly, for hospital-based doctors and dentists, the Scottish Government will work with the BMA, and seek to co-operate with the Westminster Government where appropriate, to negotiate pay, terms and conditions.

The funding and terms and conditions for General Dental Services, General Ophthalmic Services and Community Pharmacy are already devolved and fully negotiated in Scotland. These arrangements will also not change.

205. **Will Scotland continue to access services from NICE (National Institute for Clinical Excellence)?**
In Scotland, NHS Healthcare Improvement Scotland provides a similar function to that provided by NICE in England and Wales. The Scottish Medicines Consortium already delivers the functions of NICE in Scotland in relation to access to new medicines and will continue to do so.

The Scottish Government currently purchases some services from NICE via a Service Level Agreement negotiated and operated by Healthcare Improvement Scotland. This arrangement too could continue in an independent Scotland.

206. **How will an independent Scotland agree the price of medicines with the pharmaceutical industry?**
The UK Department of Health currently agrees the pricing of medicines on a UK-wide basis given that this is currently a reserved area. Negotiations on new pricing arrangements from 1 January 2014 have been agreed between the Department of Health and the Association of British Pharmaceutical Industry (ABPI). The agreement will run for a five year period in line with previous agreements.

Independence will provide the Scottish Government with an opportunity to negotiate its own pricing arrangements directly and in partnership with the pharmaceutical industry with a view to securing the best possible deal for both NHS Scotland and Scottish patients.

207. **What will happen to blood donor services in an independent Scotland?**

Scotland already has a fully independent blood donor service. NHS Blood and Transplant (NHSBT) has in place a reciprocal agreement with the Scottish National Blood Transfusion Service (SNBTS) and the other UK Blood Services to provide mutual assistance in the event of a blood shortage or unplanned event that affects their ability to supply hospitals. Following independence, this Government proposes to continue this reciprocal arrangement.

208. **How will an independent Scotland organise organ donation and transplantation services?**

Organ donation and transplant activity across the UK is co-ordinated by NHS Blood and Transplant (NHSBT) which operates in Scotland under a contractual arrangement with the Scottish Government. The Scottish Government contributes to the running costs of NHSBT and the organisation is accountable to Scottish Ministers for the organ donation and transplantation activities it undertakes in Scotland.

Donations and transplantations are organised jointly across the UK as it is in the best interests of patients to ensure that organs have the best match to recipients. We will be able to continue these arrangements following independence, in much the same way that the Health Service Executive of the Republic of Ireland currently works with NHSBT on transplants. This is the same as other parts of Europe where groups of countries work together across borders to achieve the best outcomes for their patients.

209. **Will I still be able to get specialist treatment in England?**

Yes. The NHS in Scotland already co-operates with England, as well as with other countries for some services, to provide a range of specialised services not routinely available in Scotland. Access to a range of highly specialised services in England is managed and paid for by NHS National Services Scotland. Similarly, services currently offered in Scotland to patients from England will continue in an independent Scotland.

The Westminster and Scottish Governments also have arrangements in place with a number of other nations, including the Republic of Ireland, for reciprocal treatment. It will be in everyone's interest for such arrangements and co-operation to continue in an independent Scotland.

210. **Will I be able to get NHS treatment if I am taken ill while in England?**

Yes. Following independence, should someone resident in Scotland take ill while in England, Wales or Northern Ireland they will be treated by local health services according to their clinical need, just as they are now.

Equally, visitors to Scotland from elsewhere in the UK will be cared for and treated as they are under current arrangements. EU directives protect access to such treatment.

211. **What will the law on abortion be in an independent Scotland?**

On the principle of continuation of existing law, current legislation on abortion will continue to apply within an independent Scotland until such times as that legislation is amended or repealed by the Parliament of an independent Scotland. There are no plans to change the current abortion time limit.

Housing and Regeneration

212. **What will happen to Housing Benefit in an independent Scotland?**

Housing Benefit in an independent Scotland will form part of a national social protection system. This Government's proposal is to preserve Housing Benefit as a standalone benefit rather than include it as part of a single benefit payment.

Scotland's Balance Sheet, published on 14 April 2013, shows that in 2011/12, social protection expenditure was equivalent to 14.4 per cent of economic output (GDP). This is lower than the equivalent UK figure of 15.9 per cent. In addition, spending on social protection in Scotland, as a share of the economy, has been lower than in the UK for the last five years, and is also lower than in the majority of other EU-15 countries.

213. **Will Scottish governments be able to do more to invest in affordable housing in an independent Scotland?**

Yes. There will be opportunities for more investment in affordable housing in an independent Scotland.

Full flexibility over Scotland's budgets, only available through independence, will enable future Scottish governments to:

- broaden action to make more affordable housing available to alleviate homelessness and tackle fuel poverty

- take action to further improve the quality of housing, for example in the social rented sector

- introduce different ways of supporting first time buyers

For more information see Chapter 4.

Social Justice

214. What makes you think an independent Scotland will be a fairer country?

The sort of country we become will be up to the people of Scotland. Scotland has the wealth it needs to be a fairer country. We are one of the richest nations on the planet and could choose to use that wealth in a different way than Westminster. For example, we can choose to invest in childcare instead of spending money on defence. We can choose not to impose the "bedroom tax" and to have a more efficient tax system that ensures everyone pays up their fair share. With independence we can make different choices in line with our values and the views of the people of Scotland.

To find out more about the democratic opportunities of independence, go to Chapter 1. You can find out more about this Government's commitment to a more socially just Scotland in Chapter 4.

215. Will independence mean Scotland will become a fairer society?

One of the main reasons for independence is to give Scotland the powers to make our society fairer. Scotland can make our wealth work better for the people living here and follow a different path from Westminster. The UK is now one of the ten least equal countries in the OECD. It ranks 28th out of 34 on a measure of overall inequality. OECD analysis shows that, since 1975, income inequality among working-age people has increased faster in the UK than in any other country in the organisation.

Academic analysis comparing the earnings of the worst off and those best off has found that the UK was the fourth most unequal nation amongst the world's richest countries.

These outcomes are not the result of the policies of one government, but of almost 40 years of decisions at Westminster.

With independence, Scotland can make decisions on tax, welfare and employment that help the poorest in our society, not make life worse for them.

216. How might a Scottish approach to tackling poverty be different?

This Government will not follow the same approach being adopted by Westminster which chooses to reduce support for one million Scottish households. We believe that Scotland is wealthy enough to make Scotland fairer, if we so choose. Key measures this Government proposes include:

- introducing a universal early learning and childcare system for all children aged one to school entry

- abolishing the "bedroom tax"

- reducing heating bills

- making improvements to the State Pension

217. How could an independent Scotland avoid poverty arising, as well as redressing its effects?

The political make up of the Scottish Parliament is very different from that at Westminster, where policy choices over the past forty years have resulted in an overall increase in income inequality and, most recently, with the majority of people seeing their living standards squeezed. For example, there is a consensus in the Scottish Parliament around issues like the living wage, which means more people in Scotland will receive fair reward for their hard work and efforts.

It is unlikely that a Scottish Parliament with powers over welfare and taxation would have introduced the "bedroom tax" or reduced the personal allowance for pensioners. Scotland is already taking a different path to reducing poverty by addressing the underlying causes, helping people before they reach crisis point and helping people to help themselves.

The Scottish package of universal support, including free personal care, concessionary travel, free prescriptions and the Council Tax freeze, supports those on low incomes most.

Sport

218. Will Scotland have its own Olympics and Paralympics teams?
Yes. Scotland currently meets all of the qualifying requirements of the International Olympic and Paralympic Committees (IOC), other than being an independent state.

Arrangements will be put in place to ensure that Scottish athletes were able to compete in Rio 2016 by attending any necessary qualifying events in the lead up to Rio 2016. This work would be undertaken in parallel to the wider governance arrangements required for Olympic and Paralympic accreditation, establishing Scottish Olympic and Paralympic Committees and transferring functions currently undertaken at UK level.

It is only through independence that Scotland can have its own teams for the next Olympics and Paralympics.

219. Will independence affect who can play for the Scottish rugby and football teams?
No. The criteria to play for Scotland at a sport are set by each world governing body (FIFA for football, IRB for rugby etc) and not by the Scottish or Westminster Governments.

220. Will Scottish football teams still be able to compete in FIFA and UEFA competitions?
Yes. The Scottish Football Association (SFA) is already a member of FIFA, the world governing body for football. Likewise, the SFA is also an affiliate member of UEFA (Union of European Football Associations).

221. **Will an independent Scotland still be able to host the Open Golf Tournament?**

Yes. The Royal and Ancient are responsible for determining the venue of the Open. Scotland is the home of golf and Scottish golf clubs will continue to be part of the rota to host the Open championships. Both the 2015 and 2016 events are planned for Scotland.

222. **How will an independent Scotland ensure that elite sport continues to secure appropriate levels of funding and facilities?**

Scotland already has a number of world class competition and training facilities. Our national agency for sport (**sport**scotland) has responsibility for all aspects of community and performance sport up to Commonwealth Games level.

It will be for the Parliament of an independent Scotland to decide how best to generate and deploy this resource to the benefit of Scottish sport in future.

223. **Would all Scottish athletes have to compete for Scotland or would they be free to represent the likes of "Team GB"?**

Athletes are currently free to choose which country they represent providing they meet that country's relevant qualifying criteria. Whilst the Scottish Government hopes that all athletes who are qualified to represent Scotland will do so, this is a personal decision.

Early Learning and Childcare

**224.   Could an independent Scotland provide childcare
at a reasonable cost?**
Yes. The current Scottish Government proposes a
transformation in early years learning and childcare provision.
Independence will give us the opportunity to invest more in the
supply of services, rather than subsidising demand. This is the
approach adopted in the most successful countries and will
ensure resources are spent most effectively, and make
childcare more affordable for all.

**225.   What would independence mean for early learning
and childcare?**
Independence gives us the opportunity to do more to deliver
world-class early learning and childcare. As a first step in
realising this transformational vision, this Government plans to
extend the current provision of 600 hours a year to around half
of two year olds in the first budget of an independent Scotland.
Those whose parents are currently on working tax credit or child
tax credit will benefit.

We aim, by the end of the first term of an independent Scottish
Parliament, to increase this entitlement to 1,140 hours for all
three and four year olds, and vulnerable two year olds. Our
long-term objective is that by the end of the second Parliament
all children from age one to when they enter school will have an
entitlement to 1,140 hours a year of high quality early learning
and childcare, giving young children the same number of hours
as primary school children.

**226.   What will maternity and paternity rights, and flexible
parental leave look like in an independent Scotland?**
Powers over these issues will transfer to the Scottish
Parliament on independence. On independence, parents will
continue to have the same maternity and paternity rights as
now, with future Scottish governments then able to decide how
the system of parental support should be improved.

Schools

227.   **What would independence mean for education in Scotland?**
Education is already almost fully devolved to Scotland. Our
system is performing well. Scottish pupils outperform the OECD
average in reading and science, and are similar to it in maths,
and the latest results show that we have halted a period of
relative international decline since 2000. These improvements,
achieved under devolution, show that when decisions are made
in Scotland better results are achieved for Scotland.

Our detailed proposals for education in an independent
Scotland are set out in Chapter 5.

228.   **What will independence mean for schools?**
The management of the school system in Scotland is already
fully devolved.

229.   **What educational rights would people expect in an
independent Scotland?**
This Government believes that Scotland's permanent written
constitution should include the right to education and the right
for every young person to be offered a job or training.

230.   **What will independence mean for denominational schools?**
The present system will continue. Faith-based education makes
an important and valued contribution to Scottish society and the
right of parents to make that choice for their children will remain.

231.   **What will independence mean for skills and training in
Scotland?**
Independence offers Scotland an opportunity fully to mobilise its
resources to build a skilled workforce ready to meet demand. At
the moment, the financial benefits of successful employment
initiatives by the Scottish Government – such as Modern
Apprenticeships, higher and further education funding and other
training programmes – go to Westminster in the form of reduced
welfare payments and increased taxation. With independence
we will be able to retain these benefits in Scotland and will be
able to re-invest them in our people.

232. **What will independence mean for Gaelic?**
Gaelic has been a continuing element in Scottish heritage, identity and history for many centuries. Gaelic has official recognition and it is an increasingly visible part of Scottish public life reaching into education, the arts, media and broadcasting. In an independent Scotland, Gaelic will have a central place in Scottish public life.

233. **What would the priorities be for Gaelic in an independent Scotland?**
Our aim as a government would be to continue to reverse the decline of Gaelic in Scotland. The most recent Census has demonstrated that initiatives in support of Gaelic have significantly slowed down the decline of the language. Policy and resources would continue to be directed to the priority of increasing the numbers speaking, learning and using the language.

234. **Will Gaelic be recognised as an official language in an independent Scotland?**
In Scotland, Gaelic has a significant level of official support from the Scottish Government. Official recognition for Gaelic is also provided by the 2005 Gaelic Act. In an independent Scotland this official recognition would be confirmed and maintained.

235. **Will there be more support for the Scots Language in an independent Scotland?**
The 2011 Census, for the first time, provided information on the numbers of Scots speakers. This information, in an independent Scotland, will assist in developing policy and promoting the use and status of the Scots language and supporting communities that speak Scots.

University Access, Tuition Fees and Cross-border Flow

236. **Will students resident in Scotland be able to go to university in Scotland without paying fees?**
Yes. The current Scottish Government remains committed to access to higher education for eligible Scots based on the ability to learn, not the ability to pay. This means eligible undergraduate students attending university in an independent Scotland will not have to pay tuition fees.

237.   **Would Scotland still charge students from the rest of the UK tuition fees?**

Yes. The divergence in funding policy between Scotland and England and the resulting disparity in the cost of a university education creates a huge financial incentive for students from England to study in Scotland. In that context, and to ensure Scottish students remain able to study at Scottish Higher Education Institutions, we propose maintaining the status quo by continuing our policy of allowing Scottish Higher Education Institutions to set their own annual tuition fees for students from the rest of the UK at a rate no higher than the maximum annual tuition fee rate chargeable to such students by universities in the rest of the UK.

238.   **Would charging students from the rest of the UK tuition fees in an independent Scotland be compatible with EU law?**

We believe that the unique and unprecedented position of a post-independent Scotland will enable us to continue our current policy in a way which is consistent with the principles of free movement across the EU as a whole and which is compatible with EU requirements.

239.   **Are you confident that the Court of Justice of the EU will support this position?**

Each member state is free to adopt its own domestic policies, consistent with the objectives of the EU. We believe that our fees policies contribute to student mobility across the wider EU, while addressing the consequences of the unique situation of Scottish independence. In these circumstances we believe that it will be possible to deliver our policy in a way which is compatible with EU requirements.

240.   **Will students from parts of the EU other than the rest of the UK pay tuition fees?**

Students from other parts of the EU have the same right of access to education as home students. This means EU applicants are considered for entry on the same academic basis as home students and pay the same. This will remain the case with independence.

241. **Will other international (non-EU) students be attracted to study in an independent Scotland?**
Scottish Universities are amongst the best in the world and highly attractive to overseas students. In January 2013, 21 per cent of students studying in Scotland were from outwith the UK, including 28,500 international students from outwith the EU. This world beating quality will ensure an independent Scotland continues to attract the brightest and best students from around the world to study here.

Independence will allow Scotland to develop its own immigration policies addressing the negative impact of changes to student visas implemented by the current Westminster Government. This will ensure that we benefit from the skills and enthusiasm of those highly educated young people who wish to study here and make Scotland their home.

242. **Will non-EU/international students be charged tuition fees?**
Charges for international students are at the discretion of each individual higher education institution and this will continue to be the case in an independent Scotland.

243. **Will the Westminster Government's policy on visas for international students continue to apply in an independent Scotland?**
Westminster Government decisions on student visas have deterred some international students, posing a direct threat to Scotland's universities and colleges. Independence will allow Scotland to develop its own immigration system ensuring that we benefit from the skills and enthusiasm of those highly educated young people who wish to make Scotland their home.

Our proposals on visa arrangement for international students are set out in Chapter 7.

244. Will there still be four-year degrees in an independent Scotland?

The current Scottish Government believes the flexibility of the four-year degree and potential for progression through the currently available direct entry routes is a strength of the sector. The Government intends that an independent Scotland will continue with this and will support any moves to increase choices and flexibility for our students.

245. Will UCAS continue to administer applications to Scottish universities in an independent Scotland?

Scotland's universities are autonomous institutions and currently choose to provide this service through UCAS. Independence will not affect universities' ability to make this choice.

Research Funding in an Independent Scotland

246. How will research be supported in an independent Scotland?

The excellence of Scottish universities is recognised internationally and they are highly successful in winning competitive funding grants. Building on their reputation our universities will continue to compete for substantial funding for their research on the same competitive basis as they do currently.

Our proposals to support research and innovation in Scotland are set out in Chapter 3.

247. Will an independent Scotland set up its own research councils?

There are a number of options for research funding in an independent Scotland including establishing a Scottish Research Council for the allocation of research monies or as a mechanism for directing funding into existing pan-UK research councils. We recognise the benefits – for the academic community, business and research charities across the UK – of maintaining long-term stability in research funding and systems that support initiatives of scale and researchers working together across boundaries. With independence we will seek to maintain a common research area with the rest of the UK including existing shared Research Councils.

248. **Why would UK research councils continue to fund research in an independent Scotland?**

Scotland already contributes to funding of the UK Research Councils through the tax base and this Government intends that it should continue to contribute as an independent country. The excellence of Scottish universities' research is reflected in their success in winning competitive UK Research Council grant funding.

The rest of the UK benefits from Scotland's high quality research and our centres of excellence and shared infrastructure are used by researchers from across the UK including: five Medical Research Council research centres; five Isotope facilities; the All-Waters Combined Current and Wave Test Facility; and the Roslin Institute.

Successful research depends on collaboration across boundaries, whether disciplinary, institutional or national. Research collaboration contributes directly to the competitiveness of the Scottish and UK economies through knowledge creation and exchange and direct collaboration with business, as well as supporting intellectual life and the academic aspirations of institutions and researchers.

It is in both Scotland's and the UK's interests to minimise any barriers to research collaboration and to maintain a common research area.

249. **How would the research councils be funded?**

Scotland already contributes to the funding of the Research Councils through the tax base. Following independence, Scotland would contribute directly from the Scottish Government budget giving us a clearer role in setting the strategic objectives of these bodies. With independence, we would intend to negotiate with Westminster a fair funding formula for Scotland's contribution based on population share but taking reasonable account of the fact that the amount of research funding received by Scottish institutions from the Research Councils may reflect higher or lower levels of funding.

250. **Will independence weaken university research in Scotland?**
No. We will seek to continue the current common research area
arrangements and funding through the existing research
councils. And while the UK will remain an important research
partner, Scotland can also build on the significant successes
achieved in working across European boundaries by hosting
international research centres who are increasingly attracted
to Scotland by the quality of our research base. The current
Scottish Government supports the European Commission in its
ambition for "a reinforced European research area partnership
for excellence and growth" with researchers, research
institutions and businesses moving, competing and
co-operating across borders more intensively.

Levels of public investment in university research will be
sufficient to enable our researchers and universities to remain
internationally competitive with current levels of public
investment in university research, through the Scottish Funding
Council and Research Councils, at least maintained as part of
wider and longer term plans to enhance levels of investment in
research and development in Scotland from the private sector
and other sources.

The present Scottish Government also intends to use the
powers of independence to address one of the biggest threats
to research in Scotland as a result of the policies of the current
Westminster Government. We plan to reintroduce the post-
study work visa, which was abolished by Westminster in April
2012. This visa will encourage more talented people from
around the world to further their education in Scotland,
providing income for Scotland's institutions and contributing
to a growing economy.

251. **How will Scottish research continue to benefit from UK
charities' research funding?**
Charities, like businesses, will make decisions to fund research
in an independent Scotland based upon reputation, excellence
and value for money – just as they do now.

For example, for as long as our universities and NHS research base continue to be seen as world leaders in the research and treatment of diseases – from cancer to Parkinson's – then Scotland will continue to attract funding accordingly.

UK charities, such as Cancer Research, provided competitively funded research in Scotland of £121 million in 2011/12. Scots are also generous contributors to UK charities, both financially and by way of fundraising and volunteering activities.

252. How will independence affect jobs of academics and those in related areas?
The current Scottish Government's investment in our universities has allowed them to attract an increasing number of talented researchers and academics from around the world. This has contributed to our success and independence would put our universities in an even stronger position as it would allow Scotland to remove the barriers caused by the current Westminster Government's visa regulations.

253. How will postgraduate study be supported in an independent Scotland?
Education is already fully devolved to the Scottish Parliament. The current Scottish Government has demonstrated its commitment to supporting postgraduate study and would maintain this commitment following independence.

International Relations and External Affairs

Our relationship with the rest of the UK

254. **What will the relationship be between an independent Scotland and the rest of the United Kingdom?**
Independence will enable Scotland to create a new and equal relationship with the other nations of these Isles. We will be able to update our partnership so that it meets the needs of the people of Scotland.

Under our proposals, we will keep our close links of family and friendship through an ongoing social union and will continue to share the Queen as head of state, as 16 Commonwealth countries already do, and we will share the pound as our currency.

Independence will end the parliamentary union so we will no longer send MPs to Westminster. Decisions about Scotland's future and about our economy and society will be taken in Scotland. We will be equal partners within the European Union and the common defence partnership in NATO. To find out more about our important ongoing relationship with England, Wales and Northern Ireland, see Chapter 6.

255. **Will independence mean that Scottish people require a passport to travel to England?**
No. Just as no one from the UK needs a passport to travel to Ireland now, there will be free movement across the border between Scotland and England.

The Common Travel Area has existed since the 1920s and currently allows freedom of movement for nationals of the UK, the Republic of Ireland, the Isle of Man and the Channel Islands. It will be in the interests of all partners for an independent Scotland to remain in the Common Travel Area.

Our Relationship with Europe

256. How will Scotland become an independent member of the European Union?

Following a vote for independence, the Scottish Government will immediately enter into negotiations with Westminster and EU member states to ensure that an independent Scotland achieves a smooth and timely transition to independent membership of the EU. Scotland will negotiate the terms of membership of the EU during the period we are still part of the UK and, therefore, part of the EU.

There is, within the EU Treaties, a legal framework by which Scotland, a country that has been an integral part of the EU for 40 years, may make the transition to independent EU membership in the period between the referendum and the date on which Scotland becomes an independent state. Article 48 provides a suitable legal route to facilitate the transition process, by allowing the EU Treaties to be amended through ordinary revision procedure before Scotland becomes independent, to enable it to become a member state at the point of independence.

There is no Treaty provision that would require Scotland to leave the EU on independence. It would also be against the self-interest of the EU collectively, and of the Member States individually, to seek to deprive Scotland of EU membership given that Scotland is an integral and highly valued part of the single market. Throughout its history the guiding principle of the EU has been enlargement of its membership, not contraction.

257. Why will an independent Scotland wish to be part of Europe?

Scotland has been a constituent part of the EU since the accession of the UK in 1973 and benefits greatly from the peace, security and economic opportunities provided by membership of the European Union. Over these 40 years Scotland's economy and society have become an integral and fully integrated part of the EU single market.

The best way for Scotland to be represented in the EU is as an independent nation, with our own seat at the top table. This will allow Scottish Governments to represent Scotland's interests in areas like fisheries, which have not been given sufficient priority by Westminster.

Scotland's citizens enjoy freedom of movement and the right to work and study in other member states. The ability to trade within a single market of 500 million citizens is of central importance to our strategy to stimulate growth by increasing international trade. Around 158,000 EU citizens have also chosen to live and work or study in Scotland.

The European Union continues to be Scotland's top overseas export destination – the value of exports destined for countries within the EU is estimated at £11 billion in 2011.

258. **Is the proposed transition period between the referendum and becoming independent in March 2016 enough time for Scotland to become a recognised independent member state of the European Union?**
Yes. Scotland already complies with EU laws, people in Scotland are already EU citizens and Scotland is already a member of the EU.

259. **Would an independent Scotland's voice in Europe be weaker or stronger?**
Stronger. Scotland currently has a limited voice in Europe. The Scottish Government is permitted to make an input to Westminster discussions about EU proposals that impact on devolved matters, but Westminster is under no obligation to take account of the views of the Scottish Government when determining its position at EU-level negotiations.

Independence will give Scotland our own voice in Europe, participating at every level in the EU policy process and ensuring that Scottish governments are able to promote and protect Scotland's national interests in EU affairs.

As an independent member state the Scottish Government will be able directly to promote our economic and social interests and protect our citizens by participating on equal terms with all other member states in EU affairs. Scottish Ministers would participate fully in meetings of the Council of the European Union and Scotland would have increased representation in the European Parliament, thereby increasing Scotland's voice in the two legislative bodies of the EU.

Where Scotland's interests coincide with the interests of the rest of the UK, together we will form a more powerful voice for action. When Scotland has a distinct view, we will have a new ability to build alliances and make our case, ensuring that what is right for the people of Scotland is heard.

The current Scottish Government firmly believes the only government capable of properly representing Scotland's interests in the EU decision-making process is a government elected by, and directly accountable to, the people of Scotland.

260. **Will Scotland be forced to join the Euro?**
No. In order to be considered for membership of the Eurozone, countries need to choose to include their currency in the Exchange Rate Mechanism II and there are no plans for Scotland to do this. No country can be forced to join the Euro against its will.

261. **When will Scotland begin negotiations to join the EU?**
Following a vote for independence in the 2014 referendum, the Scottish Government will immediately enter into negotiations with Westminster and EU member states to ensure that an independent Scotland achieves a smooth and timely transition to independent membership of the European Union.

262. **How long would the process of EU membership take?**
The negotiations to secure the transition to independent EU membership will be conducted between the date of the vote on 18 September 2014 and 24 March 2016 when Scotland becomes an independent state. During this period Scotland will remain part of the UK.

These negotiations will include discussions to determine the specific terms, and where necessary any transitional arrangements, under which an independent Scotland will take its place as a full EU member state.

Scotland has been a member of the EU for 40 years and already complies with its body of law. The 18 month period between the referendum and the planned date of formal independence provides sufficient time for discussions settling an independent Scotland's terms of EU membership. In the current context of devolution the Scottish Government has already demonstrated its capacity to transpose and implement the provisions of EU legislation.

263. **How does this predicted timescale compare to the process for previous accession states?**
Scotland will not be an accession state. We will negotiate the transition from being an EU member as part of the UK to becoming an independent member of the EU from within the EU. The predicted timescale compares well with the most similar sets of previous circumstances. For example, the transition to EU membership for East Germany during its reunification with West Germany took 11 months from the fall of the Berlin Wall.

264. **Will Scotland's membership of the EU require the agreement of all member states?**
Yes. The terms of Scotland's membership will be agreed with the EU and the necessary Treaty amendments will be taken forward with the agreement of member states.

265. **Will an independent Scotland continue to qualify for a European rebate?**
The EU budget has been agreed until 2020 and the Scottish Government will not seek to re-open budget discussions until the next funding cycle, at which point we will be negotiating as a full member state. Prior to 2020, the division of the share of the UK rebate will be a matter for agreement between the Scottish and Westminster Governments and the Scottish Government will argue for an equitable share.

266. **What impact will the Conservative Party proposal to have a UK referendum on EU membership have?**
It is the view of the current Scottish Government that the only real risk to Scotland's membership of the EU is the referendum proposed by the Prime Minister.

The Scottish Government does not wish Scotland to leave the EU and does not support the Prime Minister's plans to hold an in-out referendum on EU membership.

Following a vote for independence, Scotland will become an independent EU member state before the planned in-out referendum on the EU in 2017. However, if we do not become independent, we risk being taken out of the EU against our will.

Customs

267. **Will independence have a negative effect on trade between Scotland and the rest of the UK and Europe?**
No. As part of the EU, Scotland will remain part of the EU single market.

Membership of International Organisations and International Obligations

268. **Would an independent Scotland become a member of NATO, the United Nations and other international organisations?**
Following a vote for independence the Scottish Government will formally declare Scotland's intention to become a member of NATO following normal procedures. Similarly we will also signal our intention to be a member of the United Nations at that time.

Given that Scotland, as part of the UK, already meets membership requirements, we do not expect any barriers to Scotland's timely membership of international organisations.

269. **How much would an independent Scotland contribute to the budgets of international organisations such as the United Nations?**
Scotland's contribution to the budgets of the United Nations and other international organisations would be agreed as part of the membership process for each organisation. It is important to remember that Scotland already contributes to the budgets of these organisations, through our taxes, as part of the UK's contribution.

270. **How would Scotland afford international organisation memberships?**
Scotland already pays a share of the UK's membership fees for international organisations. Other states of a similar size to – and smaller than – Scotland are members of international organisations. Our membership costs would be appropriate to our size and would be determined by the funding protocol for each organisation.

271. **Would Scotland have a seat on the UN Security Council?**
An independent Scotland would not expect to have a permanent seat on the Security Council. Like other nations, Scotland would from time to time be a non-permanent member of the UN Security Council according to the existing system of election for non-permanent members by the General Assembly.

The current Scottish Government would intend to support the rest of the UK remaining a permanent member of the UN Security Council.

272. **Will independence make Scotland's voice weaker or stronger internationally?**
Stronger. Today, Scotland's Government and Parliament do not have an automatic right to speak directly on the international stage. The fundamental advantage of independence in foreign affairs is the ability always to put Scotland's interests first. Our overseas network of embassies and consulates will be working to promote Scotland's interests, in particular to develop opportunities for trade and investment.

273. **What principles would an independent Scotland follow in regard to foreign policy?**
The current Scottish Government's foreign, security and defence policies would be grounded in a clear framework of promoting sustainable economic growth, participating in rules-based international co-operation to secure shared interests and protecting Scotland's people and resources.

274. **What international legal obligations that currently apply to the UK would an independent Scotland have to adhere to?**
As an independent nation Scotland will continue to meet all legal obligations that flow from our membership of international organisations and treaties.

275. **What will the status of the UN Convention on the Rights of the Child (UNCRC) be in an independent Scotland?**
An independent Scotland will continue as a party to the UNCRC and would reflect the Convention's principles in domestic legislation and policy.

Membership of NATO

276. **Will Scotland be a member of NATO?**
It is the intention of the current Scottish Government that Scotland will be a non-nuclear member of NATO. Following a vote for independence the Scottish Government will formally declare its intention to become a member of NATO. Given Scotland's key strategic position in Europe, we expect Scotland to be welcomed as a valued partner.

277. **Why would NATO want Scotland as a member?**
Scotland is situated in a position of strategic importance, close to the Arctic channels of the High North and with the Atlantic Ocean to its west. An independent Scotland will therefore be a key partner in NATO's air and naval policing arrangements for northern Europe, and it is in both Scotland's and NATO's interests for an independent Scotland to work closely with, and to be a member of, the alliance.

Comparable non-nuclear nations can and do make significant contributions to NATO operations and deploy capabilities that are proportionate but effective – for example Denmark has had a leading role in the delivery of anti-piracy operations off the Horn of Africa and both Norway and Denmark made significant contributions of air power to the operation in Libya.

278. **Would Scotland look to participate fully in NATO activities with the exception of being a nuclear power?**
An independent Scotland will take its NATO membership seriously. The present Scottish Government's policy is that this will involve committing resources and contributing to NATO's collective defence activities and humanitarian relief missions. At all times, Scotland will work within the UN and NATO charters.

279. **Is membership of NATO consistent with removing nuclear weapons from Scotland?**
Yes. The Scottish Government's opposition to the possession of nuclear weapons is entirely consistent with the position of most NATO member states. Only three NATO members are nuclear-weapon states and 20 out of the 28 current member states neither possess nor host nuclear weapons.

280. **Would membership of the alliance result in NATO bases or activity being located in Scotland?**
Scotland will seek to play a constructive role as a member of NATO and we intend that Scotland will participate in NATO exercises and training operations, as all members of the alliance do. There are no NATO bases in Scotland as part of the UK, so it is unlikely that there will be in an independent Scotland.

281. **Why would an anti-nuclear Scotland wish to become a member of NATO as a nuclear alliance?**
An independent Scotland working within NATO will be a positive contributor to international peace and security. This position would be similar to the majority of NATO member countries who neither possess nor host nuclear weapons.

NATO's Strategic Concept states that the alliance is "resolved to seek a safer world and to create the conditions for a world without nuclear weapons" – an aim that the current Scottish Government shares.

Scotland's membership of the alliance will bring significant benefits for defence and security co-operation within our region, and will demonstrate a clear commitment towards working in close, responsible and peaceful co-operation with Scotland's neighbours and allies.

282. **Will NATO members with nuclear-armed vessels be allowed to enter Scottish waters or dock at Scottish ports?**
It is our firm position that an independent Scotland should not host nuclear weapons and we would only join NATO on that basis.

While the presence of nuclear weapons on a particular vessel is never confirmed by any country, we would expect any visiting vessel to respect the rules that are laid down by the government of an independent Scotland.

While they are both strong advocates for nuclear disarmament, both Norway and Denmark allow NATO vessels to visit their ports without confirming or denying whether they carry nuclear weapons. We intend that Scotland will adopt a similar approach as Denmark and Norway in this respect.

283. **Would Scotland provide forces to NATO as part of a collective defence (Article 5) operation?**
Yes, subject to our domestic approval arrangements. As a NATO member, Scotland will support collective defence operations (Article 5 operations), in accordance with the UN Charter, where a member of the alliance is the subject of an armed attack.

In order for NATO to invoke Article 5, each member state must be in agreement. It is for each member state to decide and agree what role they take in any military response. No member state is compelled to take part in such operations.

284. **Could NATO membership commit Scotland to taking part in military operations that it did not agree with?**
No. It is for each member state to decide and agree what role they take in any military operation.

285. **Will NATO membership make it more difficult to secure the removal of Trident?**
The removal of Trident nuclear weapons from Scotland will require negotiation with Westminster and liaison with NATO. But the aim of the current Scottish Government is clear – to secure the speediest safe removal of Trident from Scotland and to join the 20 (of 28) countries who are members of NATO without either possessing or hosting nuclear weapons.

We believe that a non-nuclear independent Scotland operating within NATO will be preferable, to the UK, NATO, and our other neighbours and allies, to a non-nuclear Scotland outside of the alliance.

286. **How long will it take to join NATO?**
Following a vote for independence in 2014, Scotland will notify
NATO of its intention to become a member of the alliance in
order to begin negotiations for Scotland's transition to becoming
an independent member of the alliance.

It will be for NATO to confirm the detailed arrangements and
timetable for Scotland's transition towards membership as an
independent country.

287. **Have there been discussions with NATO about Scotland's
membership?**
Yes. The Scottish Government has opened contact with NATO
regarding an independent Scotland's membership of the
organisation.

Foreign Policy and Representation

288. **How would an independent Scotland represent itself
internationally through embassies and consulates?**
An independent Scotland's overseas network will be
comparable to that of other nations of a similar size. The current
Scottish Government's proposed overseas representation for an
independent Scotland is set out in Chapter 6. A crucial part of
the role of our overseas offices will be to look for opportunities
to promote Scottish goods and services directly. The Team
Scotland approach will be built on and with independence our
government departments, the private sector and our diplomatic
missions will work together to promote Scotland.

289. **Will diplomatic missions be shared between an
independent Scotland and the rest of the UK?**
An independent Scotland will be represented overseas by a
network which works in the national interests of Scotland. The
current Scottish Government is open to the sharing of services
and facilities with the rest of the UK or with other countries
where this is of mutual benefit. Such arrangements already
exist between the UK and other nations, such as Canada.

290. **Would an independent Scotland recruit staff from the Foreign and Commonwealth Office to the Scottish foreign and diplomatic service?**
The Scottish Government will ensure that all its services are provided by qualified staff, who may have a range of backgrounds and experience. Recruitment opportunities may arise from existing open recruitment policies and the possibility of inward transfers, where that is appropriate.

291. **What size would the foreign and diplomatic service be in an independent Scotland?**
The current Scottish Government estimates the running costs of its initial proposed network of 70 to 90 overseas offices at £90-120 million. This is expected to be below Scotland's population share of the UK's total expenditure on overseas representation in 2016/17. Scotland would also be entitled to a fair share of the value of assets.

292. **How would an independent Scotland's diplomatic interests be represented in the period before it established its own diplomatic missions?**
The existing Scottish Development International (SDI) network of 27 overseas offices provides a firm foundation for independent Scottish international representation. Over the past five years SDI has increased Scotland's presence in emerging markets in the Middle East and Asia. The current Scottish Government proposes that the existing SDI network remains following independence, co-locating with the new diplomatic and consular services. Where SDI is currently located in a country but not in its capital city, a Scottish embassy or political mission would be established to supplement and complement the work of the trade offices.

293. **When will an independent Scotland have its own diplomatic missions up and running?**
The Scottish Government intends that Scotland will have an overseas network in place from day one of independence, building on our existing overseas offices and an appropriate share of existing UK assets.

294. **How will I get help abroad if I am Scottish? If I get stuck in Spain, will you rescue me?**
An independent Scotland will establish a network of overseas offices which will provide the same range of support and assistance to Scots abroad as currently provided by the UK. In addition, as EU citizens, Scots will have the right to request consular assistance from all other EU member states, including the UK.

295. **Under Scottish Government proposals to allow dual nationality, would people living in Scotland claiming dual Scottish/British nationality be allowed to call on the support of British embassies and consulates abroad?**
As EU citizens, Scots would have the right to request consular assistance from all other member states, including the UK. If travelling on their British passport, people with dual nationality would be entitled to call on the support of the British embassy or consulate, just as a person with dual Scottish and Irish citizenship could choose to travel on their Irish passport and request assistance from the Irish embassy or consulate.

International Development

296. **How much will an independent Scotland spend on international development?**
This is currently decided at Westminster and Scotland contributes to this spending through taxation. In an independent Scotland it will be decided by governments elected by the people of Scotland.

The current Scottish Government is committed to spending 0.7 per cent Gross National Income (GNI) on Official Development Assistance. The current Scottish Government also proposes to bring forward legislation to enshrine this as a binding target. Over the longer-term, we would work towards spending 1 per cent of GNI on aid.

297. **How could an independent Scotland afford that level of funding for international development? Is this an affordable commitment?**

This is one of the immediate priorities of the current Scottish Government for the first budget of an independent Scotland – the budget priorities of the current Government, and the proposed actions to raise revenue and reduce spending to support these priorities, are set out in Part 2 of this document. To put it in context, meeting our international aid obligation of 0.7 per cent of GNI will amount to just 70p out of every £100 of GNI. As well as the existing £9 million Scottish Government aid budget, Scottish taxes currently contribute to the UK international aid budget. The Westminster Government has committed to meet the target of 0.7 per cent of GNI within this financial year.

The 0.7 per cent target is calculated as a percentage of a country's GNI, therefore the size of the country is not relevant – the target is to spend an appropriate share of that GNI. As a country's economy becomes richer or poorer, so its contribution rises or falls.

298. **What impact will independence have on existing Department for International Development programmes?**

The Scottish Government intends to work with the UK's Department for International Development (DFID) to ensure that there is a smooth transition phase for programmes on the ground in developing countries. There will be continued funding support, where appropriate, to those DFID programmes which span the independence period to avoid any disruption to those programmes and their recipients. International Development is just one of the areas where future Scottish and Westminster governments can choose to work together to complement each other's activity. Scotland is likely to also be a significant donor to multilateral organisations reflecting similar priorities as the UK in this area.

299. **How can the Scottish Government justify spending money on international development – why aren't we spending this money at home?**
In 2012, an estimated 6.6 million children under the age of five – 18,000 a day – died from mostly preventable diseases. This huge preventable loss of life remains an urgent global problem which must be taken seriously.

Scotland is one of the wealthiest nations in the world and one of the purposes of independence is to make sure that wealth works better for the people who live here. However, we also recognise our wider international responsibilities and believe that investment in development internationally is the right thing to do.

300. **At the moment, the Scottish Government's international development funding goes directly to Scottish-based organisations and not directly to governments. Will this change if Scotland becomes independent?**
It is the view of the current Scottish Government that funding through civil society should remain a dominant feature of future Scottish development programmes.

301. **To which countries would an independent Scotland provide international development funding?**
These would be decisions for governments elected by the people of Scotland.

The current Scottish Government would consider this as we approach independence, with the Human Development Index as a central criterion in that decision-making process. We expect a geographically focussed aid policy in line with developing best practice and will develop open and objective criteria for the selection of partner countries. Ultimately, these decisions will be for the government of the day, but we hope to secure a degree of consensus regarding the criteria used to select partner countries to ensure stable and effective long-term partnerships with a small number of countries.

302. **Will an independent Scotland focus on gender equality as part of international development?**
Women and girls make up the majority of the world's poor and bear a disproportionate share of the burden of poverty and responsibility for caring for others. This Government is doing everything we can to promote equality in Scotland and we would want an independent Scotland's international policies to do the same.

303. **How will the focus on gender equality work in practice?**
Gender equality and the empowerment of women are United Nations Millennium Development Goals in their own right. They are also critical to the delivery of other key development goals including in education and health. It would therefore be right for an independent Scotland to put gender equality at the heart of its development work.

The present Scottish Government would ensure that policies put in place will be in line with international commitments and recognised good practice on gender equality.

304. **How will Scottish people know that money being spent overseas by the Scottish Government is making an impact?**
Scottish Governments will report to the Scottish Parliament regularly on Scotland's development impact.

305. **How will we know that the 'Do No Harm' approach is being implemented?**
To provide policy coherence and as an expression of the values driving our foreign policy, we propose that Scottish Government policies, on all issues, will do no harm to developing countries, will not undermine our international development aims and will ideally contribute to international development success.

This Government is committed to reporting to the Scottish Parliament on a regular basis on Scotland's development impact, including on our commitment to deliver a 'Do No Harm' approach.

Defence and Security

306. **What opportunities will independence bring to Scotland in terms of defence and security?**
Independence will enable Scotland to:

- set its own defence and security budget and maintain strong conventional defence forces to protect its people, territory, seas, airspace and national interests

- decide, with appropriate democratic oversight and respect for international law, the circumstances in which its forces are deployed overseas

- work closely with its partners – including the rest of the UK – to address global issues and contribute to international peace-keeping

- build a security and intelligence agency that is fit for purpose in the 21st century and is proportionate to, and reflects a full strategic assessment of, Scotland's needs

- legislate for, control, and oversee national security arrangements in Scotland, ensuring the constitutional rights of the Scottish people

The Scottish Government is committed to working closely with our neighbours – especially our partners across the British Isles, our trading partners, through bilateral relations with other nations and in key international institutions such as the European Union, NATO and the United Nations.

307. **What security risks would an independent Scotland face?**
Threats that countries face in the modern world tend to be international in nature. In common with other countries, an independent Scotland will require to work with partners to protect itself against international terrorism, cyber-crime and cyber-terrorism, threats that come from global instability and failed states, and international serious organised crime. Scotland will be able to build on the strong relationships we already have to promote security at home and abroad.

308. **What will Scotland's overall defence and security policy be?**

The Scottish Government's policy is for an independent Scotland to have defence and security capabilities that will, firstly, secure our territory, seas and airspace, our people and our national interests.

In light of Scotland's geography and interests, we will also have the opportunity to develop niche capabilities to support humanitarian operations, search and rescue, and other specialist land or maritime functions. These niche capabilities will support Scotland's own defence needs and also contribute to international partnerships and wider global efforts to secure peace and security.

The Scottish Government proposes to create Scotland's own domestic security and intelligence machinery sitting alongside our police service. This will see Scotland's national security arrangements being legislated for, controlled, and overseen in Scotland for the first time.

309. **Can an independent Scotland afford appropriate defence and security capabilities?**

These capabilities can be delivered from our planned annual defence and security budget of £2.5 billion. Comparable countries in Europe generally spend around 1.5 per cent of GDP on defence. In 2011/12, 1.5 per cent of Scotland's GDP was around £2.3 billion. An independent Scotland will have the right forces to defend the country properly and secure us against any threat we meet, working with our partners and allies.

With independence, Scotland will actually save on defence spending. Current UK defence policy – including spending on Trident – will cost the Scottish taxpayer £3 billion a year by 2016/17, although considerably less than this is actually spent in Scotland by Westminster.

310.   **What do you expect the implications will be for the rest
       of the UK in terms of defence and security?**
       It will be in the interests of Scotland and the rest of the UK to
       continue to work closely together to ensure the security of both
       countries. The UK will have a serious security partner in
       Scotland with effective capabilities meeting Scotland's needs
       and playing its part within NATO.

311.   **What defence and security assets would an independent
       Scotland look to inherit during independence negotiations?**
       Scotland and the rest of the UK will negotiate to ensure the
       proper defence and security of both countries from the date
       of independence. It will be in both countries' interests that this
       should be the basis of a constructive and enduring partnership
       in the months and years that follow.

       The priority will be for Scotland to secure the land, air and
       maritime capabilities – personnel and assets – that are required
       to protect our territory, people and national interests. This will
       include negotiations on a number of assets that are currently
       based in Scotland, as well as negotiation on capabilities that
       are located elsewhere, such as surface ships, air transport and
       other land, air and maritime equipment and expertise. The
       assets that the Scottish Government proposes an independent
       Scotland's army, navy, air and special forces will have are set
       out in Chapter 6.

       Scotland has invested, as part of the UK, in significant
       intelligence-gathering capabilities and would expect that
       investment to be recognised in the arrangements that will
       be developed.

Nuclear weapons and disarmament

312.   **Will an independent Scotland sign the Treaty on the
       Non-proliferation of Nuclear Weapons (NPT)?**
       Yes. It is the present Scottish Government's priority, as a good
       global citizen, to support and promote nuclear disarmament.
       That is the right thing for any responsible government to do.

We look forward to the opportunity for Scotland to add our name to those states that have ratified the Treaty, and to take forward our obligations in creating the conditions for a world without nuclear weapons.

313. **Would you sign/ratify the NPT if/while Trident nuclear weapons were still based at Faslane?**
Yes. We have made a clear commitment to secure the speediest safe withdrawal of Trident from Scotland following independence.

Scotland's ratification of the NPT will not rely on the detailed arrangements for the withdrawal of Trident.

314. **Would the removal of Trident from Scotland result in its decommissioning?**
It is the Scottish Government's preference to see Trident decommissioned, but that will be a matter for the government of the rest of the UK.

315. **How long will it take to remove Trident from Scotland and who will bear the cost?**
Nuclear weapons have been based in Scotland for almost half a century, despite the long-standing majority opposition of the people of Scotland. In addition, Scottish taxpayer contributions to Trident spending could support many more public sector jobs in Scotland than the weapons system currently brings to the Clyde, and every year therefore Scotland loses out because of the continuance of Trident nuclear weapons.

The detailed process and timetable for removal would be a priority for negotiation between the Scottish Government and the government of the rest of the UK. However, following a vote for independence, we would make early agreement on removal of nuclear weapons a priority. This would be with a view to the removal of Trident within the first term of the Scottish Parliament following independence.

Defence Forces in an Independent Scotland

316. **Will Scotland have its own army, navy and air force?**
Yes. Scotland will have its own military forces – army, navy and air force. We are committed to an independent Scotland also sharing capability with other countries through membership of NATO and other defence co-operation agreements.

317. **What size would defence forces be in an independent Scotland?**
Decisions on the size of the armed forces in an independent Scotland will be made by the Parliament and Government of an independent Scotland. The current Scottish Government believes that armed forces should build to a total of 15,000 service personnel with a reserve of 5,000 over the first 10 years of independence. The details of our proposals are set out in Chapter 6.

318. **What tasks will Scottish defence forces be expected to undertake?**
Under the Scottish Government's proposals, the main tasks for Scottish defence forces, working with other parts of government and its international partners, will be:

- securing Scotland's borders, land, airspace and sea, deterring attacks and protecting our citizens and assets from threat

- protecting Scotland's national interests and economic well being, alongside the key values and underlying principles that support Scottish society and our way of life. This task would include supporting other parts of government when necessary, for example in case of natural disasters or other national emergencies

- contributing to the protection and promotion of human rights, the rule of law, democratic values, international peace and security and Scotland's national interests as a good global citizen

319. **Wouldn't an independent Scotland's defence forces be less sophisticated than at present?**
No. Independence will give Scotland the opportunity to develop specific defence capabilities that better meet Scotland's needs and circumstances. In some areas that could mean developing capabilities that the UK currently does not have, such as maritime patrol aircraft. In other instances there are capabilities that the UK has now that Scotland would neither need nor want – such as nuclear weapons.

320. **What army will an independent Scotland have?**
The Scottish Government proposes that Scotland will have land forces incorporating infantry, light-armoured reconnaissance, and marine units, together with an army HQ function and supporting engineering, aviation, logistics and medical units. A special forces unit will also be established. Over time further capacity will be developed which can contribute to international operations. Full details are set out in Chapter 6.

321. **What air force will an independent Scotland have?**
Under the Scottish Government's proposals, Scotland will have an air force that can monitor and protect Scotland's airspace and provide transport and other support to its other armed services. Over time, capabilities will be developed that can contribute to international operations in partnership with its allies. Full details are set out in Chapter 6.

322. **Would an independent Scotland be able to maintain sophisticated air defence capabilities, as expected by NATO partners?**
Yes. Other countries of a similar size to Scotland support capable fast jets for air defence. For example, all of the Nordic countries, plus others countries such as Belgium, maintain fast jets for air defence.

Scotland has fully contributed to the development of the UK's air defence capability, which is embedded in wider NATO arrangements. Scotland will therefore inherit aspects of this resource as part of the post-referendum negotiation process. It will continue to be in the interests of the rest of the UK and an independent Scotland to work closely together on air defence, within NATO.

323. **Where will Scotland's air force be based?**
Given that the transfer of Typhoons from Leuchars will have
been largely completed before the referendum, Lossiemouth
will continue to be a main operating base for fast jet aircraft and
Scotland's air policing capability. The Scottish Government will
negotiate with Westminster to establish the joint facilities it
would be in the interests of both countries to maintain there.

324. **What navy will an independent Scotland have?**
Scotland is a nation with strong interests in its maritime
environment and will need capabilities to monitor and protect
our maritime interests. Over time, Scotland will also be able to
develop additional capabilities that will enable us to contribute
to international operations in partnership with allies, as other
small nations do.

We plan that initial capabilities, which we will negotiate from
within Scotland's share of defence assets, will include two Type
23 frigates. We will also seek to secure smaller offshore patrol
vessels and a number of inshore fast patrol boats. Full details
are set out in Chapter 6.

This Scottish Government will prioritise the procurement of four
new frigates, preferably through joint procurement with the rest
of the UK. Two of these will be ordered in the first parliamentary
term of independence and when built will bring the number of
frigates in the Scottish Navy to four (the two new frigates as well
as the inherited Type 23s). The Scottish Government believes
that is the appropriate number of frigates in the longer term, and
will order the further two frigates in time to replace the Type 23s
when they are retired from service.

325. **What special forces will an independent Scotland have?**
An independent Scotland could have special forces able to
contribute fully to the maintenance of security. We aim to work
closely with allies to maintain relevant capabilities. Scotland has
a long tradition of contribution to the UK's special forces on
which to build and we can also see from the very capable forces
developed by other small countries that it is entirely possible for
countries of Scotland's size to maintain the special forces that it
requires. Norway is particularly notable for the high reputation of

its special forces. It is our intention to have in place, as a priority and from the point of independence, a core special forces unit which will be built upon over time.

326. **Where will Scottish defence forces be based?**
This Government's intention is that all of the main defence bases inherited at the point of independence will be retained as they will, following a transitional period, be needed by Scotland's defence forces.

The current Scottish Government will also be open to discussion with the Westminster Government about continued arrangements for shared basing where that is in the joint interests of both countries.

327. **What naval vessels will be based at Faslane in an independent Scotland?**
We plan that Faslane will be an independent Scotland's main conventional navy base, and will also be home to the HQ for the navy and the Joint Forces HQ for all of Scotland's armed forces.

As a navy base, Faslane will be the main base for Scotland's major naval vessels. This will be an improvement as no major surface ships are currently stationed in Scotland. Full details of our proposal for Scotland's naval capabilities are set out in Chapter 6.

328. **Will the armament depot at Coulport remain?**
Our commitment is to securing the earliest safe withdrawal of Trident from an independent Scotland. This includes the removal of all elements of the current system, including the missiles and warheads which are stored for the Vanguard submarine fleet at Coulport.

329. **Would an independent Scotland continue to allow Faslane to host non-nuclear armed Royal Navy submarines, such as the Astute and Trafalgar, which are nuclear-powered?**
Our priority for Faslane will be to ensure the speediest and safest possible transition to its future as a conventional naval base serving the defence needs of an independent Scotland. This transition will require detailed discussion with the Government of the rest of the UK on a range of issues.

The Scottish Government strongly favours a conventional approach to Scotland's defence, with Faslane being Scotland's main conventional naval base. We do not see the continued basing of the Astute or Trafalgar fleets at Faslane, beyond the necessary transition period, to be in Scotland's interests.

The Westminster Government has signalled its intention to locate all of the Royal Navy's submarine fleet at a single base. The current proposal is for this to be HMNB Clyde. In the event of independence, it would be for the rest of the UK to decide whether to relocate its submarine fleet to the Royal Navy submarine base at HMNB Devonport or to another location.

330. **What will happen if the Westminster Government does not allow for the transfer of any of its armed forces personnel?**
The detailed arrangements for the transfer of military posts and personnel to Scottish control will be subject to agreement between the Scottish and Westminster Governments. The Westminster Government has pledged to respect the result of the referendum and to work constructively with the Scottish Government, in the interests of the people of Scotland and the rest of the UK. That will include working constructively in the interests of armed forces personnel and their families.

It is in the interests of both Scotland and the rest of the UK that the development and transition of both the rest of the UK armed forces and the Scottish armed forces happens smoothly.

331. **Would Scots personnel currently serving in UK forces be forced to join the Scottish armed forces?**
No. The Scottish Government respects the service of current personnel and will take a responsible approach to the transfer of personnel to Scottish defence forces.

In the event of a vote for independence, the detailed arrangements for the transfer of military posts and personnel to Scottish control will be subject to agreement with the rest of the UK. In relation to the army, the Scottish Government's starting point in those negotiations will be the transfer of those units mainly recruited in Scotland. We also believe that current personnel affected by these changes should be given a choice on the armed forces in which they wish to serve.

332. **What about non-Scots currently serving in 'Scottish units'?**
We believe that serving personnel should have a choice over the armed forces in which they serve.

The Scottish Government greatly respects all of those who serve in the armed forces and we demonstrate that commitment through the way we work to support armed forces communities in Scotland – work recognised as second to none in the UK. Just as individuals from many different nationalities serve in UK armed forces, so too would this Scottish Government welcome current UK service personnel into the future defence forces of an independent Scotland.

333. **Will a Scottish defence force be attractive to both current and potential future personnel?**
Scotland has a fine and longstanding tradition of providing more than its proportionate share of personnel to the UK armed forces.

Given the uncertainty that Westminster is currently creating for its armed forces personnel, it is likely that many may choose the new opportunities that Scottish defence forces will bring. Indeed, smaller armed forces – with a range of niche capabilities such as those that an independent Scotland could offer – will provide better career opportunities than those available in a larger military that is in a process of contraction. That will be enhanced by the commitment that this Scottish Government has already made that service personnel should not face compulsory redundancy during the term of their service contract.

334. **What will the terms and conditions of Scotland's armed forces be?**
This Scottish Government intends to offer terms and conditions at least as good as those offered by the UK currently. In addition, the current Scottish Government, unlike Westminster, has made the commitment that no service personnel should be faced with compulsory redundancy during the term of their service contract.

335. **Will being independent protect Scottish defence jobs?**
Currently just 7.5 per cent of UK-based MoD personnel – both
military and civilian – are based in Scotland, which is less than
Scotland's 8.4 per cent share of the UK population. Over the
first ten years of independence this Scottish Government
proposes that numbers will rise from around 11,310 regular
service personnel currently based in Scotland to 15,000.

In recent history, there has been a disproportionate reduction of
defence jobs in Scotland – for example, the number of military
and civilian MoD personnel in Scotland has dropped by around
38 per cent since 2000, compared with a fall of just 24 per cent
across the UK.

While the fundamental basis for defence and security policy
must be defence and security requirements, it is legitimate
to maximise the economic impact of defence spending. With
regard to defence procurement, recent figures confirm that,
for procurement exempt from EU competition laws, Scotland
benefits by considerably less than its population share.
Between 2007/08 and 2011/12, Scotland received £3.17 billion
out of £60 billion of these UK defence contracts. Had Scotland
benefitted in line with its population share, it would have
received approximately. £5.04 billion over the period. As a
result, Scotland received approximately £1.9 billion less than
its estimated population share.

The Scottish Government expects that the proportion of
the budget allocated for procurement of single use military
equipment will be at least equivalent to that currently allocated
by the Westminster Government (14 per cent in 2012/13).

336. **Will current MoD jobs be secure in an independent
Scotland?**
Yes. The MoD employs 15,340 people in Scotland (around
11,310 service and 4,020 civilian personnel). However, between
2000 and 2013 numbers employed by the MoD in Scotland
have fallen disproportionately – by around 38 per cent,
compared to just 24 per cent across the UK.

The MoD is currently failing to meet the commitment it made in 2011 to increase the military footprint in Scotland and successive Westminster governments have reduced the number of defence jobs in Scotland.

An independent Scotland will be better able to prioritise its defence capabilities, to secure jobs in Scotland and to ensure sustainable and appropriate defence spending levels.

337. **How will an independent Scotland support employment levels similar to those currently available at Faslane?** There are currently 6,700 military and civilian personnel at Her Majesty's Naval Base Clyde, Faslane and Coulport. Retaining Faslane as a fully operational naval base, with the addition of a Joint Forces HQ, will sustain existing military personnel numbers at the base. Significant civilian posts will also be needed to support these operations and, there will be construction work required to reshape Faslane to the needs of conventional Scottish defence forces.

338. **Will there be Ministry of Defence civilian job losses in Scotland as a result of Scotland becoming independent?** No. The current Scottish Government proposes to work with the Westminster Government to preserve continuity of employment for all staff either by way of transfer to the Scottish Government or through continued employment with the Westminster Government.

The current Scottish Government has a strong record of valuing public services in Scotland and is operating a policy of no compulsory redundancies within the public sector for which it currently has devolved responsibility. The Westminster Government has not made any similar commitment within its own areas of responsibility.

Between 2000 and 2013 Scotland saw a disproportionate decline in the number of MoD civilian staff based here – down from 9,600 to 4,020. That represents a loss of just under 60 per cent.

Impact of Defence and Security Policies on Defence Industry

339. **How will defence policies be used to help economic growth in an independent Scotland?**
The priority for defence procurement will be to ensure Scotland's security. However, like all countries, Scotland will get the best deal on any defence requirements by competing for contracts in both domestic and export markets.

Scotland does not currently get value for money in defence procurement as part of the UK. For example, for defence work awarded within the UK for reasons of national security, Westminster Government statistics show that the MoD has committed just £3.17 billion to Scotland of a total UK spend of £60 billion over the five years to 2011/12 – a shortfall of about £1.9 billion on what would have been an appropriate share.

340. **Will Scottish Governments in an independent Scotland be able to protect defence industry jobs?**
Yes. Following a vote for independence, the Scottish Government and its agencies Scottish Enterprise, Highlands and Islands Enterprise and Scottish Development International will continue to support Scotland's indigenous defence industries in existing, new and emerging markets.

We plan to make sure we have all of the defence capabilities we need. Our policy is for Scotland to work in partnership, build the necessary alliances and work with international agencies – such as the NATO 'Smart Defence Initiative' – which will allow Scotland to align our defence requirements with the collective needs and priorities of NATO allies.

The Scottish Government expects that the proportion of the budget allocated for procurement of single use military equipment will be at least equivalent to that currently allocated by the Westminster Government (14 per cent in 2012/13).

In addition, many of our defence sector companies are already successfully competing in international markets and will continue to grow their business in their traditional areas of expertise and in developing areas of business. For example, whilst refit and ship repair is still core work for Babcock Rosyth, the company is currently enhancing its position within the offshore energy and marine services markets, such as the £30 million order that BP placed for 70 subsea structures in January 2013.

The Scotland Institute's paper on 'Defence and Security in an Independent Scotland' outlines key areas in which the Scottish Government can help the diverse defence industries in Scotland to grow, including through investment in R&D, support for our niche strengths in high technology areas such as defence electronics, and science and innovation funding to maintain our global reputation.

341. **Will Scottish shipyards and other defence sectors have Scottish defence contracts to bid for?**
Yes. If in government in an independent Scotland, we will prioritise the procurement of four new frigates, preferably through joint procurement with the rest of the UK. Two of these will be ordered in the first parliamentary term of independence and when built will bring the number of frigates in the Scottish Navy to four (the two new frigates as well as the inherited Type 23s). The Scottish Government believes that is the appropriate number of frigates in the longer term, and will order the further two frigates in time to replace the Type 23s when they are retired from service.

Scotland's shipyards are amongst the most competitive and technologically advanced in the world. The MoD recognised this by awarding BAE Systems in Glasgow the £127 million contract to work on the initial design for the Type 26.

Defence companies are used to working within changing international parameters, and will continue to do so within an independent Scotland. The Scottish Government's plans for a transition to independence aim to ensure the minimum of disruption, however, while new departments, regulatory frameworks and systems are put in place.

342. **What would be the impact of independence on existing MoD contracts awarded to Scottish based companies?**
Independence will not impact on existing contracts, as contracts are offered to companies, not countries. Companies have been awarded contracts on the basis of their ability to deliver quality products within required timescales and budgets. The MoD places contracts with companies in Korea – there is no reason that it would not do so with companies in Scotland.

343. **Could Scottish companies bid for MoD contracts after independence?**
Scottish companies will be able to bid for any MoD contracts that are put out to competitive tender so UK military orders could, and should, still come to Scotland. Scotland's indigenous and global companies have the expertise to win UK and worldwide orders. There is also nothing in article 346 that would prevent the Westminster Government placing contracts exempt from EU Procurement rules in Scotland.

344. **What would an independent Scottish Government do to support Scottish companies to win contracts in export markets?**
Scottish shipyards have proved time and again that they have the skills, expertise and flexibility to build and maintain complex warships for the international market. We aim to increase Scottish opportunities and jobs through independence. There is no reason that Scotland would not attract a healthy order book.

Defence companies are strongly supported in Scotland: Scottish Enterprise provides funding for a great number of development programmes, and Scottish Development International provides targeted product support into new and emerging markets. Independence would not change this.

Many partners use manufacturing and design from other countries. For example, shipbuilders across Europe often receive orders from foreign countries – French companies make ships for Russia; a UK company has made frigates for Malaysia; Westminster has recently given a contract for MoD vessels to a Korean company. This Government's priority is to make sure that any company based in Scotland can compete in global defence markets.

345. **How will Scotland develop its own national security regulations?**
Defence is among the most regulated of all industrial sectors, with security an important element. The Scottish Government is committed to working with NATO, the EU and the United States on key issues relating to intelligence, technologies and military/industry relations through a period of transition. We will negotiate on behalf of the interests of Scotland's companies to ensure arrangements are in place which support them in winning defence contracts.

346. **Will Scottish-based companies still be able to work on secure defence contracts (the X List)?**
There are many Scottish-owned or based companies that have a long track record of working with the MoD on sensitive contracts and are already designated as 'List X' sites. This means that they have the necessary security clearance to hold information with a security marking of confidential or above.

The Scottish Government will negotiate with the Westminster Government to ensure that these arrangements continue and enable work to continue on contracts vital to the security of the Scotland and the rest of the UK.

347. **What other departments would Scotland require to support defence industries?**
Scotland's defence companies spend a great deal on research and development (R&D), as would be expected in a country known for its innovation and engineering excellence. To support this work we intend that the government of an independent Scotland will take forward work currently undertaken at a UK level to maximise the impact of science and technology for the defence and security of Scotland, including independent advice on our R&D programmes.

348. **Will Scotland replicate the three UK Security and Intelligence Agencies (MI5, MI6 and GCHQ)?**

No. Scotland will need significant independent security and intelligence capacity to ensure its security. Independence offers an opportunity to build a new model for such work, that is fit for the 21st century and provides a proportionate means of ensuring Scotland's national security.

On independence, the Scottish Government will set up a single security and intelligence agency for Scotland. The purpose of the agency will be set out in legislation, and will include the requirement to work with partners to ensure Scotland's national security. Setting up the new body will allow us to do things differently, unconstrained by historical structures and precedent. We do not propose to replicate the current UK security and intelligence agencies (the Security Service, or MI5; the Secret Intelligence Service, or MI6; and GCHQ), although Scotland will continue to work very closely with them to ensure the security of Scotland and the rest of the UK.

349. **Will Scotland be able to protect itself against terrorist attacks?**

Yes. Scotland will have the ability to protect our citizens as other independent countries do.

The primary responsibility of government is to ensure the security of its citizens and to protect them, their property and way of life against threats. An independent Scotland will have national security arrangements that reflect Scotland's specific needs and values, recognising the risks and threats we face. It will be based on a full review of security requirements and on a regular assessment of threats.

350. **Would an independent Scotland present an access route to the rest of the UK for crime and terrorism?**

No. Scotland already plays an active part in the UK Counter Terrorism Strategy and, given that responsibility for policing and justice is already devolved to the Scottish Parliament, extensive cross-border co-operation on security is already a reality. The effectiveness of these arrangements was seen in the co-operation between Scottish police forces, the Security

Service and the Metropolitan Police Service after the Glasgow Airport bombing. It will be in the mutual interests of Scotland and the rest of the UK to ensure that this cross-border co-operation continues following independence, supported by Police Scotland and a Scottish security and intelligence agency.

Under our proposals, an independent Scotland will remain part of the Common Travel Area with the rest of the UK and Ireland. As part of this, Scotland will maintain robust visa and immigration controls which will contribute to securing the external border against serious organised crime and terrorism. The arrangements to combat those seeking to exploit Scotland's ports are already delivered by Police Scotland.

351. **How will an independent Scotland ensure it has the capacity and technology required to comprehensively protect Scottish interests at home and abroad?**
An independent Scotland will have security arrangements that are proportionate, fit for purpose, and reflect a full strategic assessment of Scotland's needs and the threats Scotland may face, in the same way as comparable nations. Scotland will have an independent security and intelligence agency which will work closely with Police Scotland and with the rest of the UK to share intelligence and co-ordinate responses to threats.

352. **Will an independent Scotland benefit from shared intelligence from allies such as the rest of the UK or the USA?**
It will be in the interests of the rest of UK and other partners to work closely with Scotland on security matters, including the sharing of intelligence.

Membership of Schengen, the Common Travel Area and Port Controls

353. **Will an independent Scotland remain in the Common Travel Area with the rest of the UK, Ireland, the Isle of Man and the Channel Islands?**
Yes, that is the intention of the Scottish Government. The Common Travel Area has existed since the 1920s and allows freedom of movement for nationals of the UK, Ireland, the Isle of Man and the Channel Islands. It will be in the interests of all

partners for an independent Scotland to remain in the Common
Travel Area.

354. **Will the rest of the UK and Ireland want to remain in the
Common Travel Area with Scotland?**
It will be in their overriding interests to do so. Erecting border
controls with Scotland would be inconvenient for all Common
Travel Area partners, including Scotland and the rest of the UK,
and would not be in the interests of any party. Our shared
history, culture and borders make the Common Travel Area of
benefit to all of the territories within it.

355. **Could an independent Scotland be in the Common Travel
Area and have different immigration policies?**
Yes. Ireland currently operates a different immigration system
to the UK and this has not affected the Common Travel Area
agreement. For example, Ireland grants "green cards", which
the UK does not, and the UK has a points based system which
Ireland does not. Far from hindering the Common Travel Area,
the UK and Ireland issued a joint statement earlier this year
committing to the development of a Common Travel Area visa.

356. **Would an independent Scotland be forced to join the
Schengen Agreement?**
No. The arguments for Scotland being out of Schengen and
remaining in the Common Travel Area with the rest of the UK,
Ireland, the Isle of Man and the Channel Islands are based on
valid practical considerations of geography and working
arrangements that predate the EU and Schengen.

357. **How would Common Travel Area policy be agreed with the
rest of the UK?**
Maintaining the Common Travel Area is in the interests of all
current members and agreement would be reached as part of
negotiations with the rest of the UK.

Immigration

358. **What will independence mean for immigration in Scotland?**
Independence will enable Scotland to build a fair, robust and
secure immigration system that meets our own social, economic
and demographic needs.

359. What will an independent Scotland's policy be on immigration? How will it be different from the rest of the UK?

Scotland's differing demographic and migration needs mean that the current UK immigration system has not supported Scotland's migration priorities. The current Westminster approach is strongly focused on reducing the overall numbers of migrants and introducing number caps for certain categories of skilled individuals.

With independence, each of these decisions would, in future, be for Scottish governments, with policy choices taken on the basis of Scotland's needs and priorities.

For non-EU nationals, independence will enable us to develop and operate a controlled, transparent and efficient immigration system that best meets Scotland's needs and supports our future growth. The current Scottish Government will take forward a points-based approach targeted at particular Scottish needs.

A particular issue for Scotland is the post-study work visa. There are more than 45,000 international students from every corner of the world studying in Scotland, bringing important investment, diversity and welcome expertise to Scotland. The current Scottish Government plans to reintroduce the post-study work visa.

We plan also to lower the current financial maintenance thresholds and minimum salary levels for entry to better align them with Scottish average wages and cost of living. This will open up greater opportunities for key skilled individuals from overseas who could play important roles in our society and economy, filling vital vacancies in individual businesses.

Our detailed proposals on immigration are set out in Chapter 7.

360. I am living in Scotland on a UK visa, what would happen to me at day one of independence? Would I need to get a Scottish visa straight away?

All those legally in Scotland at independence will be able to remain in Scotland under the terms of their existing visa or

entry. When their visa expires they will be expected to leave
Scotland (and the rest of the UK) or apply for a new visa or
extension under Scottish immigration rules.

**361. Do you know how many immigrants would come to
Scotland after independence and how would Scotland
control this? Would there be a cap on the number of
migrants who can come to Scotland?**
We plan that an independent Scotland will introduce a
controlled immigration system to meet our own economic, social
and demographic priorities and needs. Each individual who
wishes to come to Scotland to work, study or live will have to
meet a set of reasonable and fair requirements to gain entry or
approval to remain in Scotland. If there are higher than required
numbers of non-European Economic Area/Swiss migrants
entering Scotland, then this can be addressed through the
points-based system using targeted changes, rather than a cap.

**362. Is there a danger that those who have been denied
permission to stay in the rest of the UK because of their
stricter policies would move to Scotland?**
Under our proposals for independence, Scotland will operate
its own visa system. Therefore anyone who is subject to
immigration controls and denied permission to stay in the rest
of the UK will have to apply for a visa to enter Scotland and
their application would be assessed under Scottish immigration
rules. They would have no automatic right to move to Scotland.

363. Do immigrants put a strain on public services?
Evidence suggests that migrants overwhelmingly pay their
way in terms of public services and make a positive financial
contribution.

The Scottish Government's policies are designed to ensure
an appropriate level of immigration based on economic needs.

**364. How will an independent Scotland's policy on immigration
impact on the diversity of Scotland as a nation?**
Scotland values our diverse ethnic minority communities, the
contribution they make and the important role they play in
enriching Scotland socially, culturally and economically.

Healthy population growth is essential for Scotland's economy. The main contributor to our population growth is from migrants who choose to make Scotland their home.

365. Will increased immigration break down community cohesion?

No. Scotland is already a welcoming society that is stronger for being a culturally rich and diverse nation and will continue to be so.

366. How will immigration rules at ports be enforced in an independent Scotland?

Under our proposals, criminal activity at ports of entry to Scotland, whether it is related to immigration, customs offences or organised crime will be dealt with in a timely and appropriate fashion by a Scottish Borders and Migration Service. Due process will be followed to detect, investigate and deal with all criminal and immigration matters at ports of entry.

Asylum

367. What will independence mean for asylum policy in Scotland?

As a nation playing a socially responsible role in the world, an independent Scotland will continue to provide a place of safety for those seeking asylum. Asylum is granted to those fleeing persecution or serious harm in their own country and in need of international protection.

Asylum is a separate issue from immigration. The current Scottish Government proposes that an independent Scotland will put in place an independent asylum agency. It will handle asylum applications from the initial submission, throughout the assessment process and make the decision on whether to grant refugee status to an individual.

The opportunity of independence will also allow Scotland to adopt a new humane approach to asylum seekers and refugees in line with our values and commitment to upholding internationally recognised human rights.

The new powers Scotland will gain at independence around
equal opportunities, including race equality and
anti-discrimination will be important in supporting Scotland's
ambition to be a progressive, welcoming and inclusive state.

368. **What makes asylum seekers different from other migrants
that come to Scotland?**
Migrants apply for visas to come to Scotland to work, study or
to join family members here. They make a decision to move to
Scotland and have to show that they have sufficient resources
to support themselves and their family while they are here.

Asylum seekers are fleeing persecution or serious harm in their
own country. They often arrive in the country in which they claim
asylum by chance and with very little forethought or preparation.
Scotland will play a responsible role as a good global citizen,
supporting vulnerable people fleeing persecution.

369. **Will an independent Scotland attract more asylum seekers
than the rest of the UK?**
There is no reason why this would be the case. Scotland will
play a responsible role as a good global citizen, supporting
vulnerable people fleeing persecution.

There is no empirical evidence to suggest that the reception
conditions provided for asylum seekers constitute a "pull factor"
or an incentive to seek protection in a particular country.

370. **Will failed asylum seekers be detained?**
Some people will fail any asylum process and there need to be
arrangements in place to deal with those people with fairness
and compassion. There is therefore no need to detain people
just because their claim has been unsuccessful and they are
awaiting removal. Detention by default, along with the practice
of dawn raids, would not form part of the current Scottish
Government's proposed approach to asylum.

Failed asylum seekers who represent a danger to the public
need to be accommodated securely whilst steps are taken to
remove them, but this should be addressed in other ways. Prison
will be a legitimate alternative in some, though very few, cases
– for example where a criminal offence has been committed.

371. **Will failed asylum seekers be forcibly removed?**
Our intention is to encourage voluntary return for failed asylum seekers wherever possible. However, we accept that there will be a need for some forced removal. Such operations will be undertaken in a sensitive and compassionate manner. There will be an end to dawn raids and a commitment not to forcibly remove vulnerable asylum seekers, such as young children or heavily pregnant women.

Citizenship

372. **What will independence mean for citizenship in Scotland?**
Our proposal is that on day one of independence, all British citizens who live in Scotland and all British citizens born in Scotland but residing elsewhere would automatically be considered Scottish citizens. Others may be able to apply for citizenship following independence through routes such as citizenship by descent or by naturalisation.

Under these proposals Scotland would not create a barrier to individuals holding Scottish citizenship alongside British or any other citizenship.

373. **What would being a Scottish citizen mean and how would I prove that I am a Scottish citizen? Would there be a registration process?**
As outlined above, all British citizens who are habitually resident in Scotland at the date of independence and all British citizens born in Scotland but resident elsewhere would automatically be considered a Scottish citizen. There would be no registration required and there are no plans to have a Scottish ID card.

We intend that the rights and responsibilities which accompany Scottish citizenship will be broadly in line with those currently aligned with British citizenship. However, there is no written record of what rights and responsibilities are associated with British citizenship. We would support the inclusion of the rights and responsibilities of Scottish citizens in the permanent written constitution of an independent Scotland. Those rights and responsibilities will reflect the European Convention of Human Rights.

374. **What different routes to citizenship will exist under the Scottish Government's proposals and who will qualify for these?**

Current Status	Scottish Citizenship?
At the date of independence	
British citizen habitually resident in Scotland on day one of independence	**Yes, automatically** a Scottish citizen
British citizens born in Scotland but living outside of Scotland on day one of independence	**Yes, automatically** a Scottish citizen
After the date of independence	
Child born in Scotland to at least one parent who has Scottish citizenship or indefinite leave to remain at the time of their birth	**Yes. Automatically** a Scottish citizen
Child born outside Scotland to at least one parent who has Scottish citizenship	**Yes. Automatically** a Scottish citizen (the birth must be registered in Scotland to take effect)
British national living outside Scotland with at least one parent who qualifies for Scottish citizenship	Can **register** as a Scottish citizen (will need to provide evidence to substantiate)
Citizens of any country, who have a parent or grandparent who qualifies for Scottish citizenship	Can **register** as a Scottish citizen (will need to provide evidence to substantiate)
Migrants in Scotland legally	May **apply** for naturalisation as a Scottish citizen (subject to meeting good character, residency and any other requirements set out under Scottish immigration law)
Citizens of any country who have spent at least 10 years living in Scotland at any time and have an ongoing connection with Scotland	May **apply** for naturalisation as a Scottish citizen (subject to meeting good character and other requirements set out under Scottish immigration law)

375. **Must I be a Scottish citizen? Can I opt out of Scottish citizenship and retain my British citizenship?**
Our proposals will allow people to opt out of Scottish citizenship. However, under international law, when setting nationality rules a country has a duty to avoid making people stateless. Therefore, those people who would automatically be considered a Scottish citizen will only be able to opt out if they already hold citizenship of another nation.

British nationality rules will be a matter for the rest of the UK. Should you qualify for British citizenship under the rest of the UK's rules post-independence then you will be able to opt out of Scottish citizenship or hold dual citizenship. Information on how to opt out will be made available before independence. We aim to keep the process simple yet robust.

376. **Can I have both Scottish and British citizenship?**
Our proposals for citizenship in an independent Scotland are based upon an inclusive model and will include dual citizenship, recognising our shared history with the UK. We will not place obstacles in the way of individuals holding Scottish citizenship alongside British or any other citizenship.

The UK allows dual or multiple citizenship for British citizens. If a British citizen acquires citizenship and a passport of another country, this does not affect their British citizenship, right to hold a British passport or right to live in the UK. It will be for the rest of the UK to decide whether it allows dual UK/Scottish citizenship, but if Westminster decided that Scottish citizens could not also be UK citizens it would be inconsistent with its approach to every other country.

377. **As a Scottish citizen could I still visit or live in the rest of the UK easily?**
Yes. Scottish citizens will be EU citizens and as such would have the right to live and work anywhere in the EU, including the rest of the UK.

378. **Would Scotland's rules be different from British citizenship rules?**
The Scottish Government's proposed rules on who is automatically a Scottish citizen are set out in Chapter 7. They will be broadly similar to existing British rules and will be based on residence and parentage.

379. **Who would qualify for citizenship by descent?**
Citizenship by descent will be open to those whose parent or grandparent was born in Scotland and qualifies, or would have qualified if living, for Scottish citizenship.

There will be a registration process for citizenship by descent and those who wish to register would have to prove their family connection with relevant documentation. Those who successfully claim citizenship by descent will have the same rights and responsibilities as other Scottish citizens, including the right to live and work in Scotland.

Passports

380. **What will the rules be on passports in an independent Scotland?**
We intend that Scottish citizens will be able to apply for a Scottish passport from the date of independence. Passport eligibility will be aligned with citizenship. If you qualify for Scottish citizenship then you will be entitled to carry a Scottish passport. Scottish passports will meet the standard requirements for EU passports.

381. **When can I get my Scottish passport?**
We plan that Scottish citizens will be able to apply for Scottish passports from the date of independence.

382. **Who will issue my Scottish passport?**
The current Scottish Government proposes a shared service agreement with HM Passport Office for a transitional period, with responsibility transferring to a new Scottish passport agency over the course of the first parliament of an independent Scotland.

383. **How much would a Scottish passport cost and how long would it last?**
Fee scales will be published prior to independence. It is the current Scottish Government's intention that passports in a newly independent Scotland will cost no more than the respective UK passport at that time.

Adult passports will last for 10 years and child passports for five years.

384. **Who can have a Scottish passport?**
Under our plans, anyone who is a Scottish citizen will be eligible for a Scottish passport.

385. **Will I need to have a Scottish passport?**
No. You will require a valid passport if you want to travel outside the Common Travel Area (Scotland, the rest of the UK, the Republic of Ireland, the Isle of Man and the Channel Islands), but we will not impose a requirement for Scottish citizens to have a Scottish passport – just as there is no requirement now to have a UK passport.

386. **What would a Scottish passport look like and would it be valid for travel around the world?**
Scottish passports will comply with EU standards for passports. They will look much the same as current UK passports in colour, size, and layout but will be identified as a Scottish passport on the front cover. Scottish passports will be recognised worldwide.

387. **I still have a number of years left of my UK passport, can I keep it? Would I be able to renew my UK passport?**
The Scottish Government plans to recognise valid UK passports until they expire. As set out above, the Scottish Government intends to allow dual nationality and would not place any obstacles in the way of individuals holding a Scottish passport alongside a UK passport.

Entitlement to UK passports will be a matter for the rest of the UK.

Borders

388. **How will an independent Scotland protect its borders from terrorist threats?**

The present Scottish Government plans that an independent Scotland will have a Scottish Borders and Migration Service which will be responsible for border control at airports and ports. Our overseas work through the consulate network, such as issuing visas, will help ensure that only those entitled to enter Scotland can do so.

As is currently the case, individuals known to be a threat to Scotland will not be allowed to enter the country. They will either be stopped at the point of application, or on attempting to enter the country. In certain cases the involvement of the police will be necessary, and there will be a key role for the Border Policing Command of Police Scotland in cases of criminality or persons wanted for criminal offences.

The Scottish Government will work with international partners to ensure that those deemed a threat to the security of Scotland are deported following proper investigation and processes. This will be consistent with relevant human rights legislation.

As a member of the EU, Scotland will uphold data and information sharing arrangements in place to contribute to, and benefit from, terrorism prevention processes such as watch lists of persons of interest.

389. **Will Scotland have security posts at the land border with England?**

No. Erecting border controls with Scotland would be inconvenient for all Common Travel Area partners, including Scotland and the rest of the UK, and will not be in the interests of any party. Our shared history, culture and borders make the Common Travel Area of benefit to all of the territories within it.

As is the case with Ireland in the Common Travel Area currently, Scotland will work with the rest of the UK to establish joint processes to manage the Common Travel Area.

390. **How will Scotland police its international border controls at ports and airports?**
Following independence, the Scottish Government's proposed Scottish Borders and Migration Service will have responsibility for ensuring that visas are issued appropriately and that only those with a right to enter Scotland can do so. In cases involving criminality there will also be a key role for the Border Policing Command of Police Scotland.

Law and Order

391. **What benefits will independence bring for law and order in Scotland?**
Scotland already has its own distinct legal system. Our justice system and institutions have a long and proud history. Scotland's justice agencies have demonstrated the benefits of having decisions taken in Scotland relevant to circumstances here.

However, powers over some key justice matters are held by Westminster, including decisions over drug classification, firearms, gambling and road traffic offences. The Westminster also controls how much of the income collected from criminals in Scotland, through fines and proceeds of crime legislation, can be retained to invest in Scottish communities.

Decisions about currently reserved issues like welfare, employment and public services also have a significant impact on the factors that lead people towards crime and make our communities vulnerable to criminals.

With independence, Scotland will have the full range of powers to tackle crime and the causes of crime in a more joined-up way, to make our communities safer.

392. **Will existing UK laws passed by Westminster still apply after independence?**
Yes. Following independence, existing laws, whether passed by Westminster or the Scottish Parliament, will continue to apply until they are amended by the independent Scottish Parliament.

393. **Will the independence of Scotland's judges and
     prosecutors be protected in an independent Scotland?**
     Yes. The roles, functions and independence of Scotland's
     judges and prosecutors will be safeguarded following
     independence. As at present, Scottish Ministers and the
     Scottish Parliament will have no powers to intervene in
     independent judicial decisions. Prosecution decisions will
     continue to be taken by the Lord Advocate.

394. **Does Scotland have the necessary skills and facilities
     to ensure law and order in an independent Scotland?**
     Yes. Scotland has its own legal profession, judiciary, police,
     prosecutors and other trained justice staff working in our courts,
     prisons and local criminal justice services.

     Crime in Scotland is at a 39 year low and violent crime has
     almost halved since 2006/07. There are fewer victims of crime
     and more people feel that their communities are safer places to
     live. The effectiveness of Scotland's justice system demonstrates
     the benefits of decisions being taken in Scotland.

     Crime and Policing

395. **Will the police still operate in the same way in an
     independent Scotland?**
     Yes. Scotland already has its own police service, Police
     Scotland, which is supervised by the Scottish Police Authority.
     Scotland's police service safeguards strong local policing in our
     communities and ensures that specialist national expertise and
     equipment – like firearms units or major investigation teams –
     are available whenever and wherever they are needed.

     Scotland has over 1,000 additional police officers in our
     communities compared with 2006/07 and crime clear-up rates
     by the police are at their highest level for 35 years.

396. **On independence, what will happen to UK police forces
     that currently operate in Scotland?**
     Following independence, the functions of UK forces currently
     operating in Scotland – the British Transport Police, Ministry
     of Defence Police and Civil Nuclear Constabulary – will come
     under Scottish control.

The Scottish Government is already seeking agreement with Westminster to integrate the functions of the British Transport Police into Police Scotland. The Scottish Government intends that, with independence, the functions of the Civil Nuclear Constabulary in Scotland will also be integrated into Police Scotland.

Just as now, policing functions in relation to defence interests will be required in an independent Scotland and posts will be needed to undertake those functions. An independent Scottish government will be able to determine the most effective and efficient way of managing those functions.

397. **Will the police in Scotland still work with forces in England, Wales and Northern Ireland after independence?**
Yes. There are existing well-established arrangements to ensure effective cross-border co-operation between Police Scotland and forces in the rest of the UK. It will be in the shared interests of Scotland and the rest of the UK to ensure that these practical arrangements continue following independence.

398. **Will I still call '999' for emergency services?**
Yes. 999 will remain the number to call for police, fire, ambulance and coastguard services in an independent Scotland.

Scotland also has its own national police non-emergency phone number – 101. People can call 101 to get advice about crime prevention or to report a crime that doesn't need an emergency response.

399. **How will Scotland's police and prosecutors deal with serious and organised crime?**
Scotland's Serious and Organised Crime Taskforce ensures that relevant agencies work together to tackle serious and organised criminals in our communities.

The new Scottish Crime Campus at Gartcosh will provide purpose-built, specialist accommodation for 1,100 staff from the police and other agencies to work together even more closely to protect Scotland from the threat of serious and organised crime.

400. **What relationship will an independent Scotland have with the UK's new National Crime Agency?**
There are existing well-established arrangements to ensure effective co-operation between Scotland's Serious and Organised Crime Taskforce and the National Crime Agency. It will be in the interests of all agencies involved in combatting serious and organised crime to continue this practical co-operation following independence.

Fire and Rescue Services

401. **Will fire and rescue services still operate in the same way in an independent Scotland?**
Yes. Scotland already has its own Scottish Fire and Rescue Service. The unified service safeguards strong local fire and rescue services in our communities and ensures specialist national expertise and equipment are available whenever and wherever they are needed.

EU and International Co-operation

402. **How will independence improve Scotland's justice agencies' work with their counterparts in the EU and internationally?**
Scotland's police and prosecutors already work effectively with their counterparts in other European countries and through EU bodies, such as Europol.

The Scottish Government opposes Westminster's plans to opt-out of EU agreements that put at risk access to the European Arrest Warrant and other practical cross-border measures for Scottish justice agencies.

Following independence, Scotland will no longer have to rely on representation on international bodies via Westminster. As an independent EU member state, Scotland will have its own voice in the development of EU justice and home affairs policy and legislation.

403. **Will Scotland be able to extradite cross-border criminals to face justice?**
Yes. The Scottish Government intends to maintain current arrangements for extradition to ensure that criminals can be pursued and brought to justice across international borders.

404. **How will an independent Scotland deal with cross-border crimes like human trafficking?**
Scotland's devolved justice agencies already work effectively with their counterparts in other countries to tackle human trafficking and other cross-border crimes.

An independent Scotland will have its own voice and will be able to participate positively and directly in EU and wider international co-operative arrangements that protect our security and help tackle cross-border crime.

Courts and Tribunals

405. **What impact will independence have on Scotland's courts?**
The civil and criminal courts in Scotland will continue to operate after independence.

Following recommendations from the Lord President, Scotland's most senior judge, the Scottish Government is already taking forward a programme of reforms to modernise and improve Scotland's courts to ensure that they are fit for the 21st century.

406. **What will happen to Scottish cases currently referred to the UK Supreme Court?**
Arrangements will be made to finalise Scottish cases already referred to the UK Supreme Court. The highest courts in an independent Scotland will be the Inner House of the Court of Session and the High Court of Justiciary (sitting as Court of Criminal Appeal), which will be known jointly as the Supreme Court of Scotland.

The UK Supreme Court will no longer have jurisdiction in Scotland. The European Court of Justice in Luxembourg and European Court of Human Rights in Strasbourg will continue to have the same jurisdiction in Scotland.

407. **Will independence mean Scotland needs new courts or new judges?**
No. Independence will not result in a need for Scotland to add to its existing courts and judiciary. As at present, following independence the total number of judges will be agreed through dialogue between Scottish Ministers and the Lord President, Scotland's most senior judge.

408. **How will tribunals change following independence?**
Scotland has its own Scottish Tribunals Service and tribunal
judiciary responsible for tribunals on devolved matters, such as
mental health. The Scottish Government intends that following
independence, tribunals for reserved matters, such as welfare
benefits and employment, will become part of the tribunal
structure in Scotland.

409. **What will happen to the income from criminal justice fines?**
The majority of income from fines applied in Scotland is
currently transferred to Westminster under UK Treasury rules.

In an independent Scotland, this fine income will be retained
by the Scottish Government and has the potential to deliver
additional net income of more than £7 million per year to
Scotland.

410. **What will happen to the money recovered from criminals
through proceeds of crime legislation in an independent
Scotland?**
Westminster currently places a cap of £30 million per year on
the amount of money recovered from criminals that can be
retained by the Scottish Government and used to reinvest in
communities in Scotland. Westminster has refused requests
to remove that cap.

In an independent Scotland there will be no cap. This means
that all money recovered from criminals will be available to be
reinvested in communities across Scotland.

Prisons

411. **What impact will independence have on prisons and
prisoners?**
Scotland already has its own Prison Service and prison officers.
As at present, criminals sentenced to prison by a Scottish court
will be sent to a Scottish prison.

412. **Will prisoner transfers continue between prisons in Scotland and England, Wales and Northern Ireland?**
Yes. There are existing arrangements in place for prisoner transfers between Scotland and the rest of the UK to enable prisoners to maintain family contact during their sentence. The Scottish Government plans to maintain these arrangements on independence. Arrangements for international prisoner transfers will also continue on the same basis as now.

Justice Workforce

413. **How will police, fire and prison officer pay be set in an independent Scotland?**
Westminster has decided to end collective bargaining for police pay and conditions in England and Wales. The current Scottish Government rejects this approach, and has introduced legislation to establish a Scottish Police Negotiating Body, ensuring that decisions about police pay and conditions are taken here in Scotland.

With independence, decisions on the pay and terms and conditions of prison officers and firefighters will be taken in Scotland, building on the strong record of partnership working with staff bodies.

414. **Will police, fire and prison officer pensions still be paid?**
Yes. The Scottish Government paper *Pensions in an Independent Scotland* made clear that in an independent Scotland all public service pension rights and entitlements which have been accrued for fully or executively devolved or reserved schemes will be fully protected and accessible. There will be no difference to how much people pay for their pensions or the level of benefits they receive as a result of the move to independence.

Independence will make it possible for a future Scottish government to consider positively the pension terms of all "uniformed" services, including the age at which they should be able to access their occupational pension.

Road Traffic Law

415. **How will the approach to drink driving limits change in an independent Scotland?**

The Scotland Act 2012 provided the Scottish Parliament with limited powers to introduce a distinct drink driving limit and a Scottish Government consultation confirmed strong public support in Scotland for a lower limit. The Scottish Government will bring forward legislation to lower the drink driving limit once technical changes to drink drive testing devices have been made.

Independence will allow all decisions on drink driving policy to be taken in Scotland.

416. **What other benefits can independence deliver for road traffic law?**

Independence will give Scotland full control over road traffic criminal law, and the ability to develop policies to reduce the number of deaths and injuries on Scotland's roads. This will include opportunities to empower our police to conduct random breath tests of drivers, create different drink drive limits for different types of driver, and to consider whether existing UK law on dangerous driving, careless driving and speeding offers a sufficient deterrent to drivers who put at risk other road users and pedestrians.

417. **How will people driving across the border know what different traffic laws apply?**

It is the responsibility of every driver to know the rules and laws of the roads on which they are driving.

Drugs

418. **How will an independent Scotland deal with illegal drug use?**

Policy on drug misuse is already devolved to the Scottish Government. Scotland's drug strategy, *The Road to Recovery,* has led the way in tackling drug problems and has received international acclaim for its positive focus on care, treatment and recovery. Drug taking in the general population is falling and drug taking among young people is at the lowest level in a decade.

With independence, responsibility for legislation on the classification of illegal drugs will also become the responsibility of the Scottish Parliament.

Gambling

419. **What will the approach to gambling be in an independent Scotland?**

With independence, responsibility for the regulation of gambling will transfer to the Scottish Parliament. An independent Scotland will have the powers to introduce additional measures to tackle problem gambling, through more effective regulation of the industry, in contrast to Westminster's approach of greater deregulation.

Firearms

420. **How will access to firearms be controlled in an independent Scotland?**

The Scotland Act 2012 provided the Scottish Parliament with limited additional powers to introduce licensing for airguns. Work is underway by the Scottish Government to introduce a licensing regime for airguns in Scotland. However, Westminster has refused requests to devolve powers fully to allow decisions on the licensing and control of firearms to be taken in Scotland.

Independence will give Scotland full powers to control firearms in Scotland. Firearms legislation and licensing in an independent Scotland will be simplified, made easier for the public to understand and for the authorities to enforce.

Energy

Scotland's Offshore Oil and Gas

421. How extensive are Scotland's oil and gas reserves?
Up to 24 billion barrels of oil and gas reserves remain under
the North Sea. Recent research by Professor Alex Kemp of the
University of Aberdeen has suggested that around 98.8 per cent
of North Sea oil production and around 60 per cent of gas
production in the 30 years from 2011 will come from Scotland's
geographical share of the current UK Continental Shelf.

422. Is it Scotland's oil and gas?
The vast majority of oil and gas in the UK comes from the
Scottish Continental Shelf and will be in Scotland after
independence. Analysis by academics at Aberdeen University
tells us that in excess of 90 per cent of the oil and gas revenues
are from fields in Scottish waters (based on well-established
principles of international law). Full details of the current
Scottish Government's position are set out in Chapter 8.

**423. How valuable are the expected tax revenues from our oil
and gas production?**
The latest Government Expenditure and Revenue Scotland
report estimates that oil and gas production in the Scottish
portion of the UK continental shelf generated £10.6 billion in tax
revenues during 2011/12. This is equal to 94 per cent of the
UK's total tax revenues from oil and gas production. Production
in Scottish waters could generate approximately £48 billion in
tax revenue between 2012/13 and 2017/18 based on industry
estimates of production and an average cash price of
approximately 113 dollars per barrel.

Oil and gas production is expected to rise to two million boe
(barrels of oil equivalent) per day towards the end of the decade
as a result of the current record levels of capital investment.
This will see the industry continue to make a substantial
contribution to tax revenues for decades to come.

424. Are oil companies still investing in the North Sea?
North Sea operators have £100 billion of capital investment
within their current business plans.

425. **What about the impacts of global recession?**
The market for oil and gas is not immune to global recessionary factors. Between 2008/09 and 2009/10, for example, North Sea tax revenues fell from £12.9 billion to £6.5 billion. However, despite this fall, Scotland continued to have a smaller fiscal deficit, as a share of GDP, than the UK as a whole. Even in years when oil revenues fell to as low as £1 billion, Scotland still generated more tax revenue per head than the average for the UK.

426. **How will an independent Scotland maximise the benefits of our oil and gas reserves?**
Careful management of Scotland's oil and gas reserves will be a key priority for an independent Scotland. Unlike successive Westminster governments, the Scottish Government recognises that an independent Scotland should provide industry with the necessary fiscal and regulatory stability and predictability for it to innovate and thrive in a globally competitive environment. We will consider how the existing fiscal regime can be enhanced to maximise oil and gas recovery, and to encourage development in the most technically challenging oil and gas fields.

427. **Will an independent Scotland establish an oil fund to safeguard the benefits of our oil and gas production?**
Yes, that is the intention of the current Scottish Government. Since the 1970s, approximately £300 billion in tax receipts (in today's prices) has gone directly to the Westminster Exchequer, with none of it being saved for the future. We cannot repeat this mistake in the future.

The Scottish Government proposes that an independent Scotland will establish a Scottish Energy Fund which will be both a stabilisation fund and long-term investment fund into which a portion of tax revenues will be invested when fiscal conditions allow. Stabilisation funds and sovereign wealth funds are common among oil and gas producing countries, with the UK being a notable exception. To find out more about our proposals for a Scottish Energy Fund, see Chapter 8.

Norway provides a good example of how a country can effectively manage its oil and gas revenues. It established its oil fund in 1990, although the first net investment was modest and was not made until 1996. The fund is now the largest sovereign wealth fund in the world, worth around £470 billion. It currently owns, on average, 2.5 per cent of every listed company in Europe, and 1.2 per cent of the world's listed companies. These investments have achieved average annual returns of 5.9 per cent over the last five years.

428.   **Is continued oil and gas production consistent with Scotland's commitments on climate change?**
Yes. In Scotland, we will need a mixed energy portfolio, including hydrocarbons, to provide secure and affordable heat and electricity for decades to come. Scotland has a target of delivering the equivalent of 100 per cent of electricity demand and 11 per cent of non-electrical heat demand from renewables by 2020. As we increase our use of renewable energy sources, we also have a duty to minimise carbon emissions in line with our world-leading climate change targets.

429.   **Will the recommendations from the Wood Review be taken forward in an independent Scotland?**
The Scottish Government welcomes the interim report produced by Sir Ian Wood in his review, *Maximisation of Recovery in the UKCS*. The report estimates that the prize from increased and effective collaboration could be an additional three to four billion barrels of oil equivalent over 20 years, which could be worth £200 billion. By addressing the challenges facing the industry and harnessing the opportunities, enormous benefits can be reaped by the industry and in tax revenues. This was recognised by the Scottish Government in our Oil and Gas Strategy published in May 2012, and in our paper *Maximising the return from Oil and Gas in an Independent Scotland* published in July 2013.

We particularly welcome the proposal to create a new regulator. This will provide the necessary skills, knowledge and authority to ensure that we maximise the potential of the wealth of resources remaining. The Expert Commission appointed by the Scottish Government will consider Sir Ian's recommendations as part of its work and will report in spring 2014.

Decommissioning

430. **How will the decommissioning costs of oil and gas platforms and other infrastructure in the North Sea be met in an independent Scotland?**
Providing a stable environment for companies to plan decommissioning is critical to delivering a dynamic and forward-looking offshore oil and gas industry. At present, North Sea operators are able to claim tax relief against the cost of decommissioning offshore facilities at the point when the decommissioning occurs.

The Scottish Government plans that decommissioning tax relief in an independent Scotland will be provided in the manner and at the rate currently provided through the current North Sea fiscal regime. This will provide long-term certainty for the industry.

Successive Westminster governments have accrued £300 billion in tax receipts (in today's prices) from North Sea oil and gas production. This Scottish Government intends that an independent Scotland will seek a commensurate contribution to the cost of decommissioning relief from the rest of the UK. This will be the subject of negotiation between the two governments, but the outcome of the negotiations will have no impact on the value of relief received by operators.

Alternative Fuels

431. **Will an independent Scotland pursue alternative fuel sources and supply, such as 'fracking' and shale gas exploration?**
The development of unconventional hydrocarbon resources is at an early stage in Scotland. Decisions on alternative fuel sources, or the appropriate energy mix, will be for future Scottish governments.

Proposals would be considered through the normal planning process and the appropriate regulatory regimes, including SEPA's updated guidance on the regulation of shale gas and coalbed methane published in December 2012.

Scottish Ministers have also recently announced a strengthening of Scottish Planning Policy in regard to unconventional gas.

432. **Will there be nuclear power generation in an independent Scotland?**
The current Scottish Government is opposed to the building of any new nuclear power stations in Scotland and will phase out existing stations in Scotland over time.

Offshore Health and Safety

433. **What will the offshore health and safety regime be in an independent Scotland?**
The offshore health and safety issues relating to the UK Continental Shelf are currently the responsibility of the UK Health and Safety Executive. This Scottish Government plans that a comparable new body will be established to perform this function in an independent Scotland. This body will maintain world-leading offshore health and safety standards as currently administered.

Oil and Gas Emissions

434. **Will an independent Scotland be able to meet statutory climate change targets?**
This Government recognises that, as an independent nation, Scotland will take responsibility for emissions from the offshore oil and gas sector within its waters. This will require primary legislation to allow the present climate change targets to reflect these additional emissions.

435. **Will carbon capture and storage be developed in an independent Scotland?**
Decisions on carbon capture and storage (CCS) will be for future governments in an independent Scotland. However, it is the current Scottish Government's view that, alongside a substantial further growth in renewable energy, it is likely there will be a need to maintain and build new power stations run on traditional fossil fuels. The scheduled closure of existing power plants, and the construction of a minimum of 2.5 GW of new or

replacement efficient fossil fuel electricity generation plants progressively fitted with CCS, will satisfy security of supply concerns and, together with renewable energy, deliver large amounts of electricity exports.

Our aim is for thermal generation in the future to be decarbonised over time through increased application of carbon capture and storage. Carbon capture and storage has the potential to substantially reduce emissions from fossil fuel power stations and will be a vital element of a decarbonised power sector.

Energy Market

436. **Will there continue to be a single GB market for energy and gas?**

Achieving security of supply for Scottish consumers will be the central priority for this Government in an independent Scotland. Provided this is not jeopardised, Scotland will continue to participate in the GB-wide market for electricity and gas, reflecting the integrated transmission networks between Scotland and the rest of the UK.

It will be in the interests of both countries for there to be an integrated market across Scotland and the rest of the UK. Scotland's transmission network is deeply interconnected with the rest of Great Britain, and Scotland will continue to export its energy to the rest of the UK. Retaining the GB energy market after independence brings the benefits of energy security to customers and businesses north and south of the border.

A single transmission operator, National Grid, can continue to balance supply and demand throughout Scotland and the rest of the UK.

This Government proposes that an independent Scotland will seek a new energy partnership with Westminster to steer energy policy jointly and to ensure proper governance of the integrated market.

Energy Prices for Consumers

437. **What effect will independence have on energy prices?**
The powers of independence will allow energy policy to be
designed to protect the interests of consumers and make sure
people are treated transparently and fairly. Appropriate
information on energy tariffs will help customers decide which
company to go with, and help make prices competitive.

Different parties will put forward proposals on energy prices and
other issues and it will be for the people of Scotland to decide
the approach they want in future elections. The current Scottish
Government proposes the transfer of responsibility for the
Energy Company Obligation and the Warm Homes Discount
from energy companies to the Scottish Government, meeting
the costs from central government budgets. By passing on
these cost reductions to their consumers, energy companies
would reduce customer bills by around five per cent or
approximately £70 per year.

The current Scottish Government will task the combined
economic regulator with ensuring an open and competitive
energy market, which protects the interests of Scottish
consumers while ensuring a fair return on investment for energy
companies. The energy arm of the Scottish Regulator could, in
principle, be based at the Scottish offices of Ofgem.

438. **Will independence help to address fuel poverty?**
Yes. The current UK regulatory model has done little to increase
households' ability to access low cost 'dual fuel' tariffs, where
gas and electricity are provided by the same supplier. Around
nine per cent of households in Scotland are without mains gas
and 43 per cent of these households live in fuel poverty.

Under the limited powers currently available to it, the current
Scottish Government is doing everything possible to meet the
statutory target to eradicate fuel poverty as far as is reasonably
practicable by 2016. With independence, and if in power
following the 2016 election, we will transfer responsibility for the
Energy Company Obligation and the Warm Homes Discount
from energy companies to the Scottish Government, meeting
the costs from central government budgets. By passing on

these cost reductions to their consumers, energy companies would be required to reduce bills by around five per cent or approximately £70 per year.

We are also committed to retaining the statutory target. Our approach is that, following independence, there should be a commitment to continue the overall levels of funding available to tackle fuel poverty – currently at least £200 million a year.

Low Carbon Energy

439. **Will an independent Scotland maintain current levels of support for renewable energy?**
The current Scottish Government's policy is that it should. Spare generating capacity throughout the UK is now at its lowest level for a generation and Ofgem forecasts it will contract even further. Without Scottish renewable energy supplies, there would already be a shortage in capacity.

Retention of the single GB-wide energy market will bring benefits of energy security to customers and businesses both north and south of the border. While detailed discussions between all parties will be necessary, we believe that it is in the interests of all that the central aspects of support for low carbon generation, as established and planned under Electricity Market Reform, should remain.

An integrated and single energy market involves customers throughout GB paying on an equitable basis for a wide range of benefits, including stable prices, security of supply and access to renewable generation. Scottish renewable production is among the most cost-effective in the UK and offers clear advantages to the rest of the UK in meeting its EU obligations, as is reflected by National Grid's decision to invest to upgrade transmission connections between Scotland and England.

440. **What will the transmission charging regime be in an independent Scotland?**
Through the Scottish regulator, an independent Scotland would seek improvements to the transmission charging methodology. The Scottish Government has long argued for an approach to transmission charging which delivers a level playing field for Scottish renewable and thermal generators, and which supports

development in areas of the highest renewables resource and on Scotland's islands. In addition to enhancing Scotland's security of supply, a fairer charging regime will support the growth of renewable generation, recognising that such capacity needs to be developed where the resource is located.

In an independent Scotland, this Government will seek to ensure that future charging regimes take our energy resources and security fully into account in a way which meets the needs of our island regions and connections.

441. **The Energy Bill is currently making its way through the UK Parliament. Will an independent Scotland continue with this regime?**
The current Scottish Government proposes that Scotland should continue to participate in an integrated market for electricity, under the terms of the Energy Bill – provided that Scottish security of supply is safeguarded.

However, as a substantial supplier to the rest of the UK, an independent Scotland will require a far greater degree of oversight of the market arrangements. Hence, the specifics of a continued GB-wide market will require detailed discussion between all parties. Through the planned Energy Partnership with Westminster, this Scottish Government will ensure that Scottish interests are protected.

442. **How will independence impact on Scotland's targets for decarbonised electricity generation in Scotland?**
These targets will remain in place on independence, and independence will give Scotland the full range of powers to develop renewable energy.

The current Scottish Government has set a target for the equivalent of 100 per cent of electricity demand to be met by renewables by 2020, and a 2030 electricity decarbonisation target to achieve a carbon intensity of 50g CO_2/kWh of electricity generation in Scotland.

Good progress is being made towards this, with renewable generation in Scotland hitting a record high of 36.3 per cent of gross consumption in 2011, well above our 31 per cent interim target for that year. Provisional figures for 2012 show a further increase to almost 39 per cent of gross consumption. Our 2030 electricity decarbonisation target could actually be hit a little earlier, perhaps closer to 2027.

443. **How will the EU's renewable energy targets be apportioned when Scotland becomes an independent member state?**
It will be for the EU to determine how the targets are split, but Scotland has a target of delivering the equivalent of 100 per cent of electricity demand and 11 per cent of non-electrical heat demand from renewables by 2020 – significantly more ambitious than the EU target.

The current Scottish Government has also committed to working with Westminster to ensure that the rest of the UK also meets its target obligations at the least cost. That will involve deploying Scottish renewable energy into the GB grid. Indeed the EU Renewable Energy Directive highlights the value of 'co-operation mechanisms' between member states.

444. **Will the Renewable Heat Incentive (RHI) operate in an independent Scotland?**
The current Scottish Government intends to continue operating the Renewable Heat Incentive (RHI) following independence. The RHI was introduced by Westminster in 2011 to incentivise the use of heat produced from renewable non-fossil fuel sources, such as wood fuel or heat pumps.

The RHI is key to an independent Scotland meeting the Scottish target of 11 per cent of heat demand from renewables by 2020, and will play a significant role in decarbonising the heat sector by 2050, with significant progress being made by 2030. The Scottish Government has developed a range of supporting actions to increase deployment of renewable heat technologies in Scotland.

445. **Will the Green Deal continue in an independent Scotland?**
The current Scottish Government proposes that schemes that are in place immediately before independence, such as this, will be inherited by an independent Scotland.

Environment and Climate Change

446. **What priority will be given to protecting the environment in an independent Scotland?**
Scotland's natural environment is important in many ways – from supporting the economy to helping to improve our health.

World-leading climate change legislation passed by the Scottish Parliament in 2009 shows that, when we have the powers, we take a more progressive approach to the protection of the environment. Scotland has had a bigger cumulative fall in emissions (29.6 per cent) than any of the EU-15 since 1990; higher than the average emissions reduction across the EU-27, and the highest of the nations in the UK.

With experience of addressing global concerns like climate change, restoring natural habitats, and managing fragile marine areas, we have an important contribution to make internationally. The current Scottish Government is committed to ensuring that an independent Scotland will deliver on its European and international obligations, while continuing to build on its reputation for positive leadership, for example by supporting inclusion of protection of the environment in the proposed written constitution.

447. **Who will pay for the cost of decommissioning civil nuclear sites in an independent Scotland?**
This Government's policy is that in an independent Scotland the decommissioning costs of Scotland's three non-operational sites (Dounreay, Hunterston A and Chapelcross) will continue to be met from the public purse. The costs of decommissioning Scotland's other two operational sites (Hunterston B and Torness) will be met by the private operators of those sites.

Following independence, the precise division of assets and liabilities will be subject to detailed negotiation between the Scottish and Westminster Governments, working together constructively in the best interests of the people of Scotland and the rest of the United Kingdom, as set out in the Edinburgh Agreement.

448. How will an independent Scotland manage its nuclear waste?

An independent Scotland will ensure that the nuclear legacy inherited from the UK is managed safely and effectively. This Scottish Government is committed to achieving that through a robust regulatory regime and effective long-term management of the decommissioning sites.

Met Office

449. What will happen to Met Office services in an independent Scotland?

The Met Office is Scotland's weather forecasting service. Scotland benefits from these weather and climate services, which improve the resilience and effectiveness of public services and communities, helping to save lives, protect property and support the national economy. The Scottish Government will seek agreement with Westminster to maintain the provision of these services on independence. The Scottish Government will make an appropriate financial contribution for the use of these services.

Agriculture, Food and Rural Communities

450. What will happen to the Crown Estate in an independent Scotland?

The Crown Estate is currently administered by a UK body, the Crown Estate Commissioners, and the revenues flow to the UK Treasury. In an independent Scotland, the current Scottish Government plans that the assets of the Crown Estate better support local economic development and provide wider community benefit in Scotland. The current Scottish Government proposes to review the management of the Crown Estate and will consult on arrangements to enhance local control of assets including greater autonomy for the islands and ownership of the foreshore and local harbours. We plan to introduce community benefit associated with Scotland's offshore renewable resource. This will deliver a direct benefit for communities across Scotland of at least half of the seabed leasing revenues and more in the islands.

451. **How will independence affect the support that Scottish farmers receive under Europe's Common Agriculture Policy (CAP)?**
As part of the UK, Scotland's farmers receive the third lowest direct payment per hectare in the European Union. Independent member states have benefitted from the European Union's principle that no member state should receive less than the minimum EU average payment rate of €196 per hectare. Had Scotland been an independent member state when the latest CAP round was agreed, this principle would have meant gaining an additional €1 billion of support between 2014 and 2020.

The following table shows how Scotland compares with EU member states before and after the recent CAP negotiations.

Table 1: Annual CAP Pillar 1 – Direct Payments per hectare – existing legislation and allocation for 2019.

Member State	Direct Payments (Existing Legislation) Per Hectare	2019 Direct Payments Per Hectare
Malta	€696	€640
Netherlands	€457	€403
Belgium	€435	€386
Italy	€404	€363
Greece	€384	€350
Cyprus	€372	€338
Denmark	€363	€332
Slovenia	€325	€302
Germany	€319	€298
France	€296	€281
Luxembourg	€275	€269
Ireland	€271	€261
Austria	€262	€253
Hungary	€260	€251
Czech Republic	€257	€249
Spain	€229	€233
Finland	€237	€230
Sweden	€235	€229
Bulgaria	€233	€228
United Kingdom	€229	€225
Poland	€215	€216
Slovakia	€206	€210
Portugal	€194	€205
Estonia	€117	€196
Latvia	€95	€196
Lithuania	€144	€196
Romania	€183	€196
Scotland	€130	€128

452.   **How will independence affect support for rural development that businesses and communities receive through the CAP?**

As part of the UK, Scotland currently receives the lowest level of rural development funding in Europe. This is because the Westminster Government does not prioritise this support in its negotiations with Europe.

With independence, Scotland will be able to negotiate for fairer allocations for rural development – similar to that achieved by many other member states. For example, despite Ireland having around 25 per cent of the agricultural land of the UK, it has successfully managed to negotiate an allocation of almost €2 billion for rural development – almost 85 per cent of the total allocation for the UK. Finland offers another example, having negotiated a €600 million uplift. This demonstrates what sovereign countries, similar in size to Scotland, can achieve within EU negotiations when they are able to reflect their own needs and priorities.

Independence will ensure that Scotland enters into the next set of CAP negotiations on an even footing with the rest of the members of the EU.

The following table shows how Scotland compares with EU member states on rural development (CAP Pillar 2) payments before and after the recent CAP negotiations.

Table 2: Annual CAP Pillar 2 payments for 2007/2013 and for 2014/2020

Member State	Average 2007/13 Rural Development Funding Per Hectare of Utilised Agricultural Area Per Annum	Average 2014/20 Rural Development Funding Per Hectare of Utilised Agricultural Area Per Annum
Malta	€ 969	€ 1,236
Croatia		€ 249
Slovenia	€ 271	€ 248
Austria	€ 182	€ 178
Cyprus	€ 205	€ 165
Greece	€ 151	€ 163
Portugal	€ 160	€ 160
Finland	€ 134	€ 148
Slovakia	€ 148	€ 141
Italy	€ 100	€ 116
Luxembourg	€ 103	€ 109
Estonia	€ 109	€ 109
Poland	€ 131	€ 107
Hungary	€ 103	€ 92
Czech Republic	€ 116	€ 88
Lithuania	€ 91	€ 83
Sweden	€ 91	€ 81
Romania	€ 82	€ 81
Latvia	€ 83	€ 77
EU 27/28 Average	€ 76	€ 76
Germany	€ 78	€ 70
Ireland	€ 78	€ 69
Bulgaria	€ 75	€ 66
Belgium	€ 51	€ 58
Spain	€ 48	€ 49
France	€ 37	€ 48
Netherlands	€ 45	€ 46
Denmark	€ 31	€ 34
United Kingdom	€ 20	€ 21
Scotland	€ 11	€ 12

453. **What will happen to CAP payments to farmers in an independent Scotland?**
With independence, farmers and crofters will continue to receive CAP payments – the budget is already set until 2020. But, crucially, with independence we will also have a direct voice in the negotiations on the post-2020 Common Agricultural Policy.

454. **Will the transition to independence disrupt CAP payments to farmers?**
No. The administration of payments for the CAP is already conducted by the Scottish Government. As the European Commission pays CAP payments in arrears, the Scottish Government plans that an independent Scotland will underwrite payments to farmers, as Westminster does today, ensuring a smooth transition for Scottish farmers.

455. **How will an independent Scotland's interests be prioritised at the Council of Ministers for Agriculture and Fisheries?**
Independence will give Scotland its own voice in Europe, participating at every level in the EU policy process and ensuring the Scottish Government is able to promote and protect Scotland's national interests in EU affairs. Fishing and agriculture are important sectors of the Scottish economy and will be priority areas for negotiation in the EU.

456. **How will Scotland's fishing quotas be determined following independence?**
Following a vote for independence, the Scottish Government will enter into negotiations with the rest of the UK and with the EU institutions to fully define our fishing rights and other key issues. At present, Scotland's fishing opportunities are provided for in a concordat among the UK nations, which gives Scotland a share of UK quotas. It will be in the interests of both Scotland and the rest of the UK to agree an appropriate and fair set of final allocations so that the normal fishing practices of each nation can continue unaffected.

457. **Will the management of Scotland's quotas be any different in an independent Scotland?**
Independence will stop Scottish-held quotas being permanently transferred out of Scotland to other parts of the UK. This is because EU rules do not allow permanent transfers of this nature from one member state to another. An independent Scotland will therefore be able to retain its quotas for the benefit of its own fishermen.

458. **Will Scottish fishing fleets still be able to declare their catch in England?**
Yes. Fishing vessels often land their catch in different countries and independence will make no difference to this.

459. **Will vessels from other EU Member States, including the rest of the UK, still be able to fish in Scottish waters and vice versa?**
Beyond 12 nautical miles, the EU's Common Fisheries Policy provides any member state's vessels with access to all member states' waters. However they can only fish in waters where they have fishing opportunities.

Within 12 nautical miles, we would expect to agree with other member states that vessels from other member states (including the rest of the UK) with historic fishing rights should be able to continue fishing in Scottish waters, and vice versa.

460. **How will independence affect Scotland's relationship with the European Common Fisheries Policy (CFP)?**
As an independent member state, Scotland will be negotiating as one of the foremost and most respected fishing nations in Europe. This status will give Scotland the opportunity to take a leadership role in driving reforms to the CFP and in negotiating annual fishing opportunities within the framework of the CFP. The government of an independent Scotland will be able to negotiate unequivocally for Scottish priorities without having to dilute these in order to suit wider UK objectives.

461. **What impact will independence have on the ability of Scottish food and drink producers to sell their produce to a UK market?**
The same opportunities will exist before and after independence. Consumers elsewhere in the UK will continue to be attracted by the world-class quality of Scottish produce. By sharing Sterling with the rest of the UK, trade will continue to be underpinned by a common currency. Scotland's status as an independent member of the European Union will ensure free movement of goods, people and services and avoid any barriers to trade with the rest of the UK or European markets.

Culture and Broadcasting

462. What will happen to the BBC following independence?

The current Scottish Government proposes that BBC Scotland will become the foundation for the establishment of a publicly-funded, public service broadcaster – the Scottish Broadcasting Service (SBS). The existing BBC charter expires on 31 December 2016, and the SBS will begin broadcasting on TV, radio and online on 1 January 2017.

The SBS would replace the BBC in Scotland in joint ventures, including those related to Freeview and Freesat. The SBS would also take on the BBC's role in the operation of relevant digital terrestrial television multiplexes in Scotland.

The SBS would also inherit a proportionate share of the BBC's commercial ventures, including BBC Worldwide Ltd, and their associated ongoing profits.

463. Would the Scottish Broadcasting Service work with the BBC?

In addition to its own TV, radio, and online services, the SBS would seek to co-operate, co-produce and co-commission with the remaining BBC network where appropriate. Currently, BBC Scotland delivers a range of programming for the BBC network: the BBC aims for 8.6 per cent of its eligible original programming to come from BBC Scotland. We propose that the SBS enter into a new formal relationship with the BBC as a joint venture, where the SBS would continue to supply the BBC network with the same level of original programming, in return for ongoing access to BBC services in Scotland.

The new joint venture relationship with the BBC would allow the SBS to continue to have the right to opt out of BBC 1 and BBC 2, as BBC Scotland can currently. The maintenance of access to the BBC will ensure that the people of Scotland will still have access to current programming such as *EastEnders*, *Doctor Who*, and *Strictly Come Dancing*, and to channels like CBeebies.

464. **Will I still get access to BBC channels following
     independence?**
     Yes. Under our proposals, a joint venture agreement between
     the SBS and the BBC would see all current BBC services
     available in Scotland continue, in addition to the TV, radio and
     online services provided by the SBS.

     If it became clear in future that Westminster did not share our
     commitment to publicly-funded public service broadcasting, the
     Scottish Government would establish a contractual arrangement
     with BBC Worldwide Ltd to secure continued availability of BBC
     services in Scotland.

     BBC channels that are available in the UK currently are also
     already available through different live transmission agreements
     in the Republic of Ireland, the Netherlands, and Switzerland.

465. **Can Scotland afford a quality publicly-financed public
     service broadcaster after independence? Would
     advertising be necessary as in Ireland?**
     £320 million is raised annually in Scotland from licence fees
     alone, but, following the implementation of the BBC's 'Delivering
     Quality First' initiative, the level of spend by the BBC in Scotland
     could be as low as £175 million in 2016/17. As a comparison
     the total annual cost of Ireland's RTÉ is around £286 million.

     In addition to the £320 million raised in licence fees in Scotland,
     around £12 million per year is made available by the Scottish
     Government for Gaelic broadcasting, and the Scottish
     proportionate share of profits of ongoing BBC commercial
     ventures is around £13 million to £19 million – approximately
     £345 million per year in total.

     On this basis, SBS would be in a position to provide a
     high-quality publicly-funded public service broadcaster
     within the resources available, without seeking revenue
     from advertising.

466. **Would the TV licence fee have to rise in an independent Scotland?**
No. The existing licence fee would be inherited on independence and is sufficient to allow a high-quality SBS service on TV, radio and online.

In future, the funding of the SBS will be determined by the government of an independent Scotland in negotiation with the broadcaster.

467. **What would happen to STV in an independent Scotland?**
STV's licence has been extended to 2025, and the current Scottish Government has been clear that existing licences will be honoured at the point of independence. Viewers in the south of Scotland will continue to be served by ITV's Borders franchise, but as part of the conditions of the renewal of that licence, ITV will now be obliged to transmit different programming to the south of Scotland and the north of England so that viewers in the south of Scotland have the same access to news and current affairs coverage about Scotland as the rest of Scotland.

These arrangements will ensure that Scottish audiences can continue to access programming such as *Coronation Street* and *X-Factor*.

468. **What would happen to Channel 4 in an independent Scotland?**
At the point of independence, it is expected that Channel 4's licence will have been extended to the end of 2024, and the established licence will be honoured. The current Scottish Government proposes to establish ownership arrangements of this public corporation which ensure that a Scottish population share of Channel 4 network original productions, by hours and by value, comes from Scotland.

469. **What would happen to Channel 5 in an independent Scotland?**
By the time Scotland becomes independent in March 2016, Channel 5's licence will have been extended to 2025. The Scottish Government intends that following independence the existing licence will be honoured.

470. **What would happen to BSkyB and other private sector cable and satellite broadcasters in an independent Scotland?**
Our intention is that existing licences will be honoured until expiry. Because of the nature of satellite technology, broadcasting over that platform will remain identical in Scotland to that in the rest of the UK, just as is the case today across the UK and Ireland.

471. **What would happen to Gaelic broadcasting in an independent Scotland?**
The Scottish Government is committed to the continuation of the BBC Alba channel and Radio nan Gáidheal, under the auspices of the Scottish Broadcasting Service.

472. **What would happen to radio in an independent Scotland?**
Our intention is that existing licences for radio stations would be honoured until expiry.

473. **Would the Scottish Broadcasting Service participate in charity fundraising drives such as Comic Relief and Children in Need?**
Yes. The SBS will seek to co-operate with the BBC and the relevant charities to continue to involve the people of Scotland in these, and similar, established telethons.

474. **Would the Scottish Broadcasting Service join the European Broadcasting Union (EBU)?**
Yes. The SBS would seek membership of the EBU and would be an active and constructive partner in the organisation. As part of this participation, we would envisage the SBS engaging with some of the EBU competitions, including Scottish entries in the Eurovision Song Contest.

475. **What will happen to cultural items related to Scotland and held in UK national collections in an independent Scotland?**
Scotland currently owns a share of all UK national collections. The national museums and galleries in both London and Scotland all hold items from different parts of the UK and collections assembled from across the world. They have long-established arrangements for loans, exchanges and

partnerships, which will be able to continue when Scotland becomes independent.

476. **What will happen to Historic Scotland in an independent Scotland?**
The Scottish Government intends that, following independence, Historic Scotland, or its successor body, will continue to provide the skills, services and visitor operations that it does at present. The merger between Historic Scotland and the Royal Commission on the Ancient and Historical Monuments of Scotland is intended to ensure the sustainability of the functions of both organisations.

477. **Will the historic environment be managed differently in an independent Scotland?**
Management of the historic environment is already within the control of the Scottish Parliament.

478. **What will happen to World Heritage Sites in an independent Scotland?**
World Heritage Sites are recognised by the United Nations Educational, Scientific and Cultural Organisation (UNESCO) as places of internationally significant cultural or natural heritage. There are currently five World Heritage Sites in Scotland – the Antonine Wall, Heart of Neolithic Orkney, New Lanark, the Old and New Towns of Edinburgh, and St Kilda, with a nomination for the Forth Bridge currently being developed. Their status will not change as a result of independence.

Future Scottish governments will continue to be able to nominate Scottish sites for world heritage status in an independent Scotland, and Historic Scotland, or its successor body, will continue to monitor the management of existing sites.

479. **Will tax incentives for cultural donations continue in an independent Scotland?**
The tax system in place immediately before independence will be inherited at that time. After that, decisions on the tax system and all specific taxes – including tax rates, allowances and credits – will be made by the parliament and government of an independent Scotland.

480. **What will happen to grants awarded under the Department of Culture, Media and Sport's Listed Places of Worship Scheme in an independent Scotland?**

The Listed Places of Worship Scheme, which is administered by the Department of Culture, Media and Sport, provides grants in respect of VAT costs incurred for eligible repairs, maintenance and alterations to places of worship across the UK. The current Scottish Government proposes that a similar scheme should operate in an independent Scotland, and will consider extending the scheme to benefit the repair and maintenance of all listed buildings.

481. **Will an independent Scotland honour existing international treaties, agreements and conventions around culture and heritage?**

Yes. The Scottish Government is committed to ensuring that, as an independent nation, Scotland will continue to meet all legal obligations that flow from its membership of international organisations and that it will continue with treaty rights and obligations. Where the UK has not signed or ratified international treaties, there will be opportunities to explore whether an independent Scotland would ratify these. The current Scottish Government is in favour, for example, of ratifying the UNESCO Convention for the Safeguarding of Intangible Cultural Heritage, as Scotland's songs, dance and stories are as important as our castles, palaces and monuments.

482. **What role will culture and heritage play in an independent Scotland?**

Culture and heritage will continue to be valued in and of itself as the heart, soul and essence of a flourishing Scotland, as well as for the wider social and economic benefits that it brings to individuals, communities and the nation.

An independent Scotland will continue to nurture and promote our culture and heritage sector, so that it can inspire and enrich lives both here and internationally.

483. **Will we have the power to reduce VAT on repair and maintenance work to dwellings in an independent Scotland?**
Independence will enable the Scottish Parliament to explore a reduction in VAT on repairs and maintenance work to homes as part of wider taxation priorities.

Powers over VAT, currently exercised by the Westminster Government, will transfer to the Scottish Parliament as a result of independence. The tax system in place immediately before independence will be inherited at that time. Thereafter decisions on the tax system and all specific taxes – including tax rates, allowances and credits for VAT and other taxes – will be made by the parliament and government of an independent Scotland.

484. **Will we need to give up specific Scottish cultural and heritage archival documents or acquire them from the UK National Archives?**
Archives across the world hold all sorts of material relating to other countries. Cross-UK advisory bodies on archives – such as the National Archives – have in practice only a limited role in Scottish terms.

National Lottery

485. **Will the National Lottery continue to operate in an independent Scotland?**
Yes, that is the current Scottish Government's intention. People will still be able to play National Lottery games, and the infrastructure enabling them to do so will remain in place.

Scotland will continue to receive a fair share of ticket sales to support good causes. Following independence, all decisions about the allocation of Scotland's share of funds will be taken in Scotland, ensuring that money raised from lottery ticket sales is used to respond to the needs of Scotland's local communities.

486. **Will I still be able to play the National Lottery?**
Yes. This Government proposes that people will still be able to play National Lottery games, and the infrastructure enabling them to do so will remain in place.

487. **Who will operate the National Lottery in Scotland?**
At present, the licence to run the National Lottery is held by
Camelot Group plc, and is in place until 2023. The Scottish
Government does not intend to change this arrangement.

488. **Will there be a Scottish Lottery? If so how will it operate?**
There are no current plans to establish a distinct Scottish
Lottery. Any decisions to do so will be the responsibility of a
future Scottish government, and will be subject to the usual
processes of consultation and consideration. Future Scottish
governments would have the powers to establish a Scottish
Lottery if there was a demand for it or in support of specific
events.

489. **In an independent Scotland, what arrangements will be
in place to distribute funds to Scottish good causes?**
The present Scottish Government's approach would be to
ensure that Scotland receives its fair share of lottery funding
and to ensure that all decisions about how good cause funds
are distributed and allocated will be taken in Scotland.

490. **Will being independent enable the same amount of money
to be generated for good causes?**
There is no reason to anticipate that this would differ because
of independence. The level of available funds depends on a
number of factors, including the number of ticket sales and the
price of those tickets.

However, there are currently no rules in place guaranteeing
Scotland any fixed proportion of National Lottery funds and
the lottery operator does not publish information on ticket sales
in Scotland. Independence would mean that future Scottish
governments will be in a position to work with the lottery
operator to ensure Scotland continues to receive a fair share
of funding.

491. **What will happen to the Big Lottery Fund in Scotland?**
The Big Lottery Fund is the largest distributor of Lottery good
cause money in Scotland and we propose that it will continue
this role after independence.

492. **How will Lottery funding for heritage be distributed?**
The Scottish Government's proposal is to build upon the good work of the Heritage Lottery Fund team based in Scotland and to give them full responsibility for the allocation and distribution of the Scottish share of lottery funding for heritage good causes. They will initially operate under a suitable shared governance system, building on the work of the current Scottish Regional Committee.

493. **What will happen to Scotland's share of Lottery funding for the arts and film and for sport in Scotland?**
Under the arrangements we propose, Scotland's share of Lottery funding for the arts and film will be distributed by Creative Scotland and for sport by **sport**scotland, as they are now.

Communications and IT Infrastructure

Postal Services

494. **What is the plan for the newly privatised Royal Mail in an independent Scotland?**
The current Scottish Government disagrees with the recent privatisation of Royal Mail. Independence will enable Scotland to restore the Royal Mail to public ownership in Scotland and the current Scottish Government intends to do so.

495. **Will universal postal services be maintained in an independent Scotland?**
Yes. This Scottish Government recognises the importance of postal services to sustaining communities across Scotland, and will maintain at least the level of service provision inherited from the United Kingdom on independence.

496. **Will the price for stamps be higher in an independent Scotland than in the rest of the UK?**
On independence, stamp prices will be the same as they are at the time in the rest of the UK. A Scottish postal service in public ownership would not need to generate profits for shareholders and so should be in a better position to ensure that postal prices and deliveries meet Scotland's needs. This applies to sending post and parcels within Scotland, to the rest of the UK and to other countries.

We know that many people and businesses will continue to send post and parcels outside Scotland and it is our intention that postal charges to the rest of the UK will not be more expensive than charges to send post within Scotland.

Communications

497. **Will I have to pay roaming charges on my mobile phone in other parts of the UK?**

No. There will be no international roaming charges across Scotland and the rest of the UK. There is no reason why companies would wish to frustrate customers on either side of the border by introducing charges.

The EU has cut charges for international voice calls, texts and internet access by 75 per cent since 2007, and the European Commission has recently published proposals to ban incoming call charges while travelling in the EU from 1 July 2014, and to abolish all other mobile roaming charges by 2016.

498. **Will I have to pay international rates to phone the rest of the UK on a landline?**

No. People in Scotland and the rest of the UK will not be subject to international rates on a fixed landline.

The European Commission has recently published proposals that would mean companies cannot charge more for a fixed call within Europe than they do for a long distance domestic call.

499. **Will my home phone number change as a result of Scotland becoming an independent country?**

No. Independence will not result in any change to local phone numbers and dialling codes for areas across Scotland (such as 01224 for Aberdeen and 01698 for Motherwell).

500. **What will the international dialling code be for an independent Scotland?**

When Scotland becomes independent, we will seek to ensure that Scotland continues to use the 0044 international dialling code, through the International Telecommunication Union. This would be similar to the current use of the 001 international dialling code which is shared by a number of North American countries including Canada and the USA.

501. Will 3G and 4G internet still be available on my mobile phone in an independent Scotland?
Yes. Powers over this issue, currently exercised by Westminster, will transfer to Scotland as a result of independence. This Scottish Government would prioritise enhancements to mobile phone coverage in an independent Scotland.

502. What impact will independence have on investment in broadband infrastructure and in satellite broadband technologies?
Public investment in broadband infrastructure at a UK level is fragmented. For example, Westminster is delivering a number of programmes – a rural broadband fund, a super-connected cities fund, and a mobile infrastructure fund.

These projects are being administered separately. They have different aims and objectives and are not fully aligned with each other. The overall investment made by Westminster is not being utilised to maximum impact. With independence, the Scottish Government will have the opportunity to direct these resources more effectively within Scotland.

503. What will happen to the UK internet domain name registration process?
There will be no impact on the UK internet domain name registration processes or the cost to businesses as anyone in the world can apply to use dotUK.

Prior to independence, a new dotSCOT top level domain will have been established and will be open to registrations from businesses, organisations and individuals from Scotland and to those with a clear Scottish connection.

An independent Scotland would also be entitled to a new two-letter country code top-level domain once new codes are in place with the International Standardization Organisation.

IT Infrastructure and Data

504. **What arrangements will be made to "share" or migrate systems with existing Westminster Government departments which currently hold data on individuals, such as on social security and tax systems?**
On independence, the short-term delivery of central government IT services would remain as it currently stands. We would work closely with Westminster departments, as envisaged in the Edinburgh Agreement, to support the best interests of the people of Scotland and the rest of the UK through continuity of service and to identify and scope any transition to new systems. This would also look at the potential for sharing existing systems, both short-term and longer-term.

The Scottish Government would look to put in place a memorandum of agreement with each of the UK departments to ensure there would be a clear understanding that data relating to Scottish citizens is entirely the responsibility of an independent Scotland, and to set out the standards required from UK departments for as long as they continue to act as processors of the data.

505. **Will independence mean there will be extra costs in terms of IT systems for public services?**
There will be transitional costs, the level of which will depend on arrangements reached with Westminster on sharing. Independence provides an opportunity to develop better integrated IT systems for public services.

506. **Will Scotland continue to have all internet traffic routed via London, or will it be necessary to create a Scottish internet hub, with direct connectivity to mainland Europe?**
This is not affected by independence and will depend on whether current connectors, mainly through London, have the bandwidth to meet the needs of Scottish businesses as they do currently. The Scottish Government has worked with industry to help create an internet exchange in Scotland, which launched in October 2013. The internet exchange point allows internet traffic to be routed through Scotland more efficiently and cost effectively, allowing Scottish businesses to connect directly to the internet more cheaply and easily, and increasing the resilience of internet infrastructure in Scotland.

The Referendum

How the Referendum will take Place

507. **Why is Scotland having a referendum on independence?**
Scotland should be independent because the best people to take decisions about Scotland's future are those of us who live and work here.

We believe the people of Scotland should have the opportunity to choose a new path for our nation. We believe that independence is the necessary next step for Scotland if our nation is to become a fairer and more prosperous place.

In May 2011, the Scottish National Party won a majority of seats in the Scottish Parliament and formed the Scottish Government. The SNP manifesto included a commitment to a referendum. The referendum on 18 September 2014 is the delivery of that commitment.

508. **What question is being asked?**
The question is "Should Scotland be an independent country?" Voters can answer Yes or No.

509. **How was the referendum question decided?**
The independent Electoral Commission tested the Scottish Government's proposed question with members of the public to ensure that people will easily understand it. It suggested a minor amendment, which we accepted. This was then agreed by the Scottish Parliament.

510. **When is the referendum going to be?**
The referendum will be held on Thursday 18 September 2014. Polls will be open from 7am until 10pm.

511. **Who can vote in the referendum?**
People who can vote in Scottish Parliamentary and local government elections will be able to vote in the referendum. The following groups are entitled to be on the electoral register for the referendum:

■ British citizens resident in Scotland.

■ Commonwealth citizens resident in Scotland who have leave to remain in the UK or do not require such leave.

- Citizens of the Republic of Ireland and other EU countries resident in Scotland.

- Members of the House of Lords resident in Scotland.

- Service personnel serving in the UK or overseas with the armed forces who are registered to vote in Scotland.

- Crown personnel serving outside the UK with HM Government who are registered to vote in Scotland.

The key difference from normal voting arrangements is that the minimum age for voting in the referendum will be 16 instead of 18. This means that people who will be 16 years old by 18 September 2014, and are otherwise eligible, can register to vote.

512. **How do I register to vote?**
The annual household canvass has been taking place in Scotland from 1 October 2013. Each household will receive a standard annual canvass form, and a young voter registration form, which will collect details of those eligible to vote in the referendum.

People can also register to vote until 11 days before the referendum through 'rolling registration'. Further information on how to register to vote is available at http://www.aboutmyvote. co.uk/

513. **How will people know their voting rights?**
The Electoral Commission has a statutory responsibility to undertake public awareness campaigns in respect of the referendum. These campaigns will cover registration and voting.

Education Scotland has a role in making sure that young people and adult learners know about the referendum and how to take part.

The electoral registration form for members of the armed forces, which is available on the Electoral Commission's website, makes clear the options available to service personnel. The Ministry of Defence also provides advice and information to service personnel on voting rights and registration options available.

514. **How and where can I cast my vote?**
    The Electoral Commission will provide factual, impartial
    guidance to voters on how to register and how to cast their vote.
    In general, votes will be cast in the same way and at the same
    places that people vote in elections.

515. **Do a certain number of people have to vote for the result to
    count?**
    Whatever the turnout in the referendum, if more than half of
    those voting vote Yes, Scotland will become independent. If
    more than half vote No, Scotland will not become independent.

516. **How will the referendum be run?**
    The referendum will be run to the highest international
    standards. There will be a Chief Counting Officer who will be
    responsible for ensuring that the referendum is run properly and
    effectively. The Chief Counting Officer will be the convener of
    the Electoral Management Board for Scotland.

    The Chief Counting Officer will appoint Counting Officers to run
    the poll at a local level.

517. **How much will the referendum cost to run?**
    The referendum will cost around £13.7 million.

    Informing My Vote

518. **What is the Scottish Government's position on the
    referendum?**
    We believe that the future prosperity and wellbeing of Scotland
    is best served by the people of Scotland voting Yes in the
    referendum so that Scotland becomes an independent country.

519. **What is the Westminster Government's position on the
    referendum?**
    The Westminster Government's position is to oppose
    independence for Scotland.

520. **What if I don't normally vote for the SNP?**
    You do not need to support the Scottish National Party to vote
    Yes. Individuals who support all the major parties – or none of
    them – support independence and will vote Yes in the
    referendum.

The decision in the referendum is not about voting for any particular political party. It is about whether decisions about Scotland should be made in Scotland or by Westminster.

The Scottish Government supports independence because we believe it will be better for us all if decisions about Scotland are taken by the people who care most about Scotland – the people who live and work here.

521. **What is the position of overseas governments and international organisations on the referendum?**
Governments of other countries, as well as international organisations, recognise that the decision about becoming an independent country is one for people in Scotland alone to make. The international community respects that the referendum is consensual and democratic.

522. **What information is available to me to help me decide how to vote?**
There is a lot of information available to help you decide how to vote:

- the independent Electoral Commission will provide information for voters about how to register and cast votes in the referendum. It also has information on its website (http://www.electoralcommission.org.uk/scotland)

- the main campaigns have dedicated websites:
    - Yes Scotland – http://www.yesscotland.net/
    - Better Together – http://www.bettertogether.net/

- the Scottish Government has a dedicated referendum website – http://www.scotreferendum.com – and has published this paper as a comprehensive guide to an independent Scotland

- the Westminster Government's Scotland Office has a dedicated website – https://www.gov.uk/government/topics/scotland

- the broadcast media must be neutral in the debate and provide information on television and online

- the print media do not have to be neutral in the debate and will be providing information and commentary in their papers and on their websites

- there are also a number of academic books available and a range of online blogs commenting on the referendum

- the main Twitter hashtag for the referendum is #indyref

523. Who will regulate the campaign?

The independent Electoral Commission will be responsible for regulating campaign activity.

During the 16 weeks prior to the referendum (the 'referendum period'), campaigners will have to follow certain rules to ensure that the referendum is fair and that it commands the confidence of both sides of the debate, including rules on how much money can be spent by different types of campaigner and where that money comes from.

524. Are there restrictions on how much can be spent on campaigning?

Yes, the Electoral Commission has recommended spending limits that will ensure a level playing field between campaigners on each side of the debate. During the 16 weeks prior to the referendum (from 29 May to 18 September 2014):

- the designated lead campaigners will be allowed to spend £1.5 million each

- other registered campaigners will be allowed to spend £150,000 each

- political parties will be entitled to spend amounts based on their level of representation in the Scottish Parliament

525. What legal advice has the Scottish Government received relating to the issues raised by independence? How has this been used to develop this guide?

This guide is consistent with, and informed by, legal advice the Government has received. The content of any legal advice is confidential. By long-standing convention, successive Scottish and Westminster governments have not disclosed the source or content of legal advice other than in the most exceptional circumstances.

526. **What are Scotland's Constitutional Arrangements now?**
At the moment, Scotland is part of the United Kingdom of Great Britain and Northern Ireland. Decisions on most rates of taxes, changes to the welfare system and policies in areas such as energy and nuclear weapons are taken by Westminster, which has only 59 Scottish MPs out of 650.

Below is a brief summary of Scotland's constitutional journey so far:

■ King James VI of Scotland also became King James I of England in 1603. This is known as the 'Union of the Crowns'. However, both Scotland and England remained independent countries at this time

■ in 1707 Scotland and England agreed to form a United Kingdom known as "Great Britain". This agreement is known as the 'Union of the Parliaments'. At this point most of Scotland's government moved from Edinburgh to London

■ in 1801 Great Britain and Ireland were united into the "United Kingdom of Great Britain and Ireland"

■ in 1885 the Scottish Office was created as a department of government whose minister, the Secretary for Scotland, was responsible for law and education. From 1892 the Secretary was in the cabinet and in 1926 the post was raised to that of Secretary of State. In 1939 the main base of the Scottish Office moved from London to Edinburgh

■ in 1922, the Irish Free State (which later became the Republic of Ireland) was formed. The remaining State became the "United Kingdom of Great Britain and Northern Ireland"

■ in 1979, the people of Scotland voted in a referendum for a national assembly for Scotland. Although a majority voted for the assembly, it was not created as a result of a technicality requiring 40 per cent of all registered voters to vote in favour

- in 1989 a Constitutional Convention was convened. The convention affirmed the sovereign right of the people of Scotland to determine the form of government best suited to their needs

- in 1997, the people of Scotland voted in a referendum for a Scottish Parliament with tax-varying powers

- in 1999, the Scottish Parliament was re-established as a devolved parliament within the United Kingdom

- in 2012, the UK Parliament passed the Scotland Act 2012 to transfer limited new powers to the devolved Scottish Parliament

More detailed information on Scotland's constitutional journey is available at Annex A.

527. In what sense would Scotland be independent if the result of the referendum is yes?

If the people of Scotland vote for independence then Scotland will become an independent state, like the other 193 states around the world. All the powers currently exercised by Westminster in Scotland, or on behalf of Scotland will be transferred to the Scottish Parliament. It will then be for the people of Scotland, through their elected representatives, to decide how these powers are exercised.

Part 1 of this guide explains this more fully.

528. How is this different from the current position?

At the moment Scotland sends 59 Members of Parliament to Westminster. The rest of the UK sends 591. Even if all Scottish MPs vote one way on an issue, they can be voted down by more than 10 to one. If Scotland was independent, our elected representatives could never be outvoted.

Since 2010, a large majority of Scottish MPs have voted against increasing VAT, austerity cuts, the privatisation of the Royal Mail, cutting child benefit, capping benefits and welfare and the introduction of the "bedroom tax". On each of these issues, Scotland's representatives at Westminster have been outvoted by a government led by a party (the Conservatives) which won only one of Scotland's 59 constituencies.

529. **What does "sovereignty of the people of Scotland" mean?**
It means that the people of Scotland have the right to choose freely their form of governance. In an independent Scotland, sovereignty would mean that the people of Scotland were the final authority and all state power and authority would be accountable to them.

530. **How is this different from the existing position in the UK?**
Under current arrangements sovereignty – supreme authority – in the UK lies with "the Crown in Parliament", rather than the people. In practice this means that the Westminster Parliament has ultimate power to do anything that it decides, including to overrule the Scottish Parliament on any matter.

531. **How would the position on sovereignty change after independence?**
With independence, sovereignty would be formally vested in the people of Scotland. Our proposal is that this would be enshrined in a written constitution.

532. **Is independence about democracy?**
Yes – and one of the arguments for independence is that the Westminster system is not democratic enough. It can be argued that it fails Scottish democracy on five counts:

- for 34 of the 68 years since 1945, Scotland has been ruled by governments that were elected by fewer than half of Scottish constituencies

- in only two of the 18 elections since 1945 (October 1964 and February 1974) – would the largest party in the UK Parliament have been different if Scotland had been independent and not returned MPs to Westminster

- the Westminster system includes the House of Lords, whose members are not elected by, or representative of, the people. Members of the House of Lords hold significant power over the people of Scotland. A single Member of the House of Lords has more say over the welfare system in Scotland, for example, than the whole of the Scottish Parliament

- the first-past-the-post electoral system, used to elect members of the Westminster Parliament, does not fully reflect the voting intentions of the people and effectively disenfranchises voters who live in constituencies where one party has a large majority

- the Westminster system is based on the principle of unlimited power, usually referred to as Parliamentary sovereignty. The Westminster Government and Parliament continue to have power to do anything – even to repeal the Human Rights Act or abolish the Scottish Parliament

533. What are the current powers of the Scottish Parliament?
The Scottish Parliament currently makes the key policy decisions in many areas, for example:

- health

- education

- justice, including the police and courts

- local government

- housing

- rural affairs and the environment

534. What powers are currently reserved to the Westminster Parliament?
Despite many decisions being made by the Scottish Parliament and Government, many key decisions are still taken by the Westminster Parliament and Government, such as:

- public finances – for example, how much tax we all pay, how much of the national debt we are paying off and how much we spend overall on public services

- welfare – for example, the level at which state benefits are paid

- pensions – for example, how much the State Pension is and at what age you are entitled to it

- defence – for example, keeping Trident nuclear weapons and going to war in countries like Iraq and Afghanistan

- foreign affairs – for example, being in the European Union and other international organisations

- energy – for example, oil and gas and the price of petrol

- most utilities – for example, decisions to privatise Royal Mail

535. Have other countries become independent in recent years?
Yes. Many countries have taken the opportunity to become independent. It is, increasingly, the natural state of affairs for nations across the world.

The number of independent states has risen dramatically in the modern era. Since the establishment of the United Nations in 1945, its membership has increased from 51 to 193 in 2011.

Of new states that have become UN members since 1945, 30 have done so following a referendum, taking an average transition period from referendum to independence of 18 months. The most recent country in Europe to become independent is Montenegro in 2006. Seven of the 28 member states of the EU have become independent countries in the last 25 years.

Following a Vote for Independence

Transition to Independence

536. What will happen if a majority vote for independence?
We propose that, if more than 50 per cent of the people who vote in the referendum vote Yes, Scotland should become an independent country in March 2016. Scotland's future will then be in Scotland's hands.

537. When will Scotland become independent?
The Scottish Government's intention is that Scotland will become independent on 24 March 2016.

538. Why should independence happen in March 2016?
Independence is about being able to make better decisions for Scotland and ensuring that our enormous wealth is put to work to make life better for the people living here.

Independence on 24 March 2016 would mean the transition process would be complete before the May 2016 Holyrood elections. This allows those elections to focus on the future and the newly elected Government and Parliament of an independent Scotland to immediately start delivering the priorities of the people of Scotland.

539.   **Is 18 months enough time to get everything in place?**
Yes. Eighteen months is a realistic timetable for the necessary preparations. International examples show that countries can make significant constitutional changes happen quickly once a democratic decision is taken. Eighteen months is comparable to the time taken by other countries making the transition to independence.

540.   **What will happen between the referendum and independence?**
There are a number of key actions for the transitional period between the referendum and Scotland becoming independent:

- agreements with the rest of the UK will be concluded, setting out the process for Scotland's independence and the terms on which Scotland will become independent

- agreements with the European Union will be concluded to change Scotland's status within the EU to that of an independent member state, the same as the existing 28 member states

- laws will be passed at both Holyrood and Westminster giving powers for Scotland to become independent and making legal changes in preparation for independence

- administrative changes will be made to enable an independent Scottish Government and Parliament to carry forward key decisions immediately after the May 2016 Scottish elections

Further detail of this transition is set out in Chapter 10.

541. **Who will be the first Government of an independent Scotland?**
The current Scottish Government will be in power until the next Scottish Parliament elections on 5 May 2016. It will be for the Scottish Government and Parliament elected in May 2016 to decide how to take an independent Scotland forward.

542. **If Scotland votes for independence, would Scots be eligible to vote in the 2015 UK General Elections?**
Yes. Sovereignty will be fully exercised by the people of Scotland from the point Scotland becomes independent on 24 March 2016. Until that point, the people of Scotland must be represented politically at the UK level. Scotland will therefore elect MPs to Westminster to represent Scotland up until the date of independence.

Negotiations with the rest of the UK

543. **Who will negotiate for Scotland in discussions with the rest of the UK?**
The Scottish Government will lead the independence negotiations. We will invite representatives from other parties in the Scottish Parliament, prominent Scottish Westminster politicians and representatives of Scottish civic society, to join the Government in negotiating the independence settlement and in ensuring the continuity of those public services currently managed at UK level.

544. **Who will negotiate for the rest of the UK?**
It will be for Westminster to decide who negotiates on behalf of the rest of the UK.

545. **Is there any precedent for negotiations between the Scottish and Westminster Governments?**
Yes. The Edinburgh Agreement, signed by the First Minister and the Prime Minister in October 2012, and the legislative changes that followed are recent, and very clear, examples of discussions between the Scottish and Westminster governments resulting in democratic and co-operative agreements. This agreement paved the way for the referendum.

546. **Will the UK General Election in May 2015 prolong the timetable for negotiations?**
There is no reason that it should do so. It will be in the interests of both countries to conclude the process in good time.

547. **What needs to be agreed before Scotland can become independent?**
Following a vote for independence in 2014, agreements will be needed between the Scottish and Westminster Governments, in the spirit of the Edinburgh Agreement, setting the parameters for Scotland's transition to independence. They will cover:

- the precise timetable towards independence day

- the constitutional platform for an independent Scotland – the laws and administrative arrangements to establish Scotland as an independent state

- the process and timetable for the negotiation and conclusion of the agreements which will form the final independence settlement

548. **What say will the people have in the independence settlement?**
A vote for independence in the referendum will give the Scottish Government and those participating on the Scottish side of the negotiations a mandate to negotiate the best possible independence settlement for Scotland.

The peoples' representatives in the Scottish Parliament will scrutinise the Government's work during the negotiations and transitional period and hold the Government to account.

549. **Are you confident that the independence negotiations will go smoothly?**
Yes. After a democratic vote for independence, it will be in the interests of both Scotland and the rest of the UK to come to a swift and co-operative settlement.

In the Edinburgh Agreement, the UK and Scottish Governments agreed that they will continue to work together constructively in the light of the outcome, whatever it is, in the best interests of the people of Scotland and of the rest of the United Kingdom.

Key to the negotiations will be issues about dividing assets and liabilities, on which the Scottish Government is committed to achieving a fair settlement.

550. **Should discussions on independence between the Scottish and Westminster Governments take place ahead of the referendum?**
The Scottish Government accepts that detailed negotiations on the independence settlement cannot begin ahead of the referendum. However, we believe that sensible discussions about the practical consequences of independence should take place to help the people of Scotland to make an informed choice and prepare the way for detailed negotiation following a vote for independence.

551. **Will an independent Scotland pay its fair share of shared liabilities?**
Yes. Scotland and the rest of the UK will agree a share of the national debt. This could be on the basis of our historical contribution to UK revenues or on the basis of our population share. Either way, our projected share of the UK debt will be smaller as a proportion of our economic output (GDP) than for the UK as a whole, which means Scotland is well placed for the future.

However, we will also be entitled to a fair share of the UK's assets, which are estimated to be worth £1,267 billion. These could be taken as physical assets, cash payments or offset against inherited National Debt.

552. **Will Holyrood or Westminster make the laws that provide for independence?**
We propose that the key legislative steps towards independence should be taken by the Scottish Parliament, following an initial transfer of powers after the referendum.

553. **Will laws need to be passed at Westminster as well as Holyrood?**
Yes, Westminster will have a role in passing legislation concerning independence.

This will not be problematic because Westminster has considerable experience of legislating for the independence of former UK territories.

Successful independent states such as Malta and Malaysia, and scores of others, had their independence legislation passed at Westminster. Scotland's situation – as part of the UK rather than an overseas territory – is different, and that is why it is appropriate that the key legislative steps are taken in the Scottish Parliament.

554. Will it cost too much to become independent?
No. Scotland already pays its share of the cost of UK-wide services, like the benefits system and the tax system. We pay our share of the UK's armed forces and overseas embassies. After independence we will no longer be paying for these UK services and bodies, but will use the money to pay for our own Scottish equivalent. We will save money on some things like defence as we will not be paying towards the UK's nuclear weapons. So money that we currently send to Westminster that is spent in other parts of the UK – or on things we in Scotland do not want – will stay in Scotland to be invested in a modern and efficient system of government for our newly independent country, and to pay for things that we do want. We might decide to continue to share some services with the rest of the UK, for a while anyway. We will pay for these as we do now.

Following a No Vote

555. What happens if there is a majority in favour of No?
If a majority of the votes cast in the referendum are No then Scotland will continue to be governed as it is now, with devolved powers exercised at Holyrood and reserved powers exercised at Westminster.

That means Scotland will lose the opportunity to, for example, remove the "bedroom tax" and to invest our offshore energy wealth. Scotland will continue to pay billions of pounds for nuclear weapons when the majority of people in Scotland wish to invest this money in things like better pensions or improved childcare.

556. **Isn't the Scottish Parliament going to get more powers anyway if Scotland votes No?**
The last time political parties opposed to Scottish independence proposed new powers for the Scottish Parliament was in 2009 when the Calman Commission reported. In 2011 the people of Scotland re-elected the current Scottish Government on a platform which proposed significant improvements to the Commission's proposals. Westminster rejected the Scottish Government's proposals, however, and the result was the Scotland Act 2012, which falls a long way short of full devolved powers in Scotland.

There has been consistent support in Scotland for the Scottish Parliament to have responsibility for taxation and the welfare system. However, none of the parties opposed to independence seem willing to offer this degree of devolution. Whatever offers of more devolution might emerge during the referendum campaign, they are likely to fall short of full powers in these vital areas of Scottish life. Nor is it clear that even limited offers of more powers would be in place by the time of the next UK General Election in May 2015 or taken forward after that.

The only way for Scotland to get all the powers needed to make Scotland a better place is through independence.

557. **If Scotland votes No, will there be another referendum on independence at a later date?**
The Edinburgh Agreement states that a referendum must be held by the end of 2014. There is no arrangement in place for another referendum on independence.

It is the view of the current Scottish Government that a referendum is a once-in-a-generation opportunity. This means that only a majority vote for Yes in 2014 would give certainty that Scotland will be independent.

Scotland as an Independent Country

Scotland on independence day

558. What will be the territory of Scotland?

Scotland's territory will remain as it is now. The borders of Scotland are well understood, extending to the areas governed by the Scottish Government and Parliament and Scottish local authorities.

559. On what basis will an independent Scotland's maritime boundaries be defined?

The setting of maritime boundaries for an independent Scotland will be guided by international law.

This matters because an independent Scotland will own oil and gas reserves within these boundaries. The vast bulk of oil and gas in the UK comes from the Scottish Continental Shelf and will be in Scotland after independence. Analysis by academics at Aberdeen University tells us that in excess of 90 per cent of the oil and gas revenues are from fields in Scottish waters, based on well-established principles of international law.

560. What will happen on the day of independence?

On the day Scotland becomes independent, the Scottish Parliament and Government will assume responsibility for matters, like the economy and welfare, that are currently decided at Westminster. The Scottish Government and Parliament will be able to use these powers to do more to improve the quality of life for people across Scotland.

Scotland already has many of the institutions that a modern independent democratic state needs: a modern parliament elected by proportional representation, a government accountable to parliament, a civil service appointed on merit and supporting the elected government and an independent judiciary and legal system.

The difference brought by independence is that powers currently exercised in Scotland by the Westminster Parliament will be transferred to the Scottish Parliament.

561. **What will Scotland's laws be on the first day of
      independence?**
      Scotland already has an independent legal system supported
      by a fully functioning court system and a legislative parliament.
      On independence, the laws of Scotland will continue in all
      areas, except where they have been changed in preparation for
      independence. After that, it will be for the elected Parliament of
      Scotland to decide on changes to the law.

562. **Won't existing UK laws on reserved matters such as tax
      or welfare need to be re-written entirely?**
      No. All laws that are in force in Scotland immediately before the
      date of independence will continue after independence until
      they are changed by the Scottish Parliament. This would cover
      all existing laws including Holyrood and Westminster legislation
      and other common laws.

      After Independence

563. **What will happen after Scotland becomes independent?**
      The Scottish Government propose that Scotland will become
      independent on 24 March 2016. Following that, the first
      elections to the Scottish Parliament of an independent Scotland
      would be held on 5 May 2016. It will be for the democratically
      elected Scottish Government and Parliament to make decisions
      about the direction of an independent Scotland.

564. **What will happen to Scottish MPs and members of the
      House of Lords in Westminster after independence?**
      With independence, Scotland will no longer send MPs to
      Westminster. Arrangements for the House of Lords will be
      for the rest of the UK to decide but the House of Lords will
      no longer be involved in legislating for Scotland.

565. **What will happen in Scotland after the 2016 elections?**
      The Government and Parliament elected in May 2016 will
      govern an independent Scotland, in accordance with the wishes
      of the people. That means that the people of Scotland will
      decide what happens – that is why the Scottish Government
      supports independence. The reason we are seeking to make
      the transition before the May 2016 elections is so that the
      government elected on 5 May 2016 will be able to immediately
      use the new powers of independence.

Scotland's Written Constitution

566. What is a constitution and why does it matter?

A constitution is the collection of principles and rules that regulates the institutions of the state, how powers are distributed amongst those institutions, and the relationship between the citizens of the country and their state, including the protection of human rights.

567. What is the UK constitution now?

In the UK at present, the constitution consists of various pieces of legislation, and constitutional rules and principles that have evolved over centuries. There is no agreement on exactly which laws, rules and principles make up the constitution. The UK is the only member of the European Union and of the Commonwealth that does not have a written constitution or a Constitution Act.

At the heart of Scotland's constitutional tradition is the fundamental principle that the people of Scotland are sovereign and have the right to determine the form of government best suited to their needs.

However, as part of the UK, the dominant constitutional rule is that Westminster can do anything it chooses, except bind its successors. Sovereignty in the UK is vested in 'the Crown in Parliament' and not in the people.

568. Are we supposed to know all this?

The UK's constitutional position is particularly complex and one of the advantages of moving to a written constitution is to make information about government structures more accessible to the people of Scotland.

569. What do other countries do?

Almost every other country in the world has a written constitution including all the other 27 European Union member states. Similarly, all the other 52 Commonwealth States have a written constitution or Constitution Act.

570. **Why is a written constitution a good thing?**
Having a written constitution means that people have clear
information about how their country works and what their rights
are and it protects these rights from being changed or removed.

571. **Should an independent Scotland have a written
constitution?**
Yes. Our proposal is that an independent Scotland would have
a written constitution which expresses Scotland's values,
embeds the rights of our citizens and sets out clearly how
institutions of state interact with each other and serve the
people.

572. **Will Scotland have a written constitution on day one
of independence?**
A permanent written constitution will be drawn up post-
independence, and everyone will have the chance to be
involved.

Before independence, a constitutional platform for Scotland will
be prepared. It will have effect from the date of independence
and will continue until the permanent written constitution has
been agreed and has come into effect. Scotland's written
constitution could only then be amended according to the
provisions of the constitution itself, therefore protecting people's
rights and liberties.

The Scottish Government set out its proposition for the
development of a permanent written constitution in *Scotland's
Future: from the Referendum to Independence and a Written
Constitution*.

573. **What should be in the written constitution?**
Scotland's written constitution should reflect our identity as
a nation and what is important to us. The present Scottish
Government will be just one of many voices contributing to
the debate to shape the content of the written constitution.
However, there are certain things that we believe should be
included, such as:

- constitutional guarantees on access to health and education, equalities and human rights, the environment, natural resources and the status of local government

- rules on war powers, providing a proper process that involves the Scottish Parliament in authorising the use of military force

- a constitutional ban on nuclear weapons being based in Scotland.

574. When should a written constitution be prepared?
The right time for a written constitution to be drafted is after independence, not before. At that point all of the people of Scotland, whatever their views in the referendum, will be able to engage fully in the process of planning for Scotland's future.

575. How would Scotland prepare a written constitution?
The process by which Scotland adopts a written constitution is as important as its content. In developing a new written constitution, Scotland will be able to learn from the innovative and participative approaches of other countries.

The process of agreeing and enacting the constitution should ensure that it reflects the fundamental constitutional principle that the people, rather than politicians or state institutions, are the sovereign authority in Scotland. The Scottish Government proposes that the newly elected independent Scottish Parliament in May 2016 should convene a Constitutional Convention to draft the written constitution.

576. Have other places had Constitutional Conventions?
In the last decade, citizen-led assemblies and Constitutional Conventions have been convened in British Columbia (2004), the Netherlands (2006), Ontario (2007) and Iceland (2010). Since December 2012, Ireland has held a citizen-based *Convention on the Constitution* to review various constitutional issues and it has met throughout 2013.

577. **Will individual people be directly involved in shaping the constitution?**
Yes. We believe the process should ensure that the people of Scotland can be directly involved in designing and determining a written constitution as the blueprint for our country's future.

A participative and inclusive process would be one where the people of Scotland, as well as politicians, civic society organisations, business interests, trade unions, local government and others, have a direct role in shaping the constitution.

Best practice for Constitutional Conventions includes live streaming and the publishing of materials (including video) online for all citizens to follow (see for example materials for Ireland's convention at www.constitution.ie).

578. **When will the Constitutional Convention process start?**
The constitutional platform we propose for independence will place a duty on the Scottish Parliament to establish the Convention soon after the Scottish Parliament elections in May 2016.

579. **How long would the Constitutional Convention take?**
It would be for the Scottish Parliament to decide whether to set a timetable for the Constitutional Convention. The Irish Convention has been asked to complete its process in 12 months.

580. **What would be the process for the permanent written constitution to become law?**
That would be for the Constitutional Convention to consider and for the Scottish Parliament then to decide.

The Monarchy

581. **Will the Queen be head of state in an independent Scotland?**
Yes. Scotland will remain a constitutional monarchy with Her Majesty The Queen as head of state. Her Majesty will be succeeded by Her heirs and successors according to law.

As is the case in the UK, if a party in favour of changing this position was to gain enough support to form a government, it would be open to it to propose a change. The current Scottish Government does not support such a change.

582. **How can Her Majesty The Queen remain Head of State of Scotland, as well as of the rest of the UK?**
The Queen is head of state of 16 Commonwealth States, including the UK. An independent Scotland would join this family of countries that share the same monarch.

583. **Will an independent Scotland pay for the Queen?**
Yes. It will be right for an independent Scotland to continue to contribute to the expenses of the Monarchy as we do already through taxes. After a vote for independence in the referendum, negotiations will take place to agree arrangements.

584. **Will the Queen grant honours in an independent Scotland?**
Yes. An honours system would continue in an independent Scotland. The current Scottish Government advocate that, as at present, nominations would be processed through the civil service and independently of politicians. We will agree with the Royal Household any amendments to the Honours system to reflect Scotland's independence.

State Institutions and Symbols

585. **What will the official name of the country be after independence?**
Scotland. On independence, the country would need a formal name by which it would be known in international bodies and by which it would join international treaties, and that name would be Scotland.

586. **What will Scotland's flag be and what will happen to the Union Flag?**
Scotland's national flag will remain the Saltire or Cross of St. Andrew. It will be for the rest of the UK to decide what its flag will be. It is possible for the rest of the UK to retain the Union Flag if that is what it wants.

The Union Flag, the first version of which dates from 1606 – before the political union of 1707 – could be used in Scotland as people think fit. For example, the Union Flag is flown in some Commonwealth countries along with the country's own national flag.

587. **What about Royal Standards, will those flags still fly on public buildings?**
As the monarchy will continue in an independent Scotland, the protocols for flying Royal Standards, for example the Lion Rampant, will continue unaffected.

588. **What will Scotland's national anthem be?**
A decision on Scotland's official national anthem will be for the first Scottish Parliament of an independent Scotland following consultation with the people of Scotland.

Songs such as "Flower of Scotland" and "Scots Wha Hae" will continue to be sung as unofficial national anthems in the meantime.

589. **What will our national languages be?**
We propose no change on independence to the status of Scotland's languages such as English, Gaelic, Scots and British Sign Language.

The Constitutional Convention appointed after independence could consider the position of Scotland's languages within the permanent written constitution.

590. **What will be the position of churches and religion in an independent Scotland?**
We propose no change to the legal status of any religion or of Scotland's churches.

Government in an Independent Scotland

Current UK Functions and Services – Continuity of Public Services

591. **Will public services continue to be delivered after independence?**
Yes. Public services will continue to be delivered in an independent Scotland. The current Scottish Government strongly believes that public services should remain in public hands rather than being privatised, as Westminster has done with Royal Mail.

592. **Who owns the public services that the UK runs now?**
UK public services are assets belonging to both Scotland and the rest of the UK. This is because tax payers in both Scotland and the rest of the UK have paid to build and maintain these services.

593. **What does Westminster run now?**
There are many services currently delivered to people in Scotland by UK (or GB) wide organisations. These include tax collection (through HM Revenue & Customs), benefits, employment services, passports and vehicle and driver licensing. The Post Office network also covers the UK, as do specialist services provided by bodies such as HM Coastguard and the air, rail and maritime investigations branches.

594. **What will happen to services that are run from elsewhere in the UK?**
The Scottish Government's priority will be the seamless delivery of public services on independence to citizens of both countries. This applies both to those services currently delivered to Scotland from locations elsewhere in the UK and to those services currently delivered from Scotland to people elsewhere in the UK.

For public services that are currently reserved, the Scottish Government proposes to negotiate arrangements for the continued delivery of services to the public across GB and the UK where this is in the interests of those who use the services. In most cases, this will be for a transitional period, but in some it may be for the longer term. The underlying principle in all cases will be that policy decisions will be made in Scotland by the Scottish Government and Scottish Parliament, accountable solely to the people of Scotland.

595. **Are there UK services that are run from Scotland?**
Yes. Important services such as tax credits and the welfare system, HM Revenue & Customs, and the Department of Work & Pensions all have assets or networks in Scotland. Other Westminster Government Departments have systems and capabilities largely outwith Scotland and the future of these will be considered in negotiations between the governments.

596. **Is it possible to 'share' public services?**
Yes. In fact Scotland and the UK already share around 60 public bodies in devolved areas now. Under the Scotland Act 1998, these bodies are known as 'cross-border public authorities'.

The UK and Ireland also share several public bodies on an all-Ireland basis (e.g. InterTradeIreland and Waterways Ireland).

597. **Will the Scottish Government take on responsibility for delivering services in an independent Scotland?**
Yes. Where a service is provided by a shared body which is currently the responsibility of Westminster, that body would in future also be accountable to the Scottish Government.

598. **How long will these sharing arrangements last?**
Many sharing arrangements will be in place for a matter of months or years while systems specific to Scotland are set up. An example of this approach is the administration of state benefits which we would intend to operate on a shared basis until 2018, though Scotland would take full control of policy decisions on benefits at the point of independence.

599. **Will there be institutions we will share with the rest of the UK on a long-term basis?**
Yes, we propose that there will be some. An example would be the Bank of England.

600. **How would sharing arrangements work?**
Agreements to share services would be formalised by either a change in the law in Scotland and the rest of the UK, or a contract or treaty between Scotland and the rest of the UK.

601. **Can two governments have a contract for services?**
Yes. The Scottish Government has several contracts now with the Westminster Government.

602. **Where there is an agreement to share a public service after independence, will the Scottish Government be able to have different policies from the rest of the UK?**
Yes. This already happens now in some instances where devolved Scotland and the rest of the UK share services. For example, the university admissions body UCAS operates across the UK but has a distinct admissions process for Scotland.

603. Will an independent Scotland have to have the agreement of the rest of the UK before changing the way shared services are provided?

The rules for changing shared services in Scotland only or in the rest of the UK only will be part of the post-referendum negotiations between Scotland and the rest of the UK.

604. What will happen to services that are currently free such as museums and libraries?

The National Museums, Galleries and Library are funded directly by the Scottish Government and entry is free to core sites. Local public libraries are provided by local authorities. These services are statutory and their provision is underpinned in legislation. Independence will not make any change to this situation.

605. How many public bodies are there currently in Scotland?

There are currently 113 public bodies that operate across Scotland in areas controlled by the Scottish Government and Parliament. There are also around 300 public bodies that act within Scotland which are controlled by Westminster.

606. How has the number of public bodies changed in recent years?

The Scottish Government has successfully simplified and streamlined the public sector landscape by reducing the number of Scottish public bodies under its control from a baseline of 199 in 2007 to 113 now.

607. How will independence affect public bodies?

Independence provides an opportunity to build on the Scottish Government's record of simplification. Scotland will certainly not recreate each of the UK's public bodies acting within Scotland which number around 300. Depending on the outcome of negotiations with the UK, the Scottish Government will further simplify the public sector landscape by transferring functions of some UK bodies to existing bodies in Scotland. Further information on this issue is available in Chapter 10.

Equality and Human Rights

608. Will I still have the same rights, including protection against discrimination, in an independent Scotland?

Yes. Indeed, they will be strengthened. Existing equality rights and human rights will continue on the date of independence. The constitutional platform we will put in place for independence will give the European Convention on Human Rights (ECHR) the same legal force for formerly reserved matters as it already has in Scotland for devolved matters. The Convention covers important human rights such as liberty, the right to a fair trial and freedom of speech, association, conscience and religion.

609. How will the rights and protection guaranteed by existing equality legislation be maintained?

Existing equality legislation will continue to apply in Scotland post-independence. The Equality Act 2010 will remain in force ensuring protection against discrimination on the same basis as at present.

Our intention is that, from the date of independence, the functions of the Equality and Human Rights Commission (EHRC) in Scotland in relation to equality will transfer to a new Scottish public body. The EHRC's human rights functions will transfer to the Scottish Human Rights Commission which will continue to act as Scotland's national human rights institution. An Equality Advisory Support Service, providing information and advice to the general public, will also continue to operate.

610. How will human rights be protected in an independent Scotland?

The Scottish Government propose that Scotland's written constitution will protect the fundamental rights and freedoms of everyone living in Scotland. At its heart will be the ECHR which contains important safeguards, covering not only rights to life and liberty but also areas as diverse as privacy, family life or freedom of speech.

ECHR protections are already central to the law of Scotland. We propose that existing arrangements under the Human Rights Act 1998 and the Scotland Act 1998 will be carried forward into the constitutional platform, which will apply from the date of independence.

It will remain possible for cases from Scotland to be heard by the European Court of Human Rights, in the normal way, and Scotland will abide by the final judgments of the Court.

An independent Scotland will accede, in its own name, to all other relevant international human rights treaties. It will fulfil its reporting obligations as a member of the United Nations and other international bodies.

611. Will there be a closer alignment between equality and human rights in an independent Scotland?
Following independence, the current Scottish Government will explore the potential for closer alignment of the equality and human rights functions in Scotland, including the option of creating a single body in line with internationally recognised principles. However, any changes would require extensive consultation. They should also form part of a broader review of options for strengthening Scotland's equality and human rights approach. That work is likely to be closely linked to the development of Scotland's permanent written constitution.

612. What about future developments? Are there plans to extend existing legislation or establish new rights?
An independent Scotland will be able to pass laws in areas that are currently reserved to Westminster. We will be able to further develop existing policies and legislation in ways that better meet Scotland's needs.

For example, areas such as employment and equal opportunities are substantially reserved to Westminster. Following independence, it will be open to the Scottish Parliament to pass new legislation in such areas. The Scottish Parliament could decide to extend existing rights.

It would also be open to an independent Scotland to develop new ways of recognising human rights, for example in the areas of education, health or housing, or in relation to the rights of disabled people. These issues could be considered by a future Constitutional Convention established to develop Scotland's permanent written constitution.

613. **Will the rights of people in Scotland differ from the rest of the UK after independence? And what will happen if current human rights or equality legislation changes before the date of independence?**

The Scottish Government proposes that fundamental rights be enshrined and protected in a written constitution. We know that senior ministers in the current Westminster Government favour abolition of the current Human Rights Act, and even complete withdrawal from the European Convention on Human Rights. The Scottish Government does not share these views and considers them to be of significant concern.

The Scottish Government is committed to maintaining at least the equality and human rights safeguards available under existing UK and Scottish legislation. If Westminster made changes before independence which reduced such safeguards and protections, the current Government would take early action to reinstate them.

614. **Will becoming independent mean more equality across public appointments in Scotland?**

The current Scottish Government has already set itself an ambition that the appointments for which it is responsible should broadly reflect the wider community. As part of that we will maintain our focus on improving the gender balance of public boards which is limited by the constraints of current Westminster legislation.

In an independent Scotland we will ensure that Scotland's institutions have equality and diversity at the heart of their governance. We will expect to see public and private institutions working to improve the diversity and gender balance of their governance. We will also consult on a target for women's representation on company and public boards and, if necessary, we will legislate as appropriate.

Parliament and Elections

615. **What will the parliamentary system be in an independent Scotland?**

The existing Scottish Parliament will become the parliament of an independent Scotland, responsible for all matters currently dealt with at Westminster.

616. **What will the electoral system be in an independent Scotland?**
On independence, the Scottish Parliament will be elected using proportional representation, as it is now.

The Constitutional Convention established by the Scottish Parliament, after independence could consider whether the electoral system should be changed as part of Scotland's permanent written constitution.

617. **Who would have voting rights after independence?**
The Scottish Government's only proposed change to voting rights is that they should be extended to 16 and 17 year olds in future Scottish Parliament elections.

The Constitutional Convention appointed by the Scottish Parliament, after independence could consider whether the rules on who can vote should be changed as part of Scotland's permanent written constitution.

618. **Who can stand for election after independence?**
The current Government proposes that the rules on standing for election will stay the same as they are now.

The Constitutional Convention appointed by the Scottish Parliament after independence could consider whether the rules on who can stand for election should be changed as part of Scotland's written constitution.

619. **Will the number of Members of the Scottish Parliament increase?**
On independence, the number of MSPs (129) will stay the same. This is broadly comparable with other independent states. For example, New Zealand with 4.5 million people has 121 MPs.

The Constitutional Convention appointed by the Scottish Parliament after independence could consider if the number of members of the Parliament should change. The current Scottish Government proposes no change.

620. **Will MSPs' salaries and expenses be changed for independence?**
No. The system of MSPs' salaries and expenses will remain the same.

621. **Will the Scottish Parliament need a bigger budget after independence?**
After independence, the Scottish Parliament will deal with the things it does now, as well as with issues currently dealt with at Westminster for Scotland. Any resulting increase in the Scottish Parliament's running costs will be more than offset by the saving Scotland will make as a result of no longer paying our share of the cost of running the Westminster parliamentary system, which currently costs the Scottish taxpayer around £50 million per year.

The Scottish Government would have a bigger budget after independence as powers and funding transfer from the Westminster Government.

622. **Will the Scottish Parliament have a second chamber?**
No. The current Scottish Government proposes that, from the date of independence, the Scottish Parliament will keep its current single chamber structure. This is similar to other comparable states which also have single chamber parliaments, such as New Zealand, Denmark, Norway and Sweden.

623. **Will Scotland have a Scottish Electoral Commission on independence?**
Yes. A stand-alone Scottish Electoral Commission will be established for the date of independence, based on the existing arrangements. That Commission will oversee the Scottish Parliamentary Elections in May 2016.

From the date of independence, the Boundary Commission for Scotland, which reviews and advises on parliamentary constituency boundaries in Scotland, will report to Scottish Ministers instead of the Secretary of State for Scotland.

Structure and Capacity of Government

624. **How many Ministers would there be in an independent Scottish Government?**
The structure of government will be a matter for future Scottish governments to decide.

The current Scottish Government's plan is to structure government into nine portfolios, each of which will comprise at least one Cabinet Secretary and supporting ministers. This structure is designed to continue the current Scottish Government's approach of more flexible and more efficient government, and will include:

- Office of the First Minister

- Finance and Economy

- Health, Wellbeing and Social Protection

- Education, Skills and Employment

- International Relations and Defence

- Justice, Security and Home Affairs

- Environment, Rural Scotland, Energy and Resources

- Culture, Communications and Digital

- Law Officers

The current system of appointing Ministers would continue. The First Minister will be appointed by Her Majesty, following nomination by a vote in the Scottish Parliament. Other Ministers will be appointed by the First Minister, with the approval of Her Majesty, but only after the Scottish Parliament has agreed.

625. **Will Ministers' salaries and expenses be changed for independence?**
No. The system of Ministers' salaries and expenses will remain the same.

626. **Will there be a bigger Scottish Government after independence?**
On independence, the Scottish Government would take responsibility for all of the things that are dealt with at Westminster and so would expand to make sure that this can be delivered.

With independence, responsibility for a wide range of currently reserved services and functions will be transferred to the Scottish Government. The Westminster Government employs nearly 30,000 civil servants in Scotland at present. By way of context NHS Scotland employs around 150,000 people; Scottish local government employs around 250,000; and the Scottish police and fire and rescue services employ 30,000.

The government of an independent Scotland will also employ additional staff to deliver its new functions on matters such as taxation, defence and employment. Some services will continue to be delivered jointly with the rest of the UK, for either a time-limited period of transition or on an ongoing basis.

627. **Will an independent Scotland replicate all the different departments operated by the Westminster Government?**
No. The functions of all Westminster Departments will transfer to the Scottish Government. The structure of government in an independent Scottish Government would not replicate the fragmented departmental structure of government at Westminster.

628. **How many people currently work for the Scottish Government and the agencies?**
There are around 16,700 public servants within the Scottish Government and its agencies, and around 14,000 staff in devolved public bodies (excluding NHS Scotland and public corporations).

629. **How many people in Scotland work for the Westminster Government?**
There are around 30,000 civil servants employed by Westminster and 6,500 UK public bodies staff working in around 30 locations in Scotland (excluding public corporations, the armed forces and financial institutions), with some providing services on a UK or GB basis.

630. **Will becoming independent create more jobs in the Scottish public sector?**
Independence will provide opportunities for employment in Scotland in government functions where jobs are currently located elsewhere in the UK. Given that the Scottish Government will be taking on a range of new responsibilities, there will be new job opportunities in the public sector in Scotland.

The current Scottish Government has a strong record of valuing public services in Scotland and is operating a policy of no compulsory redundancies within the devolved public sector.

631. **What will happen to the people working in Scotland for the Westminster Government on independence?**
Having people with the skills to deliver government priorities in Scotland is an asset. The Scottish Government will work with Westminster to preserve continuity of employment for all staff either by way of transfer to the Scottish Government or through continued employment with the Westminster Government where it continues to require their skills.

632. **How many civil servants will an independent Scotland employ?**
The final number of civil servants working in Scotland will depend on a number of factors, including agreements reached on shared services between the Scottish and Westminster Governments and decisions to be taken by the Scottish Government on the design and delivery of Scottish policies and services.

633. **How much will it cost to set up the new public services that an independent Scotland will require?**
Scotland already pays for the services we receive from Westminster and UK public bodies through our taxes. The size of the one-off investment in systems and processes that Scotland will make as a result of independence will be a small proportion of an independent Scotland's total budget, and will be offset by the opportunities that independence will provide to deliver improved government and services in the future. It will depend partly on the negotiations on apportioning assets and liabilities that will take place following a vote for independence and partly by future decisions about whether and how quickly to introduce new systems.

634. **Will the Transfer of Undertakings (Protection of Employment) Regulations 2006 (the TUPE Regulations) apply to transfers of staff from the Westminster Government to the Scottish Government on independence?**
The TUPE Regulations themselves do not cover transfers of staff between government departments, but equivalent measures are in place to protect the terms and conditions of civil service staff when their functions transfer. We will work with Westminster on the transfer of staff between the Scottish and Westminster Governments to ensure that this protection applies on independence.

Scottish Local Government

635. **What will happen to local government in an independent Scotland?**
Local government will continue to be an integral and essential element of the overall good governance of Scotland.

The current Scottish Government will guarantee the position of local government in the constitutional platform which will take effect on independence and also argue for Scotland's permanent written constitution to set out the status and rights of elected local government.

636. **Will there be any change to local authority boundaries?**
Any future proposed changes to boundaries would be for the parliament and government of an independent Scotland to consider and decide.

637. **Will local authorities be autonomous and independent of central government in an independent Scotland?**
Local authorities are democratically accountable to their local electorates, not to the Scottish Government. We expect this important principle to continue with independence, and to be reflected in the permanent written constitution of an independent Scotland.

638. **Will local authorities continue to deliver the services they do now?**
Yes. Independence itself will not change the services local government delivers. It would be for future parliaments in an independent Scotland – in consultation with local government – to decide whether there should be any subsequent changes.

639. **Will there be any change to scrutiny arrangements for local authorities?**

The process of becoming independent will not change scrutiny arrangements for local government. Since the Crerar Review in 2007, the Scottish Government has simplified arrangements, improving the way in which scrutiny is delivered and making it more proportionate and risk-based. This is still evolving as part of public service reform, and local government is directly involved with scrutiny bodies in shaping the direction of these arrangements. We expect this to continue in an independent Scotland.

640. **What will the impact of independence be on local taxation, such as business rates and council tax?**

Local taxation policy will continue to be determined by the Scottish Parliament and Government in partnership with local government. Council tax and business rates systems are already devolved to the Scottish Parliament. There will be no change to their operation as a result of becoming independent.

The current council tax system is unfair, which is why the current Scottish Government has fully funded the council tax freeze for the last six years and frozen the tax at 2007/08 levels. We are committed to continuing the freeze for the lifetime of this Parliament and will consult with others to develop options for a fairer and more progressive local tax, based on the ability to pay and would take this forward after Scotland becomes independent.

This Scottish Government acted swiftly to establish arrangements when Westminster abolished Council Tax Benefit in April 2013. Together with our local government partners, we committed a total of £40 million in 2013/14 to ensure that around 560,000 people in Scotland previously in receipt of Council Tax Benefit were protected from Westminster's 10 per cent cut in funding for successor arrangements.

The Scottish Government remains committed to Scotland continuing to be the most attractive place to do business in Europe, as demonstrated by the changes we have made to business rates arrangements.

641. **Will local government have more say on how money is spent in an independent Scotland?**
The current Scottish Government believes that local government should have the power to decide what is best for local people. Local authorities currently have the power to raise over £4 billion a year in taxes, borrow money and, since 2007, spend that money how they see fit because of reduced central 'ring fencing'.

642. **Will there be opportunities for greater local autonomy and decision-making responsibility in an independent Scotland?**
The current Scottish Government is clear that the people who live and work in Scotland are best-placed to make decisions about our future. This is the essence of self-determination, and accordingly we are committed to subsidiarity and local decision-making in public life. Our commitment to local autonomy and self-determination is central to our approach to local government.

For example, our island communities have challenges and opportunities that are different from those in other parts of the country. That is why the Scottish Government has established the Island Areas Ministerial Working Group, to engage in discussions with Orkney, Shetland and Comhairle nan Eilean Siar about the opportunities that are important for our island communities in the context of the referendum and independence.

The Group is covering issues such as energy, the Crown Estate and transport. With independence we plan to bring forward an Islands Bill to implement conclusions of this work. For any issues of interest to mainland Councils with islands, the Government has committed to separate discussions with the Councils in question.

Similarly we are working as part of the Scottish Cities Alliance – comprising the seven local authorities with cities within their boundaries – to consider how issues specific to Scotland's cities can be best tackled in the future.

643. **What will independence mean for cross-border relations with the North of England?**

An economically stronger Scotland would be a major boost for our close neighbours in the North of England and provide a counter balance to the economic draw of London. Recognising that the emergence of a successful independent Scotland could have a number of effects, North of England councils have instigated an initiative, known as "Borderlands", and are committed to working together with Scottish Borders and Dumfries and Galloway to explore synergies in tourism, transport and business links.

Scotland already has strong ties with the North of England, and it is in both our interests that these be developed and strengthened further with greater practical co-operation, for example, on transport and business links. The "Borderlands" initiative shows the co-operation possible in that context: independence and interdependence.

Charities and the Third Sector

644. **Will the third sector be supported in an independent Scotland?**

The current Scottish Government is committed to supporting the development of a capable, sustainable and enterprising Third Sector. The sector plays a key role in achieving the Government's purpose by supporting Scotland's communities and in the delivery of public services. It has specialist expertise, the ability to engage with vulnerable groups and individuals, and a flexible and innovative approach. With independence, the current Scottish Government's vision for the ector will not change – we want to continue to work with our Third Sector partners, ensuring that everyone in Scotland has a successful and fairer future.

645. **Will UK-wide/cross-border charities still be able to operate in an independent Scotland?**
Yes, just as charities currently operate cross-border between the UK and Ireland. Responsibility for the legal framework surrounding charities operating in and/or registered in Scotland is already devolved to the Scottish Government. However, income tax and corporation tax exemptions and reliefs for charities are reserved, along with legislation covering tax relief on Gift Aid, investment income, trading profits and Capital Gains tax.

The Scottish Parliament in an independent Scotland will control both charity law and tax matters. This will enable Scottish governments and the Parliament to consider taxation policy that would enhance opportunities for charitable giving.

646. **How will charities be regulated in an independent Scotland?**
The regulation of charities operating and/or registered in Scotland is already devolved. There are arrangements in place between the Office of the Scottish Charity Regulator (OSCR) and the Charity Commission to regulate and monitor charities registered in England and Wales but operating in Scotland. There is a memorandum of understanding that sets out the current operational arrangements for OSCR and the Charity Commission to work together to provide better regulation and guidance for charities that operate across England, Scotland and Wales. It will be in everyone's interests for this process to continue following independence.

647. **For cross-border charities, how will an independent Scotland ensure that a fair share of charity income is deployed in Scotland?**
Decisions on funding are for charities themselves and there are no legal provisions in place currently that require funds to be distributed in a particular way between the nations of the UK.

648. **Will UK-based charitable trusts still fund and support the work of charities operating in an independent Scotland?**
There is no reason why they will not. Trustees themselves are, and will remain, responsible for deciding which charities they fund and support.

649. Will charities continue to benefit from relief on charitable donations after independence?

Yes. The current Scottish Government will ensure that charities continue to benefit from tax relief on charitable donations.

650. Can charities get involved in the referendum process?

Charities play an important part in our society. Campaigning is a legitimate way for many charities to achieve what they were set up for, which is to further their charitable purposes. The Office of the Scottish Charity Regulator (OSCR) has published practical guidance for charity trustees to help them to decide how they may participate in the referendum process. In general, a charity may take part in the process if it can show:

- it is advancing its charitable purposes

- the charity's governing document does not prohibit such activity

- it is not advancing a political party

- Charity trustees are acting in the interests of the charity, and with due care and diligence

How can I ask more questions?

We expect you to find the answers to your questions here. However, if there is a question not covered, please visit www.scotreferendum.com/contact/ for details of how to submit your question. We will add further questions and answers to the Question and Answer section on the scotreferendum.com website.

ANNEX **A** SCOTLAND'S CONSTITUTIONAL JOURNEY

1. Scotland has a long history, both as an independent nation before the Treaty of Union, then within the United Kingdom as a recognised nation with our own institutions and legal system.

2. The history of Scotland stretches back to the eighth century, but our independence was secured through the military and diplomatic achievements of Robert the Bruce 700 years ago. Thereafter, apart from a period of incorporation into the Commonwealth of Oliver Cromwell, Scotland was an independent country until the Union of 1707.

3. The Treaty of Union between the independent kingdoms of Scotland and England came into force on 1 May 1707. The Treaty created a unified Crown and a single Parliament for the new kingdom of Great Britain. Other main provisions covered representation in the new parliament and reciprocal measures about taxation and trade, and it preserved various Scottish institutions, notably our legal system. Separate legislation guaranteed the position of the Church of Scotland.

4. Following the failure of the 1745 Jacobite rising, the issue of Scotland's place within the Union, and the stability of the succession to the throne, seemed settled. New imperatives of industrial revolution and Empire moved to the fore. Scotland played a full part in these British developments, but our nationhood was preserved by the Scottish institutions protected by the Treaty of Union.

5. In 1853, the National Association for the Vindication of Scottish Rights was formed. Although short-lived, this indicated growing interest in Scotland's position as a distinct political entity within the United Kingdom, motivated in part by the pressure for Home Rule in Ireland and by the challenges of governing the expanding British Empire.

6. The emergence of political interest in Home Rule for Scotland was accompanied by changes in the arrangements for Scotland's government, starting with the creation of the Scottish Office in 1885 and the appointment of the first Secretary for Scotland to represent Scottish interests in the Cabinet. This recognised that Scotland's distinctive culture and, institutional and political identity required specific and full-time representation. However, no national democratic assembly was developed.

7. 1886 saw the formation of a Scottish Home Rule Association. In 1888 Keir Hardie adopted a Home Rule platform at the Mid Lanark by-election, and Scotland's constitutional position has remained a central political issue since then. Home Rule for Scotland was debated on many occasions in the United Kingdom Parliament, and a number of Bills were introduced. In 1913 a Home Rule Bill passed its Second Reading, but the First World War prevented further legislative steps.

8. Following the First World War, the political relevance of Scottish Home Rule was maintained by various political parties and movements, and the Scottish National Party (SNP) was formed in 1934 from the National Party of Scotland (formed in 1928) and the Scottish Party (formed in 1932). The SNP won its first parliamentary seat at the Motherwell by-election in 1945, but held it for only three months.

9. Unionism dominated in Scotland following the Second World War, and in 1950 the Labour Party abandoned its support for Scottish Home Rule, although this remained an important issue in Scotland. The Scottish Covenant Association helped sustain popular interest in a Scottish assembly, attracting two million signatures between 1949 and 1950. However, the Association was not linked to any political party and failed to secure its objectives directly.

10. Scottish Home Rule returned as a key issue with the SNP's victory in the Hamilton by-election of 1967. Winnie Ewing won the seat with 46 per cent of the vote, marking the emergence of the SNP as an electoral force and mainstream political party.

11. Since the Hamilton by-election, each of the main political parties has, at different times, committed itself to new constitutional arrangements for Scotland. In 1968 the declaration of Perth committed the Conservatives to Scottish devolution in some form, and in 1970 the Conservative government published *Scotland's Government*, which recommended the creation of a Scottish assembly. However, Conservative support for Scottish devolution declined, and the party opposed legislative devolution for Scotland through the 1980s and 1990s. Although the party campaigned for a No vote in the referendum of 1997, the Conservatives at both Scottish and United Kingdom

level have supported the Scottish Parliament since it was established.

12.   In 1969, the Labour government commissioned a report into constitutional options for the United Kingdom. The Kilbrandon Commission did not report until 1973 by which time a Conservative government was in power. The Kilbrandon Report recommended devolved assemblies for Scotland and Wales, which led eventually to devolution being put to the electorate in a referendum in 1979. The legislation required 40 per cent of the total electorate to support devolution in the Scottish referendum; in the event 32.9 per cent supported the assembly, although this represented 51.6 per cent of those who voted – a majority of more than 77,000.

13.   Following the election of the Conservative government in 1979, devolution, and the concept of the sovereignty of the Scottish people, was taken forward first by the Campaign for a Scottish Assembly, and then, from 1989, the Scottish Constitutional Convention. In 1988 the Campaign for a Scottish Assembly published *A Claim of Right for Scotland* which asserted Scotland's cultural and historical legacy in putting forward its argument for a Scottish assembly. This was followed in 1995 by *Scotland's Parliament, Scotland's Right*, the Scottish Constitutional Convention's blueprint for a Scottish assembly, which became the basis for the devolution settlement that was enacted in 1988.

14.   The Labour Party won the 1997 general election on a platform that included a commitment to a referendum on Scottish devolution. The white paper *Scotland's Parliament* was published in July 1997, and its proposals were the basis for the referendum which was held on 11 September 1997. Over 74 per cent of those participating supported the creation of the Scottish Parliament, and over 63 per cent supported tax-varying powers for the Parliament. The Scottish Parliament that reconvened in 1999 was based on the constitutional settlement in the subsequent Scotland Act 1998.

15. Following the Scottish general elections of 1999 and 2003 Scottish administrations were formed by coalitions of the Labour and Liberal Democrat parties. These administrations introduced important reforms, such as free personal care for the elderly, the smoking ban and proportional representation for local authority elections. These measures attracted support across the Scottish Parliament. In the 2007 Scottish general election, the SNP formed the single largest party and became the first minority administration in the Scottish Parliament. That Government restored free education for Scotland's students and introduced free prescription charges and the council tax freeze. In the 2011 general election the SNP Government was returned with an absolute majority, a rare achievement in a proportional voting system.

16. The Scotland Act 1998 allowed for the powers of both the Government and Parliament to be adjusted with the consent of both the Scottish Parliament and Westminster. A number of changes have been made since 1999, most significantly devolving major responsibilities for rail in 2002. The responsibilities of the Scottish Parliament were examined following the election of the SNP Government in 2007. The Scottish Government's National Conversation considered the advantages of further devolution and independence. The Commission on Scottish Devolution (also known as the Calman Commission) established by the Labour, Liberal Democrat and Conservative parties and the Westminster Government examined further devolution only.

17. The Calman Commission's recommendations, notably to increase the taxation powers of the Scottish Parliament, led to the Westminster Scotland Act 2012, which received the Scottish Parliament's consent in April 2012 and is now being implemented.

18. In the 2011 Scottish general election, the SNP was elected on a platform of a referendum on independence. In October 2012 the Westminster and Scottish Governments signed the Edinburgh Agreement to confirm that the Scottish Parliament could legislate for the referendum, and committed to continue to work together constructively in the light of the outcome, whatever it

might be, in the best interests of the people of Scotland and the rest of the United Kingdom. The Scottish Independence Referendum (Franchise) Act 2013, which received Royal Assent in August 2013, enables 16 and 17 year olds to vote in the referendum and the legislation for the referendum itself was passed by the Scottish Parliament on 14 November 2013.

ANNEX B

B MAIN DEVOLVED AND RESERVED RESPONSIBILITIES

Responsibilities devolved to the Scottish Parliament and Government

The Scotland Act 1988 does not set out devolved subjects, but instead lists 'reserved matters' for which the UK Parliament retains responsibility. Devolved matters on which the Scottish Parliament can make laws are all those that are not specifically reserved (with certain provisos set out in the Act).

Devolved matters

- Health

- Education and training

- Local government

- Social work

- Housing

- Planning

- Tourism, economic development and financial assistance to industry

- Some aspects of transport, including the Scottish road network, bus policy and ports and harbours

- Law and home affairs, including most aspects of criminal and civil law, the prosecution system and the courts

- The police and fire services

- The environment

- Natural and built heritage

- Agriculture, forestry and fishing

- Sport and the arts

- Statistics, public registers and records

- Air guns unless classified as "specially dangerous"

- Certain forms of taxation (local taxes, such as council tax and non-domestic rates; taxes on land and building transactions; taxes on waste disposal to landfill)

The Scottish Parliament also has powers to vary the standard rate of Income Tax by up to three pence in the pound, and under the Scotland Act 2012 will have a responsibility for setting a Scottish Rate of Income Tax at a rate up to ten pence in the pound different from that elsewhere in the UK.

Scottish Government Ministers also have a range of "executively devolved" powers to make secondary legislation, such as regulations, about some of the reserved matters listed below. Otherwise the powers of the Westminster Government match those of the Westminster Parliament.

Responsibilities reserved to the Westminster Parliament

Constitutional and general reservations

The Crown, including succession to the Crown and a regency

The Union of the Kingdoms of Scotland and England

The Parliament of the United Kingdom, elections for membership of the House of Commons, the European Parliament and the Scottish Parliament

The higher courts

The Security Service, the Secret Intelligence Service and the Government Communications Headquarters

The registration and funding of political parties

Foreign affairs, international relations, and representation

The civil service

Defence

Treason

Economic and fiscal

Fiscal, economic and monetary policy, including the issue and circulation of money, taxes and excise duties (with the exceptions mentioned above), government borrowing and lending, control over United Kingdom public expenditure, the exchange rate and the Bank of England

The currency: coinage, legal tender and bank notes

Financial services

Financial markets, including listing and public offers of securities and investments, transfer of securities and insider dealing

Home affairs

Misuse of drugs

Data protection

Firearms

Classification of films and videos

Immigration and nationality, including asylum and issue of travel documents

Scientific procedures on live animals

National security, interception of communications, official secrets and terrorism

Betting, gaming and lotteries

Emergency powers

Extradition

Trade and industry

The creation, operation, regulation and dissolution of types of business association

Insolvency in relation to business associations

Regulation of anti-competitive practices and agreements; abuse of dominant position monopolies and mergers

Intellectual property

Import and export control

Regulation of sea fishing outside the Scottish zone (except in relation to Scottish fishing boats)

Consumer protection

Product standards, safety and liability

Weights and measures

Telecommunications and wireless telegraphy, including internet services

Post Office, posts and postal services

Trade and industry (contd)

Research Councils

Designation of assisted areas

Protection of trading and economic interests

Energy

Generation, transmission, distribution and supply of electricity

Oil and gas, including the ownership of, exploration for and exploitation of deposits of oil and natural gas, offshore installations and pipelines

Coal, including its ownership and exploitation, deep and opencast coal mining and coal mining subsidence

Nuclear energy and nuclear installations, including nuclear safety, security and safeguards, and liability for nuclear occurrences

Transport

Road transport

Rail transport, provision and regulation of railway services

Marine transport, including navigational rights and freedoms

Air transport

Transport of radioactive material

Social security

Social security schemes

Child support

The regulation of occupational pension schemes and personal pension schemes, including the obligations of the trustees or managers of such schemes

Regulation of the professions

Architects, health professions, auditors

Employment

Employment rights and duties and industrial relations

Health and safety at work

Job search and support

Health and medicines

Regulation of medical professions

Abortion

Xenotransplantation

Embryology, surrogacy and genetics

Medicines, medical supplies and poisons

Media and culture

Broadcasting, including the BBC

Public lending right

Government Indemnity Scheme for objects on loan
to museums, art galleries, etc

Property accepted in satisfaction of tax

Miscellaneous

Judicial remuneration

Equal opportunities

Control of nuclear, biological and chemical weapons
and other weapons of mass destruction

The Ordnance Survey

Timescales, time zones and the subject-matter of the
Summer Time Act 1972

The calendar, units of time, the date of Easter

Outer space

Regulation of activities in Antarctica

ANNEX C | SCOTLAND'S PUBLIC FINANCES

This annex provides detailed analysis of Scotland's public finances under the current constitutional framework. The analysis encompasses total public spending, public sector receipts, the overall budget balance and an implied share of UK public sector net debt.

It is clear that Scotland currently pays its way within the UK.

As we move to independence, our strong public finances will provide the foundations for policy decisions on taxation, growth and welfare.

This annex also therefore sets out forecasts for public sector expenditure and revenue for Scotland in 2016/17 based on a series of projections and plans for future expenditures and revenues.

Background

The National Statistics publication Government Expenditure and Revenue Scotland (GERS) published annually provides estimates of total public sector expenditure undertaken for Scotland, and total public sector revenue generated by economic activity in Scotland.

The analysis in GERS is based on the current constitutional framework. However, it provides a useful indication of the relative strength of Scotland's public finances as part of the UK and a starting point for discussions of Scotland's fiscal position following independence. The most recent year figures are available for is 2011/12.

The analysis in this annex assigns Scotland an illustrative geographical share of both offshore oil and gas tax receipts and GDP.

Scotland's track record

Public sector spending

Public spending for Scotland was estimated to be £64.5 billion in 2011/12 – the most recent year for which figures are available.

This reflects spending undertaken for Scotland by every tier of government, including the UK Government, the Scottish Government and Scottish local authorities. It includes a share of UK wide public spending which cannot be easily identified as benefiting any one specific part of the country. For example, Scotland is assigned a per capita share of both UK defence and debt interest spending.

Responsibility for approximately 60 per cent of the public spending undertaken for Scotland is devolved to the Scottish Government and Scottish local authorities.

Whilst responsibility for such spending is devolved, responsibility for setting the overall budget for the Scottish Government is largely reserved to the Westminster Government and is determined by the Barnett Formula.

When comparing the level of aggregate public spending across countries or over time, the standard approach is to compare the ratio of public spending to GDP. This allows the size of the public sector to be compared whilst controlling for the size of the economy.

In 2011/12, estimated public spending was equivalent to 42.7 per cent of GDP in Scotland. This is estimated to be lower than in both the UK as a whole (45.5 per cent), and the majority of EU-15 countries.

Over the period 2007/08 to 2011/12 as a whole, the ratio of public spending to GDP was estimated to be 43.0 per cent in Scotland, compared to 45.0 per cent in the UK.

Public Spending as a share of GDP: Scotland and UK (2007/08 to 2011/12)					
	2007/08	**2008/09**	**2009/10**	**2010/11**	**2011/12**
Scotland	40.1%	41.7%	46.0%	44.5%	42.7%
UK	40.7%	44.4%	47.4%	46.8%	45.5%
Source: GERS 2011/12					

Scottish tax receipts

Total tax revenue in Scotland was estimated to be £56.9 billion in 2011/12. This includes a geographical share of North Sea tax revenue, equivalent to £10.6 billion.

Income tax is estimated to be the largest onshore source of tax revenue in Scotland, raising £10.8 billion in 2011/12, 19 per cent of the Scottish total. VAT and National Insurance contributions were the second and third largest sources of onshore revenue, generating 17 per cent and 15 per cent of total estimated Scottish receipts respectively.

Total Scottish tax receipts in 2011/12 were estimated to be equivalent to £10,700 per head. This compares to a figure of £9,000 per head in the UK as a whole.

On a per head basis, total tax receipts in Scotland are estimated to have been higher than in the UK in every year since 1980/81. Over this period, total tax revenue per head in Scotland has been on average £800 a year higher than in the UK as a whole. Adjusted for inflation, the gap has averaged £1,350 over this period.

Total Tax Receipts Per Head: Scotland and UK (2007/08 to 2011/12)					
	2007/08	**2008/09**	**2009/10**	**2010/11**	**2011/12**
Scotland	£10,000	£10,600	£9,100	£9,900	£10,700
UK	£8,900	£8,600	£8,200	£8,800	£9,000
Source: GERS 2011/12 & Scottish Government Analysis					

Whilst oil and gas receipts represent an important source of Scottish tax revenue, they account for a smaller proportion of revenue than in some other major oil and gas producing countries. The table below shows the proportion of total public sector revenue attributable to oil and gas production in Scotland and Norway, the largest oil and gas producer in Europe. As the table highlights oil and gas production accounts for a higher proportion of public sector receipts in Norway compared to Scotland.

Oil and Gas Receipts as a Share of Total Public Sector Revenue					
	2007/08	**2008/09**	**2009/10**	**2010/11**	**2011/12**
Scotland	14%	21%	12%	15%	19%
Norway	36%	27%	26%	27%	31%

Source: Scottish Parliament Information Centre – Share of total tax revenue
derived from oil and gas: Scotland and Norway, and Scottish Government analysis

Scotland's overall budget balance

The budget balance measures the difference between public spending and tax revenue in a given year. It therefore determines the government's annual borrowing requirement.

The primary estimate of Scotland's overall annual budget balance is the net fiscal balance. The net fiscal balance measures the difference between total public sector expenditure and revenue. It is comparable to the estimates of UK public sector net borrowing published by the Office for National Statistics (ONS).

The table below provides estimates of Scotland's net fiscal balance between 2007/08 and 2011/12. The corresponding UK figures are also provided.

Over the five years to 2011/12 as a whole, whilst in deficit, Scotland was estimated to be in a relatively stronger fiscal position than the UK. Since 2007/08, Scotland has run an average net fiscal deficit of £8.3 billion (5.9 per cent of GDP). During the same period, the UK ran an average annual deficit of £111 billion, equivalent to 7.6 per cent of GDP.

Scotland's deficit has declined since its peak to 2009/10. In 2011/12, the latest year for which data is available, Scotland is estimated have run a net fiscal deficit equivalent to 5.0 per cent of GDP. In the same year the UK is estimated to have had a deficit of 7.9 per cent of GDP.

To put the above projections into context, the IMF report that the (weighted) average deficit across the G7 economies was 7.6 per cent of GDP in 2011, whilst the average deficit among the 35 advanced economies monitored by the IMF was 6.4 per cent of GDP.

Net Fiscal Balance: Scotland and UK (2007/08 to 2011/12) per cent GDP					
	2007/08	**2008/09**	**2009/10**	**2010/11**	**2011/12**
Scotland	-2.9%	-2.6%	-10.7%	-8.1%	-5.0%
UK	-2.6%	-6.9%	-11.2%	-9.5%	-7.9%
Source: GERS 2011/12					

Over the past five years Scotland and the UK have both run a fiscal deficit (a shortfall between government revenue and expenditure). This is not unusual. Between 1980 and 2014 there has been only one year when the 35 countries in the OECD as a whole have run an overall fiscal surplus. It is possible for a government to run an annual budget deficit (a shortfall between income and expenditure) in a manner which is sustainable. This is because if the economy is growing quicker than the rate of debt accumulation, the debt to GDP ratio will still fall. As such, the burden of the debt will be reduced, relative to the country's ability to service it.

An alternative measure of Scotland's fiscal position is the current budget balance, which is also published by the ONS for the UK. It measures the difference between current expenditure and current receipts.

The current budget balance excludes capital investment. It therefore captures the degree to which current taxpayers meet the cost of paying for the public services they consume today and a contribution to debt interest payments.

If a country is running a current budget balance or surplus it may still have to borrow to fund capital expenditure. However, such borrowing will be for long-term investment which can be expected to increase the economy's productive capacity in future years. In effect, no borrowing is being used to fund day-to-day government services.

The table opposite provides estimates of the current budget balance for Scotland and the UK between 2007/08 and 2011/12. In each year Scotland is estimated to have a relatively stronger current budget balance than the UK.

In 2007/08 and 2008/09 Scotland was either running a current budget surplus or a small deficit. In comparison, the UK was in deficit in both years. Looking at earlier years shows that Scotland also ran a current budget surplus in 2005/06 and 2006/07. In comparison, the UK has not run a current budget surplus since 2001/02.

Current Budget Balance: Scotland and UK (2007/08 to 2011/12) per cent GDP					
	2007/08	**2008/09**	**2009/10**	**2010/11**	**2011/12**
Scotland	-0.3%	0.7%	-7.2%	-5.3%	-2.3%
UK	-0.5%	-3.6%	-7.8%	-6.9%	-6.0%
Source: GERS 2011/12					

From 2009/10 onwards, the size of the current budget deficit in both Scotland and the UK increased. This reflects, in part, the impact of the financial crises and subsequent global recession which has had a significant impact on the public finances of many western economies. Scotland's public finances are expected to strengthen in the coming years as the economic recovery gathers momentum.

Scotland's national accounts on independence

To enable an informed assessment of the financial position of an independent Scotland, the Scottish Government has prepared projections of Scotland's public finances under the current constitutional framework in 2016/17, the year when Scotland will become independent. Such projections reflect the decisions and priorities of the Westminster Government.

In contrast, the strength of Scotland's public finances in the years after 2016/17 will depend on the economic and fiscal decisions of future Scottish governments and our ability to grow the economy.

The financial position that Scotland will inherit upon independence will depend in part on negotiations between the Scottish and Westminster Governments following a Yes vote. For example, the proportion of UK public sector debt which an independent Scotland will assume responsibility for.

To reflect the range of possible outcomes, the analysis here uses two scenarios for Scotland's share of UK public sector debt and annual interest payments.

- Scotland's share of UK public sector net debt could be apportioned by reference to the historic balance of public spending and taxation since 1980/81. This provides a measure of our contribution to the UK's finances over the years.

- Alternatively, Scotland could take responsibility for a population share of UK public sector net debt.

In addition, the following core projections are used:

- Indicative total public receipts in Scotland 2016/17 of between £64 billion and £65 billion are projected. This is split £57 billion onshore and £7 to 8 billion offshore.

- Onshore tax revenues in Scotland are projected to follow the path forecast for the UK as a whole and grow by approximately £5 billion (10 per cent) in real terms between 2011/12 and 2016/17. For each of the onshore revenue streams in GERS, the average ratio of Scottish to UK receipts in the three years to 2011/12 has been calculated and applied to the forecasts by the Office for Budget Responsibility (OBR) for the individual UK tax receipts in future years.

- Forecasts for North Sea revenues are based on scenarios published in the Scottish Government Oil and Gas Analytical Bulletin.

- Indicative non-debt interest total managed expenditure (TME – all public spending on behalf of Scotland based on the existing constitutional framework) is estimated at approximately £64 billion. This is based on the Westminster Government's current spending plans, which will see such spending fall by 4 per cent in real terms between 2011/12 and 2016/17. Scottish TME in future years has been estimated by applying the average share of UK TME undertaken for Scotland over the three years to 2011/12 to the totals for future UK TME. Spending on individual spending lines for Scotland have been estimated based on the projected growth in the corresponding UK totals.

- Current devolved expenditure is estimated to be £37 billion, based on known expenditure plans. Estimates of reserved social protection (including welfare and pensions) are projected at £19 billion in 2016/17 based on existing OBR forecasts.

- Of reserved expenditures, defence is estimated at £3 billion (a per person share of assumed UK spend of £36 billion in 2016/17).

- The cash value of Scottish onshore GDP is assumed to grow in line with the OBR forecasts for UK GDP. Scottish offshore GDP has been estimated by projecting forward outturn data using the assumptions about future production and prices underpinning the forecasts for North Sea tax receipts.

Summary of Scotland's projected fiscal position

Table - Estimates of Scotland's financial position (2016/17) £ Billions – under current constitutional arrangements	
Total Expenditure (Non-Debt Interest)	**£63.7**
Currently Devolved	£37.3
Defence	£3.0
Reserved Social Protection	£18.8
Other Reserved Spending	£4.6
Public Sector Debt Interest[1]	**£3.9 to £5.5**
Total Public Sector Receipts	**£63.7 to £64.8**
Onshore Receipts	£56.9
Offshore Receipts	£6.8 to £7.9
Net Fiscal Balance[2]	
Including historical share of debt interest payments	-£2.7 to -£4.0
As percentage of GDP	-1.6 per cent to -2.4 per cent
Including population share of debt interest payments	-£4.3 to -£5.5
As percentage of GDP	*-2.5 per cent to -3.2 per cent*
UK Public Sector Net Borrowing[3]	*-£61*
As percentage of GDP	*-3.4 per cent*
Figures are rounded to the nearest hundred million and therefore may not sum	
[1] Range based upon historical or population share	
[2] Scottish Government projections	
[3] Office for Budget Responsibility – March 2013 Economic and Fiscal Outlook	

Scotland's deficit is forecast to fall to between 1.6 per cent and 2.4 per cent of GDP in 2016/17 with a historical share of UK debt and to be between 2.5 per cent and 3.2 per cent of GDP if we take on a population share of UK public sector debt. The OBR forecasts that the UK will run a deficit of 3.4 per cent of GDP in the same year. The IMF estimates that the average deficit across the G7 economies will be 3.2 per cent in 2016.

Scotland's current budget balance is also projected to improve in the coming years. Assuming a share of debt interest payments based upon Scotland's historical contribution to the UK public finances, Scotland's current budget balance is estimated to be between 0.1 per cent (i.e. a surplus) and -0.7 per cent of GDP in 2016/17. Assuming a per capita share of debt interest payments, Scotland's current budget balance in 2016/17 is projected to be between -0.8 per cent and -1.5 per cent of GDP. This compares to the OBR's forecast for the UK as a whole of -1.9 per cent.

These forecasts outline Scotland's potential fiscal position under the current constitutional framework. However, independence would provide the opportunity to implement a range of policies to reflect the preferences and needs of Scottish households and businesses. Such policy changes could have an impact on the public finances of an independent Scotland. Although in some cases their initial impact on 2016/17 would be limited with the full change not being observed on the public finances for a number of years.

Public sector net debt
When considering the sustainability of a country's public finances, it is important to consider the overall stock of debt, as well as the level of borrowing in a specific period.

Under the current fiscal framework, UK public sector net debt is incurred for the country as a whole, and not directly for Scotland or any other part of the UK.

As such, there are no outturn figures for the share of UK debt incurred on behalf of Scotland. Two approaches which can be used to allocate a notional share of UK net debt to Scotland are presented below.

Population share
GERS allocates Scotland a per head share of UK debt interest payments. The same approach could therefore be used to allocate Scotland a share of the corresponding debt.

UK public sector net debt at the end of 2016/17 is forecast to stand at £1.6 trillion. Scotland's per head share would be equivalent to approximately £130 billion (76 per cent of GDP).

This would represent a lower debt to GDP ratio than for the UK as a whole (86 per cent), reflecting the fact that Scotland has a higher level of GDP per capita (including North Sea oil) than the UK.

Historical share

A country's public sector net debt can be viewed as the sum of its historic annual borrowing, minus any debt repayment. Therefore, an alternative way to calculate Scotland's notional share of UK public sector debt is to base it on Scotland's historical fiscal position.

During the early 1980s, Scotland ran a substantial net fiscal surplus, driven by the significant growth in North Sea revenues. Scotland's fiscal position weakened through the 1990s but since 2001/02 has been broadly in line with that of the UK.

As approximately 90 per cent of UK public sector net debt has been incurred since 1980, assessing Scotland's fiscal position over this period gives an indication of the amount of UK net debt which has been incurred on behalf of Scotland.

Between 1980/81 and 2016/17, Scotland is estimated to run a cumulative net fiscal deficit equivalent to approximately £85 billion. This means that over this period as a whole, total public spending for Scotland will exceed tax revenue by £85 billion. This equates to around 6 per cent of the cumulative UK deficit over the same period (£1,400 billion).

Applying this ratio to UK public sector net debt in 2016/17 would result in a notional share for Scotland of approximately £100 billion, this is equivalent to 55 per cent of Scottish GDP.

ANNEX D | EQUALITY CONSIDERATIONS

Scotland's strong commitment to equality is reflected in this guide to an independent Scotland. It is an integral part of our vision for a modern, democratic Scotland. It underpins our aspirations for a society which is fair and just and informs our ambitions for a dynamic successful nation, caring for its people and resources and occupying its place in the world.

As an independent nation, Scotland can choose a more modern approach to government, including a written constitution. This will put issues such as wage equality and protection against discrimination at the very heart of our legal system, and in the very foundations of our new nation. We will have in Scotland all the powers we need to ensure equality of opportunity in the workplace including, for example, improved representation for women in leadership roles at board level in companies.

The Scottish Government is proposing that equality and human rights should be embedded in Scotland's written constitution. Existing legislation, protection and rights will be maintained on independence. Changes will be subject, as now, to consultation and democratic decision-making, including equality impact assessment.

The specific policies set out in this guide indicate what will be possible in an independent Scotland. The importance we attach to equality is reflected in the approach we propose, for example, to welfare and to pensions.

Being independent will mean we can deliver important advantages for people across Scottish society, with women seeing some of the clearest gains. For older women, a Scottish pension will have a guaranteed triple lock increase protecting its value beyond 2015 (when the triple lock comes to an end in the UK). Entitlement based on a spouse's contribution will also be maintained.

With independence the Scottish Parliament will also be able to reduce energy bills, and this Scottish Government's proposals will save an average household £70. For parents with young families, independence will allow us to deliver a transformational change in early years education and childcare. This will cut childcare costs and make it easier for mothers to enter the labour market.

Following independence, decisions about what policies or proposals should be adopted in Scotland will be a matter for the Scottish Parliament. They will be subject to the appropriate consultation and scrutiny and to assessment of their impact on equality.

ANNEX E

OTHER SCOTTISH GOVERNMENT PUBLICATIONS ON CONSTITUTIONAL REFORM

Scotland's Future is the Scottish Government's comprehensive guide to an independent Scotland and what it means for you. It builds on the Scottish Government's previous publications *Choosing Scotland's Future* (2007) and *Your Scotland, Your Voice* (2009). In addition to this guide, the Scottish Government has published a series of other documents focussing on particular areas. These are all available to view on the Scottish Government's dedicated referendum website www.scotreferendum.com. They are:

- *Scotland's Future: from the Referendum to Independence and a Written Constitution,* February 2013

- *Fiscal Commission Working Group Report – Macroeconomic Framework,* February 2013

- *Economic and Competition Regulation in an Independent Scotland,* February 2013

- *Scotland's Balance Sheet,* April 2013

- *Currency Choices for an Independent Scotland,* April 2013

- *Scotland's Economy: the case for independence,* May 2013

- *Expert Working Group on Welfare Report,* June 2013

- *Maximising the Return from Oil and Gas in an Independent Scotland,* July 2013

- *Consumer Protection and Representation in an Independent Scotland: Options,* August 2013

- *Pensions in an Independent Scotland,* September 2013

- *Fiscal Commission Working Group Report – Stabilisation and Savings Funds For Scotland,* October 2013

- *Fiscal Commission Working Group Report – Principles for a Modern and Efficient Tax System in an Independent Scotland,* November 2013

- *Fiscal Commission Working Group Report – Fiscal Rules and Fiscal Commissions,* November 2013

- *Building Security and Creating Opportunity: Economic Policy Choices in an Independent Scotland,* November 2013

ENDNOTES

1   Even after the new tax powers of the Scotland Act 2012, the Scottish Parliament will only be responsible for around 15% of taxes raised in Scotland. Scottish Government (2013) Scotland's Balance Sheet. http://www.scotland.gov.uk/Publications/2013/06/9241/downloads

2   The Barnett Formula allocates to Scotland a population share of changes in comparable spending programmes in England. Comparability is the extent to which services delivered by Whitehall departments correspond to services delivered by the devolved administrations. Barnett only applies to expenditure classified within Departmental Expenditure Limits – about 85 per cent of Scotland's total budget.

3   Institute for Fiscal Studies: Child and Working-Age Poverty in Northern Ireland from 2010 to 2020. http://www.ifs.org.uk/comms/r78.pdf

4   Amongst OECD economies, Scotland would be ranked 8th in terms of output per head. Scottish Government (2013) Scotland's International GDP Per Capita Ranking – 2011. http://www.scotland.gov.uk/Topics/Economy/Publications/GDP-Per-Capita

5   The Organisation for Economic Co-operation and Development: www.oecd.org

The mission of the Organisation for Economic Co-operation and Development (OECD) is to promote policies that will improve the economic and social well-being of people around the world.

There are currently 34 members: Australia, Austria, Belgium, Canada, Chile, Czech Republic, Denmark, Estonia, Finland, France, Germany, Greece, Hungary, Iceland, Ireland, Israel, Italy, Japan, Korea, Luxembourg, Mexico, Netherlands, New Zealand, Norway, Poland, Portugal, Slovak Republic, Slovenia, Spain, Sweden, Switzerland, Turkey, United Kingdom and United States.

The OECD provides a forum in which governments can work together to share experiences and seek solutions to common problems. It works with governments to understand what drives economic, social and environmental change, and, drawing on facts and real-life experience, it recommends policies designed to make the lives of ordinary people better.

6   Life expectancy at birth in Scotland was 1.8 years lower than in the UK for females and 2.5 years lower for males in 2013. Source: Period expectations of life (years). Based on historical mortality rates from 1981 to 2010 and assumed calendar year mortality rates from the 2010-based principle projections.

UK data: http://www.ons.gov.uk/ons/rel/lifetables/period-and-cohort-life-expectancy-tables/2010-based/a1--2010-based-period-expectation-of-life--1981-2060--principal-projection--uk.xls

Scotland data: http://www.ons.gov.uk/ons/rel/lifetables/period-and-cohort-life-expectancy-tables/2010-based/rft-a6-scoperiod10.xls.

7   In 2011/12, 710,000 people (14% of the population) were living in relative income poverty before housing costs in Scotland. Scottish Government (2013) Poverty and income inequality in Scotland 2011-12. http://www.scotland.gov.uk/Publications/2013/06/2493

8   OECD Statistics – 2012 GDP per capita, US$, current prices, current PPPs. Norway, Sweden, Denmark and Finland are ranked in the top 15.

9   OECD Statistics – 2010 data on Gini coefficient (after taxes and transfers). Data not available for all countries, so 2009 figures used for Chile, Hungary, Ireland, Japan, New Zealand, Switzerland and Turkey.

10   OECD: Divided We Stand: Why Inequality Keeps Rising. http://www.oecd.org/unitedkingdom/49170234.pdf

11   Currently nine of the top 15 advanced economies measured by income per capita are small countries with populations less than 10 million. OECD Statistics – 2012 GDP per capita, US$, current prices, current PPPs. Luxembourg, Norway, Switzerland, Austria, Ireland, Sweden, Denmark, Finland and Iceland are ranked in the top 15.

12   Paragraph 30. http://www.scotland.gov.uk/About/Government/concordats/Referendum-on-independence

13   "Supporters of independence will always be able to cite examples of small, independent and thriving economies across Europe such as Finland, Switzerland and Norway. It would be wrong to suggest that Scotland could not be another such successful, independent country" http://www.telegraph.co.uk/comment/personal-view/3639114/Scots-and-English-flourish-in-the-Union.html

14   Scottish Government (2013) Scotland's Balance Sheet. http://www.scotland.gov.uk/Publications/2013/06/9241/downloads

15   Office for Budget Responsibility – Economic and Fiscal Outlook – March 2013.

16   International Monetary Fund – World Economic Outlook Database – October 2013.

17   ONS Wealth and Assets Survey 2008-10. http://www.ons.gov.uk/ons/rel/was/wealth-in-great-britain-wave-2/wealth-of-the-wealthiest--2008-10/wealth-of-the-wealthiest-households--great-britain--2008-10.html#tab-The-South-East-has-biggest-share-of-the-wealthiest-households

18   OECD statistics – 2010 data on Gini coefficient (after taxes and transfers). Data not available for all countries, so 2009 figures used for Chile, Hungary, Ireland, Japan, New Zealand, Switzerland and Turkey.

19   United Nations Development Programme (2013) Summary – Human Development Report 2013 The Rise of the South:Human Progress in a Diverse World. New York: UNDP. http://hdr.undp.org/en/media/HDR2013_EN_Summary.pdf

20   Oil and Gas UK, Economic Report 2013. http://www.oilandgasuk.co.uk/2013-economic-report.cfm

21   2020 Routemap for Renewable Energy in Scotland. http://www.scotland.gov.uk/Resource/Doc/917/0118802.pdf

22   Based on current projections, Scotland is projected to have a lower dependency ratio than the UK until approximately 2032 (the dependency ratio is based on the pension age/child (under 16) population relative to the working-age population). In 2012 there were 588 dependents per 1,000 persons of working age in Scotland compared to 615 in the UK as a whole. Source: NRS and ONS 2012-based population projections.

23   In estimating total public spending undertaken for Scotland, GERS includes all spending undertaken directly for Scottish residents and businesses by every tier of government, including the Westminster and Scottish Governments and Scottish Local Authorities. This includes a share of UK wide public spending which cannot be easily identified as benefiting any one specific part of the country. For example, Scotland is allocated a population share of UK defence expenditure, on the basis that all areas of the UK benefit equally from such spending. Further information is available from http://www.scotland.gov.uk/gers

24   Fiscal Commission Working Group, (2013) – First Report – Macroeconomic Framework, Paragraph 4.19.

25   Scotland's balance sheet, Scottish Government, April 2013, Table 1.2. http://www.scotland.gov.uk/Resource/0041/00418420.pdf

26   In cash terms.

27   Government Expenditure and Revenue Scotland 2011-12, Table 3.1.

28   Analysis based on Scottish Government, March 2013: Government Expenditure and Revenue Scotland 2011-12.

29   Government Expenditure and Revenue Scotland 2011-12, Table 2.5.

30   Government Expenditure and Revenue Scotland 2011-12, Box 2.3.

31   For further discussion of Scotland's public finances and international comparisons please see the Scottish Government report 'Scotland's Balance Sheet'. http://www.scotland.gov.uk/Resource/0042/00425599.pdf

32   Scotland's Balance Sheet, Scottish Government, April 2013, Paragraph 4.16. http://www.scotland.gov.uk/Resource/0041/00418420.pdf

33   The Fiscal Commission Working Group is a sub-group of the Scottish Government's Council of Economic Advisers which has advised on the development of a robust fiscal and macroeconomic framework for an independent Scotland. Its membership includes two Nobel Laureates. http://www.scotland.gov.uk/Topics/Economy/Council-Economic-Advisers/FCWG. It is referred to as the Fiscal Commission in the rest of this paper.

34   Fiscal Commission Working Group: Stabilisation and Savings Funds for Scotland, Annex A. http://www.scotland.gov.uk/Resource/0043/00435303.pdf.

35   Fiscal Commission Working Group: Fiscal Rules and Fiscal Commissions, Paragraph 2.25 (November 2013).

36   OECD Economic Outlook Database.

37   Fiscal Commission Working Group: Fiscal Rules and Fiscal Commissions, Paragraph 2.26 (November 2013).

38   Government Expenditure and Revenue Scotland 2011-12, Table E.4

39   http://www.oecd-ilibrary.org/economics/government-deficit_gov-dfct-table-en (There are 34 OECD members in total, however, OECD data for 2012 is not reported for Chile, Mexico and Turkey).

40   Projections of public spending and onshore tax receipts are based on the Office for Budget Responsibility forecasts in the March 2013 Economic and Fiscal Outlook.

41   A further discussion on Scotland's historic and per head share of UK public sector net debt is provided in Scotland's Balance Sheet, Scottish Government (April 2013). http://www.scotland.gov.uk/Resource/0041/00418420.pdf

42   Office for Budget Responsibility – Economic and Fiscal Outlook – March 2013.

43   UK forecasts are taken from Office for Budget Responsibility – Economic and Fiscal Outlook – March 2013.

44   The Scottish Government's Oil and Gas Analytical Bulletin, March 2013, provides further information on these forecasts.

45   Office for Budget Responsibility – Economic and Fiscal Outlook – March 2013.

46   International Monetary Fund – World Economic Outlook Database – October 2013

47   Fiscal Commission Working Group Reports. http://www.scotland.gov.uk/Topics/Economy/Council-Economic-Advisers/FCWG

48   Fiscal Commission Working Group Report: Macroeconomic Framework, Chapter 5. http://www.scotland.gov.uk/Resource/0041/00414291.pdf

49   Fiscal Commission Working Group – First Report –
        Macroeconomic Framework (2013), paragraph 3.1.
        http://www.scotland.gov.uk/Publications/2013/02/3017

50   ONS – Regional Gross Value Added (December 2012).
        http://www.ons.gov.uk/ons/rel/regional-accounts/regional-gross-
        value-added--income-approach-/december-2012/stb-regional-
        gva-2011.html#tab-Regional--NUTS1--GVA-estimates

51   Scottish Government Analysis – Scottish National Accounts
        Project.

52   Scottish Government Analysis – Scottish National Accounts
        Project.

53   Scottish Government (2013) Scotland's International GDP Per
        Capita Ranking – 2011. http://www.scotland.gov.uk/Topics/
        Economy/Publications/GDP-Per-Capita

54   Ernst & Young UK Attractiveness Survey 2013. http://www.
        ey.com/UK/en/Issues/Business-environment/2013-UK-
        attractiveness-survey

55   Scottish Government (2013) Scotland's Balance Sheet.
        http://www.scotland.gov.uk/Resource/0041/00418420.pdf

56   http://www.scotland.gov.uk/Topics/Business-Industry/Energy/
        Facts

57   Oil and Gas UK, 2013 Economic Report.
        http://www.oilandgasuk.co.uk/2013-economic-report.cfm.

58   For example in 2010, of the 10 OECD countries with the lowest
        income inequality (measured by the Gini coefficient in 2010),
        8 have populations less than 10 million. 7 out of the 10 OECD
        countries with the highest GDP per capita (measured by $US,
        current prices, current PPPs) in 2010 were small countries.
        Norway, Denmark, Austria and Sweden ranked the top ten for
        both GDP per capita and income inequality whilst the UK was
        ranked 28th for income inequality and 15th for GDP per capita.
        Source: OECD statistics – 2010 figures have been used as
        more recent Gini coefficient figures were not available at the
        time of publication.

59   Between 1977-2007 Scotland's onshore GDP per head grew
        at an annual rate of 2.48% in real (volume) terms. The average
        rate among small European countries was 2.61%, a gap of

0.12% each year. Over a 30 year period the compounded effect of this gap totals 3.8% of GDP £900 per person in 2011 prices. The small countries used for comparison are: Austria, Denmark, Finland, Iceland, Ireland, Luxembourg, Norway (mainland only), Portugal and Sweden. Sources: Scottish Government, GDP and SNAP statistics; OECD, GDP and population statistics; Statistics Norway, mainland GDP statistics.

60   OECD statistics - 2010 data on Gini coefficient (after taxes and transfers). Data not available for all countries, so 2009 figures used for Chile, Hungary, Ireland, Japan, New Zealand, Switzerland and Turkey.

61   In 2011, the OECD reported that income inequality among working age people increased more quickly in the UK than in any other OECD economy since 1975. OECD (2011) Divided We Stand: Why Inequality Keeps Rising. http://www.oecd.org/unitedkingdom/49170234.pdf

62   The Fiscal Commission Working Group highlighted how "Such patterns of inequality will continue to have a negative impact on growth and prosperity in the long-term". http://www.scotland.gov.uk/Resource/0041/00414291.pdf

63   In 2011, output per head in London was over 70% higher than the UK average. http://www.ons.gov.uk/ons/rel/regional-accounts/regional-gross-value-added--income-approach-/december-2012/stb-regional-gva-2011.html#tab-Regional--NUTS1--GVA-estimates

64   Scottish Government (2013) Scotland's Balance Sheet. http://www.scotland.gov.uk/Publications/2013/06/9241/downloads

65   In 1999, excluding the North Sea, Scotland was ranked 4th out of the 12 UK countries and regions for output per head (95% of UK figure). In 2011, Scotland had risen to 3rd with output per head at 99% of the equivalent UK figure. Source: GVA per head at current basic prices on workplace basis, UK figure excluding extra-regio. http://www.ons.gov.uk/ons/publications/re-reference-tables.html?edition=tcm%3A77-265236

66   http://www.davidhumeinstitute.com/images/stories/Spring_2013/Small-countries.pdf

67   Scottish Government (2013) Scotland's International GDP Per Capita Ranking – 2011. http://www.scotland.gov.uk/Topics/Economy/Publications/GDP-Per-Capita In 2011 Luxembourg, Norway, Switzerland, Ireland, Austria, Sweden, Denmark, Finland and Iceland are ranked in the top 15.

68   Human Development Index 2012 Rankings. http://hdr.undp.org/en/statistics/ Norway, New Zealand, Ireland, Sweden, Switzerland, Hong Kong, Iceland, Denmark, Israel, Austria and Singapore are ranked in the top 20.

69   http://hdr.undp.org/en/statistics/

70   ONS Labour Productivity, Q2 2013. http://www.ons.gov.uk/ons/dcp171778_326680.pdf

71   http://www.scotland.gov.uk/About/Performance/scotPerforms/purpose/productivity

72   In Norway, the average unemployment rate was 3.3% between 2004 and 2012, and in Iceland the average employment rate was 81.6% over the same period. Source: Eurostat

73   http://www.scotlandscensus.gov.uk/documents/censusresults/release1b/rel1bsb.pdf

74   The working age population in Scotland is projected to increase by 3.4% compared to 10.9% in the UK between 2012 and 2035. ONS/NRS 2012-based population projections.

75   In 2011/12 the Gini coefficient for Scotland was 32, lower than the UK which was 34. Source: Family Resources Survey, DWP.

76   2010 data from OECD on international Gini comparisons. Data not available for all countries, so 2009 figures used for Chile, Hungary, Ireland, Japan, New Zealand, Switzerland and Turkey. Data for Scotland based on 2010-2011. Note that the 2010/11 Gini coefficient for Scotland was lower, at 30, than the 2011/12 value, however OECD data is only currently available for 2010.

77   Data from the ONS Annual Survey of Household Earnings for 2011 shows that median manufacturing gross annual salaries were 24% higher than those in the service sector, and 19% higher than the average across all industries.

78   Scottish Government Supply and Use Tables 1998-2009 balanced accounts.

79   Business Enterprise Research and Development 2011 Tables Expenditure on R&D performed within businesses in Scotland. http://www.scotland.gov.uk/Topics/Statistics/Browse/Business/RD/BERDTables

80   Helper, S. Krueger, T. and Wial, H. (2012) Why does manufacturing Matter? Which Manufacturing Matters?

81   Scottish Government (2013) Scotland's Global Connections Survey 2011. http://www.scotland.gov.uk/Resource/0041/00412570.pdf

82   Analysis conducted on behalf of the Scottish Government by aviasolutions.

83   York Aviation. The Impact of Air Passenger Duty on Scotland, Final Report October 2012. Commissioned by a Consortium of Scottish Airports. http://www.glasgowairport.com/static/Glasgow/Downloads/PDF/APD-York_Aviation-report-Oct-2012.pdf http://corporate.easyjet.com/~/media/Files/E/Easyjet-Plc-V2/pdf/content/APD-study-Abridged.pdf

84   http://www.taoiseach.gov.ie/eng/News/Archives/2010/Taoiseach's_Speeches_2010/Speech_by_the_Taoiseach_at_the_Opening_of_Terminal_2_T2_Dublin_Airport_on_19_November_2010.html

85   http://www.sdi.co.uk/

86   Scottish Government (2013) Scotland's Global Connections Survey 2011. http://www.scotland.gov.uk/Resource/0041/00412570.pdf

87   There are 92,381 recipients of Small Business Bonus Scheme (SBBS) relief in 2013-14. http://www.scotland.gov.uk/Topics/Statistics/Browse/Local-Government-Finance/NDR-Rates-Relief/SBBS2013

88   Scottish Government (2013) Economic and Competition Regulation in an Independent Scotland. http://www.scotland.gov.uk/Resource/0041/00415411.pdf

89   Protecting Consumers, Audit Scotland, January 2013. http://www.audit-scotland.gov.uk/docs/local/2013/nr_130131_protecting_consumers.pdf

90   Aghion and Howitt, 2009, "The Economics of Growth Theory", provides an overview of the economic theory of growth and the importance of technological progress as the main driver. More recently, NESTA's Plan i from 2012 underlines how "decades of research have shown that innovation is the most important driver of long term productivity and prosperity".

91   Gross Expenditure on Research and Development Data for Scotland, Table 4a. http://www.scotland.gov.uk/Topics/Statistics/Browse/Business/RD/GERDTables

92   Scottish Government (2013) Gross Expenditure on Research and Development Data for Scotland, Table 4a. http://www.scotland.gov.uk/Topics/Statistics/Browse/Business/RD/GERDTables

93   See Table 4a and Table 4b. http://www.scotland.gov.uk/Topics/Statistics/Browse/Business/RD/GERDTables

94   In 2011 49% of expenditure on R&D was performed in Higher Education in Scotland. Scottish Government (2013) Gross Expenditure on Research and Development Data for Scotland. Table 1. http://www.scotland.gov.uk/Topics/Statistics/Browse/Business/RD/GERDTables

95   Scottish Government (2013) Gross Expenditure on Research and Development Data for Scotland, Table 4c. http://www.scotland.gov.uk/Topics/Statistics/Browse/Business/RD/GERDTables

96   http://www.davidhumeinstitute.com/images/stories/Spring_2013/Small-countries.pdf

97   OECD 2012, "Inequality in labour income – What are its drivers and how can it be reduced?", OECD Economics Department Policy Notes. http://www.oecd.org/eco/public-finance/49417273.pdf

98   Workers on Board, The case for workers' voice in corporate governance. TUC. http://www.tuc.org.uk/sites/default/files/Workers_on_board.pdf

99   http://www.legislation.gov.uk/ukdsi/2013/9780111540169/regulation/3

100   http://www.gov.uk/government/uploads/system/uploads/
      attachment_data/file/182602/bis-13-p135-women-on-
      boards-2013.pdf

101   http://ec.europa.eu/justice/gender-equality/files/
      womenonboards/factsheet-general-2_en.pdf

102   Households Below Average Income dataset. UK figures:
      1996/7 to 2011/12.

103   Public Sector Employment in Scotland – Q2 2013.
      http://www.scotland.gov.uk/Publications/2013/09/2277

104   http://www.scotland.gov.uk/News/Releases/2012/11/
      Livingwage051112

105   Joint Labour Market Study by Scottish Government
      and STUC – June 2013. http://www.scotland.gov.uk/
      Resource/0042/00425244.pdf

106   Based on SG analysis of ASHE micro-data. ASHE, ONS.

107   Based on the additional gross earnings of an individual working
      full time.

108   http://www.tuc.org.uk/economic-issues/economic-analysis/
      corporate-governance/chancellors-shares-rights-gimmick-could-
      cost

109   http://www.ft.com/cms/s/0/4ff7a5ac-42ea-11e2-a3d2-
      00144feabdc0.html#axzz2kF5hJR4P

110   Fiscal Commission Working Group (2013) First Report –
      Macroeconomic Framework. http://www.scotland.gov.uk/
      Resource/0041/00414291.pdf

111   Page 19 Fiscal Commission Working Group (2013) First Report
      – Macroeconomic Framework. http://www.scotland.gov.uk/
      Resource/0041/00414291.pdf

112   Fiscal Commission Working Group (2013) First Report – Annex:
      Assessment of key currency options. http://www.scotland.gov.
      uk/Resource/0041/00414366.pdf

113   Chapter 7 – Fiscal Commission Working Group (2013) First
      Report – Macroeconomic Framework. http://www.scotland.gov.
      uk/Resource/0041/00414291.pdf

114   Fiscal Commission Working Group (2013) Fiscal Rules and Fiscal Commissions. http://www.scotland.gov.uk/Resource/0043/00437469.pdf

115   Fiscal Commission Working Group (2013) Stabilisation and Savings Funds for Scotland. http://www.scotland.gov.uk/Resource/0043/00435303.pdf

116   Box 7.03 Fiscal Commission Working Group (2013) First Report – Macroeconomic Framework. http://www.scotland.gov.uk/Resource/0041/00414291.pdf

117   OECD Tax Database Table II.1 http://www.oecd.org/ctp/tax-policy/tax-database.htm#C_CorporateCaptial

118   Scottish Government (2013) Scotland's Balance Sheet. http://www.scotland.gov.uk/Publications/2013/06/9241/downloads

119   Fiscal Commission Working Group (2013) Principles for a Modern and Efficient Tax System in an Independent Scotland. http://www.scotland.gov.uk/Resource/0043/00434977.pdf

120   In the last year which data is available, which is more exposed to fluctuations in tax revenues and GDP, costs per revenue are 0.83 in the UK, 0.71 in Denmark, 0.40 in Sweden, and 0.80 in Finland. See page 37 Fiscal Commission Working Group (2013) Principles for a Modern and Efficient Tax System in an Independent Scotland. http://www.scotland.gov.uk/Resource/0043/00434977.pdf

121   http://corporate.easyjet.com/~/media/Files/E/Easyjet-Plc-V2/pdf/content/APD-study-Abridged.pdf

122   Scottish Government: Devolving Corporation Tax in the Scotland Bill (2011). http://www.scotland.gov.uk/Resource/Doc/919/0120770.pdf

123   http://www.resolutionfoundation.org/blog/2013/oct/21/who-will-benefit-tax-break-married-couples/

124   http://www.ifs.org.uk/publications/6869

125   In the UK, the tax gap is estimated to have been around £35 billion, or 7 per cent of the total due in 2011-12. 11 per cent of this, £4 billion, is reported to arise through tax avoidance schemes. HMRC (2013) Measuring Tax Gaps. http://www.hmrc.gov.uk/statistics/tax-gaps/mtg-2013.pdf

126   Fiscal Commission Working Group (2013) Principles for a Modern and Efficient Tax System in an Independent Scotland. http://www.scotland.gov.uk/Resource/0043/00434977.pdf

127   For example see analysis released on impact of HS2 on different parts of the UK obtained by the BBC via FOI. www.bbc.co.uk/news/uk-24589652

128   Statistical Bulletin - Transport Series. Transport and Travel in Scotland 2012. Table S1 [% refers to the change between 2004-5 and 2012-13]. http://www.transportscotland.gov.uk/strategy-and-research/publications-and-consultations/j281378-08.htm#tableS1

129   Transport Scotland (2012) Scottish Ferries Service: Ferries Plan (2013 – 2022). http://www.transportscotland.gov.uk/files/documents/reports/j254579_1.pdf

130   https://www.gov.uk/government/uploads/system/uploads/attachment_data/file/244672/qep511.xls

131   http://www.nats.aero/about-us/what-we-do/our-ownership-2/

132   Scottish Government (2013) Economic and Competition Regulation in an Independent Scotland. http://www.scotland.gov.uk/Resource/0041/00415411.pdf

133   Relative poverty is defined here as individuals living in households whose equivalised income is below 60% of UK median income in the same year, before housing costs.

134   Scottish Government (2013) *Poverty and income inequality in Scotland 2011-12*. http://www.scotland.gov.uk/Publications/2013/06/2493

135   Institute for Fiscal Studies: Child and Working-Age Poverty in Northern Ireland from 2010 to 2020. http://www.ifs.org.uk/comms/r78.pdf

136   Dorling D: Inequality and Injustice: Some News from Britain. Urban Geography 33.5 (2012). http://bellwether.metapress.com/content/m10m3736514222q5/fulltext.pdf

137   Period expectations of life (years). Based on historical mortality rates from 1981 to 2010 and assumed calendar year mortality rates from the 2010-based principle projections. UK data. http://www.ons.gov.uk/ons/rel/lifetables/period-and-cohort-life-expectancy-tables/2010-based/a1--2010-based-

period-expectation-of-life--1981-2060--principal-projection--uk.xls
Scotland data: http://www.ons.gov.uk/ons/rel/lifetables/period-
and-cohort-life-expectancy-tables/2010-based/rft-a6-scoperiod10.
xls

138   http://www.scotpho.org.uk/population-dynamics/healthy-life-
expectancy/key-points

139   http://www.gcph.co.uk/publications/391_still_the_sick_man_of_
europe

140   Scotland and European Health for All Database 2012.
http://www.scotpho.org.uk/comparative-health/scotland-and-
european-hfa-database

141   Audit Scotland (2012) Health Inequalities in Scotland.

142   http://www.scottish.parliament.uk/parliamentarybusiness/28862.
aspx?r=7902&mode=pdf

143   Scottish Government (2013) UK Government cuts to
welfare expenditure in Scotland. http://www.scotland.gov.uk/
Resource/0041/00417011.pdf

144   Internal Scottish Government analysis of the 2012 Autumn
Budget Statement and Resolution Foundation (2012)
Resolution Foundation analysis of the 2012 Autumn Statement.
http://www.resolutionfoundation.org/publications/resolution-
foundation-analysis-2012-autumn-stateme/

145   Scottish Government (2013) Impact of UK Government Welfare
Reforms on families. http://www.scotland.gov.uk/Topics/People/
welfarereform/analysis/wrimpactonfamilies

146   Based on initial analysis at http://www.scotland.gov.uk/
Topics/Built-Environment/Housing/supply-demand/chma/
Benefitchanges/underoccupancy updated to reflect actual rather
than projected impacts.

147   Scottish Government (2013) Impact of Planned Benefit
Changes on Under-Occupied Disabled Households
in Scotland. http://www.scotland.gov.uk/Topics/Built-
Environment/Housing/supply-demand/chma/Benefitchanges/
BenefitChangesDisabledHouseholds

148   http://news.scotland.gov.uk/News/-Bedroom-Tax-help-543.aspx

149   Scottish Government (2013) Empowering Scotland: the Government's Programme for Scotland 2013-14. http://www.scotland.gov.uk/Publications/2013/09/8177

150   http://www.scotland.gov.uk/Topics/People/welfarereform/scottishwelfarefund

151   The Pensions Commission (2005) A New Pension Settlement for the Twenty-First Century. London: TSO.

152   OECD (2011), Pensions at a Glance 2011: Retirement-income Systems in OECD and G20 Countries, Part II Chapter 2 (Pension Entitlements), OECD Publishing. http://dx.doi.org/10.1787/pension_glance-2011-en

153   Pensions Commission, 2005.

154   Maer, L. and Thurley, D. (2009) House of Commons Library Standard Note SN/BT/1759. Last updated: 9 March 2009

155   http://www.moneymarketing.co.uk/analysis/raid-review/131072.article

156   Department for Work and Pensions (2013) *Framework for the analysis of future pension incomes.* https://www.gov.uk/government/uploads/system/uploads/attachment_data/file/238978/framework-analysis-future-pension-incomes.pdf

157   ONS (2013) *Pension Trends – Chapter 7: Private Pension Scheme Membership.* http://www.ons.gov.uk/ons/dcp171766_314955.pdf

158   HMRC (2013) *Personal pensions – estimate number of individuals contributing by country and region.* http://www.hmrc.gov.uk/statistics/pension-stats/pen5.xls

159   LCP (2013) *Accounting for Pensions 2013.* LCP. http://www.lcp.uk.com/media/636443/lcp_afp2013_interactivepdf.pdf

160   Department for Work and Pensions (2013) *Framework for the analysis of future pension incomes.* https://www.gov.uk/government/publications/framework-for-the-analysis-of-future-pension-incomes

161   Scottish Government (2013) *Poverty and income inequality in Scotland 2011-12.* http://www.scotland.gov.uk/Publications/2013/06/2493

162 Scottish Government (2013) *Pensions in an Independent Scotland.* http://www.scotland.gov.uk/Publications/2013/09/3492

163 Scottish Government (2013) *Scotland's Balance Sheet*

164 DWP tabulation tool: Pension Credit Caseload – number of beneficiaries: Region by Time Series by Type of Pension Credit. Note that future interaction between Guarantee Credit and the single tier pension makes prediction of future number of recipients difficult.

165 The benefits will be lower if individuals do not qualify for the full Savings Credit. Note that entitlement for couples depends on both partners' incomes; the maximum Savings Credit entitlement for couples is currently £22.89 per week.

166 Dependency ratios should be interpreted carefully. While a simple interpretation is that the ratio reflects the number of older people or children who are 'dependent' on people aged 16 to 64, that interpretation assumes that most older people and children are not economically active. The reality is more complex, for example not everyone of working age is employed and economically active (some are at school or university and others are unemployed); and the age at which people retire varies greatly. A large number of factors will affect future dependency ratios and the further ahead projections are made, the less accurate they are likely to be.

167 NRS/ONS (2013) 2012-based population projections.

168 Population projections have limitations. A projection is a calculation showing what happens if particular assumptions are made. The population projections are trend-based. They are, therefore, not policy-based forecasts of what the government expects to happen. Many social and economic factors influence population change, including policies adopted by both central and local government. The relationships between the various factors are complex and largely unknown.

169 NRS/ONS (2013) 2012-based population projections.

170 Family Resources Survey, 2011/12.

171 United Nations Development Programme (2013) *Summary – Human Development Report 2013 The Rise of the South:Human Progress in a Diverse World*. New York: UNDP. http://hdr.undp.org/en/media/HDR2013_EN_Summary.pdf

172   http://www.davidhumeinstitute.com/images/stories/Spring_2013/
       Small-countries.pdf

173   In brief, 'social protection' covers pensions and other welfare
       spending. More broadly, the term describes help given to those
       in need or at risk of hardship. Regarded as a safety net meant
       to provide a minimum decent standard of living, it is designed to
       protect the vulnerable in society such as those affected by, for
       example, illness, low income, family circumstances or age.

174   Pensions in an Independent Scotland.
       http://www.scotland.gov.uk/Publications/2013/09/3492

175   Scottish Government (April 2013) *Public Spending for Scotland.*
       http://www.scotland.gov.uk/Resource/0041/00418131.pdf
       Analysis assigns Scotland a geographical share of GDP from
       North Sea oil and gas production.

176   Scottish Government (April 2013) Public Spending for Scotland.
       http://www.scotland.gov.uk/Resource/0041/00418131.pdf

177   HC (Deb) 15 Jan 2013: Column 715W.
       http://www.publications.parliament.uk/pa/cm201213/cmhansrd/
       cm130115/text/130115w0003.htm#13011576000093

178   Scottish Government (September 2013) Annual Report for the
       Child Poverty Strategy for Scotland 2013. http://www.scotland.
       gov.uk/Publications/2013/09/2212

179   Scottish Government (2013) *The Gender Impact of Welfare
       Reform.* http://www.scotland.gov.uk/Resource/0043/00432337.
       pdf

180   http://www.scotland.gov.uk/Publications/2013/02/3017

181   Fiscal Commission Working Group (2013) First Report:
       Macroeconomic Framework, p.24.

182   Scottish Executive (1999) *Social Justice: A Scotland where
       Everyone Matters*, Rt Hon Donald Dewar MSP, 1999.
       http://scotland.gov.uk/Resource/Doc/158142/0042789.pdf

183   Expert Working Group on Welfare Report, June 2013.
       http://www.scotland.gov.uk/Publications/2013/06/8875

184   Scottish Government (2013) *Government Expenditure and
       Revenue Scotland 2011/12.* http://www.scotland.gov.uk/
       Publications/2013/03/1859. Figure relates to 2011/12.

185   Department for Work and Pensions, 2012. https://www.gov.uk/
       government/organisations/department-for-work-pensions/series/
       welfare-reform-act-2012-equality-impact-assessments

186   Gender Impact of the UK Welfare Reforms. http://www.
       scotland.gov.uk/Topics/People/welfarereform/analysis/
       welfarereformanalysisgenderimpact

187   http://www.scotland.gov.uk/Topics/People/welfarereform/
       EXPERTWORKINGGROUPONWELFARE

188   Institute for Fiscal Studies (July 2013) *Government spending on
       benefits and state pensions in Scotland: current patterns and
       future issues.* http://www.ifs.org.uk/bns/bn139.pdf

189   Office for National Statistics (June 2011) The effects of taxes
       and benefits on income inequality, 1980-2009/10. http://www.
       ons.gov.uk/ons/taxonomy/search/index.html?newquery=*&nscl=
       Income+Inequality+of+Households&nscl-orig=Income+Inequalit
       y+of+Households&content-type=publicationContentTypes&sort
       Direction=DESCENDING&sortBy=pubdate

190   Fiscal Commission Working Group: Principles for a Modern and
       Efficient Tax System in an Independent Scotland. (November
       2013) http://www.scotland.gov.uk/Publications/2013/10/4839

191   Fiscal Commission Working Group – Principles for a Modern
       and Efficient Tax System in an Independent Scotland
       (November 2013), page 11.

192   http://www.scotland.gov.uk/Topics/Government/Finance/
       scottishapproach/lbtt

193   Numbers as at May 2013. http://www.scotland.gov.uk/
       Topics/Built-Environment/Housing/supply-demand/chma/
       Benefitchanges/underoccupancypenalty

194   Internal Scottish Government analysis based on DWP estimates
       of impact of changes under Universal Credit (UC) in Scotland
       available in Welfare Reform (Further Provision) (Scotland) Act
       2012, Initial Report – 2013

195   Scottish Government analysis based on Resolution
       Foundation (2012) Gaining from Growth –The final report
       of the Commission on Living Standards. http://www.
       resolutionfoundation.org/publications/final-report-commission-
       living-standards/

196 Expert Working Group on Welfare (June 2013) Expert Working Group on Welfare Report. http://www.scotland.gov.uk/Publications/2013/06/8875

197 Healthy Living Survey 2013. http://www.scotland.gov.uk/Publications/2013/06/7503/0

198 Fiscal Commission Working Group –Principles for a Modern and Efficient Tax System in an Independent Scotland (November 2013). http://www.scotland.gov.uk/Publications/2013/10/4839

199 The Expect Working Group's current Call for Evidence is available at http://www.scotland.gov.uk/Topics/People/welfarereform/EXPERTWORKINGGROUPONWELFARE/

200 Source: Department of Work and Pensions (2012) Work Programme evaluation: Findings from the first phase of qualitative research on programme delivery. https://www.gov.uk/government/publications/work-programme-evaluation-findings-from-the-first-phase-of-qualitative-research-on-programme-delivery-rr821

201 National Audit Office (2013) Universal Credit: Early Progress. http://www.nao.org.uk/report/universal-credit-early-progress/

202 http://www.cpag.org.uk/content/stop-work-poverty Households Below Average Income dataset 2011/12, DWP

203 Expert Working Group on Welfare (June 2013) Expert Working Group on Welfare Report. http://www.scotland.gov.uk/Publications/2013/06/8875

204 Expert Working Group on Welfare (June 2013) Expert Working Group on Welfare Report. http://www.scotland.gov.uk/Publications/2013/06/8875 – paragraph 4.50

205 Expert Working Group on Welfare (June 2013) Expert Working Group on Welfare Report. http://www.scotland.gov.uk/Publications/2013/06/8875

206 See for example the Scottish Index of Multiple Deprivation (SIMD). http://www.scotland.gov.uk/Topics/Statistics/SIMD/

207 Scottish Government: Scotland's People Annual Report: Results from 2012 Scottish Household Survey. http://www.scotland.gov.uk/Publications/2013/08/6973/3

208   http://www.ifs.org.uk/publications/6818 p.27

209   Table 4, Scottish House Condition Survey: Key Findings 2011. http://www.scotland.gov.uk/Publications/2012/12/4995

210   Table 27, Scottish House Condition Survey, Key Findings 2011. http://www.scotland.gov.uk/Publications/2012/12/4995

211   Dorling D (2013) In Place of Fear: Narrowing health inequalities.

212   http://www.ashscotland.org.uk/what-we-do/supply-information-about-tobacco-and-health/resources/national-evaluation-of-scotland%27s-smoke-free-legislation.aspx

213   http://www.scotland.gov.uk/About/Performance/programme-for-government/2013-14/Food-Standards-Scotland-Bill

214   These are: Royal Caledonian Curling Club, Scottish Football Association, Scottish Rugby Union, Basketball Scotland, Scottish Volleyball Association, Amateur Boxing Scotland, Badminton Scotland, SGU/SLGA (golf), Scottish Hockey, Table Tennis Scotland & Weightlifting.

215   *Programme for International Student Assessment (PISA) 2009: Highlights from Scotland's Results*, Scottish Government, December 2010.

216   *Scottish Government analysis 2013: UK Government cuts to welfare expenditure in Scotland* Scottish government, March 2013. http://www.scotland.gov.uk/Resource/0041/00417011.pdf

217   Scottish Government (September 2013) *Annual Report for the Child Poverty Strategy for Scotland 2013.* http://www.scotland.gov.uk/Publications/2013/09/2212

218   Gourtsoyannis, R (2012) *UK immigration policy is "poisonous gun" pointed at universities.* http://www.holyrood.com/2012/11/uk-immigration-policy-is-poisonous-gun-pointed-at-universities

219   Scottish Parliament (2012) Education and Culture Committee *Official Report 2 October 2012*: Column 1514. http://www.scottish.parliament.uk/parliamentarybusiness/28862.aspx?r=7652&mode=pdf

220   Family and Daycare Trust (2013) *The 2013 Scottish childcare report.* http://www.familyandparenting.org/Resources/FPI/Documents/FCT_Scottish_Childcare_Costs_13.pdf. Based on average costs.

221   Scottish Government (2013) *Summary statistics for attainment,
       leaver destinations and healthy living*, No. 3: 2013 Edition.
       http://www.scotland.gov.uk/Publications/2013/06/7503/4#tb3

222   Scottish Qualifications Authority (2013) *Pre-appeals National
       Course and Awards Results Statistics 6 August 2013.*
       http://www.sqa.org.uk/sqa/64717.4239.html

223   http://www.scotland.gov.uk/About/Performance/scotPerforms/
       indicator/youngpeople

224   Scottish Government (2012) Summary Statistics for Schools
       in Scotland, No.3: 2012 Edition. http://www.scotland.gov.uk/
       Publications/2012/12/2355/19

225   Scottish Government analysis using http://www.
       timeshighereducation.co.uk/world-university-rankings/ and
       http://data.worldbank.org/indicator/SP.POP.TOTL

226   Research Assessment Exercise 2008 Scottish results available
       at http://www.sfc.ac.uk/research/research_assessment/
       research_assessment.aspx

227   Scottish Development International (2013) *Scotland's Education
       Sector.* http://www.sdi.co.uk/~/media/SDI/Files/documents/
       education/scotlands-education-sector-brochure

228   Skills Development Scotland (2009) *Life Sciences Key
       Sector Report.* http://www.skillsdevelopmentscotland.co.uk/
       media/116740/key%20sector%20report%20-%20life%20
       sciences.pdf

229   British Council Scotland (2013) *A Strategic Analysis of the
       Scottish Higher Education sector's distinctive assets.* http://
       www.britishcouncil.org/scotland-report-a-strategic-analysis-of-
       the-scottish-higher-education-sectors-distinctive-assets.pdf

230   Higher Education Statistics Authority (2013) *HE finance
       plus* Figure available at http://www.hesa.ac.uk/index.
       php?option=com_content&task=view&id=1900&Itemid=239

231   Scottish Government (2012) *Opportunities for All Supporting all
       young people to participate in post-16 learning, training or work.*
       http://www.scotland.gov.uk/Publications/2012/11/7618

232   http://oecdeducationtoday.blogspot.co.uk/2013/02/making-
       education-more-equitable.html

233   Mostafa, T. and Green, A., *Measuring the Impact of Universal Pre-School Education and Care on Literacy Performance Scores*. Institute of Education (2012).

234   www.europa.eu/countries/index_en.htm

235   European Commission (2013) *Barcelona objectives The development of childcare facilities for young children in Europe with a view to sustainable and inclusive growth.* EU:Luxembourg

236   Daycare Trust and Family and Parenting Institute (2013) *Childcare Cost Survey 2013.* http://www.daycaretrust.org. uk/data/files/Research/costs_surveys/Childcare_Costs_ Survey_2013.pdf

237   Scottish Government (2013) *Early Childhood Education and Care Provision: International Review of Policy, Delivery and Funding.* http://www.scotland.gov.uk/ Publications/2013/03/4564/0

238   British Council Scotland (2008) *Tracking the University and College Experience in Scotland.* http://www.britishcouncil.org/ scotland-learning-igraduate-international-student-summary- report-26-06-08.pdf

239   Scottish Funding Council (2013) *Higher Education Students and Qualifiers at Scottish Institutions 2011-12.* http://www.sfc. ac.uk/web/FILES/ReportsandPublications/HE_Students_and_ Qualifiers_publication_11-12.pdf

240   UCAS (2013) *Interim assessment of UCAS acceptances by intended entry year, country of institution and qualifications held.* http://www.ucas.com/news-events/news/2013/interim- assessment-ucas-acceptances-intended-entry-year-country- institution-0

241   UCAS, Interim assessment of UCAS acceptances, 24 September 2013.

242   Higher Education Statistics Authority (2013) *HESA Finance Plus 2011/12, Table 5b.* http://www.hesa. ac.uk/index.php?option=com_pubs&task=show_pub_ detail&pubid=1710&Itemid=276 plus SFC estimate of Total Research Funding

243   Research Assessment Exercise 2008 Scottish results available at http://www.sfc.ac.uk/research/research_assessment/research_assessment.aspx

244   Running from 2014 to 2020, Horizon 2020 has a budget of just over €70 billion – including some €24 billion to support top-level research.

245   Higher Education Statistics Authority (2013) *HESA Finance Plus 2011/12, Table 5b.* http://www.hesa.ac.uk/index.php?option=com_pubs&task=show_pub_detail&pubid=1710&Itemid=276 Plus SFC estimate of Total Research Funding

246   The Anholt-GfK Roper Nation Brands Index (NBI). http://www.scotland.gov.uk/Publications/2012/12/4188/downloads#res409519

247   FCO Annual Report 2012/13. https://www.gov.uk/government/uploads/system/uploads/attachment_data/file/210136/HC_32_v0_2.pdf

248   Joint Statement by PM David Cameron and Taoiseach Enda Kenny on 12 March 2012, "British Irish relations – the next decade".

249   Golub, J (2012) the Journal of European Public Policy, vol 19:9, p1294-1315.

250   Scottish Government (2013) Global Connections Survey 2011.

251   http://www.scotlandscensus.gov.uk/en/censusresults/downloadablefilesr2.html

252   Bailes, A. JK., Thorhallsson, B., and Johnstone R. L. 2011. Scotland as an independent small state: Where would it seek shelter. Fraedigreinar, Stornmal & Stornsysla.

253   http://www.norden.org/en/about-nordic-co-operation/agreements/treaties-and-agreements/basic-agreement/the-helsinki-treaty

254   On 20 March 2013, the Scottish Parliament voted conclusively 61 in favour, 16 against and 31 abstentions) in support of the UN Secretary-General's five point plan for nuclear disarmament and called on the Westminster Government to acknowledge the Parliament's opposition to Trident.

255 Estimated direct MOD expenditure in Scotland in 2007-08 was £1.57 billion (House of Commons written answer, 6 April 2010: Column 1200W).

256 Government Expenditure and Revenue Scotland (GERS) 2011-12 estimates, Scotland's defence and security contribution within the UK. Scotland's combination to UK defence & security budgets is estimated to be £3 billion by 2016/17, based on the methodology set out in Chapter 2.

257 Oral statement to the House of Commons by the Secretary of State for Defence, Philip Hammond, MP, on 5 March 2013.

258 Oral statement to the House of Commons by then Secretary of State for Defence, Liam Fox, MP, on 18 July 2011.

259 MoD Personnel Bulletin 2.03 – service and civilian personnel – 2013.

260 The National Asset Register, HM Government, 2007, page 269.

261 The plans set out here are based on a process of policy development by the Scottish Government that has drawn appropriately on expert advice at a number of stages. The process involved development of an underpinning framework for defence and security policy, based on an understanding of Scotland's geopolitical context and analysis of threats and risk. Plans for specific defence and security capabilities were then developed based on that framework, drawing on a range of expert inputs.

262 The Secretary of State for Defence announced in the House of Commons on 6 November 2013 that the Westminster Government had signed an agreement in principle with BAE Systems for three new Offshore Patrol Vessels.

263 Scotland Analysis: Defence, UK Government, page 30.

264 This does not refer to the timeframe for the withdrawal of Trident nuclear weapons and/or the Vanguard submarine fleet, which would be decided and delivered separately as quickly as it can be both safely and responsibly secured.

265 Scotland Analysis: Defence, UK Government, p32.

266 Disarming Trident – A practical guide to de-activating and dismantling the Scottish-based Trident nuclear weapons system, Scottish CND, June 2012.

267 Cancelling Trident - The Economic And Employment Consequences For Scotland. http://www.stuc.org.uk/files/STUC%20-%20CND%20Trident%20Report%202007/STUC-CND%20Trident%20Report.pdf

268 Scotland Analysis: Defence, UK Government, p41. The Westminster Government defines single use military equipment as that "which only has a military use, such as warships, fighting vehicles and fighter aircraft."

269 The Westminster Government has set out a 10-year defence equipment plan including almost £160 billion of procurement. Joint arrangements would support delivery of this plan without the direct contribution of Scottish tax receipts.

270 http://www.scotland.gov.uk/Topics/Justice/public-safety/17141/cashback

271 Scottish Government: Crime and Justice Survey 2010-11 Main Findings (2011) - 74% of adults thought that the local crime rate stayed the same or improved in their local area in 2010-11, an increase from 71% in 2009-10. http://www.scotland.gov.uk/Publications/2011/10/28142346/0

272 Scottish Government: Recorded Crime in Scotland 2012-13, (2013). http://www.scotland.gov.uk/Publications/2013/06/9697

273 Scottish Government: Homicide in Scotland 2012-13, (2013). http://www.scotland.gov.uk/Resource/0043/00435280.pdf

274 Scottish Government: Recorded Crime in Scotland 2012-13, (2013). http://www.scotland.gov.uk/Publications/2013/06/9697

275 Scottish Government: Police Officer Quarterly Strength Statistics 30 June 2013, (2013). http://www.scotland.gov.uk/Topics/Statistics/Browse/Crime-Justice/PublicationPoliceStrength/POQS2013Q2

276 Scottish Government: Letting Our Communities Flourish. (2009): http://www.scotland.gov.uk/Publications/2009/06/01144911/0

277 For example, the principles set out by the Geneva Centre for the Democratic Control of Armed Forces (DCAF) in *Overseeing Intelligence Services: A Toolkit*. http://www.dcaf.ch/Publications/Overseeing-Intelligence-Services-A-Toolkit. DCAF is an international foundation whose mission is to assist the international community in pursuing good governance and reform of the security sector.

278 Scottish Government: What Works to Reduce Reoffending: A Summary of the Evidence. (2011). http://scotland.gov.uk/Resource/0038/00385880.pdf

279 http://webarchive.nationalarchives.gov.uk/20100921035225/http:/northreview.independent.gov.uk/

280 Scottish Health Survey 2012 - Summary of Main Findings (2013): http://www.scotland.gov.uk/Publications/2013/09/4693/1

281 http://www.parliament.uk/business/committees/committees-a-z/commons-select/culture-media-and-sport-committee/news/120724-gambling-report-publication/

282 Scottish Government: Scottish Crime and Justice Survey Drug Use Report 2010-11. (2012). http://www.scotland.gov.uk/Publications/2012/03/2775/5

283 Scottish Schools Adolescent Lifestyle and Substance Misuse Survey (SALSUS) National Report (2010). http://www.drugmisuse.isdscotland.org/publications/local/SALSUS_2010.pdf

284 Including Belgium, the Czech Republic, Denmark, Finland, Germany, the Netherlands, New Zealand, Norway, Sweden and Switzerland.

285 The plans set out here are based on a process of policy development by the Scottish Government that has drawn appropriately on expert advice at a number of stages. The process involved development of an underpinning framework for defence and security policy, based on an understanding of Scotland's geopolitical context and analysis of threats and risk. Plans for specific defence and security capabilities were then developed based on that framework, drawing on a range of expert inputs.

286   As indicated by Professor Sir David Omand, evidence at Foreign Affairs Committee 4 December 2012: "It is part of our history that we helped both Australia and Canada develop significant capability over a period of very many years".

287   http://www.scotland.gov.uk/Publications/2011/03/21095856/0

288   HM Government, October 2013, *Scotland analysis: Security*. https://www.gov.uk/government/publications/scotland-analysis-security

289   http://www.legislation.gov.uk/ukpga/2000/23/contents and http://www.legislation.gov.uk/asp/2000/11/section/31

290   Intelligence Services Commissioner, the Interception of Communications Commissioner, and the Office of the Surveillance Commissioners.

291   For example, the principles set out by the Geneva Centre for the Democratic Control of Armed Forces (DCAF) in *Overseeing Intelligence Services: A Toolkit*. http://www.dcaf.ch/Publications/Overseeing-Intelligence-Services-A-Toolkit

292   The control principle is that intelligence received from another country must not be passed on to a third party country without the originating country's consent. The importance of this was highlighted, for example, by the Intelligence and Security Committee in their Annual Report 2011-12 (paragraph 154): "whilst UK Agencies are given foreign intelligence material by those with whom they co-operate, it does not then belong to us and is not ours to do with as we wish. It is not therefore up to the UK to decide who else we might share it with – that decision rests with the country that 'owns' the material". http://isc.independent.gov.uk/committee-reports/annual-reports.

293   *Security and Intelligence Agencies: Financial Statement 2012-13*. http://www.official-documents.gov.uk/document/hc1314/hc00/0027/0027.pdf)

294   ONS/NRS (2013) 2012-based population projections.

295   http://www.scotland.org/study-in-scotland/why-study-in-scotland

296   *Habitually resident* is a term used in international law including the European convention on Nationality. The term has been equated with the term "ordinarily resident" which is currently

used to define "settled in the UK" in the British Nationality Act 1981. *[Note: "settled" is defined by the British Nationality Act 1981 as requiring ordinary residence AND without being subject under immigration laws to any restriction on the period for which the person may remain i.e. a person with indefinite leave to remain.]* The test for ordinary residence is satisfied where the person has habitually and normally resided for a settled purpose apart from temporary or occasional absences. "Settled purpose" is defined as one which has "a sufficient degree of continuity to be properly described as settled".

297   Highlands and Islands Enterprise, A Minimum Income Standard for Remote Rural Scotland. www.hie.co.uk/regional-information/economic-reports-and-research/archive/a-minimum-income-standard-for-remote-rural-scotland.html

298   Scottish Government, Economic Report on Scottish Agriculture 2013, Section 2 – Geography and Structure. www.scotland.gov.uk/Publications/2013/06/5219/3

299   Scottish Agricultural Census. www.scotland.gov.uk/Publications/2013/10/5891

300   Comparison of Scotland's rate per hectare of €130 with rates in other Member States. http://register.consilium.europa.eu/pdf/en/11/st12/st12734.en11.pdf

301   Table CAP Pillar 1 – Scottish Government, Common Agricultural Policy Payments. http://www.scotland.gov.uk/Topics/farmingrural/Agriculture/CAP/cap-resources/CAP-payments See also in the Environment, Rural Scotland, Energy and Resources section of the Q&A.

302   Table CAP Pillar 2 – Comparison of 2007-2013 Scottish per hectare average to average Rural Development funding across EU. http://ec.europa.eu/agriculture/statistics/rural-development/2012/full-text_en.pdf and Eurostat area statistics. See also in the Environment, Rural Scotland, Energy and Resources section of the Q&A.

303   Scottish Government, CAP budget negotiations - the facts. www.scotland.gov.uk/Topics/farmingrural/Agriculture/CAP/CAPEurope10112012/budget-facts31102012

304 See http://www.scotland.gov.uk/Topics/farmingrural/Agriculture/
     CAP/cap-resources/CAP-payments

305 Eurostat: 2011 Utilized agricultural area (UAA).

306 http://www.europarl.europa.eu/committees/en/studiesdownload.
     html?languageDocument=EN&file=94213

307 http://www.europarl.europa.eu/committees/en/studiesdownload.
     html?languageDocument=EN&file=94213

308 Key Stocks' are the most valuable quota stocks of the three
     species types: demersal, pelagic and shellfish. These include
     the North Sea and West of Scotland quota stocks for Cod,
     Haddock, Monkfish, Nephrops, Herring and Mackerel. Scottish
     Government, Scottish Sea Fisheries Statistics 2012.
     www.scotland.gov.uk/Publications/2013/09/2502/downloads

309 55m euros of a total EFF budget of 4.3bn euros.

310 Total EU landings 2010 4.9m tonnes (source Eurostat); total
     landings by Scottish vessels 2010 367,400 tonnes (source
     Scottish Sea Fisheries Statistics): 7.48 per cent of EU total.

311 Total EU aquaculture production 2009 1.3m tonnes (latest
     figures, source Eurostat); total Scottish aquaculture production
     2009, 158,000 tonnes (source Marine Scotland): 11.9 per cent
     of EU total.

312 Scottish aquaculture production 167,000 tonnes out of a UK
     total of 201,000 tonnes (2010, source DEFRA).

313 Drink exports are defined as exports of Scotch Whisky from the
     UK.

314 HMRC Overseas and Regional Trade Statistics.
     www.uktradeinfo.com/Pages/Home.aspx

315 Scotch Whisky Association.
     www.scotch-whisky.org.uk/what-we-do/facts-figures/

316 Scottish Government Growth Sector Database.
     www.scotland.gov.uk/Topics/Statistics/Browse/Business/
     Publications/GrowthSectors/Database

317 Scottish Global Connections Survey. www.scotland.gov.uk/
     topics/statistics/browse/economy/exports/GCSIntroduction

318 GVA statistics are available for Scotland as a whole and on a regional basis. They are not available for individual local authorities or according to the Scottish Government urban rural classification. Rural GVA figures are therefore estimated by classifying NUTS 3 regions into rural regions and the rest of Scotland regions. These figures are based on the Office for National Statistics Regional Accounts GVA in current basic prices. Further details on this calculation can be found on the following paper: http://www.scotland.gov.uk/Publications/2010/07/30093457/0

319 Citizen's Advice Scotland (2012), *The Postcode Penalty*. www.cas.org.uk/publications/postcode-penalty

320 Scottish Government: www.scotland.gov.uk/News/Releases/2013/06/landreform07062013

321 Rural Development in the EU Statistical and Economic Information Report 2012. http://ec.europa.eu/agriculture/statistics/rural-development/2012/full-text_en.pdf

322 Rural Development National Strategy Plan 2007-2013 - United Kingdom. www.scotland.gov.uk/Publications/2010/11/19093802/5. The 443m euro figure quoted is the total in the Scotland table (679m) minus the 'Voluntary modulation for the UK" in the Scotland table (236m). This deduction enables comparison to be made with the EU allocation for other countries.

323 Climate Change (Scotland) Act 2009. www.legislation.gov.uk/asp/2009/12/contents

324 EEA Greenhouse Gas Emissions Data Viewer. http://www.eea.europa.eu/data-and-maps/data/data-viewers/greenhouse-gases-viewer. Greenhouse Gas Inventories for England, Scotland, Wales and Northern Ireland 1990-2011. http://naei.defra.gov.uk/reports/reports?report_id=756

325 Scottish Government, Low Carbon Scotland - Meeting our Emissions Reduction Targets 2013-2027, the second Report on Proposals and Policies. www.scotland.gov.uk/Topics/Environment/climatechange/scotlands-action/lowcarbon/meetingthetargets

326 Ofgem Spare Capacity Margin projections 2013.

327 https://www.gov.uk/government/news/davey-announces-29-billion-boost-to-economy-and-makes-the-case-for-scotland-to-remain-in-the-united-kingdom UK Department for Energy and Climate Change (DECC), July 2012

328 http://www.scotland.gov.uk/Publications/2013/06/5757

329 http://www.scotland.gov.uk/Resource/0041/00415411.pdf

330 http://www.scotland.gov.uk/Topics/Business-Industry/Energy/resources/ExpertCommission

331 UKCS Maximising Recovery Review - Wood Review. http://www.woodreview.co.uk/documents/UKCS_Maximising_Recovery_Review_Interim_Report_11.11.13_LOCKED.PDF

332 For a discussion of international examples of stabilisation funds and sovereign wealth funds, see Fiscal Commission Working Group (2013) - Stabilisation and Savings Funds For Scotland. http://www.scotland.gov.uk/Publications/2013/10/7805

333 Scottish Government (2013) – Scottish National Accounts Project.

334 FTSE 100 Factsheet, 30 April 2013.

335 Elsewhere in this guide, the term "North Sea" refers to the UK Continental Shelf. References to the Scottish share of the North Sea are based on the median line principle as employed in 1999 to determine the boundary between Scotland and the rest of the UK for fishery demarcation purposes. A map showing this boundary can be found at figure 4.1 of the Government Expenditure and Revenue Scotland 2011-2012 Report. http://www.scotland.gov.uk/Publications/2013/03/1859/6. Discussion of alternative methods of demarcation can be found at paragraphs 3.16 to 3.18 of Maximising Return from Oil and Gas in an Independent Scotland. http://www.scotland.gov.uk/Resource/0042/00428074.pdf

336 For a further discussion of oil and gas reserves in Scotland see the Scottish Government March 2013 Oil and Gas Analytical Bulletin.

337 http://www.scotland.gov.uk/Publications/2013/07/5746

338 http://www.scotland.gov.uk/Resource/0043/00435303.pdf

339 *The BBC Trust's Review and Assessment 2012*, page 35, available at http://downloads.bbc.co.uk/annualreport/pdf/2012-13/bbc-bbctrust-annualreport-review-and-assessment-2012-13.pdf

340 *Public Attitudes to Broadcasting in Scotland* available at http://www.scotland.gov.uk/Publications/2010/01/21104900/0]

341 UK Trade & Investment/PACT UK Television Exports 2012 available at http://www.pact.co.uk/support/document-library/television-exports-report-2012/

342 MG Alba Annual report 2012-13, page 24, available at http://www.mgalba.com/downloads/reports/annual-report-12-13.pdf; Scottish Government News Release of 26 September 2013 available at http://news.scotland.gov.uk/News/A-f%C3%A0s-le-G%C3%A0idhlig-48b.aspx

343 The Availability of Communications Services in the UK, 2013. http://stakeholders.ofcom.org.uk/binaries/research/markets-infrastructure/economic-geography.pdf

344 Glasgow is a UNESCO City of Music, Edinburgh is the world's first designated UNESCO City of Literature, and Scotland is home to five UNESCO World Heritage Sites, with the Forth Bridge due to be nominated as a sixth in 2014.

345 http://www.scottishten.org/

346 Growth Sector Database, Scottish Government – Table 2.2. http://www.scotland.gov.uk/Topics/Statistics/Browse/Business/Publications/GrowthSectors/Database

347 Economic Impact of the Historic Environment in Scotland – A Final Report by ECOTEC for the Historic Advisory Council for Scotland, pages 3-4, available at http://www.heacs.org.uk/documents/2009/ecotec.pdf

348 http://www.museumsgalleriesscotland.org.uk/research-and-resources/resources/publications/publication/503/economic-data-for-the-museums-galleries-scotland-national-strategy http://www.scotland.gov.uk/Topics/Statistics/Browse/Business/Publications/GrowthSectors/Database

349 *Edinburgh Festivals Impact Study* Final Report May 2011. BOP Consulting. http://www.eventscotland.org/funding-and-resources/downloads/get/56

350   http://makeabignoise.org.uk/sistema-scotland/

351   http://www.scotland.gov.uk/Publications/2013/05/1373/0

352   http://www.scotland.gov.uk/News/Speeches/Culture-Heritage05062013

353   BBC commercial ventures combined profit before interest and tax was £155 million in 2012/13, and £222 million in 2011/12. Scotland's population share would therefore be around £13 million to £19 million. Page 4. http://downloads.bbc.co.uk/annualreport/pdf/2012-13/bbc-annualreport-complete-2012-13.pdf

354   The arrangement could be similar to STV and ITV or that between the German broadcaster Arbeitsgemeinschaft der öffentlich-rechtlichen Rundfunkanstalten der Bundesrepublik Deutschland (ARD) and regional public service broadcasters in Germany.

355   http://stakeholders.ofcom.org.uk/binaries/consultations/renewal-c4-licence/summary/c4.pdf

356   OFCOM Communications Market Report 2013. Scotland. http://stakeholders.ofcom.org.uk/binaries/research/cmr/cmr13/Scotland_2.pdf

357   See http://www.scotland.gov.uk/Resource/0041/00415411.pdf.

358   £410 million is made up of £284 million from public sector sources (Scottish Government, ERDF, Department for Culture, Media and Sport, and all of Scotland's local authorities) and £126 million from BT.

359   http://www.pts.se/upload/Faktablad/En/Factsheet_3G_Sweden.pdf

360   Ofcom Communication Market Report 2010: Scotland. http://stakeholders.ofcom.org.uk/market-data-research/market-data/communications-market-reports/cmr10/scotland/

361   Digital Agenda Scoreboard 2013: Commission Staff Working Document. https://ec.europa.eu/digital-agenda/sites/digital-agenda/files/DAE%20SCOREBOARD%202013%20-%20SWD%202013%20217%20FINAL.pdf

362   The Availability of Communications Services in the UK, 2013. http://stakeholders.ofcom.org.uk/binaries/research/markets-infrastructure/economic-geography.pdf

363   http://www.scotland.gov.uk/Publications/2013/09/6141

364   http://maps.ofcom.org.uk/mobile-services/

365   http://www.scotland.gov.uk/Resource/0041/00415411.pdf

366   https://www.gov.uk/government/publications/scotland-analysis-business-and-microeconomic-framework

367   https://ec.europa.eu/digital-agenda/en/news/communication-commission-european-parliament-council-european-economic-and-social-committee-a-0

368   The Governments formed in 1945, 1950, 1951 and 1955 (two Labour and two Conservative) each won between 35 and 37 of Scotland's 71 seats. In contrast, the Conservative Governments between 1979 and 1997 won 22 out of 71, 21 out of 72, 10 out of 72 and 11 out of 72 Scotland seats while the current Coalition Government won 12 out of 59 seats.

369   In the October 1964 election, instead of a Labour majority, there would have been a hung Parliament with 279 Conservative MPs and 274 Labour MPs. In the February 1974 election, instead of a Labour minority government there would have been a hung Parliament with 276 Conservative MPs and 261 Labour MPs.

370   The Conservatives won 16.7% of the vote in Scotland in 2010.

371   http://www.legislation.gov.uk/ukpga/2012/11/contents/enacted

372   http://www.scotland.gov.uk/About/Government/concordats/Referendum-on-independence

373   http://www.scotland.gov.uk/Publications/2013/02/3017

374   UK Whole of Government Accounts 2011-12.

375   http://www.scotland.gov.uk/Resource/0043/00434502.pdf

376   Fiscal Commission Working Group (2013) – First Report – Macroeconomic Framework. http://www.scotland.gov.uk/Resource/0041/00414291.pdf; see pages 169-174.

377   By the Succession to the Crown Act 2013.

378   Although the Scottish Parliament has some powers to legislate in relation to human rights and to take action to encourage and promote equal opportunities, key existing statutes such as the Human Rights Act 1998 or the Equality Act 2010 are reserved.

379   For example the Convention on the Elimination of all forms of Discrimination Against Women (CEDAW), the Convention on the Rights of Persons with Disabilities (CRPD) and the Convention on the Rights of the Child (CRC).

380   National Public Bodies Directory. http://www.scotland.gov.uk/Topics/Government/public-bodies/about/Bodies

381   Public Sector Employment in Scotland – Q2 2013. http://www.scotland.gov.uk/Publications/2013/09/2277

382   Source: Scottish Government, (June 2013) Police Officer Quarterly Strength Statistics Scotland, Change since 2007

383   Source: Information Services Division, (August 2013) NHS Scotland Workforce. Change since 2007.

384   Public Sector Employment in Scotland – Q2 2013. http://www.scotland.gov.uk/Publications/2013/09/2277

385   http://www.scotland.gov.uk/About/Review/publicservicescommission

386   http://news.scotland.gov.uk/News/Lerwick-Declaration-2a7.aspx

387   Article 2: http://www.conventions.coe.int/Treaty/en/Treaties/Html/122.htm

IMAGE CREDITS

Our thanks goes to the following organisations for photography contributions:

Chris Close Photography
Edinburgh's Festivals
Michael Boyd Photography
NHSScotland Photo Library
PA Images
Scottish Viewpoint
Simple Photography